ARCO TEST NEWS BULLETIN FOR THE GMAT

Just recently the GMAT, administered by the Educational Testing Service, included a new analytical question-type — the Validity of Conclusion. Through reports from people who have taken this latest examination, we are able to provide you with the most detailed information available about this type of question. The current official GMAT *Bulletin of Information* does not discuss the Validity of Conclusion question.

The Educational Testing Service may sometimes vary the types of questions on this exam. And all people taking the GMAT do not necessarily receive the same test booklet at the examination center. Therefore, the Validity of Conclusion question may or may *not* be on the test you take. It may also be included as an experimental question-type (and therefore not affect your GMAT score). However, since it may very well be an important part of your examination, you must be thoroughly prepared to face and work out this type of question.

A format of a recent GMAT was as follows:

SECTION	TYPE OF QUESTION	NO. OF QUESTIONS	TIME
I	Reading Comprehension	30	30
II	Mathematics	55	40
III	Practical Business Judgment	25 (appx.)	20
IV	Data Sufficiency	20	20
V	English Usage	30	20
VI	Practical Business Judgment	25 (appx.)	20
VII	Validity of Conclusion	40	30
	total time		180 min. (3 hrs.)

The Validity of Conclusion questions in the ARCO Bulletin will approximate those given at the actual examination in number, level of difficulty, as well as in the length of time needed for working them out. On page 2 of this Bulletin a sample Validity of Conclusion question is presented and explained step by step. This will prepare you for the two sample test sections that follow. Explanatory answers are given at the end of each test section. However for your own benefit complete each test section before checking your answers. If you work out the Validity of Conclusion test sections in conjunction with the model exams offered in this book, you will have ample preparation for taking the Graduate Management Admissions Test.

WHAT THE VALIDITY OF CONCLUSION QUESTION MEASURES

No formal training in logic or methods of analysis is required for you to work out Validity of Conclusion problems. As with other types of questions on the Graduate Management Admissions Test, this is a measure of your mental abilities for the study of management at the graduate level, not a measure of achievement or knowledge in any specialized area.

The analytical Validity of Conclusion question can be used to measure your ability:

1. to recognize logical relationships (for example between evidence and a hypothesis, between premises and a conclusion, or between stated facts and possible explanations);

2. to judge the consistency of interrelated statements;

3. to draw conclusions from a complex series of statements;

4. to use a sequential procedure to eliminate incorrect choices in order to reach a conclusion; and

5. to draw inferences from statements expressing relationships in order to reach a conclusion.

FORMAT OF THE VALIDITY OF CONCLUSION QUESTION

The format of the Validity of Conclusion question-type is as follows: You are first given a brief reading passage which describes a particular situation, usually involving such concerns as increasing profits, expansion, relocation, or marketing a new product. The situation is likely to detail several proposed courses of action and factors affecting these proposals. The passage will be followed by a conclusion based on the facts in the passage, or a description of a decision taken regarding the situation. The conclusion will be followed by 10 statements which have a possible bearing on the conclusion. For each state-

ment, you are to determine whether:

(A) The statement proves the conclusion, in which case you would choose answer (A) and mark the answer sheet appropriately.
(B) The statement supports the conclusion but does not prove it. If so, choose (B).
(C) The statement disproves the conclusion. If so, choose (C).
(D) The statement weakens the conclusion but does not disprove it. If so, choose (D).
(E) The statement has no relevance to the conclusion. If so, choose (E).

SAMPLE VALIDITY OF CONCLUSION QUESTION WITH EXPLANATORY ANSWERS

DIRECTIONS: Read the following passage. As you read, try to formulate a clear idea of the prime objective involved and the various means available for achieving the objective.

SAMPLE SET

D. Rivers, the president of WAS Airlines, sent a memorandum to all WAS stockholders on January 13 describing three alternative plans for continued profits on their roundtrip, New York to London flight. The price of WAS's London flight had for some time been $400, but a rival firm, Camel Airlines, had recently introduced a 279-dollar bargain flight from New York to London. Plan 1 called for the investment of one million dollars in new luxury items for WAS planes. Rivers felt that many people would rather pay more money for a flight to Europe

if they would be provided with wider seats, free champagne, and flight attendants dressed in designer uniforms. Plan 2 suggested lowering the price of the flight to $325. Rivers felt that, although this price was higher than Camel's, he would be able to sell more flights than Camel on the basis of WAS's reputation as the safest and most reliable airline in the business. Plan 3 was to lower the fare to $278, while increasing the number of seats on the planes by 15%.

CONCLUSION: Plan 3 was put into effect on February 15, 1977.

QUESTIONS

DIRECTIONS: For each of the following statements, choose from options below the one which best describes the relationship between the statement and the conclusion:

(A) The statement proves the conclusion.
(B) The statement supports the conclusion but does not prove it.
(C) The statement disproves the conclusion.
(D) The statement weakens the conclusion but does not disprove it.
(E) The statement is irrelevant to the conclusion.

1. Sixty percent of the stockholders preferred Plan 2.

   The correct answer is D — the statement weakens the conclusion. Because 60% constitutes a majority, one might be inclined to think that the statement disproves the conclusion. However, this is not necessarily the case. For example, there is a chance that the decision would be made by those stockholders holding majority shares of WAS stock. These stockholders could have preferred Plan 3.

2. On January 17, the Civil Aeronautics Board prohibited airline fares below $325.

   The correct answer here would be C — the statement disproves the conclusion. If fares below $325 were prohibited, Plan 3, which called for a fare of $278, could not be put into effect.

3. On March 2, 1977, Jenny Malone paid her travel agent $278 for her roundtrip, New York–London ticket on WAS airlines.

   This statement proves the conclusion (answer A). The amount paid to the travel agent is exactly the airfare called for by Plan 3.

4. The public relations department at WAS began receiving complaints on February 25 about cramped conditions on their New York to London flight.

   This statement supports the conclusion (answer B). Plan 3 called for increased seating on the New York to London flights and this could engender complaints. This statement, however, does not absolutely prove the conclusion. For example, WAS could have decided to add more seats with Plan 2. The passage does not preclude this possibility.

5. Molly Parks, a stewardess on WAS airlines, loved her designer uniform so much that she wore it to a party after working hours.

   This statement weakens the conclusion (answer D). Plan 1 is the plan which called for designer uniforms. However, as was the case in question 4, there is a possibility that WAS decided to include the new uniforms as part of Plan 3. While it is unlikely that a budget plan such as Plan 3 would include designer uniforms, this unlikeliness does not constitute a disproof.

6. In 1978, WAS merged with Balia Airlines.

   A merger with Balia is irrelevant to the conclusion (answer E).

7. Joe Buck celebrated his anniversary and WAS's new low fares by taking his wife to London.

   This statement supports the conclusion (answer B), but does not prove it. Plan 2, as well as Plan 3, called for lowered fares.

8. WAS announced increased profits in 1978, despite the competition from Camel Airlines.

   Irrelevant (answer E). All three plans were intended to increase profits. This statement offers no specific information regarding Plan 3.

9. While drinking free champagne and watching the flight attendants in their designer uniforms, Todd Craig fell asleep in his extra wide seat on WAS Airlines' Flight #345 to London, feeling that WAS Airlines was certainly justified in charging $400 for so much service.

   This statement disproves the conclusion (answer C). It mentions all of the options which were a part of Plan 1.

10. On January 25, 1977, Camel Airlines raised the price of their New York to London charter flight to $300.

    This statement weakens the conclusion (answer D). The prime reason for the proposals to lower WAS's fare was the competition from Camel. If Camel raised their price to $300, it is not likely that WAS would find it necessary to lower their rates to $278. They might, however, have wanted to do so anyway.

ANSWER SHEET FOR PRACTICE TEST 1

(answer grid: items 1–40, options A B C D E)

PRACTICE VALIDITY OF CONCLUSION QUESTIONS

TEST 1

TIME ALLOWED: 30 Minutes

To simulate a complete examination experience, take the following section of Validity of Conclusion questions in sequence after having completed the First Practice Examination in this book. Use the answer sheet above for the practice Validity of Conclusion questions.

DIRECTIONS: Each of the following 4 sets consists of a reading passage followed by a conclusion drawn from the passage. Each conclusion is followed by 10 statements which have a possible bearing on the conclusion. For each statement, you are to choose from the following the option which best expresses the relationship between the statement and the conclusion:

(A) The statement proves the conclusion.
(B) The statement supports the conclusion but does not prove it.
(C) The statement disproves the conclusion.
(D) The statement weakens the conclusion.
(E) The statement is irrelevant to the conclusion.

SET 1

Bill Chamberlain, a graduate student of American History at Scaradango University in California, contracted to drive a car for Dri-Con Auto Transporters (DCAT) from New York to San Francisco. The contract stated that Bill would receive $250 and the use of the car for 7 days. Section 4 of the contract stated that Bill could carry no passengers in the car. It was further stipulated that the company had the right not to pay any contractee who violated any part of the contract.

On the evening of April 14, Bill was stopped by state police for erratic driving. Bill refused to take a breath analysis test and so was taken into custody with the car. He was released 10 days later.

CONCLUSION: DCAT refused to pay Bill.

QUESTIONS

1. Bill had been stopped for drunken driving two times in the past.

2. The car was not delivered on time.

3. When he was arrested, Bill called a friend who consented to drive the car to its destination within the prescribed 7 days. The authorities, after having the situation explained to them and verifying the story with DCAT, consented to release the car to Bill's friend.

4. Walter Spivek, a hitch-hiker Bill picked up in New Jersey, called DCAT on the phone while Bill was in jail to explain the difficulty.

5. April 14 was three days after the car had already been delivered.

6. Bob Preston, the man at DCAT who contracted Bill, knew Bill's father and did not like him.

7. When officials at Scaradango University heard of the charges against Bill, they suspended him for one semester.

8. When Christie Brinkley returned her DCAT car 2 days late, she did not receive payment.

9. Bill used the money he received from DCAT to pay his bail.

10. Bill was contracted a second time by DCAT the following September.

SET 2

Ted Johnson owns a small grocery business that has been on the decline for over a year since the advent of a large supermarket in a nearby town. He is seriously considering accepting an offer made by the owner of the adjoining store, Frank North. North, a prospering hardware dealer and an avid fishing and boating enthusiast, wants more space to accommodate a line of fishing tackle and boating accessories. North has told Johnson that he has received a substantial demand for boating and fishing equipment which he has been unable to meet and he wants to expand his business to cater to this market. North offers to buy Johnson's property and take him in as a partner in the new boating and fishing business. Johnson, who wants an active and prosperous business and who is strongly against retirement, sees two alternatives open to him: either maintaining his present business or accepting North's offer.

CONCLUSION: Of the visible alternatives open to him, Johnson concludes that it is in his best interest to reject North's offer and maintain his present business.

QUESTIONS

11. The Conservation Department is about to release a report that recommends the banning of all water sports in the area for at least the next five years. There is every indication that this recommendation will be acted upon.

12. A recreational development is being planned for the area and a number of people from nearby cities have decided to purchase tracts of land in the area to take advantage of the new boating and fishing opportunities.

13. Kramer, another hardware dealer in the area, tells Johnson that he never receives calls for fishing or boating equipment.

14. Johnson learns that North, before he was successful in the hardware business, had gone bankrupt in the sporting goods business.

15. It is learned that another supermarket is about to open nearby.

16. The chain that owns the large supermarket has been unhappy with the store's business and will sell the store to a large sporting goods chain who will stock the store in boating and fishing equipment.

17. Johnson learns that North's wife has strong moral objections against fishing and hunting activities.

18. Johnson learns that North is expected to live only a year, and North's wife, who will be taking over his business interests, has moral objections against hunting and fishing activities.

19. A number of fishermen tell Johnson that North, who claims to be a very successful fisherman, cannot be expected to tell the truth about the size and number of his catch.

20. The Be Kind to All Animals Society has recently become active in the area and intends to disrupt those businesses that are involved with game sports.

SET 3

When the Secretary of Commerce of the United States received a report stating that the country's stockpiles of copper had increased from a quarter of a million tons in 1988 to 1.5 million tons in 1993, he became alarmed. World stockpiles of copper, and copper prices, had remained stable during the past years. Because of the higher quality of American copper, it had always been 3 cents per pound more expensive than the rest of the world's copper, the price of which was determined by the London Metal Exchange. The secretary had three ideas to choose among in order to remedy the situation. He considered lowering the price of American copper by 1.5 cents per pound. He felt that, because of the higher quality of American copper, the copper-buying corporations of the world would start to purchase American copper at this reduced price. Next, he considered mixing the copper with a cheaper metal so that he could drop prices to below the world standard. His third idea was to request that the United States Treasury Department issue copper quarters rather than silver ones. This course of action would have

the beneficial effect of reducing American stockpiles of copper, and would thus keep the price of copper at its current level. At the same time, it would help to build up silver stockpiles which had recently fallen to a critically low level.

CONCLUSION: Now that the price of American copper has been reduced by 1.5 cents per pound, stockpiles have started to decrease.

QUESTIONS

21. A scientific investigation committee could discover no metal which could successfully be mixed with copper.

22. The secretary received a pledge from 89% of the world's copper-buying corporations that they would start and continue to buy American copper if the price were lowered to 1.5 cents per pound.

23. The president of the London Metal Exchange informed the secretary that, in his opinion, the quality of the world's copper was sufficient to meet any need.

24. The president of Boeing Airlines informed the secretary that he could substitute copper for steel in his planes, but that he would only purchase American copper if the price were dropped.

25. At the end of the fiscal year, the secretary received a report that silver stockpiles in the United States had started to increase for the first time in four years.

26. Liechtenstein, a small country in Europe, announced that it would continue to buy its copper from the London Metal Exchange.

27. The new copper quarter was issued in 1994. It had a picture of the Secretary of Commerce on one side.

28. Carl Saunders, a scientist in Pascal, North Dakota, discovered that he could mix titanium, a cheap metal, with copper, and the resulting compound would have all the properties of copper.

29. The President of the United States refused to allow the quality of American copper to be reduced. He also vetoed the proposal to issue copper quarters.

30. The London Metal Exchange kept the price of copper constant in 1994 and 1995.

SET 4

In June of 1976, when Alexi Winston graduated from the University of Arizona with a B.A. degree in psychology, she owed $10,000 to the Third National Bank. The first payment on this loan, which she had taken out to pay for college, was due in 1977. If accepted into the University of Minnesota's psychology Ph.D. program, she would need another $10,000 loan. When Alexi graduated in 1976, her father, Herbert Winston, offered her a high-paying job in his advertising agency. Before Alexi could make her plans for September 1976, she needed to know if she had been accepted for a fellowship at the Anna Freud Psychoanalytic Institute in Zurich, Switzerland.

CONCLUSION: On September 15, 1976, Alexi Winston stood in line to register for classes at the University of Minnesota.

QUESTIONS

31. Alexi was refused the fellowship at the Anna Freud Institute because of her lack of experience with child analysis.

32. When Herbert Winston saw how disappointed Alexi was that she had not received the fellowship, and how she did not want to work for him, he payed the loan for her, and payed for graduate school.

33. The U.S. Secretary of Labor and Commerce predicted that employment opportunities for women would rise precipitously from 1976 to 1980.

34. The income differential between psychology B.A.'s and Ph.D.'s was reportedly narrowing.

35. The Third National Bank raised its interest rates on loans to 15½% in 1976.

36. In November 1976, Alexi Winston received a raise after procuring the Carl's Soda account for the advertising company.

37. The University of Minnesota psychology department received a three million dollar grant from the Ford Foundation in August 1976.

38. Herbert Winston announced at the July 1976 board meeting of his company that he had convinced two major oil companies to let his firm represent them.

39. Carl Adler, Alexi's fiance, enrolled at the University of Minnesota in September 1976.

40. On September 14, 1976, Alexi was arrested in Jose, Mexico for possession of marijuana; she spent the next 17 days in a Mexican jail.

ANSWER KEY FOR PRACTICE TEST 1

1. E	11. A	21. B	31. B
2. A	12. D	22. A	32. A
3. D	13. B	23. D	33. E
4. A	14. B	24. B	34. D
5. D	15. D	25. D	35. D
6. B	16. A	26. E	36. C
7. E	17. E	27. C	37. B
8. B	18. B	28. D	38. E
9. C	19. E	29. A	39. B
10. D	20. B	30. E	40. C

EXPLANATORY ANSWERS FOR PRACTICE TEST 1

SET 1

1. **(E)** Irrelevant. Bill's previous driving-convictions have no bearing on the situation at hand.

2. **(A)** This statement proves the conclusion. If the car was not delivered on time, Bill would not have fulfilled the contract and would therefore not be entitled to payment.

3. **(D)** This statement would tend to weaken the conclusion. If the car were returned on time, this would be a factor in favor of Bill's receiving payment. However, the contract stated that Bill could not bring passengers into the car, and we do not know how DCAT would feel about someone other than Bill driving the car. Hence, the statement does not totally disprove the conclusion.

4. **(A)** This statement proves the conclusion. The contract stated that Bill could not have passengers. When Spivek called to explain the situation, DCAT would have found out that he was a passenger and that Bill had therefore broken his contract: a suitable reason for not paying him.

5. **(D)** This statement would weaken the conclusion. If the car had been delivered on time, Bill should have received payment. However, we do not know if the car was returned on time. We are only told that it was returned before Bill was arrested.

6. **(B)** This statement would support the conclusion. If Preston used his dislike of Bill's father against Bill, the chances are slim that Bill would have been given the benefit of the doubt in any dispute over his fulfillment of the contract.

7. **(E)** Events at Scaradango College are irrelevant to the conclusion.

8. **(B)** This statement indicates that DCAT usually abided by their policy of refusing payment in any case of breach of contract. It would therefore tend to support the conclusion. However, it is not established that the car was returned late or that Bill violated any other part of his contract. Hence, the statement does not prove the conclusion.

9. **(C)** This statement disproves the conclusion. If Bill used the money from DCAT to pay his bail, it is safe to say that he was indeed paid by DCAT.

10. **(D)** This statement tends to weaken the conclusion. It is not likely that Bill would be contracted a second time by DCAT if there had been any problem the first time he drove a car for them. If there had been no problem, they would have been willing to pay him.

SET 2

11. **(A)** This statement proves the conclusion. A ban on all water sports would completely rule out the option of going into the boating and fishing supplies business.

12. **(D)** This statement weakens the conclusion. New recreational opportunities in the area would provide a good reason for Johnson to accept North's offer. But, of course, such a new development should contribute to other sorts of business as well, including the grocery business.

13. **(B)** This statement supports the conclusion. The information provided by Kramer calls into question North's contention that there will be a large demand for boating and fishing equipment. We do not know, however, if Kramer's statement is accurate or if Kramer's experience is applicable to Johnson's situation.

14. **(B)** This statement supports the conclusion. It can be taken as an indication that North does not have a good business judgment in the area of sporting goods. However, it is possible that the bankruptcy did not have anything to do with the type of business and may have been due to conditions which are no longer present.

15. **(D)** This statement weakens the conclusion. The added competition would make Johnson's business an even greater risk and hence provide some reason for accepting North's offer.

16. **(A)** This statement proves the conclusion. It removes the initial condition which made Johnson consider leaving the grocery business and, at the same time, makes North's proposal more of a risk.

17. **(E)** Irrelevant. It is North's attitude, not his wife's, which is relevant to the success of the proposed business.

18. **(B)** This statement supports the conclusion. It would seem undesirable for Johnson to be involved, as he inevitably would be, in a business venture with someone who has moral qualms about such a venture.

19. **(E)** North's fish stories would have no relevance to his reliability as a businessman.

20. **(B)** This statement supports the conclusion. Such disruptions would no doubt have some negative effect on the proposed business and hence provide some reason for rejecting North's offer.

SET 3

21. **(B)** This statement supports the conclusion. If no metal could be found that would mix successfully with copper, the secretary's second option would be eliminated. This leaves the option of reducing the price by 1.5 cents per lb., and that of issuing copper quarters. As the statement makes no mention of copper quarters one way or the other, this possibility cannot be excluded, and the conclusion, therefore, is not absolutely proven.

22. **(A)** This statement proves the conclusion. The main objective set up in the passage is to find a way to sell more copper. A pledge on the part of 89% of the world's copper-buying nations to buy American copper if the price were lowered gives the secretary ample reason to adopt the course of action mentioned by the conclusion.

23. **(D)** This statement weakens the conclusion. If the president of the London Metal Exchange were correct in his belief that the lower quality copper was sufficient for any purpose, then it would make no sense for the United States to produce higher-priced, better quality copper. The statement does not disprove the conclusion, however, because we do not know if the president's statement is accurate.

24. **(B)** This statement supports the conclusion. The secretary might have decided to drop the price to accommodate Boeing. He could have assumed that if Boeing were willing to buy the copper at the reduced price, others would as well. He also could have decided, however, that Boeing was not a large enough company to warrant this decision, and could therefore have opted for one of the other alternatives.

25. **(D)** This statement weakens the conclusion. If silver stockpiles increased, as the statement asserts, it could have been due to a decision to mint copper quarters (and, implicitly, a decision not to reduce copper prices). The increased silver stockpiles, however, could have been the result of any number of other causes.

26. **(E)** The statement asserts that Liechtenstein is a small country. The announcement that it would continue to buy copper from the Metal Exchange would therefore have little effect on the secretary's decision, and is, consequently, irrelevant to the conclusion.

27. **(C)** This statement disproves the conclusion. The passage tells us that the secretary had to choose among three options. If copper quarters were issued, we can deduce that the price of copper was not changed.

28. **(D)** This statement weakens the conclusion. If a cheaper alloy having all the properties of copper could be made, the secretary might have decided to use this alloy in the future, lower prices below world levels, and thereby build up stockpiles. There is no conclusive proof, however, that this was his course of action.

29. **(A)** This statement proves the conclusion by eliminating all courses of action other than the one mentioned in the conclusion.

30. **(E)** This statement is irrelevant to the conclusion. There is no indication in the passage that the secretary's decision was in any way contingent upon the future activities of the London Metal Exchange.

SET 4

31. **(B)** This statement supports the conclusion, but does not prove it. Once refused the fellowship, Alexi was left with two choices: graduate school and working for her father. We know she wants to continue her education since she has applied to graduate school, but that she will need a loan. We also know that she owes $10,000 to the bank, which might provide incentive for her to take the job. The chances are that, if she received the loan, she would go to school. There is not, however enough information to prove that this is so.

32. **(A)** This statement proves the conclusion. The statement eliminates the fellowship, and tells us how the financial problems are solved so that Alexi can go to graduate school.

33. **(E)** Irrelevant. A prediction about employment opportunities for women between 1976–1980 has nothing to do with Alexi's plans.

34. **(D)** This statement weakens the conclusion. The narrowing income differential between Ph.D.'s and B.A.'s might be a reason for Alexi not to go to graduate school. It is also possible, however, that Alexi did not care about the money and wanted to further her education to enrich herself.

35. **(D)** This statement weakens the conclusion. We know that Alexi already owes $10,000 and that she will need another $10,000 to go to graduate school. An increase in the interest rates might persuade her to take the job so that she could pay back the first loan, before starting to owe more money. It is possible that the increase in rates was not large. The statement does not mention what the former rate of interest was. It is also possible that the increase in rates would not affect her choice.

36. **(C)** This statement disproves the conclusion. The statement tells us that Alexi received a raise a month after graduate school was to start. We can therefore assume that she took the advertising job rather than going to school.

37. **(B)** This statement supports the conclusion. Money from the grant might have been used as fellowships, which could have helped Alexi if she received one.

38. **(E)** This statement is irrelevant. New accounts procured by Herbert Winston have no effect on Alexi's decision.

39. **(B)** This statement supports the conclusion. There is a chance that if Alexi's fiance enrolled at the University of Minnesota, she would decide to go there.

40. **(C)** This statement disproves the conclusion. If Alexi was in jail in Mexico on September 14, 1976 and for the next 17 days, she could not have stood in line to register for classes on September 15, 1976.

ANSWER SHEET FOR PRACTICE TEST 2

PRACTICE VALIDITY OF CONCLUSION QUESTIONS

TEST 2

TIME ALLOWED: 30 MINUTES

To simulate a complete examination experience, take the following section of Validity of Conclusion questions in sequence after having completed the Second Practice Examination in this book. Use the answer sheet above for the practice Validity of Conclusion questions.

DIRECTIONS: Each of the following 4 sets consists of a reading passage followed by a conclusion drawn from the passage. Each conclusion is followed by 10 statements which have a possible bearing on the conclusion. For each statement, you are to choose from the following the option which best expresses the relationship between the statement and the conclusion:

(A) The statement proves the conclusion.
(B) The statement supports the conclusion but does not prove it.
(C) The statement disproves the conclusion.
(D) The statement weakens the conclusion.
(E) The statement is irrelevant to the conclusion.

SET 1

In 1975, Walter Hinckle, the sole owner of the Handy-Dandy Dry Cleaning Company, located outside Keene, New Hampshire, began investigating various options which would allow him to expand his business and increase his profits. A vacant lot adjacent to the left side of his building was for sale. If he expanded his business into this lot, he would be able to stay in the same location while having enough space for a much needed parking lot. However, a friend in the real estate business told Hinckle about a piece of land available closer to the university in town which would be suitable for a dry cleaning business. Also, because many of his relatives and friends had moved to Florida, Hinckle considered the option of moving his business to Fort Lauderdale.

CONCLUSION: In 1976, construction of a new addition to the Handy-Dandy Dry Cleaning Company was completed on the parking lot adjacent to the former establishment.

QUESTIONS

1. After investigating, Hinckle was not able to find a suitable location for his business in Fort Lauderdale.

2. Silas Silverman built a fast food store on the lot adjacent to the Handy-Dandy Dry Cleaning Company.

3. Pride Cleaner Company opened a store in 1974 across the street from Handy-Dandy.

4. The interest rate on municipal bonds rose 7% between 1974 and 1976.

5. The dry cleaning business relies heavily on customer loyalty.

6. Census reports showed a reflux of population into the University district of Keene, New Hampshire.

7. Hinckle hired the Wellington Construction Company to erect the addition and new parking lot in the lot adjacent to his building.

8. Figures published by the U.S. Department of Commerce showed that the rate of failure of small businesses is higher in the Northeast than in the Southeast.

9. Land values in the University district were rising during this period.

10. The new Democratic mayor of Keene promised strong affirmative action programs.

SET 2

Field Ballet Company, based in New York City, has in a short time become one of the leading performing dance groups in the country. This ascendancy is due primarily to their having signed a number of leading European dance stars whom American audiences were eager to see. Nonetheless, maintaining a number of European dance stars has been expensive and the company must now raise a substantial sum of cash. Fred Field, the director of the company, sees two alternatives open to him, either of which would solve his problem. One alternative is not to renew the contracts of Rudolf Zahn and his wife Nina, two of the European dancers who joined the company upon receiving lucrative contracts. Though their release would make a substantial amount of money available, the Zahns have become very popular and along with the other European stars have played a role in attracting audiences. The other alternative is to completely reorganize the company's school, at which the dancers train and rehearse, in order to open up large classes to the general public. If such classes become popular, they can provide a substantial income. However, such expansion would involve a risk, since it is always possible that the classes might not become popular. Also, public classes would to some extent disrupt the company's class and rehearsal schedule.

CONCLUSION: After carefully considering both alternatives open to him, Field concludes that it is in the best interest of the company not to renew the contract of the Zahns rather than open its school to the public.

QUESTIONS

11. Field learns that a substantial number of dancers in the company have come to resent the Zahn's popularity and plan some sort of disruption if the Zahns are once again offered a lucrative contract.

12. Four other major dance companies in New York have realized significant financial success by opening their classes to the general public.

13. Tom and Kristin Baker, who understudy the Zahns and receive a third of their salary, have received critical acclaim and are thought by the company ballet teachers to have even greater talent than the Zahns.

14. It is discovered that Rudolf Zahn is an alcoholic and has been unable to control his drinking as he and his wife become more and more homesick.

15. The Zahns have become popular national figures and a television network plans to make Field an attractive offer to gain the right to televise Zahn performances.

16. It is learned that Zahn has contracted a serious knee injury and is certain to be out for at least six months. Nina will not appear in any role unless her husband is in the male lead.

17. Several European newspapers have criticized European dance stars for leaving their European companies in order to make more money in America.

18. Nancy Kellman, a strong supporter of the company, learns of Field's plans and offers to donate the sum of the Zahn's salary if Field opens his school to the public.

19. It is learned that all of the European dancers, including the Zahns, have strong objections to opening classes to the general public and threaten to leave the company if such a policy is adopted.

20. It seems that, if the Zahn's contract is not renewed, the rest of the European dancers will also leave the company in protest.

SET 3

Automotive engineers working at the Nelson Motor Company recently designed a new compact car. They experienced numerous problems with the steering mechanism. Other motor companies had successful designs for steering mechanisms which they had already used successfully in their previous models. American buyers, given recent gas shortages and resultant high prices, are buying compact cars at an increasing rate. The executive committee at Nelson realizes that, on the one hand, the demand for compacts is continually increasing, but, on the other hand, that, unless the problems with their steering mechanism are corrected, it will be impossible for them to have a compact model ready for next year's line.

CONCLUSION: The executive committee decides that designs for a steering mechanism should be bought from another company.

QUESTIONS

21. The profit from the sale of the Nelson compact will be much greater than a small royalty on the steering designs.

22. The contract for the royalty for the steering mechanism is for one year.

23. The high costs of research on steering mechanisms has created substantial financial problems for the company in the past.

24. The Government has recently passed legislation requiring a full warranty on all new products.

25. The Nelson Research Department corrected all problems with the steering mechanism.

26. The demand for compacts is expected to double and royalties are to be at their lowest in ten years.

27. Research engineers expect a breakthrough before production starts.

28. The Nelson Motor Company has the technical ability to produce a new steering mechanism within several years.

29. The steering mechanism is made of titanium tetraoxide.

30. The Nelson Motor Company has shown consistent losses on all of its other compact cars.

SET 4

Bob Martin has recently been hired to manage the West Side Health Spa. One of his first problems is what to do about Tom Brenner, an assistant manager who helps run the club and is in charge of selling new memberships. The only two women on the staff and several members of the club have asked that Brenner be dismissed on the grounds that he does not give equal treatment to the women members of the health club. Martin decides that he will dismiss Brenner if he finds that Brenner has not given equal consideration to women, either in selling new memberships or in his treatment of women in the club.

CONCLUSION: Martin decides to dismiss Brenner on the grounds that he has not given equal consideration to women.

QUESTIONS

31. In the men's locker room, Brenner has often been heard to make disparaging remarks about some of the women he is acquainted with.

32. The membership list shows that the West Side Health Spa has five times as many male members as female.

33. Fifteen women applicants who had been denied membership had been closely questioned by Brenner about their views on the women's movement.

34. It is well known that Brenner is fond of his mother.

35. Brenner has been in charge of maintenance problems in the health club, and almost a third of the women's exercise equipment is seriously in need of repair, whereas all of the men's equipment is in good-working condition.

36. Brenner has been instrumental in organizing a number of special days for women at the health spa and setting up workshops of particular interest to women.

37. Brenner was correctly quoted in a national health club magazine as saying that women, be-cause of their physique and lack of stamina, receive little or no benefit from health clubs and their presence only interferes with the health programs that clubs are able to provide for male members.

38. During a brief period in which there was a fuel shortage, Brenner had ordered the closing of the women's whirlpool, sauna, and steam room so that it would not be necessary to cut back any of those services in the men's area.

39. Brenner has consulted with a number of women in the health club business to determine how he might increase female membership and make the club more attractive for women. He took subsequent steps to implement some of the suggestions he received.

40. Brenner, operating on the assumption that clean facilities are more important to women than men, has attempted to keep the women's locker room and exercise area immaculate.

ANSWER KEY FOR PRACTICE TEST 2

1. B	11. B	21. B	31. E
2. C	12. D	22. E	32. B
3. D	13. B	23. B	33. A
4. E	14. B	24. B	34. E
5. B	15. C	25. C	35. B
6. D	16. A	26. A	36. D
7. A	17. E	27. D	37. B
8. D	18. C	28. B	38. A
9. B	19. A	29. E	39. C
10. E	20. C	30. D	40. D

EXPLANATORY ANSWERS FOR PRACTICE TEST 2

SET 1

1. **(B)** This statement supports the conclusion that Hinckle remained where he was. It does not prove it, however, because from the information given, Hinckle still had the option to relocate closer to the city of Keene.

2. **(C)** This statement disproves the conclusion. If Silverman had bought the lot adjacent to the Handy-Dandy Dry Cleaning Company, then it would be impossible for Hinckle to buy it and expand his building.

3. **(D)** This statement weakens the conclusion. If the Pride Cleaner Company were competing for the business in Hinckle's location, it is not like-ly that he would want to remain there.

4. **(E)** Irrelevant. There is no relationship between municipal bonds and the dry cleaning business.

5. **(B)** This statement supports the conclusion. It offers a reason why Hinckle would want to stay where he was and keep the clientele he already had.

6. **(D)** This statement weakens the conclusion. If the population of the University district of Keene was growing, then it would be a good idea for Hinckle to take the option of relocating closer to the city.

7. **(A)** The hiring of a construction company to build the addition proves the conclusion.

8. **(D)** This statement weakens the conclusion. It offers a reason why Hinckle would want to move his business to Fort Lauderdale.

9. **(B)** This statement supports the conclusion. The price of relocating the Handy-Dandy Dry Cleaning Company in the University district where land values had increased might have proved too expensive.

10. **(E)** Irrelevant. The new mayor's promise of strong affirmative action programs has nothing to do with the dry cleaning business.

SET 2

11. **(B)** This statement supports the conclusion. Dissent among company members would affect the performance of the company and could even endanger its future. Still, it is possible that the company could survive a period of dissent and enjoy the benefits of keeping the Zahns.

12. **(D)** This statement weakens the conclusion. It provides some reason for thinking that the Field Company could solve its financial problems in a manner similar to that of the other companies mentioned. It does not constitute a disproof, however, since there may be features about the Field Company and its situation which are unique.

13. **(B)** This statement supports the conclusion by opening up the possibility that the Zahns' departure would not really hurt the company since the Zahns could be replaced by the popular and promising Bakers. There can be no guarantee, however, that the Zahns' departure would not hurt the company.

14. **(B)** This statement supports the conclusion. The Zahns' personal problems could make them a liability rather than an asset in the future. There is no certainty, however, that these problems are irremediable.

15. **(C)** This statement disproves the conclusion. With this new and unexpected source of income, there is no longer any reason to take either of the undesirable options.

16. **(A)** This statement proves the conclusion. If Zahn will be unable to dance, and his wife will not dance, there would be no advantage to renewing their contract. Not renewing their contract will solve the problem of funds.

17. **(E)** The attitudes expressed in the European papers have no relevance to Field's decision regarding the Zahns.

18. **(C)** This statement disproves the conclusion. Since the cash problem is solved by this new condition, there is no longer any reason to give up the Zahns.

19. **(A)** This statement proves the conclusion. Since the Zahns' attitude about open classes makes it impossible for Field to keep them and also open up classes, Field has no choice but to not renew their contract.

20. **(C)** This statement disproves the conclusion. Choosing to not renew the Zahns' contract would seem to be disasterous for the company since its success seems dependent upon the European dancers. The option of not renewing the Zahns' contract, therefore, is not in the best interest of the company.

SET 3

21. **(B)** This statement supports the conclusion. As long as the royalty for the designs is a nominal amount, the expected large profit on the sale of the car will more than cover the royalty. However it is not certain that the car will bring in a large profit.

22. **(E)** Irrelevant. The key issue is how much the royalty will cost for next year's model. The fact that the term of the contract is one year does not enter into this cost analysis.

23. **(B)** This statement supports the conclusion. If research expenses have been so high as to become a problem, it would seem advisable to procure a steering mechanism by other means. The statement does not prove the conclusion, however, because we do not know how the cost of buying designs compares with the cost of continued research.

24. **(B)** This statement supports the conclusion. The government regulation puts even more pressure on the company to procure a steering mechanism on which it can rely. To purchase designs for a steering mechanism which has been proven successful is a feasible way for the company to produce a car which it can fully guarantee.

25. **(C)** This statement disproves the conclusion. The development of a successful steering mechanism makes it no longer necessary to buy any designs.

26. **(A)** This statement proves the conclusion. If the demand is to double, then it is logical to assume that a new line of compacts must be brought out immediately. The expected low royalty makes the purchase of a design for a steering mechanism especially advantageous.

27. **(D)** This statement weakens the conclusion. If a problem-free mechanism can be designed, then another company's design is no longer necessary. Nevertheless, we cannot say that this statement definitely disproves the conclusion until the breakthrough by the research department actually occurs.

28. **(B)** This statement supports the conclusion. The company needs the steering mechanism within a year and it will take longer than that to develop the mechanism independently. The company might, however, decide to wait until it can do so and take the risk that there will still be a large demand for compact cars in several years.

29. **(E)** It is irrelevant that the mechanism is made of titanium tetroxide.

30. **(D)** This statement weakens the conclusion. If the company has a poor record with regard to compact cars, it should be cautious about producing any more compacts. However, there is no certainty that the company will continue to suffer losses with their compact cars.

SET 4

31. **(E)** Irrelevant. The remarks may only indicate certain personal dislikes and in no way reflect his general attitude toward potential and actual female members of the club.

32. **(B)** This statement would support the conclusion. By no means, however, does it constitute a proof. The figure cited means little until we know the number of men and women applicants. Brenner may well be doing everything he can be reasonably expected to do to make memberships attractive to women.

33. **(A)** This statement proves the conclusion. This is not an appropriate question to ask a health club applicant. The relatively large number of these occurrences, moreover, makes it feasible for Martin to accuse Brenner of discriminating against women.

34. **(E)** Irrelevant. This fact tells us nothing about Brenner's treatment of women with respect to the health club.

35. **(B)** This statement supports the conclusion. To actually prove, however, that he has intentionally neglected the women, we need to know to what extent he has attempted to remedy the situation. Perhaps he has been unsuccessful in obtaining certain parts needed for repairs.

36. **(D)** This statement weakens the conclusion. It certainly seems to indicate that he has an interest in the women members, but it is possible that he has initiated such activities to direct attention away from some other unfair practices for which he is responsible.

37. **(B)** While this statement clearly supports the conclusion, it does not prove it. Though such a statement does establish that Brenner does not think that women should be given equal treatment, it may nevertheless be true that Brenner, in his capacity as assistant manager at the spa, carries out a policy of equal treatment, even though he does not in fact endorse such a policy.

38. **(A)** This statement proves the conclusion. Such an action does constitute unequal treatment.

39. **(C)** This statement disproves the conclusion. If Brenner sought advice on how to increase female membership and actually took action to do so he cannot reasonably be said to discriminate against women with regard to club membership.

40. **(D)** This statement weakens the conclusion but does not disprove it. Though Brenner's action certainly indicates a concern for the women members, it is still possible that Brenner has discriminated against women in other considerations, such as exercise programs, special work shops, etc.

THE COMPLETE STUDY GUIDE
FOR SCORING HIGH

GRADUATE MANAGEMENT ADMISSION TEST

BY DAVID R. TURNER, M.S. in Ed.

arco 219 Park Avenue South
New York, N.Y. 10003

Second Edition (B3518)
Fourth Printing, 1979

Copyright © 1976, 1977
by Arco Publishing, Inc.

Published by Arco Publishing, Inc.
219 Park Avenue South, New York, N. Y. 10003

Library of Congress Cataloging in Publication Data

Turner, David Reuben, 1915–
    Graduate management admission test.

    1. Management--Examinations, questions, etc.
2. Business--Examinations, questions, etc. I. Title.
HD30.4.T87 1977   658'.0076   77-7368
    ISBN 0-668-04352-0 (Library Edition)
    ISBN 0-668-04360-1 (Paper Edition)

Printed in the United States of America

CONTENTS

HOW TO USE THIS INDEX
Slightly bend the right-hand edge
of the book. This will expose
the corresponding Parts
which match the index, below.

PART

1

2

3

4

5

How this book was prepared: what went into these pages to make them worth your while. How to use them profitably for yourself in preparing for your test. The essentials of successful study.

PART ONE
PRELIMINARY INFORMATION AND ADVICE

Essential information about your test: how it is constructed, how questions are to be answered, how the test scores are evaluated, and how the candidate should prepare for it.

Master each of these methods—they apply to question types you may meet on your exam. Practice them when testing yourself in this book

PART TWO
THREE MODEL EXAMS TO DIRECT YOUR STUDY

The first big step in your journey. Quite similar to the Exam you'll actually take, this one is a professionally constructed yardstick for measuring your beginning knowledge and ability. Score yourself objectively and plan further study to concentrate on eliminating your weaknesses.

...continued on next page

CONTENTS continued

PART

1

2

3

4

5

PART THREE
A PRACTICAL COURSE OF SELF-INSTRUCTION

PART FOUR
EXTRA PRACTICE WITH
SUBJECTS LIKELY TO GIVE YOU TROUBLE

A new kind of test. It deals with actual business problems, and requires that you make the judgments and decisions. Each test includes a Business Situation, a Data Application Quiz, and a Data Evaluation Quiz. Key and explanatory answers are provided for all questions.

All the mathematical processes you will need to know for your test. Includes fractions. decimals. percents. Each chapter contains practice problems and key answers followed by fully explanatory answers. Q and A keyed to similar problems to insure ease of learning.

Tests of reasoning ability. You must determine, from the information given, whether or not the problem can be solved.

PART FIVE
ANOTHER MODEL EXAM AND FINAL ADVICE

Test-taking strategy for successful exam performance.   How to prepare yourself emotionally, factually, physically.   During the exam . . . budgeting your time . . . following directions.   "Musts" for the master test-taker.

You'll want to consult this list of Arco publications to order other invaluable career books related to your field. The list also suggests job opportunities and promotions that you might want to go after with an Arco self-tutor.

WHAT THIS BOOK WILL DO FOR YOU

To get the greatest help from this book, please understand that it has been carefully organized. You must, therefore, plan to use it accordingly. Study this concise, readable book earnestly and your way will be clear. You will progress directly to your goal. You will not be led off into blind alleys and useless fields of study.

If you are planning to take the Graduate Management Admission Test (GMAT) this book is indispensable for a higher score.

You are well aware that the GMAT is one of the most important examinations that you will have ever taken. The results of this test will determine, in great measure, whether you will be admitted to the graduate school of your choice. Your entire future may well depend on the results of the GMAT.

There will be many other candidates taking the Graduate Management Admission Test—and not all will score well enough to be accepted by the graduate schools of their choice. There simply are not enough places in the nation's better graduate schools to accommodate all applicants, worthy as they may be.

This book is designed to guide you in your study so that you will SCORE HIGH.

This claim—that you will get a higher rating—has both *educational and psychological validity for these reasons:*

CAN YOU PREPARE YOURSELF FOR YOUR TEST?

We believe, most certainly, that you *can* with the aid of this "self-tutor!"

It's not a "pony." It's not a complete college education. It's not a "crib sheet," and it's no HOW TO SUCCEED ON TESTS WITHOUT REALLY TRYING. There's nothing in it that will give you a higher score than you really deserve.

It's just a top quality course which you can readily review in less than twenty hours . . . a digest of material which you might easily have written yourself after about five thousand hours of laborious digging.

To really prepare for your test you must motivate yourself . . . get into the right frame of mind for learning from your "self-tutor." You'll have to urge *yourself* to learn and that's the only way people ever learn. Your efforts to score high on the test will be greatly aided by the fact that you will have to do this job on your own . . . perhaps without a teacher. Psychologists have demonstrated that studies undertaken for a clear goal . . . which you initiate yourself and actively pursue . . . are the most successful. You, yourself, want to pass this test. That's why you bought this book and embarked on this program. Nobody forced you to do it, and there may be nobody to lead you through the course. Your self-activity is going to be the key to your success in the forthcoming weeks.

Arco Publishing Company has followed testing trends and methods ever since the firm was founded in 1937. We have specialized in books that prepare people for tests. Based on this experience it is our modest boast that you probably have in your hands the best book that could be prepared to help *you* score high. Now, if you'll take a little advice on using it properly, we can assure you that you will do well.

To write this book we carefully analyzed every detail surrounding the forthcoming examination . . .

* official and unofficial announcements concerning the examination

* all the available previous examinations

* many related examinations

* technical literature that explains and forecasts the examination.

As a result of all this (which you, happily, have not had to do) we've been able to create the "climate" of your test, and to give you a fairly accurate picture of what's involved. Some of this material, digested and simplified, actually appears in print here, if it was deemed useful and suitable in helping you score high.

But more important than any other benefit derived from this research is our certainty that the study material, the text and the practice questions are right for you.

The practice questions you will study have been judiciously selected from hundreds of thousands of previous test questions on file here at Arco. But they haven't just been thrown at you pell mell. They've been organized into the subjects that you can expect to find on your test. As you answer the questions, these subjects will take on greater meaning for you. At the same time you will be getting valuable practice in answering test questions. You will proceed with a sure step toward a worthwhile goal: high test marks.

Studying in this manner, you will get the feel of the entire examination. You will learn by "insight," by seeing through a problem as a result of experiencing *previous similar situations*. This is true learning according to many psychologists.

In short, what you get from this book will help you operate at top efficiency . . . make you give the best possible account of yourself on the actual examination.

ORIGIN AND PURPOSE

The initiative which led to the development of GMAT came from officials of prominent graduate schools of business who shared the belief that a single, uniform test, made available several times a year on a national and international scale, would help to ensure the fairness and effectiveness of their admissions procedures. Representatives of these schools in consultation with the Educational Testing Service agreed on certain important mental abilities which they judged to be essential to success in the study of business at the graduate level and also on types of test material which would satisfactorily measure those abilities. On the basis of these decisions the first forms of the test were designed. Subsequently the test has been revised and improved as the result of careful experimentation with other types of test material.

Used correctly, your "self-tutor" will show you what to expect and will give you a speedy brush-up on the subjects peculiar to your exam. Some of these are subjects not taught in schools at all. Even if your study time is very limited, you should:

● Become familiar with the type of examination you will meet.

● Improve your general examination-taking skill.

● Improve your skill in analyzing and answering questions involving reasoning, judgment, comparison, and evaluation.

● Improve your speed and skill in reading and understanding what you read—an important part of your ability to learn and an important part of most tests.

● Prepare yourself in the particular fields which measure your learning.

This book will tell you exactly what to study by presenting in full every type of question you will get on the actual test. You'll do better merely by familiarizing yourself with them.

This book will help you find your weaknesses and find them fast. Once you know where you're weak you can get right to work (before the test) and concentrate your efforts on those soft spots. This is the kind of selective study which yields maximum test results for every hour spent.

This book will give you the *feel* of the exam. Almost all our sample and practice questions are taken from actual previous exams. Since previous exams are not always available for inspection by the public, these sample test questions are quite important for you. The day you take your exam you'll see how closely this book follows the format of the real test.

This book will give you confidence *now*, while you are preparing for the test. It will build your self-confidence as you proceed. It will beat those dreaded before-test jitters that have hurt so many other test-takers.

This book stresses the modern, multiple-choice type of question because that's the kind you'll undoubtedly get on your test. In answering these questions you will add to your knowledge by learning the correct answers, naturally. However, you will not be satisfied with merely the correct choice for each question. You will want to find out why the other choices are incorrect. This will jog your memory . . . help you remember much you thought you had forgotten. You'll be preparing and enriching yourself for the exam to come.

Of course, the great advantage in all this lies in narrowing your study to just those fields in which you're most likely to be quizzed. Answer enough questions in those fields and the chances are very good that you'll meet a few of them again on the actual test. After all, the number of questions an examiner can draw upon in these fields is rather limited. Examiners frequently employ the same questions on different tests for this very reason.

If you find that your reasoning ability or your ability to handle mathematical problems is weak, there are ways of improving your skill in these fields.

There are other things which you should know and which various sections of this book will help you learn. Most important, not only for this examination but for all the examinations to come in your life, is learning how to take a test and how to prepare for it.

HOW THIS BOOK WILL HELP

1. **YOU WILL KNOW WHAT TO STUDY** — A candidate will do better on a test if he knows what to study. The Sample Tests and GMAT-type questions in this book will tell you what to study.

2. **YOU WILL SPOTLIGHT YOUR WEAKNESSES** — In using this book, you will discover where your weaknesses lie. This self-diagnosis will provide you with a systematic procedure of study whereby you will spend the greater part of your time where it will do you the most good.

3. **YOU WILL GET THE "FEEL" OF THE EXAM** — It is important to get the "feel" of the entire examination. Gestalt (meaning *configuration* or *pattern*) psychology stresses that true learning results in a grasp of the *entire situation*. Gestaltists also tell us that we learn by "insight." One of the salient facets of this type of learning is that we succeed in "seeing through" a problem as a consequence of experiencing *previous similar situations*. This book contains hundreds and hundreds of "similar situations" — so you will discover when you take the actual examination.

4. **YOU WILL GAIN CONFIDENCE** — While preparing for the exam, you will build up confidence, and you will retain this confidence when you enter the exam room. This feeling of confidence will be a natural consequence of reason "3" above (getting the "feel" of the exam).

5. **YOU WILL ADD TO YOUR KNOWLEDGE** — "The learned become more learned." In going over the practice questions in this book, you will not — if you use this book properly — be satisfied merely with the answer to a particular question. You will want to do additional research on the other choices of the same question. In this way, you will broaden your background to be adequately prepared for the exam to come, since it is quite possible that a question on the exam which you are going to take may require your knowing the meaning of one of these other choices. Thorndike's principle of "identical elements" explains this important phase of learning — particularly as it applies to examination preparation.

GRADUATE MANAGEMENT ADMISSION TEST

1

PART ONE

Preliminary Information and Advice

GRADUATE MANAGEMENT ADMISSION TEST

A PREVIEW

HOW TO PREPARE FOR THE TEST

The Graduate Management Admission Test measures abilities and skills that are developed over a long period of time. It is not designed to test specific knowledge in specialized academic subjects. Normal undergraduate training, therefore, should provide sufficient general knowledge to deal adequately with the test questions which, basically, require you to think clearly and systematically.

Cramming or specialized study for the test is not recommended. The best preparation is careful and continuous study throughout your undergraduate years.

On the other hand, some familiarity with the types of questions on the test should be helpful. For this reason, we advise you to use this book in the following way:

1. Take a Sample Test .

2. Determine your areas of weakness .

3. Answer the practice questions in these "soft" areas .

4. Take the second Sample Test .

5. Again determine existing weaknesses.

6. Again remedy those weaknesses by answering practice questions.

7. Proceed in the same manner with the third and fourth Sample Tests.

APPLYING FOR THE TEST

Sometime during the month before you are to take the test, Educational Testing Service will send you a ticket of admission bearing the date of the test and the exact address of the center to which you should report for assignment to a testing room. You will not be admitted to the test center without your ticket of admission. If you should lose your ticket, write or wire the ETS Princeton office immediately for special authorization to take the test. ETS cannot guarantee last-minute authorization, but will make every effort to help you.

Stapled to the ticket of admission you receive from ETS will be a mailing label giving you information about what time to report for the test, what kind of pencils you should bring, and other important details. This form also bears *your examination number* — the number that identifies all your papers and records at ETS.

It is *extremely important* that you take this form, as well as your ticket of admission, with you to the test center, because you will have to copy your examination number onto your answer sheet before you take the test. If you do not have your examination number, or do not copy it correctly, there may well be considerable delay in identifying your test score and reporting it promptly.

RULES FOR CONDUCT OF THE TEST

So that all candidates may be tested under equally favorable conditions, standard procedures and regulations are observed at every test center. The arrangements supervisors are asked to make, and the regulations examinees are required to observe, are these:

Supervisors are asked to arrange for testing rooms free from noise or disturbance. All visitors will be excluded.

If possible, each testing room should have a clock plainly visible to all candidates. Candidates should bring watches.

All tests at all centers will be given strictly according to the same schedule. No candidate will be permitted to continue any test beyond the time limit allowed for that test.

Candidates should bring with them three or four sharpened No. 2 pencils or a mechanical pencil with soft lead, and an eraser. *No pencils or erasers will be furnished at the center.*

Candidates will not be permitted to bring books or papers of any kind (including scratch paper) into the examination room and are strongly urged not to bring them to the examination center at all. Similarly, the use of dictionaries, slide rules, protractors, compasses, rulers, or stencils is not permitted. If a candidate is found to have such material with him in the room during the test, he will not be allowed to continue the test. Scratchwork may be done in the margins of the test books.

Candidates wishing to leave the room during a rest period or while the test is in progress should secure permission from the supervisor.

A candidate who gives or receives assistance during the progress of the test will be required to leave the examination room and will not be permitted to return. His test book and answer sheet will be taken from him to be returned to ETS with a note of explanation, and the facts will be made known to the business schools he has named to receive a score report.

All test books and answer sheets must be turned in at the close of the examination. No test materials, documents, or memos of any sort are to be taken from the room. Disregard of this rule will be considered as serious an offense as cheating.

HOW TO TAKE THE TEST

Perhaps the most important point to remember when you take the test is to be sure to read carefully the directions for each section. If you skip over these instructions too hastily, you may miss a main idea and thus lose credit for an entire section.

Although the test stresses accuracy more than speed, it is important for you to use your time as economically as possible. Work steadily and as rapidly as you can without becoming careless. Take the questions in order, but do not waste time in pondering over questions which contain extremely difficult or unfamiliar material. If you complete a section of the test before time is called, it is wise to go back and reconsider any questions about which you were not certain at first.

NO "PASSING" OR "FAILING" GRADE

The test is so designed that the average person taking it will answer correctly only about two-thirds of the questions. No one is expected to get a perfect score, and there is no established "passing" or "failing" grade. Your score compares your performance with that of all other candidates taking the test, and the report to the business school shows how far you stand above or below the "average" score for all candidates. The business school considers your total record of college work, references, recommendations, and interviews, as well as your test score, in determining your admission. Each business school will use the test score as it sees fit for this purpose.

SHOULD YOU GUESS?

Many candidates wonder whether or not to guess the answers to questions about which they are not certain. In this test a percentage of the wrong answers will be subtracted from the number of right answers as a correction for haphazard guessing. It is improbable, therefore, that mere guessing will improve your score significantly; it may even lower your score, and it does take time. If, however, you are not sure of the correct answer but have some knowledge of the question and are able to eliminate one or more of the answer choices as wrong, your chance of getting the right answer is improved, and it will be to your advantage to answer such a question.

HOW IMPORTANT ARE THE TEST SCORES?

1. Since the test scores provide valuable information about fitness for the study of business, many business schools give preference to applicants who have relatively high scores. It should be emphasized, however, that no business school admits students solely on the basis of test scores. Consideration is always given to other sources of information about applicants, such as undergraduate record, application forms, the results of interviews, letters of recommendation, and so forth.

2. Many business schools look for a high standard of performance on the test in making scholarship awards.

3. Admissions officers often find the test scores useful in discussing with applicants the advisability of attempting the study of business. The test scores may also prove helpful in counseling and guidance work with admitted students.

HOW THE TEST BENEFITS BUSINESS SCHOOLS AND CANDIDATES

The test scores have two very important characteristics: 1) They are a dependable measure of certain mental abilities which have been found to be important in the study of business. 2) The scores are based on the same standard for all candidates, regardless of when they take the test. This uniformity of standards differentiates the scores from undergraduate averages, the meaning of which varies markedly depending on the grading standards of the institution from which they come. By virtue of these two characteristics the test scores provide business schools with a means of increasing the accuracy of comparisons made among applicants. Thus the use of the test scores as a criterion for admission can help a business school to select from among its applicants those who are most likely to do well in their studies.

From the applicant's point of view, the use of the test scores makes it more likely that his abilities will be fairly evaluated. Thus an applicant with only a moderately high undergraduate record from a college with high grading standards is not so likely to lose out when compared with an applicant having a high record from a college where grading standards are relatively low.

Some people look with suspicion on the test, viewing it as an obstacle intended to make it more difficult for them to reach a desired goal. This is understandable among business school applicants who have been rejected partly on the basis of test scores or among candidates for the test who fear that this might happen. However, such an attitude toward the test is based on a misinterpretation of its purpose and function. Properly used, it can bring about a large saving in time, money and energy both for the business school and for the applicant who may not be adequately equipped to pursue profitably the study of business. It is much better that an applicant be forewarned of probable difficulty in a business school he has applied to than to struggle through his first year only to fail at the end of it.

WHAT THE TEST MEASURES

As with any test, the scores on this test can be best understood by thinking of the purpose for which the scores are used. Many faulty interpretations of test scores can be traced to a misunderstanding of the job the test is supposed to do. The test was designed primarily to predict success in graduate business schools. The test has been judged successful in performing its job because it has been found that the higher a student scores, the better are his chances of succeeding in business school. The name Graduate Management Admission Test was chosen to describe this primary function of the test.

It may help to clarify this question of purpose if we consider for a moment the kinds of information that cannot be expected from the test scores. First

of all, the Graduate Management Admission Test (GMAT) is not an intelligence test. Although many of the items in the test are similar to those that are used in intelligence tests, it would be particularly unfortunate to interpret any of your scores as an I. Q. The test does not have as its aim the classification of students into categories of intelligence, nor has any formal evidence been collected to determine whether the test could be used successfully for such a purpose. No doubt, the abilities and aptitudes generally thought of as making up general intelligence are related to success in business school and are also related to scores on the Graduate Management Admission Test (GMAT), but this does not justify interpreting the scores as I. Q.'s.

A second unfortunate misinterpretation would be to think of the test scores as an indication of probable success on a job. No formal evidence has been collected relating scores on this test to job success in the fields of business, much less in other fields. Again, it seems safe to assume that there is *some* relationship between test scores and success in business—since the test does predict success in business school and since we have every reason to believe that success in business school is related to success in business—but the extent of the relationship is unknown.

Having considered what the scores do *not* tell us, let us now return to what they do tell us. It was mentioned earlier that it has been found that, in general, the higher a student's score the better his chances of succeeding in business school. E.T.S. has established this relationship between test scores and success in business school by experimental studies. A number of business schools throughout the country required their applicants to take the test. The test scores of accepted students were kept on file until grades were available for these same students. Then grades and test scores were compared to determine whether the scores could be used effectively to sort out the better business students from the poorer students. This kind of analysis is known as a validity study.

The validity studies of the test demonstrated that it effectively predicts which students are most likely to do well at business school. The correlation between test scores and grades is not perfect; we cannot be *certain* that an applicant will or will not perform well. The scores must be interpreted in terms of the probability of an applicant's success. That is, when a school receives an applicant's score, it is possible to state the odds that he will successfully complete his course work at that business school. The higher the score the more favorable the odds.

HOW THE SCORES ARE INTERPRETED

There are many reasons why we cannot expect a test to provide perfect predictions of performance in graduate business schools. The most obvious is that it is impossible for a test to measure all of the factors that are instrumental in determining whether an individual student will be successful. We do not know all of these factors; and among those that we do know at present there are some that are not amenable to testing of the kind done in the present program.

Because the business schools are well aware that the test does not measure all of the relevant characteristics, they use the test as a source of only one kind of information in a large pool of information about each applicant. The evidence indicates that undergraduate record is, on the average, at least as good a predictor as the test scores and most schools give it as much weight as the scores. Indeed, an admissions officer may on occasion discount mediocre test scores when they are counter-balanced by good college grades from an institution in which he has confidence. Information as to your interest in business, your willingness to apply yourself, and your character, as obtained from your application, interviews, and letters of recommendation, is also included in the pool of information. In general, letters of recommendation and interviews are given the least weight in the pool of information but they could be the deciding factors in a choice between two applicants whose test scores and undergraduate records and averages are quite similar.

ETS does not set a passing or failing score on the test. Each school evaluates the scores in its own way. Of course, a total score of 700 would be considered high at any school and a score of 300 would be low, but there is a wide range of scores around 500 which cannot be considered high or low in any absolute sense. Different schools judge the scores by different standards and what may be considered a mediocre score at one school may be considered quite satisfactory at another.

In a few cases, there may be special circumstances which the admissions officer will want to keep in mind when considering a test score. He may, for example, give weight to special conditions, such as illness at the time of taking the test. which may have handicapped a candidate.

Obviously you cannot expect to be told your chances of succeeding at every business school in the country. One important practical implication does follow, however, from this discussion. You should apply to several schools. It is an unfortunate mistake to give up when a business school turns you down because your score is too low. The school that turns you down may have had an unusually large number of applicants, or it may place more weight on the score than do other schools. It is a common occurrence for students rejected by some schools to be accepted by others. Your undergraduate advisor may be very helpful in this connection. Possibly on the basis of his experience he may be able to suggest schools to which it would be most suitable for you to apply.

EVALUATING THE SCORES

The score scales for the Graduate Management Admission Test were established during the first two years of the test's existence. A reference or standardization group of examinees was chosen and the numbers 200 through 800 were assigned to their papers in accordance with the total raw scores they had received and in such a way that 500 was the average total score and about two-thirds of the group received scores between 400 and 600.

With your scores, you will receive a memorandum describing the score system and giving distributions of the scores for a large group of applicants. The distributions of scores, which give the percentages of candidates whose scores fall below each of several selected scores, will enable you to determine your standing among all applicants who have taken the test over a number of years. If your scores are very high in this group your chances of being accepted are quite good, whereas if your scores are very low you are less likely to be accepted although the exact degree of likelihood will vary depending on the schools to which you apply.

When you compare your scores with the distributions or if you should compare scores with your friends, there is one point you should remember: scores on the Graduate Management Admission Test , and in fact scores on any test, are not perfectly reliable. You should think of your score as representing a small range of scores within which your true score lies. In other words, if your score total is 500, it would be appropriate to say that your true score lies somewhere between 470 and 530. Thought of in this way, your score of 500 is not really different from scores of 515 and 490 obtained by two of your friends.

HOW TO BE A MASTER TEST TAKER

It's really quite simple. Do things right . . . right from the beginning. Make successful methods a habit by practicing them on all the exercises in this book. Before you're finished you will have invested a good deal of time. Make sure you get the largest dividends from this investment.

SCORING PAPERS BY MACHINE

A typical machine-scored answer sheet is shown below, reduced from the actual size of 8¼ x 11 inches. Since it's the only one that reaches the office where papers are scored, it's important that the blanks at the top be filled in completely and correctly.

The chances are very good that you'll have to mark your answers on one of these sheets. Consequently, we've made it possible for you to practice with them throughout this book.

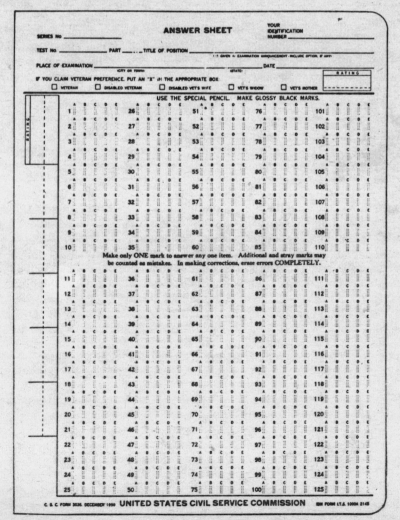

FOLLOW DIRECTIONS CAREFULLY

It's an obvious rule, but more people fail for breaching it than for any other cause. By actual count there are over a hundred types of directions given on tests. You'll familiarize yourself with all of them in the course of this book. And you'll also learn not to let your guard down in reading them, listening to them, and following them. Right now, before you plunge in, we want to be sure that you have nothing to fear from the answer sheet and the way in which you must mark it; from the most important question forms and the ways in which they are to be answered.

HERE'S HOW TO MARK YOUR ANSWERS ON MACHINE-SCORED ANSWER SHEETS:

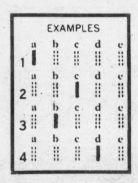

Make only ONE mark for each answer. Additional and stray marks may be counted as mistakes.
In making corrections, erase errors COMPLETELY. Make glossy black marks.

(b) Each mark must be in the space between the pair of dotted lines and entirely fill this space.

(c) All stray pencil marks on the paper, clearly not intended as answers, must be completely erased.

(d) Each question must have only one answer indicated. If multiple answers occur, all extraneous marks should be thoroughly erased. Otherwise, the machine will give you *no* credit for your correct answer.

(a) Each pencil mark must be heavy and black. Light marks should be retraced with the special pencil.

MULTIPLE CHOICE METHODS

Multiple choice questions are very popular these days with examiners. The chances are good that you'll get this kind on your test. So we've arranged that you practice with them in the following pages. But first we want to give you a little help by explaining the best methods for handling this question form.

You know, of course, that these questions offer you four or five possible answers, that your job is to select *only* the *best* answer, and that even the incorrect answers are frequently *partly* correct. These partly-true choices are inserted to force you to think . . . and prove that you know the right answer.

USE THESE METHODS TO ANSWER MULTIPLE CHOICE QUESTIONS CORRECTLY:

1. Read the item closely to see what the examiner is after. Reread it if necessary.

2. Mentally reject answers that are clearly wrong.

3. Suspect as being wrong any of the choices which contain broad statements hinging on "cue" words like

absolute
absolutely
all
always
axiomatic
categorical
completely
doubtless
entirely
extravagantly
forever
immeasurably
inalienable
incontestable
incontrovertible
indefinitely
indisputable
indubitable
inevitable
inexorable
infallible
infinite
inflexible

inordinately
irrefutable
inviolable
never
only
peculiarly
positive
quite
self-evident
sole
totally
unchallenged
unchangeable
undeniable
undoubtedly
unequivocal
unexceptionable
unimpeachable
unqualified
unquestionable
wholly
without exception

If you're unsure of the meanings of any of these words, look them up in your dictionary.

4. A well-constructed multiple choice item will avoid obviously incorrect choices. The good examiner will try to write a cluster of answers, all of which are plausible. Use the clue words to help yourself pick the *most* correct answer.

5. In the case of items where you are doubtful of the answer, you might be able to bring to bear the information you have gained from previous study. This knowledge might be sufficient to indicate that some of the suggested answers are not so plausible. Eliminate such answers from further consideration.

6. Then concentrate on the remaining suggested answers. The more you eliminate in this way, the better your chances of getting the item right.

7. If the item is in the form of an incomplete statement, it sometimes helps to try to complete the statement before you look at the suggested answers. Then see whether the way you have completed the statement corresponds with any of the answers provided. If one is found, it is likely to be the correct one.

8. Use your head! Make shrewd inferences. Sometimes with a little thought, and the information that you have, you can reason out the answer. We're suggesting a method of intelligent guessing in which you can become quite expert with a little practice. It's a useful method that may help you with some debatable answers.

NOW, LET'S TRY THESE METHODS OUT ON A SAMPLE MULTIPLE-CHOICE QUESTION.

1. Leather is considered the best material for shoes chiefly because
   (A) it is waterproof
   (B) it is quite durable
   (C) it is easily procurable
   (D) it is flexible and durable
   (E) it can be easily manufactured in various styles.

Here we see that every one of the answer statements is plausible: leather is waterproof if treated properly; it is relatively durable; it is relatively easily procurable; it bends and is shaped easily, and is, again, durable; it constantly appears in various styles of shoes and boots.

However, we must examine the question with an eye toward identifying the key phrase which is: *best* for shoes *chiefly*.

Now we can see that (A) is incorrect because leather is probably not the *best* material for shoes, simply because it is waterproof. There are far bet-

ter waterproof materials available, such as plastics and rubber. In fact, leather must be treated to make it waterproof. So by analyzing the key phrase of the question we can eliminate (A).

(B) seems plausible. Leather is durable, and durability is a good quality in shoes. But the word *quite* makes it a broad statement. And we become suspicious. The original meaning of *quite* is completely, wholly, entirely. Since such is the case we must reject this choice because leather is *not completely* durable. It does wear out.

(C) Leather is comparatively easy to procure; but would that make it *best* for shoes? And would that be the *chief* reason why it is used for making shoes? Although the statement in itself is quite true, it does not fit the key phrase of the question and we must, reluctantly, eliminate it.

(D) is a double-barreled statement. One part, the durability, has been suggested in (B) above. Leather is also quite flexible, so both parts of the statement would seem to fit the question.

(E) It is true that leather can be manufactured in various styles, but so can many other materials. Again, going back to the key phrase, this could be considered one, but not the *chief* reason why it is *best* for shoes.

So, by carefully analyzing the *key* phrase of the question we have narrowed our choices down to (D). Although we rejected (B) we did recognize that durability is a good quality in shoes, but only one of several. Since flexibility is also a good quality, we have no hesitation in choosing (D) as the correct answer.

The same question, by slightly altering the answer choices, can also call for a *negative* response. Here, even more so, the identification of the key phrase becomes vital in finding the correct answer. Suppose the question and its responses were worded thus:

2. Leather is considered the best material for shoes chiefly because
   (A) it is waterproof
   (B) it is easily colored
   (C) it is easily procurable
   (D) it can easily be manufactured in various styles
   (E) none of these.

We can see that the prior partially correct answer (B) has now been changed, and the doubly-correct answer eliminated. Instead we have a new response possibility (E), "none of these."

We have analyzed three of the choices previously and have seen the reason why none of them is the *chief* reason why leather is considered the *best* material for shoes. The two new elements are (B) "easily colored," and (E) "none of these."

If you think about it, leather *can* be easily colored and often is, but this would not be the chief reason why it is considered *best*. Many other materials are just as easily dyed. So we must come to the conclusion that *none* of the choices is *completely* correct—none fit the key phrase. Therefore, the question calls for a negative response (E).

We have now seen how important it is to identify the key phrase. Equally, or perhaps even more important, is the identifying and analyzing of the key *word*—the qualifying word—in a question. This is usually, though not always, an adjective or adverb. Some of the key words to watch for are: *most, best, least, highest, lowest, always, never, sometimes, most likely, greatest, smallest, tallest, average, easiest, most nearly, maximum, minimum, chiefly, mainly, only, but* and *or*. Identifying these key words is usually half the battle in understanding and, consequently, answering all types of exam questions.

Rephrasing the Question

It is obvious, then, that by carefully analyzing a question, by identifying the key phrase and its key words, you can usually find the correct answer by logical deduction and, often, by elimination. One other way of examining, or "dissecting," a question is to restate or rephrase it with each of the suggested answer choices integrated into the question.

For example, we can take the same question and rephrase it.
- (A) The chief reason why leather is considered the best material for shoes is that it is waterproof.
  or
- (A) Because it is waterproof, leather is considered the best material for shoes.
  or
- (A) Chiefly because it is waterproof, leather is considered the best material for shoes.

It will be seen from the above three new versions of the original statement and answer that the question has become less obscure because it has been, so to speak, illuminated from different angles. It becomes quite obvious also in this rephrasing that the statement (A) is incorrect, although the *original* phrasing of the question left some doubt.

The rules for understanding and analyzing the key phrase and key words in a question, and the way to identify the *one* correct answer by means of intelligent analysis of the important question-answer elements, are basic to the solution of all the problems you will face on your test.

In fact, perhaps the *main* reason for failing an examination is failure to *understand the question*. In many cases, examinees *do* know the answer to a particular problem, but they cannot answer correctly because they do not understand it.

METHODS FOR MATCHING QUESTIONS

In this question form you are actually faced with multiple questions that require multiple answers. It's a difficult form in which you are asked to pair up one set of facts with another. It can be used with any type of material . . . vocabulary, spatial relations, numbers, facts, etc.

A typical matching question might appear in this form:

Directions: Below is a set of words containing ten words numbered 1 to 10, and twenty other words divided into five groups labeled Group A to Group E. For each of the numbered words select the word in one of the five groups which is most nearly the same in meaning. The letter of that group is the answer for that numbered item.

Although this arrangement is a relatively simple one for a "matching" question, the general principle is the same for all levels of difficulty. Basically, this type of question consists of two columns. The elements of one of the columns must be matched with some or all of the elements of the second column.

1. fiscal
2. deletion
3. equivocal
4. corroboration
5. tortuous
6. predilection
7. sallow
8. virtuosity
9. scion
10. tenuous

Group A
indication, ambiguous
excruciating   thin

Group B
confirmation   financial
phobia   erasure

Group C
fiduciary   similar
yellowish   skill

Group D
theft   winding
receive   procrastination

Group E
franchise   heir
hardy   preference

Correct Answers

1. B	4. B	6. E	8. C
2. B	5. D	7. C	9. E
3. A			10. A

There are numerous ways in which these questions may be composed, from the simple one shown to the most difficult type of arrangement. In many cases the arrangement of the question may be so complicated that more time may be spent upon the comprehension of the instructions than on the actual question. This again, points up the importance of fully and quickly understanding the instructions before attempting to solve any problem or answer any question.

Several general principles apply, however, when solving a matching question. Work with one column at a time and match each item of that column against all the items in the second column, skipping around that second column looking for a proper match. Put a thin pencil line through items that are matched so they won't interfere with your later selections. (This is particularly important in a test that tells you to choose any item only once. The test gets real tricky, however, when you are asked to choose an item more than once.)

Match each item very carefully—don't mark it unless you are certain—because if you have to change any one, it may mean changing three or four or more, and that may get you hopelessly confused. After you have marked all your *certain* choices, go over the unmarked items again and make a *good* guess at the remaining items, if you have time.

USE CONTROLLED ASSOCIATION when you come to an item which you are not able to match. Attempt to recall any and all facts you might have concerning this item. Through the process of association, a fact recalled might provide a clue to the answer.

GRADUATE MANAGEMENT ADMISSION TEST

PART TWO

Three Model Exams

The time allotted for each Test in each Examination in this book is based on a careful analysis of all the information now available. The time we allot for each test, therefore, merely suggests in a general way approximately how much time you should expend on each subject when you take the actual Exam. We have not, in every case, provided precisely the number of questions you will actually get on the examination. It's just not possible to know what the examiners will finally decide to do for every Test in the Examination. It might be a good idea to jot down your "running" time for each Test, and make comparisons later on. If you find that you're working faster, you may assume you're making progress. Remember, we have timed each Test uniformly. If you follow all our directions, your scores will all be comparable.

I. A VERISIMILAR EXAM

To begin your studies, test yourself now to see how you measure up. This examination is similar to the one you'll get, and is therefore a practical yardstick for charting your progress and planning your course. Adhere strictly to all test instructions. Mark yourself honestly and you'll find where your weaknesses are and where to concentrate your study.

The time allowed for the entire examination is 3½ hours.

In constructing this Examination we tried to visualize the questions you are *likely* to face on your actual exam. We included those subjects on which they are *probably* going to test you.

Although copies of past exams are not released, we were able to piece together a fairly complete picture of the forthcoming exam.

A principal source of information was our analysis of official announcements going back several years.

Critical comparison of these announcements, particularly the sample questions, revealed the testing trend; foretold the important subjects, and those that are likely to recur.

In making up the Tests we predict for your exam, great care was exercised to prepare questions having just the difficulty level you'll encounter on your exam. Not easier; not harder, but just what you may expect.

The various subjects expected on your exam are represented by separate Tests. Each Test has just about the number of questions you may find on the actual exam. And each Test is timed accordingly.

The questions on each Test are represented exactly on the special Answer Sheet provided. Mark your answers on this sheet. It's just about the way you'll have to do it on the real exam.

As a result you have an Examination which simulates the real one closely enough to provide you with important training.

Proceed through the entire exam without pausing after each Test. Remember that you are taking this Exam under actual battle conditions, and therefore you do not stop until told to do so by the proctor.

Certainly you should not lose time by trying to mark each Test as you complete it. You'll be able to score yourself fairly when time is up for the entire Exam.

Correct answers for all the questions in all the Tests of this Exam appear at the end of the Exam.

Don't cheat yourself by looking at these answers while taking the Exam. They are to be compared with your own answers *after* the time limit is up.

ANALYSIS AND TIMETABLE: I. VERISIMILAR EXAMINATION

The timetable below is both an index to your practice test and a preview of the actual exam. In constructing this examination, we have analyzed every available announcement and official statement about the exam and thus predict that this is what you may face.
It is well known that examiners like to experiment with various types of questions, so the test you take may be slightly different in form or content. However, we feel certain that if you have mastered each subject covered here, you will be well on your way to scoring high.

SUBJECT TESTED	*Time Allowed*
READING RECALL	35 minutes
DATA INTERPRETATION & PROBLEM SOLVING	75 minutes
VERBAL ABILITY	20 minutes
DATA SUFFICIENCY	15 minutes
READING COMPREHENSION	20 minutes
ENGLISH USAGE	15 minutes
PRACTICAL BUSINESS JUDGMENT	25 minutes

READING RECALL

TEST I. READING PASSAGES

TIME: 15 Minutes

DIRECTIONS: This is a test to determine your ability to remember main ideas and significant details. You are to read the passages that follow in a period of 15 minutes altogether. It is suggested that you divide your time equally among the passages. When the time is up, you will be asked to recall certain ideas and facts about the passages. You will not be able to refer back to the passages after 15 minutes.

PASSAGE 1

The job of attracting the right young people into business will be facilitated if businessmen and the world at large understand the real benefits of an education designed to prepare young people for business and the fact that such an education does breed the broad-gauge man who can stand with feet planted in both Column A and Column B. The continued success of our business democracy requires no less.

Education for business must avoid the purely intellectual for something with a more pragmatic focus. And what is wrong with an education that has a pragmatic focus? Plato—in his *Republic*—was far more pragmatic than we ever think of being.

But even if education for business should be unashamedly pragmatic, it cannot be an end in itself. Any young person entering management, from school, regardless of what degree he has earned, is going to have to continue his education throughout his life. Things are happening too fast today for anyone to feel fully educated after four years, or six years, or ten years! What he will have to do is to be retrained or retooled as the years go by. The kind of education needed is that which opens the young person's eyes to the need for a lifetime of study and gives him the foundations on which his continued study can be based.

Rather than being narrowly vocational, modern business education in many ways leads in the liberality of its approach. Beginning with courses in human relations, and ending up permeating all its activities, is the concept of participative management. Why? Because as business becomes more scientific, more intellectual, more complex, no one man can have the total knowledge required to make sound decisions arbitrarily. When things become so highly complex, group management is the logical answer.

It is in modern business education that this type of leadership is taught and researched. This is of crucial importance to the well-being of our nation, because if the leaders of our business democracy cannot meet the challenge of the collective economy which boasts it will bury us, we may indeed be buried—and not just economically. Modern business education teaches how to lead without a sacrifice of freedom; how to exercise control and direction, while at the same time respecting opinions of others more qualified in highly specialized areas, as well as respecting their essential dignity as humans; and how to learn to lead by freeing the latent potentialities of gifted advisers—not by stifling them.

Perhaps it will be the business schools of this nation which will remind American education not only that democracy and strong leadership are *not*

29

contradictory terms, but that leadership can and *must* be taught. No other part of our university system seemingly is paying much, if any, attention to *doing* something about, rather than talking about, education for democratic leadership. To some faculties, leadership itself is a jingoistic word harking back echoes of Teddy Roosevelt. Not so to the faculties of our modern business schools—and not so to the masses of American students who are revolting against the lofty disengagement of many academics from the complex—and often unclean—realities of our world.

Thus business will be serving the nation's interest as well as its own—*if* it recognizes that the *right* kind of young people it needs for tomorrow's managers are the brighter students who are not purely intellectual, or purely pragmatic; *if* it offers them a career that will satisfy their values; and *if* it does what it can to encourage their development.

PASSAGE 2

While the Soviet regime has accepted monetary incentives and self-interest as key motivating forces for both managers and workers for decades, the Chinese regime takes a less sanguine view toward such rewards. During the 1952–1957 period, great stress was placed on monetary incentives for spurring productivity. Many workers were put on piece-rate schemes, and enterprise managers as well as party officials were paid bonuses primarily in relation to gross output results. This led to some complaints in the press and journals about undesirable managerial practices similar to those found in Russia.

During the Great Leap Forward of 1958–1961, the regime tried to wipe out self-interest—and hence monetary incentives—as a key motivating force. With the Reds in charge, it was felt that they could organize and motivate the work force to respond to nonmaterial stimuli. When the experts once again gained favor in 1961, worker as well as managerial incentives were also revived.

However, profit rather than gross output became the key success indicator. Profit could be a reasonably meaningful measure of efficiency, it was felt, since enterprise managers were given greater independence over product decisions, marketing, and procurement, and more say in the pricing of their products. By 1964 some articles had begun to appear about the ideological conflict involved in stressing profit as the key success indicator and in emphasizing monetary incentives and personal gain. That was at a time when economic conditions were once again favorable and when China and Russia were engaged in an open, heated feud about proper ideology and revisionism.

I found during my visits to 38 Chinese factories that piece-rate incentives for workers had been completely abolished. However, at about 80% of the factories, workers could still earn monthly or quarterly bonuses. And, interestingly enough, such bonuses were not based solely upon productivity; politics and helping co-workers were also key criteria.

PASSAGE 3

Middle level managers, such as department heads and workshop directors, can still earn bonuses at about 80% of the factories surveyed. It is the middle managers who are usually the experts because of their formal education and training. (By contrast, the director of a factory is likely to be more Red than expert, and the vice directors are typically a mixture of Reds and experts.) For middle managers to earn bonuses, the fulfillment of certain enterprise targets is a required condition at only about 20% of the factories; they are more commonly evaluated for their "contribu-

tions" rather than on the basis of overall enterprise performance. Where enterprise targets have to be fulfilled for bonuses to be paid, in most cases profit is not the only success indicator. Quantity and value of production, sales, production costs, labor productivity, and/or quality are other key success indicators at various enterprises.

During the past few years, directors, vice directors, and party secretaries have not been eligible to receive bonuses at any enterprises. Can top-level enterprise managers (or middle managers, too, for that matter) be adequately motivated over time to perform efficiently without bonuses? I doubt it. At present there seems to be considerable dedication, zeal, patriotism, and other nonmaterial stimuli motivating many of them to do the b~~--- ---~~ey can. But these stimuli cann~~-- --- --- --- -~~ or long. Compoun~~---- --- --- --- --~~y is the fact that salar~~--- ---~~rs, and living conditions of top man-~~--~~gers are relatively low in relation to those of their subordinates.

Just as the nonmanager is dependent on his boss for motivational opportunities, so is the manager dependent on his boss for conditions of motivation which have meaning at his level. Since the motivation of an employee at any level is strongly related to the supervisory style of his immediate boss, sound motivation patterns must begin at the top. Being closer to the policy-making level, the manager has more opportunity to understand and relate his work to company goals. However, high position alone does not guarantee motivation or self-actualization.

Motivation for the manager, as well as the non-manager, is usually both a consequence and a symptom of effective job performance. Job success is dependent on cyclical conditions created by inter-personal competence, meaningful goals, and helpful systems. After sustained conditioning in the developmental cycle, an individual has amazing capacity and incentive to remain in it. Moreover, if forced into the reductive cycle, unless he has pathological needs to remain there, organizational conditions must be remarkably and consistently bad to suppress his return to the developmental cycle.

Sustained confinement of a large percentage of the work force in the reductive cycle is symptomatic of organizational illness. It is usually a culmination of a chain of events beginning with top management, and is reversible only by changes at the top. Consequences of reductive conditions such as militant unionism and other forms of re-active behavior usually provoke management into defensive and manipulative behavior which only reinforces the reductive cycle. The vicarious pleasure sought by the rank and file through seeing the management giant felled by their union is a poor substitute for the self-actualization of being a whole person doing a meaningful job, but, in the absence of motivational opportunities, it is an understandable compromise.

The seeds of concerted reactive behavior are often brought to the job from broadly shared frustrations arising from social injustice, economic deprivation, and moral decadence either to sprout in a reductive climate or become infertile in a developmental climate. Hence, the unionization of a work group is usually precipitated by management failure to provide opportunities for employees to achieve personal goals through the achievement of organization goals. Organizations survive these failures only because most other companies are equally handicapped by the same failures.

Management failures in supervision do not, of course, stem from intentional malice. They may result, in part, from a lingering tradition of "scientific management" which fractionated tasks and "protected" employees from the need to think, and perpetrated management systems based on automaton conformity. But more often such failures stem from the manager's insensitivity to the needs and perceptions of others, particularly from his inability to see himself as others see him.

Insensitivity or the inability to empathize is manifested not only as interpersonal incompetence, but also as the failure to provide meaningful goals, the misuse of management systems, or a combination of both. Style of supervision, then, is largely an expression of the personality characteristics and mental health of the manager, and his potential for inducing developmental or reductive cyclical reactions.

END OF SECTION

*If you finish before the allotted time is up, work on this part only.
When time is up, proceed directly to the next part and do not
return to this part.*

TEST I. READING QUESTIONS

TIME: 20 minutes

DIRECTIONS: Answer the following questions in accordance with the contents of the preceding passages. You are not to turn back to the passages.

QUESTIONS ON PASSAGE 1

1. According to the author, the business community can be best served by the student who is
   (A) practical
   (B) intellectual
   (C) a Liberal Arts major
   (D) practical as well as intellectual
   (E) jingoistic

2. The passage implies that
   (A) a business education is better than a Liberal Arts education
   (B) business schools are in the forefront in the matter of liberalizing curricula
   (C) a Liberal Arts education is superior to a Technical education
   (D) education is of little importance to success in the business world
   (E) business is not challenging to most students

3. According to the passage, the economic health of our country depends mainly on
   (A) businessmen
   (B) business school faculties
   (C) government supervision
   (D) the general public
   (E) group management

4. According to the author,
   (A) business is an end in itself
   (B) the college-trained business leader should continue his education throughout life
   (C) the role of the businessman in business education has not been clearly defined
   (D) Plato disengaged himself from the realities of life
   (E) business education is essential to success in the business world

5. Which of the following describes business education today?
   I. Interest in human relations
   II. Realization of individual limitations
   III. Concept of participative management

   (A) I only   (B) II only
   (C) II and III only   (D) I and III only
          (E) I, II, and III

6. It is obvious that
   (A) our business leaders are incapable of competing with the collective economy system
   (B) things are going along at an unwholesome rate of speed
   (C) business is growing less complex
   (D) Teddy Roosevelt is favorably regarded by the author
   (E) students prefer that their professors take an active role in solving world problems

7. The author views the business schools of this country as a prod to education to see to it that
   (A) the ability to lead must be part of the curriculum
   (B) business education is just as important as any other type of education
   (C) professors get off their "high horses" and teach realistically
   (D) a new emphasis is to be placed upon innovation
   (E) businessmen must not be disregarded in what they have to offer educators

8. The author indicates that
   (A) business methods have drastically changed in the last decade
   (B) there has been too much government interference in business
   (C) the larger universities are far too impersonal in their dealings with students
   (D) the importance of vocational education is much over-rated
   (E) business success, in the final analysis, spells success for the entire nation

9. Businessmen, according to the passage, must recognize that
   (A) they must set an example for young people
   (B) greater financial support of business schools is necessary
   (C) business schools must be autonomous to function properly
   (D) a primary result of a business education should be the development of individuals with a wide range

(E) government intervention in business schools is inevitable

10. The most appropriate title for this passage is
    (A) Businessmen and Business Schools
    (B) Youth and Business
    (C) Business Schools
    (D) Bright Students and Business
    (E) The Relationship between Business Education and Business

QUESTIONS ON PASSAGE 2

11. The "Great Leap Forward" period was characterized by
    (A) the emergence of intellectual leadership
    (B) the attempt to eliminate the stimulus of money as a spur to production
    (C) a series of one-year plans
    (D) the acceptance of some capitalistic innovations
    (E) a wave of corruption among the managers

12. During the period 1958-1961, who was in charge of China's production facilities?
    (A) the workers   (B) Soviet engineers
    (C) Chinese experts   (D) the proletariat
            (E) the Communist Party

13. The feud between China and Russia, which came out into the open in 1964, concerned itself with
    (A) monetary vs. non-material incentives
    (B) trading with the West
    (C) ideology
    (D) military matters
    (E) border disputes

14. In the period 1952-1957 in China, which of the following were incentives for encouraging greater production?
    I. Piece-rate schemes
    II. Bonuses to managers in relation to gross output
    III. Bonuses to managers in relation to profits
    (A) I only   (B) II only
    (C) III only   (D) I and II only
            (E) II and III only

15. The author's attitude toward production techniques now used by the Chinese is

(A) sanguine   (B) gloomy
(C) indifferent   (D) sarcastic
            (E) biased

16. When the writer visited the factories in China, he found that
    (A) the factories were badly in need of repair
    (B) most workers were still offered monetary incentives
    (C) the level of intelligence among the workers was high
    (D) politics played no part in the granting of bonuses
    (E) most workers were discontented

17. In 1961, the major change from previous incentive plans was the emphasis on
    (A) profits
    (B) output
    (C) better living conditions
    (D) working comforts
    (E) social opportunities

18. According to the passage, where enterprise targets have to be fulfilled for bonuses to be paid to middle management, which of the following are success indicators?
        I. Profits   II. Sales
            III. Production costs
    (A) I only   (B) II only
    (C) III only   (D) I and II only
            (E) I, II, and III

19. Who is usually the factory expert in China's economic system?
    (A) the director
    (B) the middle manager
    (C) the party secretary
    (D) the vice director
    (E) whoever proves that he has the greatest ability

20. Who cannot receive a bonus in any enterprise?
    I. the director   II. the worker
    III. the middle manager

(A) I only   (B) II only
(C) III only   (D) I and III only
          (E) I, II, and III

QUESTIONS ON PASSAGE 3

21. Managers and other employees are most often dependent upon whom for their motivation?
    (A) Wives   (B) Owner of the firm
    (C) Their union (D) Their fellow-workers
          (E) Themselves

22. The writer is especially critical of
    (A) automation   (B) unions
    (C) employees   (D) managers
          (E) owners

23. A reductive cycle is one in which
    (A) an employer attempts to reduce costs
    (B) the work-force is gradually reduced in number
    (C) costs decrease as a firm gains experience
    (D) a union, step-by-step, takes over control of a business
    (E) there is less productive effort on the part of employees

24. The passage brings out that job success is contingent upon cyclical conditions created by which of the following?
    I. interpersonal competence
    II. meaningful goals
    III. monetary rewards
    (A) I only   (B) II only
    (C) I and II only   (D) I and III only
          (E) I, II, and III

25. If a substantial number of the employees remain in the reductive cycle, one may assume that
    (A) the organization is enjoying increased business
    (B) the personnel department has been functioning effectively
    (C) the boss is not giving sufficient attention to the business
    (D) there is an unwholesome behavior pattern among the employees
    (E) the managers lack know-how

26. Which of the following is likely to result initially from reductive conditions in an organization?
    I. militant unionism
    II. pension plans
    III. higher wages

(A) I only   (B) II only
(C) I and II only   (D) I and III only
          (E) I, II, and III

27. The passage indicates that the unionization of a work group is most commonly brought about by management's failure to provide
    (A) opportunities for the workers to realize individual objectives by way of group objectives
    (B) opportunities for the workers to achieve a feeling of self-identification
    (C) more pleasant working surroundings including modern conveniences available both at their work and during rest-periods and lunch-periods
    (D) greater fringe benefits including more more holidays and health insurance
    (E) opportunities for socialization during working hours as well as after work

28. According to the author, management failures in supervision are mainly attributable to
    (A) currying favor with the boss
    (B) a soft-hearted attitude
    (C) ignorance
    (D) lack of consideration
    (E) inability to gain respect

29. The style of supervision is
    I. an expression of the manager's personality
    II. an expression of the manager's mental health
    III. an expression of the manager's own job skills
    (A) I only   (B) II only
    (C) III only   (D) I and II only
          (E) II and III only

30. Employees will get together to seek an improvement of conditions because of dissatisfactions stemming from
    I. social injustice
    II. economic deprivation
    III. moral decadence
    (A) I only   (B) II only
    (C) I and II only   (D) I and III only
          (E) I, II, and III

END OF PART

QUANTITATIVE PART

55 questions- 75 minutes

TEST II. DATA INTERPRETATION

TIME: 15 minutes

DIRECTIONS: Read each test question carefully. Each one refers to the following graph, and is to be answered solely on that basis. Select the best answer among the given choices and blacken the proper space on the answer sheet.

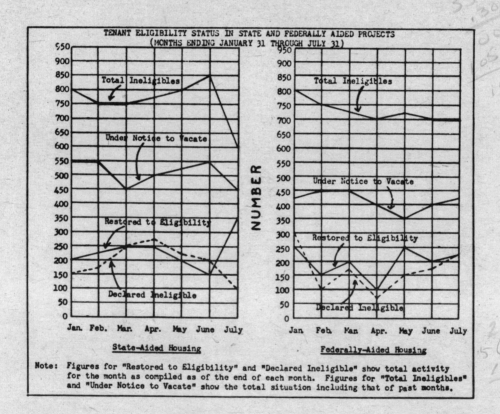

TENANT ELIGIBILITY STATUS IN STATE AND FEDERALLY AIDED PROJECTS
(MONTHS ENDING JANUARY 31 THROUGH JULY 31)

Note: Figures for "Restored to Eligibility" and "Declared Ineligible" show total activity for the month as compiled as of the end of each month. Figures for "Total Ineligibles" and "Under Notice to Vacate" show the total situation including that of past months.

1. In Federally-aided housing, the average number of tenants restored to eligibility during the first six months of the year is, most nearly
   (A) 100　　(B) 192　　(C) 188
   (D) 196　　(E) 200

2. For the months covered by the graphs, in State-aided housing, the ratio of the average number of total ineligibles to the average number under notice to vacate is, most nearly
   (A) 1:2　　(B) 2:3　　(C) 3:2
   (D) 2:1　　(E) 3:1

3. Assume that, at the end of March, in State-aided housing, the total number of ineligibles was 10% greater than shown on the graph, and that this 10% increase was due entirely to a greater number of tenants being declared ineligible in that month than is shown on the graph. Under this assumption, the percentage increase in the number *declared ineligible*, as compared with the figure in the graph, would be, most nearly,
   (A) 3%　　(B) 30%　　(C) 17%
   (D) 23%　　(E) 10%

35

4. For State-aided housing, assume that it has been decided to predict figures for the end of August and the end of September on the basis that the number of tenants expected to be declared ineligible in each future month will be 30% less than the average for the previous three months. The number of tenants expected to be declared ineligible during the month of September is expected to be, most nearly,

(A) 122   (B) 100   (C) 141

(D) 158   (E) 175

5. Of the four categories of tenant status in the graph, the number of categories in which, at the end of May as compared with the end of April, there was a greater *numerical* increase in State-aided housing as compared with the same category in Federally-aided housing, is

(A) 1

(B) 0

(C) 2

(D) 3

(E) 4

Questions 6 to 13 are to be answered on the basis of information contained in the chart and table below. The chart shows the percentage of annual expenditures for equipment, supplies, and salaries. The table shows the annual expenditures for each of the years 1957-1961.

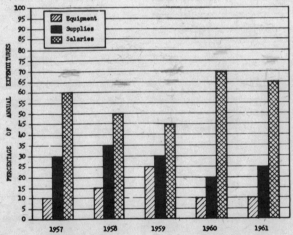

The bureau's annual expenditures for the years 1957-1961 are shown in the following table:

Year	Expenditures
1957	$ 800,000
1958	1,200,000
1959	1,500,000
1960	1,000,000
1961	1,200,000

Equipment, supplies, and salaries were the only three categories for which the bureau spent money.

6. On the following, the year in which the bureau spent the greatest amount of money on supplies was

(A) 1961   (B) 1957

(C) 1958   (D) 1959

7. Of the following years, the one in which there was the greatest increase over the preceding year in the amount of money spent on salaries is

(A) 1958   (B) 1961

(C) 1960   (D) 1959

8. The information contained in the chart and table is sufficient to determine the

   (A) average annual salary of an employee in the bureau in 1958
   (B) decrease in the amount of money spent on supplies in the bureau in 1957 from the amount spent in the preceding year
   (C) changes, between 1959 and 1960, in the prices of supplies bought by the bureau
   (D) increase in the amount of money spent on salaries in the bureau in 1961 over the amount spent in the preceding year

9. In 1959 the bureau had 125 employees. If 20 of the employees earned an average annual salary of $8,000, then the average annual salary of the other 105 employees was, most nearly,

   (A) $6,400   (B) $4,900
   (C) $4,100   (D) $5,400

10. Of the bureau's expenditures for equipment in 1961, one-third was used for the purchase of mailroom equipment and the remainder was spent on miscellaneous office equipment. How much money did the bureau spend on miscellaneous office equipment in 1961?

    (A) $400,000   (B) $40,000
    (C) $800,000   (D) $80,000

11. If the percentage of expenditures for salaries in one year is added to the percentage of expenditures for equipment in that year, a total of the two percentages for that year is obtained. The two years for which this total is the same are

    (A) 1958 and 1960   (B) 1957 and 1959
    (C) 1957 and 1960   (D) 1958 and 1961

12. If there were 120 employees in the bureau in 1960, then the average annual salary paid to the employees in that year was, most nearly,

    (A) $4,345   (B) $4,960
    (C) $5,835   (D) $8,080

13. Assume that the bureau estimated that the amount of money it would spend on supplies in 1962 would be the same as the amount it spent on that category in 1961. Similarly, the bureau estimated that the amount of money it would spend on equipment in 1962 would be the same as the amount it spent on that category in 1961. However the bureau estimated that in 1962 the amount it would spend on salaries would be 10 per cent higher than the amount it spent on that category in 1961. The percentage of its annual expenditures that the bureau estimated it would spend on supplies in 1962 is most nearly

    (A) 27.5%   (B) 22.5%
    (C) 23.5%   (D) 25%

END OF TEST

Go on to the next Test in the Examination, just as you would do on the actual exam. Check your answers when you have completed the entire Examination. The correct answers for this Test, and all the other Tests, are assembled at the conclusion of this Examination.

TEST III. PROBLEM SOLVING

TIME: 60 Minutes

DIRECTIONS: For each of the following questions, select the choice which best answers the question or completes the statement.

1. In two hours, the minute hand of a clock rotates through an angle of

   (A) 60°
   (B) 90°
   (C) 180°
   (D) 360°
   (E) 720°

2. Which of the following fractions is less than one-third?

   (A) $\frac{22}{63}$
   (B) $\frac{4}{11}$
   (C) $\frac{15}{46}$
   (D) $\frac{33}{98}$
   (E) $\frac{102}{303}$

3.

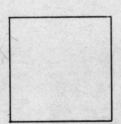

The length of each side of the square above is $\frac{2x}{3} + 1$. The perimeter of the square is

   (A) $\frac{8x + 4}{3}$ (B) $\frac{8x + 12}{3}$

   (C) $\frac{2x}{3} + 4$ (D) $\frac{2x}{3} + 16$

   (E) $\frac{4x}{3} + 2$

4. An individual intelligence test is administered to John A when he is 10 years 8 months old. His recorded M.A. (mental age) is 160 months. What I.Q. should be recorded?

   (A) 80   (B) 125
   (C) 128   (D) 148
          (E) 160.

5. When it is noon at prime meridian on the equator, what time is it at 75° north latitude on this meridian?

   (A) 12 noon
   (B) 3 P.M.
   (C) 5 P.M.
   (D) 7 A.M.
   (E) Midnight.

Questions 6-9 are to be answered with reference to the following diagram:

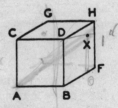

The diagram shows a cube. Each corner has been identified by a letter. Corner E is not shown, but its location is the one corner not shown in the diagram. The cube has a 1″ side.

6. The distance from A to D is

   (A) 1 inch   (B) 2 inches
   (C) $\sqrt{2}$ inches   (D) $\sqrt{3}$ inches

          (E) $\frac{1}{\sqrt{2}}$ inches

7. There is a dot X on the BDHF face of the cube. If we let the cube rotate 180° in a clockwise direction on an axis running through A and H, the

(A) cube will be standing on corner C
(B) dot X will appear in the plane where face ABCD is now shown
(C) dot X will be in the plane where face CDGH is now shown
(D) cube will return to its position as shown in the diagram
(E) corner C will appear in the place where corner F is now shown.

8. The distance from A to X is

(A) more than 2 inches
(B) less than 1 inch
(C) between 1 and $\sqrt{3}$ inches
(D) between $\sqrt{3}$ and 2 inches
(E) exactly $\sqrt{3}$ inches.

9. If the cube is successively rotated 180° on axes going through the center of faces ABCD and EFGH, faces AECG and BFDH, and faces CDGH and ABEF, where will the face containing point X be?

(A) where face BDHF was at the start of the operation
(B) Where face AECG was at the start of the operation
(C) Where face EFGH was at the start of the operation
(D) Where face ABEF was at the start of the operation
(E) Where face ABCD was at the start of the operation.

10. A carpenter needs four boards, each 2 feet, 9 inches long. If wood is sold only by the foot, how many feet must he buy?

(A) 9
(B) 10
(C) 11
(D) 12
(E) 13

11. CMXLIX in Roman numerals is the equivalent of

(A) 449
(B) 949

(C) 969
(D) 1149
(E) 1169.

Questions 12-16 are to be answered with reference to the graph below:

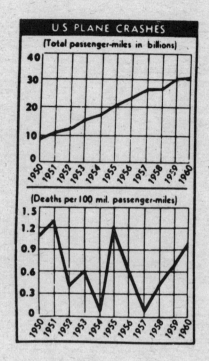

12. The period with the smallest increase in total passenger-miles was

(A) 1951-52
(B) 1954-55
(C) 1955-56
(D) 1957-58
(E) 1958-59.

13. It is *not* true that

(A) excluding 1960, there were more deaths in the aggregate, per 100 million passenger-miles, during the odd years than during the even years
(B) there was an increase in passenger-miles flown from 1950 to 1957
(C) there has been an increase in passenger-deaths every year since 1950
(D) there were more passenger-deaths in 1960 than in 1950
(E) 30 billion passenger-miles were flown in 1959

14. The greatest and the least number of passenger-deaths occurred during

 (A) 1950 and 1957
 (B) 1954 and 1960
 (C) 1952 and 1955
 (D) 1953 and 1956
 (E) 1954 and 1957

15. In 1955, passenger-deaths numbered approximately

 (A) 24
 (B) 240
 (C) 2400
 (D) 24,000
 (E) 240,000

16. The sharpest drop in passenger-deaths was during the period of

 (A) 1951-1952
 (B) 1953-1954
 (C) 1954-1955
 (D) 1955-1956
 (E) 1957-1958

Questions 17-21 are to be answered with reference to the following paragraph:

Five geometric figures have been drawn: An isosceles triangle with base equal to its altitude = a, a square with side = a, a circle with a radius = a, a regular hexagon with each side = a, and a semicircle with a diameter = a. (The figures are not drawn to scale. All the questions assume the stated dimensions.)

17. Which figure has the greatest area?

 (A) △
 (B) □
 (C) ○
 (D) ○
 (E) ◠

18. Which figure has the shortest perimeter?

 (A) □
 (B) △
 (C) ○
 (D) ○
 (E) ◠

19. Which of the following statements is true?

 (A) ○ can be inscribed inside □
 (B) □ can be inscribed inside △
 (C) ○ can be inscribed inside □
 (D) ○ can be inscribed inside ○
 (E) △ can be inscribed inside ◠

20. Which of these statements is true? The area of

 (A) △ is just ⅙ the area of ○
 (B) △ is just ½ the area of □
 (C) □ is just ½ the area of ○
 (D) ○ is just ¾ the area of ○
 (E) ◠ is just ½ the area of O ○

21. The ratio of the areas of ◠ and ○ is

 (A) 1:8
 (B) 1:6
 (C) 1:4
 (D) 1:2
 (E) 1:1

22. A motorist travels 120 miles to his destination at the average speed of 60 miles per hour and returns to the starting point at the average speed of 40 miles per hour. His average speed for the entire trip is

 (A) 53 miles per hour
 (B) 50 miles per hour
 (C) 48 miles per hour
 (D) 45 miles per hour
 (E) 52 miles per hour

23. A snapshot measures 2½ inches by 1⅞ inches. It is to be enlarged so that the longer dimension will be 4 inches. The length of the enlarged shorter dimension will be

 (A) 2½ inches
 (B) 3 inches
 (C) 3⅜ inches
 (D) 2⅝ inches
 (E) none of these

24. From a piece of tin in the shape of a square 6 inches on a side, the largest possible circle is cut out. Of the following, the ratio of the area of the circle to the area of the original square is closest in value to

 (A) ⅘
 (B) ⅔
 (C) ⅗
 (D) ½
 (E) ¾

25. The approximate distance, s, in feet that an object falls in t seconds when dropped from a height is obtained by use of the formula $s = 16\,t^2$. In 8 seconds the object will fall

(A) 15,384 feet
(B) 1,024 feet
(C) 256 feet
(D) 2,048 feet
(E) none of these

26. In the figure, $AB = BC$ and angles BAD and BCD are right angles. Which one of the following conclusions may be drawn?

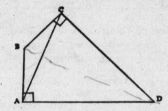

(A) angle BCA=angle CAD
(B) angle B is greater than angle D
(C) AC=CD
(D) AD = CD
(E) BC is shorter than CD.

Questions 27-30 are to be answered with reference to the following explanatory paragraph:

Suppose in the place of a number system a symbol system were instituted which had digits □,∧,Z,≤,▷,5,∂,∨,× and ⊖ corresponding respectively to the digits 0, 1, 2, 3, 4, 5, 6, 7, 8 and 9. The digit □ is used in the same fashion as the 0 in the decimal system, e.g., ∧□ = 10.

27. Which is equal to 10^2?

(A) ∧□□
(B) ∂▷
(C) ∧□∧
(D) 5≤
(E) ×□∧

28. What is the sum of ▷ + ∂ + ≤ ?

(A) Z∧
(B) ∧≤
(C) ≤▷
(D) ∧∂
(E) ∧∧

29. Which of the following indicates three-quarters of an inch?

(A) $\dfrac{5}{∧□}$ inches

(B) $\dfrac{∂}{×}$ inches

(C) $\dfrac{∨}{∧□}$ inches

(D) $\dfrac{∨}{∧□□}$ inches

(E) $\dfrac{∂5}{□□}$ inches

30. What is the value of

$$∧Z∂ - ▷∨ + \frac{∧□}{Z} \ ?$$

(A) ▷∂
(B) 5∨
(C) ×▷
(D) ∨□
(E) ⊖Z

31. A pound of water is evaporated from 6 pounds of sea water containing 4% salt. The percentage of salt in the remaining solution is

(A) $3\frac{1}{3}$
(B) 4
(C) $4\frac{4}{5}$
(D) 5
(E) none of these

32. The product of 75^3 and 75^7 is

(A) $(75)^{10}$
(B) $(150)^{10}$
(C) $(75)^{21}$
(D) $(5625)^{10}$
(E) $(75)^5$

33. The scale of a map is: ¾ of an inch = 10 miles. If the distance on the map between two towns is 6 inches, the actual distance is

(A) 45 miles
(B) 60 miles
(C) 80 miles
(D) 75 miles
(E) none of these

34. If $d = m - \dfrac{50}{m}$, and m is a positive number which increases in value, d

    (A) increases in value
    (B) decreases in value
    (C) remains unchanged
    (D) increases,then decreases
    (E) decreases, then increases

35. If a cubic inch of a metal weighs 2 pounds, a cubic foot of the same metal weighs

    (A) 8 pounds
    (B) 24 pounds
    (C) 288 pounds
    (D) 96 pounds
    (E) none of these

Questions 36-38 are to be answered with reference to the following illustrations:

Here are three views of a single cube:

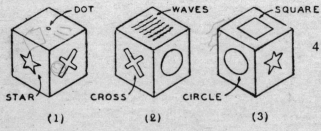

(1)   (2)   (3)

36. What symbol is opposite the dot?
    (A) circle
    (B) cross
    (C) square
    (D) waves
    (E) star

37. What symbol is opposite the cross?
    (A) circle
    (B) dot
    (C) square
    (D) waves
    (E) star

38. What symbol is on the bottom of figure 3?
    (A) cross
    (B) dot
    (C) star
    (D) waves
    (E) none of these

39. If the number of square inches in the area of a circle is equal to the number of inches in its circumference, the diameter of the circle is

    (A) 4 inches
    (B) 2 inches
    (C) 1 inch
    (D) π inches
    (E) none of these

40. The least common multiple of 20, 24, 32 is
    (A) 960
    (B) 1920
    (C) 15,360
    (D) 240
    (E) none of these

41. Six quarts of a 20% solution of alcohol in water are mixed with 4 quarts of a 60% solution of alcohol in water. The alcoholic strength of the mixture is
    (A) 80%
    (B) 40%
    (C) 36%
    (D) 48%
    (E) none of these

42. To find the radius of a circle whose circumference is 60 inches

    (A) multiply 60 by π
    (B) divide 60 by 2π
    (C) divide 30 by 2π
    (D) divide 60 by π and extract the square root of the result
    (E) multiply 60 by $\dfrac{\pi}{2}$

VERBAL ABILITY PART

38 questions- 20 minutes

TEST IV. ANTONYMS

TIME: 5 Minutes

DIRECTIONS: For each question in this test, select the appropriate letter preceding the word that is opposite in meaning to the capitalized word.

1. FETID ~Foul odor~

    (A) in an embryonic state
    (B) easily enraged
    (C) acclaimed by peers
    (D) reduced to skin and bones
    (E) having a pleasant odor

2. CHIMERICAL ~imaginary~

    (A) nimble (B) realistic
    (C) powerful (D) underrated
    (F.) remarkable

3. APOCALYPTIC ~a revelation~

    (A) concealed (B) pure
    (C) steep (D) paralyzed
    (E) authentic

4. ABERRANCE ~deviate~

    (A) refusal (B) criticism
    (C) adherence (D) exhuming
    (E) easing

5. DISCRETE ~seperate~

    (A) orderly (B) antisocial
    (C) crude (D) joking
    (E) grouped

6. CONTUMACIOUS ~rebellious~

    (A) swollen (B) scandalous
    (C) sanguine (D) concise
    (E) obedient

7. CAMARADERIE ~fellowship~

    (A) deviation (B) glee
    (C) aristocracy (D) noise
    (E) plunder

8. DOUR ~stern~

    (A) gay (B) sweet
    (C) wealthy (D) responsive
    (E) noiseless

9. MENDACIOUS ~false, deceitful~

    (A) charitable (B) efficacious
    (C) truthful (D) destructive
    (E) brilliant

10. ENERVATE ~weakens~

    (A) debilitate (B) fortify
    (C) introduce (D) conclude
    (E) escalate

11. POLTROON ~coward~

    (A) plutocrat (B) hero
    (C) amateur (D) partisan
    (E) sage

12. PUNCTILIOUS ~precise~

    (A) late (B) scrupulous
    (C) disorganized (D) apathetic
    (E) repulsive

13. VILIFY ~slander~

    (A) sing the praises of
    (B) show satisfaction with
    (C) regard with distrust
    (D) welcome with glee
    (E) accept halfheartedly

14. IRASCIBLE ~irritable~

    (A) placid (B) fortuitous
    (C) shameless (D) entrancing
    (E) yielding

43

TEST V. VERBAL ANALOGIES

TIME: 7 Minutes

DIRECTIONS: In these test questions each of the two CAPI-
TALIZED words have a certain relationship to each other.
Following the capitalized words are other pairs of words, each
designated by a letter. Select the lettered pair wherein the words
are related in the same way as the two CAPITALIZED words are
related to each other.

1. DIETING : OVERWEIGHT ::
   (A) overeating : gluttony
   (B) gourmet : underweight
   (C) poverty : sickness
   (D) doctor : arthritis
   (E) resting : fatigue

2. HOUSE : MORTGAGE ::
   (A) car : lien
   (B) inventory : merchandise
   (C) word : promise
   (D) security : price
   (E) equity : interest

3. MONEY : EMBEZZLEMENT ::
   (A) bank : cashier
   (B) writing : plagiarism
   (C) remarks : insult
   (D) radiation : bomb
   (E) success : deference

4. FOIL : FENCE ::
   (A) pencil : mark
   (B) road : run
   (C) gloves : box
   (D) train : travel
   (E) bow : bend

5. CLIMB : TREE ::
   (A) row : canoe
   (B) ascend : cliff
   (C) throw : balloon
   (D) file : finger
   (E) rise : top

6. LION : CUB ::
   (A) duck : drake
   (B) rooster : chicken
   (C) human : child
   (D) mother : daughter
   (E) fox : vixen

7. DIET : WEIGHT ::
   (A) food : fat
   (B) dinner : supper
   (C) bread : starchy
   (D) drug : pain
   (E) reduce : increase

8. STREPTOCOCCI : PNEUMONIA ::
   (A) boat : trip
   (B) quinine : malaria
   (C) cause : sickness
   (D) malnutrition : beriberi
   (E) medicine : sickness

9. HYGROMETER : BAROMETER ::
   (A) water : mercury
   (B) snow : rain
   (C) humidity : pressure
   (D) temperature : weather
   (E) forecast : rain

10. CORRESPONDENCE : CLERK ::
    (A) office : manager
    (B) secretary : stenographer
    (C) orders : accountant
    (D) records : archivist
    (E) paper : author

11. FRAME : PICTURE ::
    (A) cup : saucer
    (B) table : floor
    (C) radio : sound
    (D) cover : book
    (E) base : lamp

12. ROOM : HOUSE ::
    (A) refrigerator : kitchen
    (B) chair : room
    (C) cabin : ship
    (D) wheel : chair
    (E) cockpit : plane

TEST VI. SENTENCE COMPLETIONS

TIME: 8 Minutes

DIRECTIONS: Each of the completion questions in this test consists of an incomplete sentence. Each sentence is followed by a series of lettered words, one of which best completes the sentence. Select the word that best completes the meaning of each sentence, and mark the letter of that word opposite that sentence.

1. An _____ study should reveal the influence of environment on man.
   (A) ecumenical   (B) endemic
   (C) ecological   (D) epiigraphic
   (E) incidental

2. The researcher in the field of _____ was interested in race improvement.
   (A) euthenics   (B) euthanasia
   (C) euphuism   (D) euphonics
   (E) philology

3. _____ concerns itself with _____ of plants.
   (A) etiology . . . eating
   (B) ethnology . . . drying
   (C) etiolation . . . blanching
   (D) epistemology . . . collecting
   (E) cardiology . . . sifting

4. Through a _____ circumstance, we unexpectedly found ourselves on the same steamer with Uncle Harry.
   (A) fortuitous   (B) fetid
   (C) friable   (D) lambent
   (E) habitual

5. I had a terrible night caused by an _____ during my sleep.
   (A) epilogue   (B) insipidity
   (C) insouciance   (D) optimum
   (E) incubus

6. The Romans depended on the _____ for the _____ of their homes.
   (A) lares . . . protection
   (B) caries . . . painting
   (C) aborigines . . . blessing
   (D) mores . . . erection
   (E) resilience . . . insolvency

7. In the study of grammatical forms, the _____ is very helpful.
   (A) syllogism   (B) mattock
   (C) paradigm   (D) pimpernel
   (E) palladium

8. The _____ method is used to _____ admission.
   (A) plutonic . . . offer
   (B) Socratic . . . elicit
   (C) sardonic . . . bar
   (D) Hippocratic . . . prepare
   (E) refrigerant . . . desist

9. They had a wonderful view of the bay through the _____.
   (A) nadir   (B) behemoth
   (C) oriel   (D) fiat
   (E) pastorate

10. There is no reason to insult and _____ the man simply because you do not agree with him.
    (A) depict   (B) enervate
    (C) defame   (D) distort
    (E) enhance

11. Almost every citizen of a large city suffers from the _____ of organized crime.
    (A) debility   (B) tenuousness
    (C) depredations   (D) fortuitousness
    (E) depletion

12. He failed the examination because none of his answers was _____ to the questions asked.
    (A) pertinent   (B) omniscient
    (C) referential   (D) implacable
    (E) elusive

S1583

DATA SUFFICIENCY PART

15 questions - 15 minutes

TEST VII. DATA SUFFICIENCY

TIME: 15 minutes

DIRECTIONS: Each question below is followed by two numbered facts. Decide whether the data given is sufficient for answering the question. Sometimes the two facts do not give enough information to answer the question. Sometimes the two facts give just enough data to answer the question. And sometimes one of the facts alone is sufficient to answer the question. Read each question and the two facts that follow it; then mark your answer on the answer sheet that follows.
Mark "A" if statement 1 alone is sufficient to answer the question, but statement 2 alone is not sufficient.
Mark "B" if statement 2 alone is sufficient to answer the question, but statement 1 alone is not sufficient.
Mark "C" if both statements together are needed to answer the question, but neither statement alone is sufficient.
Mark "D" if either statement by itself is sufficient to answer the question asked.
Mark "E" if not enough facts are given to answer the question.

Note: *In the data sufficiency problems which follow, the diagrams are generalized illustrations and are not necessarily drawn to scale.*

1. How many students are in the auditorium?

    (1) There are 210 girls in the auditorium.
    (2) 30% of those in the auditorium are boys.

2. How many students passed geometry this year?

    (1) Last year 450 passed geometry.
    (2) This year there was a 10% increase over last year in the number passing geometry.

3.

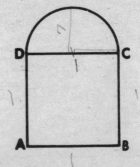

The figure above represents a square and a semicircle. What is the combined area of the above figure?

    (1) The radius of the semicircle is 7.
    (2) A side of the square is 14.

4. If a and b are integers, is a + b an odd number?

   (1) 8 < a < 11
   (2) 7 < b < 10

5. A guidance counselor wishes to choose one Junior and one Senior to represent the school at a PTA meeting. From which class, Junior or Senior, is the counselor more likely to choose a boy?

   (1) The Senior class has 300 boys and the Junior class has 250 boys.
   (2) The Junior class has 200 girls and the Senior class has 200 girls.

6.

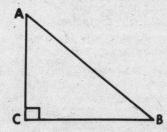

What is the perimeter of the above triangle?

   (1) △ABC is a right triangle.
   (2) The hypotenuse of the triangle is 5.

7. Which car was reduced by the largest number of dollars?

   (1) The big American car was reduced 10%.
   (2) The little foreign car was reduced 5%.

8. How many feet long is the edge of a certain cubical box?

   (1) The number of cubic feet in its volume is 9 times the number of feet in its edge.
   (2) The number of square feet in its total surface area is 18 times the number of feet in its edge.

9. Is there a common point between all 3 triangles, A, B, and C?

   (1) There is a point between triangles A and B.
   (2) There is a point between triangles B and C.

10.

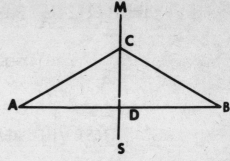

In the figure above, line MS bisects segment AB at D. Is MS ⊥ AB?

   (1) AC = CB
   (2) AD = DB

11. Does T = 24?

   (1) The average (average mean) of A, B, and T is 8.
   (2) −A = B

12.

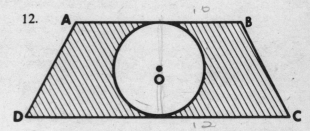

In the above figure, circle O is inscribed in trapezoid ABCD whose bases are 10 and 12. Find the area of the shaded portion.

   (1) The trapezoid is isosceles.
   (2) The circumference of the circle is 14.

13. Is the radius of circle O a whole number?

   (1) The circumference of circle O is 12π.
   (2) The ratio of the circumference of circle O to the area of circle O is $\frac{1}{4}$.

14. What percent of all the marbles in the bag are black?

   (1) The ratio of black to white marbles was 3:4.
   (2) There were exactly 5 brown marbles in the bag.

15. How many people heard Al's joke?

   (1) Al told the joke to 3 friends, each of whom repeated it to 4 friends who did not repeat it.
   (2) No one heard the joke twice.

READING AND GRAMMAR PART

47 Questions 35 Minutes

TEST VIII. READING COMPREHENSION

TIME: 20 Minutes

DIRECTIONS: Below each of the following passages, you will find questions or incomplete statements about the passage. Each statement or question is followed by lettered words or expressions. Select the word or expression that most satisfactorily completes each statement or answers each question in accordance with the meaning of the passage. Write the letter of that word or expression on your answer paper.

The standardized educational or psychological tests, that are widely used to aid in selecting, classifying, assigning, or promoting students, employees, and military personnel have been the target of recent attacks in books, magazines, the daily press, and even in Congress. The target is wrong, for in attacking the tests, critics divert attention from the fault that lies with ill-informed or incompetent users. The tests themselves are merely tools, with characteristics that can be measured with reasonable precision under specified conditions. Whether the results will be valuable, meaningless, or even misleading depends partly upon the tool itself but largely upon the user.

All informed predictions of future performance are based upon some knowledge of relevant past performance: school grades, research productivity, sales records, batting averages, or whatever is appropriate. How well the predictions will be validated by later performance depends upon the amount, reliability, and appropriateness of the information used and on the skill and wisdom with which it is interpreted. Anyone who keeps careful score knows that the information available is always incomplete and that the predictions are always subject to error.

Standardized tests should be considered in this context. They provide a quick, objective method of getting some kinds of information about what a person has learned, the skills he has developed, or the kind of person he is. The information so obtained has, qualitatively, the same advantages and shortcomings as other kinds of information. Whether to use tests, other kinds of information, or both in a particular situation depends, therefore, upon the empirical evidence concerning comparative validity, and upon such factors as cost and availability.

In general, the tests work most effectively when the traits or qualities to be measured can be most precisely defined (for example, ability to do well in a particular course or training program) and least effectively when what is to be measured or predicted cannot be well defined (for example, personality or creativity). Properly used, they provide a rapid means of getting comparable information about many people. Sometimes they identify students whose high potential has not been previously recognized. But there are many things they do not do. For example, they do not compensate for gross social inequality, and thus do not tell how able an underprivileged youngster might have been had he grown up under more favorable circumstances.

Professionals in the business and the conscientious publishers know the limitations as well as the values. They write these things into test manuals and in critiques of available tests. But they have no jurisdiction over users; an educational test can be administered by almost anyone, whether he knows how to interpret it or not. Nor can the difficulty be controlled by limiting sales to qualified users; some attempts to do so have been countered by restraint-of-trade suits.

In the long run it may be possible to establish better controls or to require higher qualifications. But in the meantime, unhappily, the demonstrated value of these tests under many circumstances has given them a popularity that has led to considerable misuse. Also unhappily, justifiable criticism of the misuse now threatens to hamper proper use. Business and government can probably look after themselves. But school guidance and selection programs are being attacked for using a valuable tool, because some of the users are unskilled.

—by Watson Davis, Sc.D., Director of Science Service
(reprinted with permission)

1. The essence of this article on educational tests is:
   (A) These tests do not test adequately what they set out to test.
   (B) Don't blame the test—blame the user.
   (C) When a student is nervous or ill, the test results are inaccurate.
   (D) Publishers of tests are without conscience.
   (E) Educators are gradually losing confidence in the value of the tests

2. Tests like the College Entrance Scholastic Aptitude Test are, it would seem to the author,
   (A) generally unreliable
   (B) generally reliable
   (C) meaningless
   (D) misleading
   (E) neither good nor bad

3. The selection implies that, more often, the value of an educational test rests with
   (A) the interpretation of results
   (B) the test itself
   (C) the testee
   (D) emotional considerations
   (E) the directions

4. Which statement is not true, according to the passage, about educational tests?
   (A) Some students "shine" unexpectedly
   (B) Predictions do not always hold true
   (C) Personality tests often fail to measure the true personality
   (D) The supervisor of the test must be very well trained
   (E) Publishers cannot confine sales to highly skilled administrators

5. According to the passage, the validity of a test requires most of all
   (A) cooperation on the part of the person tested
   (B) sufficient preparation on the part of the applicant
   (C) clearcut directions
   (D) one answer—and ony one—for each question
   (E) specificity regarding what is to be tested

When television is good, nothing—not the theatre, not the magazines, or newspapers—nothing is better. But when television is bad, nothing is worse. I invite you to sit down in front of your television set when your station goes on the air and stay there without a book, magazine, newspaper, or anything else to distract you and keep your eyes glued to that set until the station signs off. I can assure you that you will observe a vast wasteland. You will see a procession of game shows, violence, audience participation shows, formula comedies about totally unbelievable families, blood and thunder, mayhem, more violence, sadism, murder, Western badmen, Western goodmen, private eyes, gangsters, still more violence, and cartoons. And, endlessly, commercials that scream and cajole and offend. And most of all, boredom. True, you will see a few things you will enjoy. But they will be very, very few. And if you think I exaggerate, try it.

Is there no room on television to teach, to inform, to uplift, to stretch, to enlarge the capacities of our children? Is there no room for programs to deepen the children's understanding of children in other lands? Is there no room for a children's news show explaining something about the world for them at their level of understanding? Is there no room for reading the great literature of the past, teaching them the great traditions of freedom? There are some fine children's shows, but they are drowned out in the massive doses of cartoons, violence, and more violence. Must these be your trademarks? Search your conscience and see whether you cannot offer more to your young beneficiaries whose future you guard so many hours each and every day.

There are many people in this great country, and you must serve all of us. You will get no argument from me if you say that, given a choice between a Western and a symphony, more people will watch the Western. I like Westerns and private eyes, too—but a steady diet for the whole country is obviously not in the public interest. We all know that people would more often prefer to be entertained than stimulated or informed. But your obligations are not satisfied if you look only to popularity as a test of what to broadcast. You are not only in show business; you are free to communicate ideas as well as to give relaxation. You must provide a wider range of choices, more diversity, more alternatives. It is not enough to cater to the nation's whims—you must also serve the nation's needs. The people own the air. They own it as much in prime evening time as they do at 6 o'clock in the morning. For every hour that the people give you—you owe them something. I intend to see that your debt is paid with service.

> —excerpt from speech by Newton N. Minow, chairman of the Federal Communications Commission, before the National Association of Broadcasters.

6. The wasteland referred to describes
    (A) Western badmen and Western goodmen
    (B) average television programs
    (C) the morning shows
    (D) television shows with desert locales
    (E) children's programs

7. The author's attitude toward television is one of
    (A) sullenness
    (B) reconciliation   (D) rage
    (C) determination   (E) hopelessness

8. The National Association of Broadcasters probably accepted Minow's remarks with
    (A) considerable enthusiasm
    (B) shocked wonderment
    (C) complete agreement
    (D) some disagreement
    (E) absolute rejection

9. The Federal Communications Commission chairman is, in effect, telling the broadcasters that
    (A) the listener, not the broadcaster, should make decisions about programs
    (B) children's shows are worthless

(C) mystery programs should be banned
(D) television instruction should be a substitute for classroom lessons
(E) they had better mend their ways

10. Concerning programs for children, Minow believes that programs should
    (A) eliminate cartoons
    (B) provide culture
    (C) be presented at certain periods during the day
    (D) eliminate commercials
    (E) not deal with the West

11. The statement that "the people own the air" implies that
    (A) citizens have the right to insist on worthwhile television programs
    (B) television should be socialized
    (C) the government may build above present structures
    (D) since air is worthless, the people own nothing
    (E) the broadcasters have no right to commercialize on television

12. It can be inferred from the passage in regard to television programming that the author believes
    (A) the broadcasters are trying to do the right thing but are failing
    (B) foreign countries are going to pattern their programs after ours
    (C) there is a great deal that is worthwhile in present programs
    (D) the listeners do not necessarily know what is good for them
    (E) 6 A.M. is too early for a television show

If Johnny can't write, one of the reasons may be a conditioning based on speed rather than respect for the creative process. Speed is neither a valid test of nor a proper preparation for competence in writing. It makes for murkiness, glibness, disorganization. It takes the beauty out of the language. It rules out respect for the reflective thought that should precede expression. It runs counter to the word-by-word and line-by-line reworking that enables a piece to be finely knit.

This is not to minimize the value of genuine facility. With years of practice, a man may be able to put down words swiftly and expertly. But it is the same kind of swiftness that enables a cellist, after having invested years of efforts, to negotiate an intricate passage from Haydn. Speed writing is for stenographers and court reporters, not for anyone who wants to use language with precision and distinction.

Thomas Mann was not ashamed to admit that he would often take a full day to write 500 words, and another day to edit them, out of respect for the most difficult art in the world. Flaubert would ponder a paragraph for hours. Did it say what he wanted it to say—not approximately but exactly? Did the words turn into one another with proper rhythm and grace? Were they artistically and securely fitted together? Were they briskly alive, or were they full of fuzz and ragged edges? Were they likely to make things happen inside the mind of the reader, igniting the imagination and touching off all sorts of new anticipations? These questions are relevant not only for the established novelist but for anyone who attaches value to words as a medium of expression and communication.

E. B. White, whose respect for the environment of good writing is exceeded by no word-artist of our time, would rather have his fingers cut off than to be guilty of handling words lightly. No sculptor chipping away at a granite block in order to produce a delicate curve or feature has labored more painstakingly than White in fashioning a short paragraph. Obviously, we can't expect our schools to make every Johnny into a White or a Flaubert or a Mann, but it is not unreasonable to expect more of them to provide the conditions that promote clear, careful, competent expression. Certainly the cumulative effort of the school experience should not have to be undone in later years.

—by Norman Cousins, Editor of
Saturday Review (reprinted
with permission)

13. According to the passage, competence in writing is
(A) an art that takes practice
(B) a skill that requires dexterity
(C) a technique that is easy to learn
(D) a result of the spontaneous flow of words
(E) an inate ability that few people have

14. The main purpose of the passage is to
(A) present an original idea
(B) describe a new process
(C) argue against an established practice
(D) comment on a skill and its techniques
(E) urge the reader to action

15. Our schools, according to the passage,
(A) are providing proper conditions for good writing
(B) should not stress writing speed on a test
(C) should give essay tests rather than multiple-choice tests
(D) teach good writing primarily through reading
(E) correlate art and music with writing instruction

16. In describing White as a "word-artist," the author means that White
(A) was also a cartoonist
(B) illustrated his stories
(C) was colorful in his descriptions
(D) had artistic background
(E) was a great writer

17. It can be inferred from the passage that the author values good literature primarily for its ability to
(A) relieve the boredom of everyday life
(B) accurately describe events as they occur
(C) prevent disorder in society
(D) communicate ideas and experience
(E) provide individuals with skills for success

END OF TEST

Go on to the next Test in the Examination, just as you would do on the actual exam. Check your answers when you have completed the entire Examination. The correct answers for this Test, and all the other Tests, are assembled at the conclusion of this Examination.

TEST IX. ENGLISH USAGE

TIME: 8 Minutes

DIRECTIONS: *This is a test of standard written English. The rules may differ from everyday spoken English. Many of the following sentences contain grammar, usage, word choice, and idiom that would be incorrect in written composition. Some sentences are correct. No sentence has more than one error. Any error in a sentence will be underlined and lettered; all other parts of the sentence are correct and cannot be changed. If the sentence has an error, choose the underlined part that is incorrect, and mark that letter on your answer sheet. If there is no error, mark E on your answer sheet.*

1. If he <u>had had</u> the <u>forethought</u> to arrange an <u>appointment</u>,
        A   B   C

   his reception <u>would have been</u> more friendly. <u>No error.</u>
              D   E

2. His education had filled him <u>with anger</u> against those
                          A

   <u>whom</u> he <u>believed</u> had hurt or <u>humiliated</u> him. <u>No error.</u>
     B   C   D   E

3. The train <u>having stopped</u> several times during the night,
              A

   <u>we couldn't</u> even <u>lay</u> down <u>to sleep.</u> <u>No error.</u>
     B   C   D   E

4. <u>Admirers</u> of American ballet have made the claim that
     A

   <u>its</u> stars can dance <u>as well or</u> <u>better than</u> the best of the
     B   C   D

   Russian artists. <u>No error.</u>
                 E

5. Rather <u>than go</u> <u>with John,</u> he <u>decided</u> to stay <u>at home.</u>
        A   B   C   D

   <u>No error.</u>
     E

6. <u>You telling</u> the truth in the face of such <u>dire consequences</u>
     A   B

   <u>required</u> great <u>moral</u> courage. <u>No error.</u>
     C   D   E

7. The following description, together with the drawings,
   A
   present a master plan for the development of the airport.
   B   C   D
   No error.
   E

8. For conscience' sake he gave himself up, though no sus-
   A   B   C
   picion had been directed toward him. No error.
   D   E

9. I am depending on the medicine being delivered without
   A   B   C
   delay. No error.
   D   E

10. His father was disturbed to find that the boy had lied
    A   B   C
    rather than telling the truth. No error.
    D   E

11. Neither tears or protests effected the least change in their
    A   B   C
    parents' decision. No error.
    D   E

12. We thought the author of the letter to Aunt Mame to
    A   B   C
    be him. No error.
    D   E

13. The victim's mother, besides herself with grief, could
    A   B   C
    give no coherent account of the accident. No error.
    D   E

14. The children smiled at him, the laborer's greeted him by
    A   B
    waving their hats, and even the dogs licked his hand.
    C   D
    No error.
    E

15. Every sheet of ruled paper and every sheet of unruled
    A   B   C
    paper is carefully examined before it is returned.
    D
    No error.
    E

END OF TEST

TEST X. ENGLISH USAGE

TIME: 7 Minutes

DIRECTIONS: This is a test of standard written English. The rules may differ from everyday spoken English. Many of the following sentences contain grammar, usage, word choice, and idiom that would be incorrect in written composition. Some sentences are correct. No sentence has more than one error. Any error in a sentence will be underlined and lettered; all other parts of the sentence are correct and cannot be changed. If the sentence has an error, choose the underlined part that is incorrect, and mark that letter on your answer sheet. If there is no error, mark E on your answer sheet.

1. I saw Mr. Davis, him whom you pointed out last evening.
   A   B   C   D
   No error.
   E

2. When you have done your report, will you return this
   A   B
   memoranda as soon as possible? No error.
   C   D   E

3. This applicant lacks a few months' experience, otherwise
   A   B   C
   he is qualified for the position. No error.
   D   E

4. That scientist must be ingenuous to be able to arrive at
   A   B   C
   such valid conclusions. No error.
   D   E

5. She flouts her mink coat whenever she goes out with us
   A   B
   so that we'll think she's very wealthy. No error.
   C   D   E

6. Granting this to be true, what would you imply from the
   A   B   C
   statement which he has made? No error.
   D   E

7. We objected to him scolding us for our good, especially
   ——A———————————————————B—
   when he said it hurt him more than us. No error.
   ————C——————————————D———E

8. I was quite disappointed in his words, for I had always
   ————A——————————————————B———C——
   treated him like he was my brother. No error.
   ——————D——————————————E

9. Precisely the same thought sent the three of us into two
   ———A—
   different directions—they to West Berlin and me to
   ——B———————————C——————————————————D—
   Paris. No error.
   ——E

10. Many a box of oranges have been sent to New York by
    ————A——————————B———————————C——
    enthusiastic Californians. No error.
    ————D——————————————E

11. Let me say once and for all that between you and I
    —A—————————————————————————————B
    there can be no further friendship. No error.
    ——C——————————D——————————E

12. He proved to his own satisfaction that he was as shrewd as,
    ——A———————————B—————————————————C
    if not shrewder than, she. No error.
    ————D——————————E

13. The award should go to the pupil who we think the
    ——A————————————————————B
    parents had intended it for. No error.
    ——C——————D——————————E

14. We insist upon your telling us who else's signature ap-
    ——A————————B——————————C
    peared on this petition besides yours. No error.
    ——————————————D——————————E

15. The child felt very bad when his teacher criticized him
    —————A——————B
    before the entire class. No error.
    ——C——————D—————————E

END OF PART

PRACTICAL BUSINESS JUDGMENT

30 questions - 25 Minutes

DIRECTIONS: In testing your aptitude for business, they will ask you to evaluate a Situation and a Decision. You will be quizzed on goals, assumptions, conclusions, information, predictions, problems, options, and opinions. First, you will read a comprehensive analysis of a business situation; and then you will take two subtests based on your analysis: Data Application Quiz, and Data Evaluation Quiz.

Business Situation   To Bid or Not to Bid.

The Company. Wingfleet, Inc., is the fourth largest aircraft manufacturer in the world. Last year, the company's sales revenues were slightly under two billion dollars. Wingfleet, an old company in terms of aviation history, started production in 1921, struggled through the depression, and entered World War II a medium-sized company. Thousands of fighters and bombers rolled out of Wingfleet factories. It gained a worldwide reputation for well-designed and well-constructed military aircraft and continued to grow until the late 1960s. It now employs over 100,000 people in many plants throughout the U.S. The suppliers of Wingfleet employ another 75,000 workers. In short, Wingfleet is a solid supporter of the nation's economy.

Opportunity: The 2L-1000. John Franco, chairman of the Board of Directors of Wingfleet, carefully studies a lengthy proposal by an executive committee, consisting of three board members and three vice-presidents, recommending that the company bid on a new military-transport plane, the 2L-1000. This will be the largest and one of the fastest transport planes in the world. It will take at least six years to design, test, and bring into full production the 115 planes to be built for the government. The project will provide jobs for 25,000 Wingfleet workers, plus 20,000 jobs for Wingfleet suppliers.

Advantages. Nearly 90% of Wingfleet's business is with the U.S. government. Therefore the aircraft manufacturer's sales revenue is dependent on the federal budget. During times of national emergency (such as the cold war, the Vietnam and Korean conflicts), Wingfleet does very well. But lately Congress has cut defense expenditures, and these cuts have greatly reduced Wingfleet earnings. In 1966, for example, Wingfleet showed a profit of 51 million dollars. But last year, the company lost 33 million.

Thus it would be advantageous for Wingfleet to enter the commercial aircraft field to diversify its sources of revenue, and, paradoxically, this is one of the reasons why the executive committee recommends going all out to get the 2L-1000 contract. The huge transport, with slight alteration in design, will make an excellent commercial passenger plane, the committee claims.

In this connection, a preliminary survey of major airlines showed that nine domestic and foreign airlines indicated their willingness to order 201 of these commercial planes. Furthermore, should Wingfleet get the government contract, these airlines would order the planes and place immediate and substantial down payments.

Wingfleet has a tentative, but exclusive, contract with the Ponzol Company, one of Europe's leading engine manufacturers, to design and produce the plane's engines. This contract depends, of course, on whether Wingfleet decides to bid on the military contract and gets it. The fact that Ponzol engines will power the 2L-1000 should make the Pentagon regard the Wingfleet bid favorably.

Dangers. John Franco ponders the possible problems that might arise should Wingfleet take on this enormous project. In order to get the contract against vigorous competition, Wingfleet must make the lowest bid, which is estimated at 1.7 billion dollars if everything goes perfectly. Therefore, the executive committee suggests a bid of 2 billion dollars. But John Franco is aware, after 33 years with the company, that it is rare when actual development costs do not exceed estimates. He realizes that two or three major structural problems would quickly eat up the million-dollar gross profit.

On the other hand, he figures, costs over bid might not be disastrous. It is possible to renegotiate a government contract when cost overruns occur. Wingfleet has done this many times. In fact, cost overruns average 50% over accepted bids, and these have usually been made up by the government. However, John Franco wonders if Congress in its present anti-military spending mood would approve an appropriation to make up the difference.

Franco is also uneasy about the Ponzol Company. He has no doubt about the quality of Ponzol engines, but the foreign firm is nationalized. Its profits have been almost nonexistent for the past few years, and governments, he has discovered, are far less patient with losses than capitalist shareholders. Suppose the European government that owns Ponzol decides to liquidate the engine company in the middle of the 2L-1000 contract? He shudders at the thought.

Even though the airlines put down substantial payments for the 201 civilian planes, this money will not solve Wingfleet's poor cash position. The company must depend on 25 banks to advance half a billion dollars for the 2L-1000 project, and this will add substantially to Wingfleet's overall debt.

Finally, Wingfleet has tried to enter the commercial airplane field three times without success. The failures could not be blamed on inefficiency or lack of knowledge of the market, because careful surveys preceded each attempt. Yet each time Wingfleet guessed incorrectly. Could this happen again?

Decision. Despite his many misgivings, John Franco decides to recommend to the full Board of Directors that Wingfleet make a 2-billion-dollar bid for the 2L-1000 contract.

TEST XI. DATA APPLICATION

DIRECTIONS: Based on your understanding of the Business Situation, answer the following questions testing your comprehension of the information supplied in the passage. For each question, select the choice which best answers the question or completes the statement. When you understand the data and interpret it correctly, you will be better prepared to evaluate Data, as required by the second part of this test.

1. Most of Wingfleet's income is derived from sales to

   (A) foreign governments
   (B) the U.S. government
   (C) domestic airlines
   (D) manufacturing companies
   (E) private agencies

2. According to the passage, Wingfleet's earnings are erratic because of
   (A) poor management
   (B) cost overruns
   (C) the vagaries of the federal budget
   (D) attempts to enter the commercial aircraft field
   (E) high bank debt

3. One of the advantages of the 2L-1000 contract for Wingfleet would be that
   (A) the contract will lead to other government contracts
   (B) Congress doesn't particularly care what the cost will be
   (C) the contract will keep Wingfleet from going bankrupt
   (D) the military plane can also be sold to foreign governments
   (E) a change of design can change the military plane to a commercial one

4. A preliminary survey of major airlines shows that they
   (A) see no advantage in purchasing a commercial counterpart of 2L-1000

   (B) will purchase 201 planes of the 2L-1000 type with substantial down payments
   (C) will consider purchasing passenger planes after the 2L-1000 is produced
   (D) have no funds to buy new planes
   (E) are willing to lend money to Wingfleet to manufacture the 2L-1000

5. Regarding the 2L-1000 contract, the Wingfleet executive committee suggests that it

   (A) make a bid for the 2L-1000 contract

   (B) postpone a decision until there is further study of the project

   (C) turn down the contract

   (D) make a low bid to secure the contract

   (E) try to sell more of the commercial counterpart of the 2L-1000

6. John Franco considers the problem with cost overruns is that
   (A) Congress has frowned on paying these costs in the past
   (B) the loss would have to be sustained by Wingfleet
   (C) in its present mood Congress might not approve these extra costs
   (D) the government has little experience with overruns since they happen so infrequently
   (E) they would indicate that Wingfleet is very inefficient

S3329

7. One reason that the Pentagon might favor Wingfleet is that

   (A) Wingfleet has an excellent reputation in manufacturing commercial planes
   (B) The national economy might be thrown into chaos if Wingfleet does not get the contract
   (C) so many banks are willing to back Wingfleet
   (D) Wingfleet has already built a plane very similar to the 2L-1000
   (E) Ponzol engines will be used

8. Which of the following is a major concern of John Franco's regarding the 2L-1000 project?

   (A) Wingfleet does not have have the technical ability to produce such a plane as the 2L-1000.
   (B) The Wingfleet bid might be too high.
   (C) Wingfleet's suppliers in the U.S. might become bankrupt before the project is finished.
   (D) Ponzol might be liquidated.
   (E) A commercial counterpart of the 2L-1000 might be impractical.

9. Which of the following best describes Wingfleet's financial situation in its consideration of the 2L-1000 contract?

   (A) Wingfleet will have to depend on many banks to produce the 2L-1000.
   (B) Wingfleet's cash position is excellent because of recent high profits.
   (C) Wingfleet will need to obtain foreign capitol.
   (D) Wingfleet has little bank credit.
   (E) The down payments from the commercial airlines will provide enough cash to Wingfleet to see it through the 2L-1000 contract.

10. Which of the following best describes Wingfleet's past experiences in aircraft manufacturing?

   (A) Wingfleet has had little luck in entering the commercial aircraft industry.
   (B) Wingfleet was most successful in the commercial aircraft field, but gave this market up.
   (C) The company avoided military plane production.
   (D) The manufacturer has shown consistent losses on government aircraft contracts.
   (E) Wingfleet saw no reason to produce commercial aircraft.

END OF TEST

Go on to the next Test in the Examination, just as you would do on the actual exam. Check your answers when you have completed the entire Examination. The correct answers for this Test, and all the other Tests, are assembled at the conclusion of this Examination.

TEST XII. DATA EVALUATION

DIRECTIONS: Based on your analysis of the Situation, classify each of the following conclusions in one of five categories. Check:

(A) *if the conclusion is a MAJOR OBJECTIVE in making the decision; that is, the outcome or result sought by the decision maker.*

(B) *if the conclusion is a MAJOR FACTOR in arriving at the decision; that is a consideration, explicitly mentioned in the passage that is basic in determining the decision.*

(C) *if the conclusion is a MINOR FACTOR in making the decision; that is, a secondary consideration that affects the criteria tangentially, relating to a Major Factor rather than to an Objective.*

(D) *if the conclusion is a MAJOR ASSUMPTION made in deliberating; that is a supposition or projection made by the decision maker before weighing the variables.*

(E) *if the conclusion is an UNIMPORTANT ISSUE in getting to the point; that is a factor that is insignificant or not immediately relevant to the situation.*

11. Entrance into the commercial aircraft market.

12. Possible cost overruns of 2L-1000.

13. A projected six years to produce the 2L-1000.

14. The ability of the 2L-1000 to be modified to a commercial plane.

15. The possible liquidation of Ponzol.

16. Ninety per-cent of Wingfleet's business has been with the United States government.

17. Down payments by airlines.

18. The willingness of airlines to order 201 planes.

19. Diversification of market.

20. Possible cost overruns of 50%.

21. Recent drop in Wingfleet's profit.

22. Banks' willingness to lend $500,000.

23. Wingfleet's experience in producing military planes.

24. Congress's possible disapproval of cost overruns.

25. John Franco's 33-year experience with Wingfleet.

26. Wingfleet's lack of success in the commercial aircraft field.

27. Estimate that Wingfleet could produce the 2L-1000 for 1.7 billion dollars.

28. Government reduction of federal defense expenditures.

29. Exclusive contract with Ponzol.

30. Securing the 2L-1000 contract.

END OF EXAMINATION

CORRECT ANSWERS FOR VERISIMILAR EXAMINATION I.

(Please make every effort to answer the questions on your own before look-ing at these answers. You'll make faster progress by following this rule.)

TEST I. READING QUESTIONS

1.D	6.E	11.B	16.B	21.B	26.A
2.B	7.A	12.E	17.A	22.E	27.A
3.E	8.E	13.C	18.E	23.E	28.D
4.B	9.D	14.D	19.B	24.C	29.D
5.E	10.E	15.B	20.A	25.D	30.C

TEST II. DATA INTERPRETATION

1.B	3.B	5.A	7.A	9.B	11.B	13.C
2.C	4.B	6.D	8.D	10.D	12.C	

TEST III. PROBLEM SOLVING

1.E	7.A	13.C	19.D	25.B	31.C	37.C
2.C	8.C	14.B	20.B	26.D	32.A	38.A
3.B	9.A	15.B	21.A	27.A	33.C	39.A
4.B	10.C	16.A	22.C	28.B	34.A	40.E
5.A	11.B	17.C	23.B	29.B	35.E	41.C
6.C	12.D	18.E	24.A	30.C	36.A	42.B

TEST III. EXPLANATORY ANSWERS

1. **(E)** Every hour, the minute hand of a clock goes around once, or 360°. In two hours, it rotates 720°.

2. **(C)** $^{15}/_{45}$ would be $\frac{1}{3}$. With a larger denomin-ator, the fraction $^{15}/_{46}$ is less than $\frac{1}{3}$.

3. **(B)** Since the perimeter of a square is four times the length of a side, it is

$$4x \left(\frac{2x}{3} + 1 \right), \text{ or } \frac{8x + 12}{3}$$

4. **(B)** IQ is 100 times this result: the mental age of a person divided by his chronological age. This is $100 \times 160 \div 128$, which equals 125.

5. **(A)** Time does not vary with latitude (dis-tance from the equator), but only with longi-tude (distance from the prime meridian).

6. **(C)** ABD forms a right triangle with both legs equal to 1 inch. By the Pythagorean Theorem, AD = $\sqrt{2}$.

7. **(A)** Imagine the triangle ACH rotated 180° about AH. C will be lower than the present position of the ABEF plane.

8. **(C)** AX must be shorter than AH, which is $\sqrt{3}$, and longer than AB, which is 1.

9. **(A)** The first rotation puts X where ACGE was. The second leaves X in the same plane. The third rotation returns X to its original position.

10. **(C)** The carpenter needs a total of 33 inches for each board. The total length is 132 inches, or 11 feet.

11. **(B)** CM equals 1000 − 100, or 900. XL equals 50 − 10, or 40. IX equals 10 − 1, or 9. Their sum is 949.

12. **(D)** The line in the top graph is almost horizontal between 1957 and 1958. In the other years, the line is rising.

13. **(C)** In 1955, there were 1.2 deaths per 100 million passenger-miles, and 20 billion passenger-miles, which means there were 240 deaths. In 1956, there were 0.6 deaths per 100 million passenger-miles, and about 24 billion passenger-miles, which means there were about 144 deaths.

14. **(B)** In 1954, there were only 18 deaths, and in 1960, there were 300.

15. **(B)** See calculations for #13.

16. **(A)** In the period from 1951-1952, the death rate dropped to about $\frac{1}{3}$ of its previous level.

The answers to 17-21 can be readily seen from the diagram below.

17. C

18. E

19. D

20. B

21. A

22. **(C)** In the first trip, the motorist travels 120 miles at 60 m.p.h., which takes 2 hours. On the way back, he travels the same distance at 40 m.p.h., which takes 3 hours. His average rate is the total distance (240 miles) divided by the total time (5 hours), which yields 48 m.p.h.

23. **(B)** The proportion to be solved is $2\frac{1}{2}:4 = 1\frac{7}{8}:x$, where x is the length of the shorter dimension of the enlargement. Solving, x=3.

24. **(A)** The area of the circle is π times the square of the radius, or 9π. The area of the square is 36. Thus, the ratio is $\frac{9\pi}{36}$, or $\frac{\pi}{4}$. Approximating π as 3.14, we divide and obtain .785, which is closest to $\frac{4}{5}$.

25. **(B)** By simple substitutions, s=16×8×8, or 1024.

26. **(D)** If angles BAD and BCD are right angles, they are equal. Angle BAC equals angle BCA, since they are base angles of an isosceles triangle. Subtracting equals from equals, angle DAC equals angle DCA. Therefore, ACD is an isosceles triangle, and AD=CD.

27. **(A)** 10^2=100, or $\wedge\ \square\square$

28. **(B)** $\triangleright + \dashv + \lessgtr = 4+6+3=13 = \wedge\lessgtr$

29. **(B)** $\dfrac{\dashv}{\times} = \dfrac{6}{8} = \dfrac{3}{4}$

30. **(C)** $\wedge Z \dashv\ -\triangleright\ulcorner + \dfrac{\wedge\square}{Z} = 126-47+19\frac{1}{2} = 84 = \times\triangleright$

31. **(C)** The original 6 pounds contained .24 pounds of salt. Now, the same .24 pounds are in 5 pounds of solution, so the percentage is $\frac{24}{5}$, or $4\frac{4}{5}$.

32. **(A)** By the Law of Exponents, $(75)^3\times(75)^7 = (75)^{3+7}=(75)^{10}$.

33. **(C)** This is a proportion→ ¾ in.:6 in.=10 mi.:x. Solving, x=80 miles.

34. **(A)** If <u>h</u> is any positive quantity, then letting $\underline{d}' = (m + h) - \left(\dfrac{50}{m + h}\right)$, we can see that $\underline{d}'$ is greater than $\underline{d}$, since <u>h</u> is greater than zero, and $\dfrac{50}{m}$ is greater than $\dfrac{50}{m + h}$. Therefore, d increases as m does.

35. **(E)** One cubic foot equals 12^3 cubic inches, or 1728. Thus, one cubic foot of the metal would weigh 3456 pounds.

This is an unfolded view of the cube in questions 36-38:

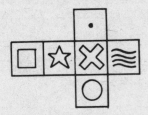

36. **(A)**

37. **(C)**

38. **(A)**

39. **(B)** The area of the circle is πr^2, and the circumference is $2\pi r$. If the area equals the circumference, solve the equation $\pi r^2 = 2\pi r$, so $r = 2$. The diameter is 2r, or 4 inches.

40. **(E)** $20 = 2 \times 2 \times 5$; $24 = 2 \times 2 \times 2 \times 3$; $32 = 2 \times 2 \times 2 \times 2 \times 2$. The least common multiple is found by taking the highest power of each factor, and multiplying the results. The highest power of 2 is 2^5, the highest power of 3 is 3^1, and the highest power of 5 is 5^1. The answer is $2^5 \times 3^1 \times 5^1$, or 480.

41. **(C)** The total volume is ten quarts. In the first solution, there are 20% of 6 quarts of alcohol, or 1.2. In the second solution, there are 60% of 4 quarts, or 2.4. Thus, there are 3.6 quarts of alcohol in 10 quarts of solution, and the percentage is 36%.

42. **(B)** If the circumference is 60 inches, since $C = 2\pi r$, substitute $C = 60$; therefore, $r = \dfrac{60}{2\pi}$

TEST IV. ANTONYMS

1.E	3.A	5.E	7.D	9.C	11.B	13.A
2.B	4.C	6.E	8.A	10.B	12.C	14.A

TEST V. VERBAL ANALOGIES

1.E	3.B	5.B	7.D	9.C	11.D
2.A	4.C	6.C	8.D	10.D	12.C

TEST VI. SENTENCE COMPLETIONS

1.C	3.C	5.E	7.C	9.C	11.C
2.A	4.A	6.A	8.B	10.C	12.A

TEST VII. DATA SUFFICIENCY

1.C	3.D	5.C	7.E	9.E	11.C	13.D	15.C
2.C	4.E	6.E	8.D	10.A	12.B	14.E	

TEST VII. EXPLANATORY ANSWERS

1. (C)

By statement (2) if 30% are boys, 70% are girls. Using statement (1) let x = number of students.

.70x = 210
70x = 21,000
  x = 300

2. (C)

Using both statements take 10% of 450 = 45. Add 45 to 450 and 495 passed geometry this year.

3. (D)

By statement (1) if the radius of the semicircle is 7, then the side of the square is 14. Hence the areas of both geometric figures can be found. By statement (2) if the side of the square is 14, then the radius of the semicircle is 7 and both areas again can be found.

4. (E)

By statement (1) a could equal a 9 or 10. By statement (2) b could equal an 8 or 9. Hence whether a + b is odd cannot be determined.

5. (C)

Using both statements

Statement (1) $\dfrac{\text{Seniors}}{300 \text{ boys}}$ $\dfrac{\text{Juniors}}{250 \text{ boys}}$

Statement (2) $\frac{200}{300}$ girls $\frac{200}{450}$ girls
  Totals
Seniors = $\frac{300}{500} = \frac{3}{5}$ Juniors $\frac{250}{450} = \frac{5}{9}$
Since $\frac{3}{5} > \frac{5}{9}$, the probability lies with the Senior class.

6. (E)

Using both statements only one side of the triangle is known. Hence the perimeter cannot be determined.

7. (E)

The price of both cars would have to be known before the question could be answered.

8. (D)

By statement (1)

$V = e^3$
$e^3 = 9e$
$e^2 = 9$
 $e = 3$

By statement (2)

 $A = 6e^2$
$6e^2 = 18e$
$6e = 18$
 $e = 3$

9. (E)

Since the triangles are not determined as being collinear, it is impossible to determine if there is a point common between all three triangles.

10. (A)

By statement (1) if AC = CB, then any point on a ⊥ bisector is equidistant from the ends of the line segment.

11.   (C)

By statement (1)

$$\frac{A + B + T}{3} = 8$$

$$A + B + T = 24$$

By statement (2)

$$-A = B$$

substituting in statement (1)

$$A + (-A) + T = 24$$
$$T = 24$$

12.   (B)

To find the area of the shaded portion, you must subtract the area of the circle from the area of the trapezoid. To find the area of a circle, you need its radius ($A = \pi r^2$). To find the area of a trapezoid, you need both bases and its height. $A = \frac{1}{2}h(b_1 + b_2)$. By statement (2) given the circumference 14π, the radius is 7. If the radius is 7, the height of the trapezoid is 14.

13.   (D)

By statement (1)

$$C = 12\pi$$
$$2\pi r = 12\pi$$
$$2r = 12$$
$$r = 6$$

By statement (2)

$$\frac{2\pi r}{\pi r^2} = \frac{1}{3}$$
$$\frac{2}{r} = \frac{1}{3}$$
$$r = 6$$

14.   (E)

No mention is made if the black, white, and brown are the only colors in the bag.

15.   (C)

Statement (2) is necessary to eliminate two people having the same friend in statement (1).

TEST VIII. READING COMPREHENSION

1.B	4.D	7.C	10.B	13.A	16.E
2.B	5.E	8.D	11.A	14.D	17.D
3.A	6.B	9.E	12.D	15.B	

TEST IX. ENGLISH USAGE

1.E	4.C	7.B	10.D	13.B
2.B	5.E	8.E	11.A	14.B
3.C	6.A	9.B	12.E	15.E

TEST X. ENGLISH USAGE

1.B	4.B	7.A	10.B	13.B
2.E	5.A	8.D	11.B	14.C
3.C	6.C	9.C	12.E	15.E

TEST XI. TEST XII. DATA APPLICATION AND EVALUATION

1.B	6.C	11.A	16.C	21.B	26.C
2.C	7.E	12.D	17.C	22.C	27.E
3.E	8.D	13.E	18.B	23.C	28.B
4.B	9.A	14.B	19.A	24.C	29.B
5.A	10.A	15.C	20.C	25.E	30.B

TEST XI. TEST XII. EXPLANATORY ANSWERS

Elucidation, clarification, explication and a little help with the fundamental facts covered in the Previous Test. These are the points and principles likely to crop up in the form of questions on future tests.

1. **(B)** It is stated that nearly 90% of Wingfleet's business is done with the U.S. government.

2. **(C)** It is emphasized that Wingfleet has had to depend on defense contracts which can greatly fluctuate from year to year.

3. **(E)** By being able to modify 2L-1000, the company can enter the commercial aircraft field, which is seen as an advantage.

4. **(B)** Commercial airlines are said to be ready to purchase 201 passenger planes and are willing to make immediate down payments if Wingfleet gets the 2L-1000 contract.

5. **(A)** It is stated that the executive committee suggests making a bid for the 2L-1000 contract, a recommendation which Franco decides to carry to the Board of Directors.

6. **(C)** It is stated that Congress is in an anti-military mood and might frown on paying cost overruns. **(A)** is incorrect because Congress has been generous with cost overruns before. In **(B)**, the important word is "would," to indicate that Wingfleet would have to pay for the cost overruns. **(E)** might be true but is not so stated. **(D)** is obviously untrue.

7. **(E)** The fact that Ponzol engines would be used in the 2L-1000 is assumed to carry great weight with the Pentagon. **(A)** is wrong; Wingfleet's reputation has not been made in the commercial aircraft field. **(B)** is exaggerated; many people might be thrown out of work, but failure to get the contract would not throw the huge U.S. economy into a state of chaos. As far as **(C)** is concerned, many banks would back Wingfleet should it receive the contract, but it is not stated that this fact would influence the Pentagon's decision. **(D)** is obviously incorrect.

8. **(D)** John Franco is worried about Ponzol because it is a nationalized company whose foreign government might liquidate it at any time. **(B)**, **(C)**, and **(A)** are obviously wrong. **(E)** is incorrect because it is stated that Wingfleet tried three times to enter the commercial aircraft field without success.

9. **(A)** It is true that 25 banks would have to lend half a billion dollars for Wingfleet to produce the 2L-1000. **(B)** is wrong; recently Wingfleet has experienced a deficit. It is stated that John Franco has been with Wingfleet for 33 years, so **(C)** is incorrect. Since **(A)** is correct, **(D)** and **(E)** are wrong.

10. **(A)** It is stated that Wingfleet tried to enter the commercial aircraft field three times without success. Therefore **(B)** and **(E)** are incorrect. **(C)** is wrong; 90% of the company's business has been in the military plane field. **(D)** must be wrong since Wingfleet would not have been able to remain in business had it shown consistent losses on government contracts.

LETTER CODE FOR EVALUATING DATA

(A) means that the Conclusion is a Major Objective;
(B) means that the Conclusion is a Major Factor;
(C) means that the Conclusion is a Minor Factor;
(D) means that the Conclusion is a Major Assumption;
(E) means that the Conclusion is an Unimportant Issue.

11. **(A)** It is stated that Wingfleet wishes to enter the commercial aircraft field, which is a major reason to try to secure the 2L-1000 contract.

12. **(D)** It is not absolutely certain that the 2L-1000 will not be produced at the bid price, although John Franco is dubious that it can.

13. **(E)** The length of time it will take to produce the 2L-1000 does not seem to concern anyone.

14. **(B)** The possibility that the 2L-1000 can be converted to a commercial plane is a major factor contributing to a major objective of Wingfleet to enter the commercial market.

15. **(C)** The possible liquidation of Ponzol by a foreign government is a factor relating to the exclusive contract held by Wingfleet.

16. **(C)** Since 90% of Wingfleet's business is with the government, government reductions in military spending is a major reason why Wingfleet wishes to enter the commercial field.

17. **(C)** The willingness by airlines to make substantial down payments is a minor factor leading to the major factor of a purchase order of 201 passenger planes, which, in turn, influences the major objective of Wingfleet's entrance into the commercial aircraft field.

18. **(B)** The order for 201 passenger planes is a major factor influencing the major objective of Wingfleet's entrance into the commercial aircraft field.

19. **(A)** Diversification is a major objective since Wingfleet has had to depend on the single market of government contracts.

20. **(C)** Cost overruns are a concern in the decision to obtain the contract.

21. **(B)** The drop in Wingfleet's profits caused by the vagaries of defense budgets is a major factor in Wingfleet's desire to diversify.

22. **(C)** That the banks are willing to lend half a billion dollars is a minor but necessary factor in securing the 2L-1000 contract. Without such loans, Wingfleet could not build the plane.

23. **(C)** Wingfleet's experience in military plane production involves its ability to seek and obtain the 2L-1000 contract.

24. **(C)** Congress's disapproval of cost overruns is a variable considered in seeking the contract.

25. **(E)** Franco's experience is unimportant in the deliberations.

26. **(C)** Wingfleet's lack of success in the commercial aircraft field is a factor considered in its ability to be successful in this venture.

27. **(E)** Although Franco doubts the estimate of 1.7 billion dollars to produce the 2L-1000, he puts this factor aside in arriving at his decision to recommend to the Board of Directors that Wingfleet try to secure the government contract.

28. **(B)** Governmental budget reductions are very important in Wingfleet's desire to enter the commercial aircraft field.

29. **(B)** Wingfleet believes that having an exclusive contract with Ponzol will have a direct bearing on securing the 2L-1000 contract, which is a major factor.

30. **(B)** Securing the 2L-1000 contract is a major factor in entering the commercial aircraft field.

GRADUATE MANAGEMENT ADMISSION TEST

II. A VERISIMILAR EXAM

This Verisimilar Examination is patterned after the actual exam. In all fairness we must emphasize that it is not a copy of the actual exam, which is guarded closely and may not be duplicated. The exam you'll take may have more difficult questions in some areas than you will encounter on this Verisimilar Exam. On the other hand, some questions may be easier, but don't bank on it. This book is supposed to give you confidence . . . not over-confidence.

The time allowed for the entire examination is 3½ hours. In order to create the climate of the test to come, that's precisely what you should allow yourself . . . no more, no less. Use a watch and keep a record of your time, especially since you may find it convenient to take the test in several sittings.

ANALYSIS AND TIMETABLE: II. VERISIMILAR EXAMINATION

This table is both an analysis of the exam that follows and a priceless preview of the actual test. Look it over carefully and use it well. Since it lists both subjects and times, it points up not only what to study, but also how much time to spend on each topic. Making the most of your study time adds valuable points to your examination score.

SUBJECT TESTED	Time Allowed
READING RECALL	35 minutes
DATA INTERPRETATION & PROBLEM SOLVING	75 minutes
VERBAL ABILITY	20 minutes
DATA SUFFICIENCY	15 minutes
READING COMPREHENSION	20 minutes
ENGLISH USAGE	15 minutes
PRACTICAL BUSINESS JUDGMENT	25 minutes

READING RECALL

4 passages-27 questions

TEST I. READING PASSAGES

TIME: 15 Minutes

DIRECTIONS: This is a test to determine your ability to remember main ideas and significant details. You are to read the four passages that follow in a period of ten minutes altogether. It is suggested that you divide your time equally among the four passages. When the time is up, you will be asked to recall certain ideas and facts about the four passages. You will not be able to refer back to the passages after 15 minutes.

PASSAGE 1

What is to happen about transport? Evidently there are huge and important changes in prospect. A decade or so from now, there will have been yet another transformation in the way in which people and their goods are moved from place to place. Old techniques are being faced with attenuation or even extinction, sometimes because better methods of travelling have come along but sometimes simply because the old methods have become intolerable.

The development of recent decades most obviously likely to be continued is the tendency for alternative methods of travel to co-exist, and so to offer potential travellers a choice. Within large cities, underground transport is usually an alternative to several ways of travelling on the surface. Roads, railways and airlines are in competition, and there are still people who cross the North Atlantic by sea. (Most freight goes that way, of course.) Choices between co-existing alternatives are usually made on rational grounds, although this does not imply that cheapness is all that matters.

In circumstances like these, even minor technical developments can trigger off marked changes in the pattern of transport. In Britain, electric traction promises to increase the distance over which railways can win passengers from airlines. Quite modest improvements of public transport in cities could do much to diminish congestion from motor cars. Oil tankers displacing 300,000 tons like that ordered from a Japanese yard by Gulf Oil could decisively affect the pattern of petro-leum distribution from the major oilfields and —at the same time—encourage the pipeline operators, who offer the simplest and often the cheapest means of bulk transport. Then, there is the Boeing 747 aircraft, which is likely to do for people what the huge tankers will do for petroleum—trunk route transport will flourish, but getting off the beaten track will be increasingly troublesome. All these changes, promised or merely possible in the pattern of transport, have in common what is, in the broadest sense, an economic stimulus.

From this point of view, the benefits of new technical developments may be different from what their supporters intend. Thus, ironically, it could be that the first—and perhaps even the only—beneficial consequence of the Anglo-French project to build the *Concord* supersonic airliner will be to ensure that the operating costs of slower aircraft are steadily reduced. More soberly, there could well be a time, in the early 'seventies, when huge subsonic aircraft ply across the North Atlantic and similar routes, and smaller and faster aircraft travel less busy but longer routes. (It does not, of course, follow that the British and French Governments will recover their expenditure on the *Concord*.) Yet again, diversity seems to promise that the pattern of transport will be helped to find its most economic form. But what kind of diversity would be best?

Fast transport between cities separated by a few hundred miles is becoming urgently necessary in densely populated areas, particularly in Eu-

71

rope, North America and Japan. The United States Government is financing a number of exploratory investigations bearing on specific problems such as linking the major cities on the Atlantic seaboard. However, it remains to be seen whether the result will really reach beyond schemes for patching up the existing railway network to some of the more ambitious schemes which are sometimes heard of—monorails, pneumatic tubes with trains inside, and deep-bored tunnels intended to enable trains to oscillate from one city to another with no expenditure of energy except for overcoming friction and air resistance. One difficulty is that these transport studies, although well supported, are not being given the kind of attention lavished, for example, on getting to the Moon. In Britain, the somewhat comparable development of hovercraft, also likely to be important over distances of a few hundred miles (by sea or dry land), is not moving forward as vigorously as it might because of a tendency to expect that this device should show a profit from the beginning. Then intra-city transport systems of radically new design are being explored chiefly on the backs of envelopes.

There may eventually be even greater benefits to be won by planning cities, and indeed whole countries, in such a way that the advantages of novel kinds of transport networks can be exploited to the full. Within existing cities, for example, populations tend to be uniformly distributed on the ground, although with a density decreasing outwards from some central zone. The interactions between the distribution of population and an existing transport network tend to be limited to the proclivity for population to distribute itself, over the course of time, in such a way that all transport links are equally congested. It is, however, entirely conceivable that some quite different pattern of population would lend itself more easily to the use of fast transport links. If, within cities, populations were to be gathered into a number of more or less separate concentrations, it might be possible to win great advantages from potentially fast means of travel—monorails for example—which are not likely to be economic as simple replacements for existing underground railways. In other words, there is a strong case for asking that the fabric of a city and the means of transport used within it be designed as a delicately integrated whole. Similarly, cities should be designed or encouraged to develop in such a way as to cater more efficiently for the need to move people and goods easily from one to the next. This, after all, is how the great oil companies organize their affairs (although even they find it difficult to regulate the disposition of the eventual users of petroleum products).

PASSAGE 2

Chemical engineering was not originally science-based in the same sense as electrical engineering. Although the chemical industry was firmly based on the science of chemistry, the role of the chemical engineer was originally merely to provide vessels, pipes, pumps and so on to enable a reaction to be carried out under the conditions specified by the chemist. It is true that there are early examples in which the engineering interacted with and influenced the process—for example, the lead-chamber sulphuric acid process, the Solvay ammonia-soda process and the Haber-Bosch ammonia synthesis. In general, however, the chemical engineer had little influence on the process, and there was very little science involved in chemical engineering. The most difficult part of the job was the choice of the right materials of construction—but until quite recently science has been of little help in this respect.

The type of chemical engineer I have just described—typical, perhaps, of the year 1900—has given way to someone who occupies a very different position. The scientific and unspecialized nature of the training of the chemical engineer fits him for employment in many industries apart from the chemical industry—for example, combustion engineering, food processing and extraction metallurgy. The proportion of chemical engineers employed in non-chemical industries in our country has risen steadily in the past decade, and now amounts to about 25 per cent. This wider dissemination of the philosophy of chemical engineering is an important feature of the development of the profession, and is likely to be of great benefit to certain industries which have been somewhat isolated from the mainstream of technological development.

I shall use the phrase "chemical engineering science" to mean the science employed by chemical engineers in their various activities. It is clear that the chemical engineer does not himself always have to develop scientific methods for solving the problems which he encounters. For example, although he is professionally very deeply concerned with the properties of materials, he is not usually thought to be responsible for developing the science and technology of materials—metallurgy, corrosion, refractories, and so on. Other technologists have assumed this responsibility, which on the whole requires a different scientific background from that of the chemical engineer. Chemical engineering science is, therefore, the body of applied science developed by chemical engineers for their own purposes, in fields not covered by other branches of technology. It would be a great mistake to think of the content of chemical engineering science as permanently fixed. It is likely to alter greatly over the years in response to the changing requirements of industry and to the occasional technological "break-through."

The functions of chemical engineering science are mainly economic. One is the development of quantitative design procedures, so that full-scale plants can be designed by calculation, if necessary with the help of laboratory-scale experiments, but if possible without the need for expensive and time-consuming pilot-scale experiments. The more precise the design procedures which can be developed, the more precisely is it possible to optimize the design of plant, and the narrower becomes the wasteful margin of safety imposed by ignorance. There is also the need to improve the efficiency of processes and of the plant in which they are carried out—for example, to obtain a higher yield in a chemical reaction, a higher plate-efficiency in a distillation column, or a machine which will produce granular material of a more nearly uniform size. There is also the matter of true invention, leading to quite new processes and devices. Although science may not always provide the inspiration for inventions, it must usually be called in to develop them properly. Finally, there is the need to develop not only automatic but also self-optimizing processes and plants; in the chemical factory of the near future we shall have replaced not only the workman but the management by instruments.

PASSAGE 3

Educators are seriously concerned about the high rate of dropouts among the doctor of philosophy candidates and the consequent loss of talent to a nation in need of Ph.D.s. Some have placed the dropout loss as high as 50 per cent. The extent of the loss was, however, largely a matter of expert guessing.

Last week a well-rounded study was published. It was based on 22,000 questionnaires sent to former graduate students who were enrolled in 24 universities between 1950 and 1954 and seemed to show many past fears to be groundless.

The dropout rate was found to be 31 per cent, and in most cases the dropouts, while not completing the Ph.D. requirements, went on to productive work.

They are not only doing well financially, but, according to the report, are not far below the income levels of those who went on to complete their doctorates.

The study, called "Attrition of Graduate Students at the Ph.D. Level in the Traditional Arts and Sciences," was made at Michigan State University under a $60,000 grant from the United States Office of Education. It was conducted by Dr. Allan Tucker, former assistant dean of the university and now chief academic officer of the Board of Regents of the State University System of Florida.

Discussing the study last week, Dr. Tucker said the project was initiated "because of the concerns frequently expressed by graduate faculties and administrators that some of the individuals who dropped out of Ph.D. programs were capable of completing the requirements for the degree.

"Attrition at the Ph.D. level is also thought to be a waste of precious faculty time and a drain on university resources already being used to capacity. Some people expressed the opinion that the shortage of highly trained specialists and college teachers could be reduced by persuading the dropouts to return to graduate school to complete the Ph.D. program."

"The results of our research," Dr. Tucker concluded, "did not support these opinions."

The study found that:

(1) Lack of motivation was the principal reason for dropping out.

(2) Most dropouts went as far in their doctoral programs as was consistent with their levels of ability or their specialties.

(3) Most dropouts are now engaged in work consistent with their education and motivation.

(4) The dropout rate was highest in the humanities (50%) and lowest in the natural sciences (29%)—and is higher in lower-quality graduate schools.

Nearly 75 per cent of the dropouts said there was no academic reason for their decision, but those who mentioned academic reasons cited failure to pass qualifying examinations, uncompleted research and failure to pass language exams.

"Among the single most important personal reasons identified by dropouts for noncompletion of their Ph.D. program," the study found, "lack of finances was marked by 19 per cent."

As an indication of how well the dropouts were doing, a chart showed that 2 per cent whose studies were in the humanities were receiving $20,000 and more annually while none of the Ph.D.'s with that background reached this figure. The Ph.D.'s shone in the $7,500 to $15,000 bracket with 78 per cent at that level against 50 per cent for the dropouts. This may also be an indication of the fact that top salaries in the academic fields, where Ph.D.'s tend to rise to the highest salaries, are still lagging behind other fields.

In the social sciences 5 per cent of the Ph.D.'s reached the $20,000 plus figure as against 3 per cent of the dropouts but in the physical sciences they were neck-and-neck with 5 per cent each.

Academic institutions employed 90 per cent of the humanities Ph.D.'s as against 57 per cent of the humanities dropouts. Business and industry employed 47 per cent of the physical science Ph.D.'s and 38 per cent of the physical science dropouts. Government agencies took 16 per cent of the social science Ph.D.'s and 32 per cent of the social science dropouts.

As to the possibility of getting dropouts back on campus, the outlook was glum.

"The main conditions which would have to prevail for at least 25 per cent of the dropouts who might consider returning to graduate school would be to guarantee that they would retain their present level of income and in some cases their present job."

PASSAGE 4

It is a part of the charm of little Tahiti, or Otaheite, whose double island is not more than a hundred miles about, that it has been the type of the oceanic island in story.

With its discovery begins the interest that awoke Europe by the apparent realization of man in his earliest life—a life that recalled the silver if not the golden age. Here men and women made a beautiful race, living free from the oppression of nature, and at first sight also free from the cruel and terrible superstitions of many savage tribes. I have known people who could recall the joyous impression made upon them by these stories of new paradises, only just opened; and both Wallis's and Bougainville's short and official reports are bathed in a feeling of admiration, that takes no definite form, but refers both to the people and the place and the gentleness of the welcome.

The state of nature had just then been the staple reference in the polemic literature of the latter part of the eighteenth century. The refined and dry civilization of the few was troubled by the confused sentiments, the dreams, and the obscure desires of the ignorant and suffering many. Their inarticulate voice was suddenly phrased by Rousseau. With that cry came in the literary belief in the natural man, in the possibility of analyzing the foundations of government and civilization, in the perfectibility of the human race and its persistent goodness when freed from the weight of society's blunders and oppressions.

Later, Byron:—

"—the happy shores without a law,
Where all partake the earth without dispute,
And bread itself is gathered as a fruit;
Where none contest the fields, the woods, the streams:
The goddess age, where gold disturbs no dreams."

There is no doubt that at the moment of the discovery our islanders had reached the full extent of their civilization; that, numerous, splendid, and untainted in their physical development, they seemed to live in a facility of existence, in an absence of anxiety emphasized by their love of pleasure and fondness for society,—by a simplicity of conscience which found no fault in what we reprobate,—in a happiness which is not and could not be our own. The "pursuit of happiness" in which these islanders were engaged, and in which they seemed successful, is the catchword of the eighteenth century.

People were far then from the cruel ideas of Hobbes; and the more amiable views of the nature of man, and of his rights, echo in the sentimentality of the eighteenth century like the sound of the island surf about Tahiti.

The name recalls so many associations of ideas, so much romance of reading, so much of the history of thought, that I find it difficult to disentangle the varying strands of the threads. There are many boyish recollections behind the charm of Melville's *Omoo* and Stoddard's *Idylls,* or even the mixed pleasure of Loti's *Marriage.*

I believe too that my feelings are intensified because they are directed towards an island, a word, a thing of all time marked by man as something wherein to place the ideal, the supernatural, the home of the blest, the abode of the dead, the fountain of eternal youth, as in Heine's song about the island of Bimini:

> "Little birdling Colibri,
> Lead us thou to *Tahiti!*"

END OF SECTION

If you finish before the allotted time is up, work on this part only. When time is up, proceed directly to the next part and do not return to this part.

TEST 1. READING QUESTIONS

TIME: 20 minutes

DIRECTIONS: Answer the following questions in accordance with the contents of the preceding passages. You are not to turn back to the passages.

QUESTIONS ON PASSAGE 1

1. Basically, transportation plans for the future are made in the light of
   (A) economic considerations
   (B) government regulations
   (C) moral and ethical standards
   (D) political interrelations
   (E) anticipated growth of cities

2. The article brings out that
   (A) there is much less intra-city transport congestion in the small cities than in the large cities
   (B) population increases as one leaves the center of an average-sized city
   (C) the next ten years should, if we are to judge by what has happened in the last decade, bring few changes in the means of transportation
   (D) eventually there will, for reasons of efficiency, be only one mode of transportation
   (E) transportation of commercial goods from Boston and New York to London and Paris is, for the most part, by boat

3. The selection makes it clear that our government is spending money so that it will be easier in the future to transport goods and passengers between New York,
   (A) Los Angeles, and San Francisco
   (B) Minneapolis, and Omaha
   (C) Chicago, and Kansas City
   (D) Savannah, and Jacksonville
   (E) Denver, and Tulsa

4. The least expensive way to ship oil is most often by
   (A) freighter   (B) plane
   (C) railroad   (D) truck
           (E) none of the above

5. The helicopter type of transportation for distances shorter than the customary jet plane flight
   (A) is being developed with unexpected rapidity
   (B) shows little chance of eventual success
   (C) is slow in development because immediate profits are not being realized
   (D) is being seriously considered for flights to the moon some time in the 1970's
   (E) is of little interest to transport planners because of its poor safety record

6. The author states or implies that
   (A) an innovator of a transportation technique may find such a technique advantageous, but not in the way originally anticipated
   (B) the giant British jet planes are now actively transporting oil but ships are still being used by Britain for oil transportation
   (C) Japanese oil tankers are, at the present time, being rapidly replaced by pipelines for the transportation of oil
   (D) supersonic planes will, before long, carry freight rather than passengers
   (E) railroads are doomed as more efficient means of transportation are developed

S1361

7. The writer would *not* agree that
   (A) future communities should be planned with transportation efficiency as a major consideration
   (B) the replacement of current railways by monorails would save money in a short period of time
   (C) an oil company would do well to use more than one type of transportation for its product

   (D) we should divert some of the money being used for putting a man on the moon to the improvement of transportation in our own country

   (E) electric locomotives have helped to make railroad transportation more "palatable" to the passenger

QUESTIONS ON PASSAGE 2

8. The general tenor of the article is that
   (A) the chemical engineer does not have the prestige of the other engineers
   (B) great strides have been made—and will continue to be made—in the chemical engineering profession
   (C) engineering, in general, is a profession which does not receive adequate recognition financially as well as socially
   (D) there is much difference of opinion among scientists in regard to whether chemical engineering is a true science
   (E) the most trying field of all engineering is chemical engineering

9. The word "refractories" in the third paragraph means materials which

   (A) rust readily
   (B) do not behave as expected
   (C) crack easily
   (D) are highly resistant to intense heat
   (E) are made in a chemical factory

10. "The functions of chemical engineering science are mainly economic." This statement implies that

    (A) chemicals are more costly today than ever before
    (B) other engineering sciences are relatively uninterested in the profit motive
    (C) the chemical engineer is not concerned with moral issues
    (D) chemical engineering is the most lucrative of all engineering professions
    (E) chemical engineering, by securing maximum efficiency, will save money

11. The author implies that

    (A) faith plays as important a part as science in chemical engineering
    (B) the chemical engineer should not be concerned with working with metals

    (C) the science of chemical engineering is far from set in regard to its function
    (D) the chemical engineer ought not to employ a scientific method
    (E) more often than not, the chemical engineer has the same content background as the electrical engineer

12. At the beginning of the twentieth century, the chemical engineer
    (A) knew little about science
    (B) did not put his scientific background to much use
    (C) was not capable of selecting appropriate materials to do the job required
    (D) frequently did the work of the electrical engineer
    (E) was not required to have a degree

13. The selection indicates that
    (A) chemical engineering is an art rather than a science
    (B) about one-fourth of the nation's engineers are chemical engineers
    (C) the prototype of all engineers was the chemical engineer
    (D) the chemical engineer no longer concerns himself with pumps and pipes
    (E) the development of certain processes required a scientific approach on the part of the chemical engineer

14. After reading this article, one would think that the writer
    (A) is opposed to labor unions
    (B) believes that creativity is to be discouraged among engineers
    (C) feels that the majority of chemical engineers have selfish interests
    (D) stresses the need for a technological revolution
    (E) urges chemical engineers to develop their own procedures to solve problems —not to depend on other technologists

QUESTIONS ON PASSAGE 3

15. The author would agree that

    (A) steps should be taken to get the drop-
    outs back to school particularly in cer-
    tain disciplines
    (B) since the dropout does just about as
    well financially as the Ph.D. degree-
    getter, there is no justifiable reason for
    the former to return to his studies.
    (C) the high dropout rate is largely attrib-
    utable to the lack of stimulation on the
    part of faculty members
    (D) the dropout should return to a lower
    quality school to continue his studies
    (E) the Ph.D. holder is generally a better
    adjusted person than the dropout

16. The article states that

    (A) not having sufficient funds to continue
    accounts for more Ph.D. dropouts than
    all the other reasons combined
    (B) in fields such as English, philosophy,
    and the arts, the dropouts are doing
    better in the higher salary brackets
    than the Ph.D.'s
    (C) at the $10,000 earning level, there is a
    higher percentage of dropouts than the
    percentage of Ph.D.'s
    (D) in physics, geology, and chemistry, the
    Ph.D.'s are twice as numerous in the
    higher salary brackets than the drop-
    outs
    (E) the government agencies employ twice as
    many dropouts as they do Ph.D's

17. Research has shown that

    (A) dropouts are substantially below
    Ph.D.'s in financial attainment
    (B) the incentive factor is a minor one in
    regard to pursuing Ph.D. studies
    (C) the Ph.D. candidate is likely to change
    his field of specialization if he drops
    out
    (D) about one-third of those who start
    Ph.D. work do not complete the work
    to earn the degree
    (E) there are comparatively few dropouts
    in the Ph.D. humanities disciplines

18. Meeting foreign language requirements for
the Ph.D.

    (A) is the most frequent reason for drop-
    ping out
    (B) is more difficult for the science candi-
    date than for the humanities candidate
    (C) is considered part of the so-called
    "qualification" examination
    (D) is an essential for acquiring a Ph.D.
    degree
    (E) does not vary in difficulty among uni-
    versities

19. Dr. Tucker felt that

    (A) a primary purpose of his research proj-
    ect was to arrive at a more efficient
    method for dropping incapable Ph.D.
    applicants
    (B) a serious aspect of the dropout situa-
    tion was the deplorable waste of pro-
    ductive talent
    (C) one happy feature about the dropout
    situation was that the dropouts went
    into college teaching rather than into
    research
    (D) his project should be free of outside
    interference and so he rejected outside
    financial assistance for the project
    (E) Ph.D. dropouts were responsible for
    considerable loss of time and money
    on the part of the university

20. After reading the article, one would refrain
from concluding that

    (A) colleges and universities employ a sub-
    stantial number of Ph.D. dropouts
    (B) Ph.D.'s are not earning what they de-
    serve in nonacademic positions
    (C) the study, *Attrition of Graduate Stu-
    dents at the Ph.D. Level in the Tradi-
    tional Arts and Sciences,* was con-
    ducted with efficiency and validity
    (D) a Ph.D. dropout, by and large, does not
    have what it takes to earn the degree
    (E) optimism reigns in regard to getting
    Ph.D. dropouts to return to their pur-
    suit of the degree

QUESTIONS ON PASSAGE 4

21. Tahiti
    (A) adjoins the island of Otaheite
    (B) is more or less circular with a diameter of approximately 100 miles
    (C) was visited by Rousseau
    (D) was known for the beauty of its women
    (E) had among its natives many well-educated persons

22. Byron looks upon Tahiti as a land where
    (A) individuals are loath to complete their tasks
    (B) money is relatively of little importance
    (C) lawlessness prevails
    (D) inhabitants substitute fruit for bread
    (E) the people live in dire poverty

23. Thomas Hobbes (1588-1679), the English philosopher, believed that
    (A) of the three forms of sovereignty—monarchy, aristocracy, democracy—the latter is the most effective in securing peace
    (B) to achieve the good life, a man must cultivate the virtues
    (C) the ruler is limited to the making of general laws—he is not to pass judgment upon individuals
    (D) pleasure is the standard by which every good and every right action is to be judged
    (E) in a state of nature, one must expect a war of every man against every other man

24. Wallis and Bougainville were primarily
    (A) scientists   (B) historians
    (C) navigators   (D) philosophers
         (E) missionaries

25. Literature in the latter part of the eighteenth century was characterized by
    (A) stress on the importance of the individual
    (B) a reversion to classical patterns by imitating the Latin and Greek poets
    (C) religious views comparable to those of the early theologians
    (D) bold references to the vices of mankind
    (E) a divorcement from the realities of life

26. The author considers the Tahitians
    (A) superstitious and savage until visitors to their island showed them a better way of life
    (B) a backward race who were happy in their stupidity
    (C) a troubled people suffering from lack of adequate diet and deprived of the comforts of civilization
    (D) a well-adjusted folk who did not especially benefit from the influence of the visiting white men
    (E) a refined community, highly civilized, quite unlike the natives of other Pacific islands

27. A recently published documentary which brings out what happened eventually to the Tahiti natives as a result of the visiting Englishmen, has the appropriate title:
    (A) *A New World*
    (B) *Eden Revisited*
    (C) *The Pursuit of Happiness*
    (D) *Intermarriage*
    (E) *The Fatal Impact*

END OF PART
If you finish before the allotted time is up, work on this part only.
When time is up, proceed directly to the next part and do not
return to this part.

QUANTITATIVE PART

59 questions- 75 minutes

TEST II. DATA INTERPRETATION

TIME: 7 minutes

DIRECTIONS: Read each test question carefully. Each one refers to the following graph, and is to be answered solely on that basis. Select the best answer among the given choices and blacken the proper space on the answer sheet.

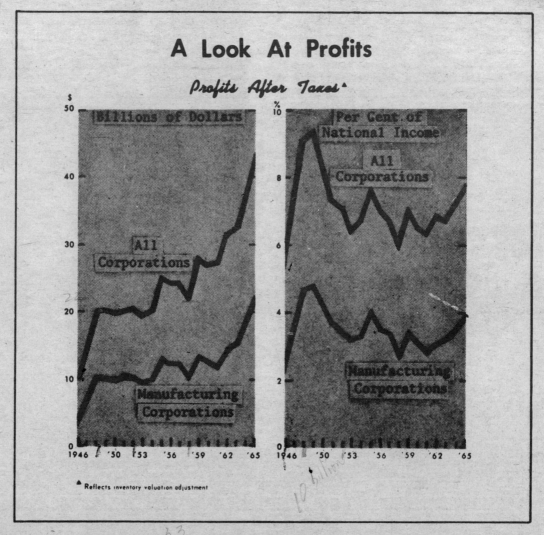

A Look At Profits

Profits After Taxes

▲ Reflects inventory valuation adjustment

1. In 1958, the profits of *non*-manufacturing corporations was

   (A) $8 billion   (B) $10 billion
   (C) $12 billion   (D) $14 billion
          (E) none of the above

2. The percents of the National Income for all corporations and for manufacturing corporations show a paired rise or a paired fall in every year *except*

   (A) 1950-1951   (B) 1953-1954
   (C) 1956-1957   (D) 1961-1962
          (E) 1962-1963

3. What was the National Income in 1946?

   (A) $10 billion   (B) $17 billion
   (C) $60 billion   (D) $170 billion
          (E) $6 trillion

4. Between 1948 and 1952, the National Income

   (A) more than doubled
   (B) increased, but did not double
   (C) decreased by more than 50%

   (D) decreased by less than 50%
   (E) remained practically the same

5. The *average* income of a manufacturing corporation in 1959

   (A) was more than twice that of a non-manufacturing corporation in 1948
   (B) was greater than that of any corporation in 1946
   (C) was less than 4% of the National Income in that year
   (D) was approximately $14 billion
   (E) was greater than 4% of the National Income in that year

6. As the number of corporations doubled between 1946 and 1948, how was the average profit affected?

   (A) It remained fairly constant.
   (B) It rose by about 50%.
   (C) It rose by about 100%.
   (D) It fell by about 50%.
   (E) It fell by about 100%.

END OF TEST

Go on to the next Test in the Examination, just as you would do on the actual exam. Check your answers when you have completed the entire Examination. The correct answers for this Test, and all the other Tests, are assembled at the conclusion of this Examination.

TEST III. PROBLEM SOLVING

TIME: 68 minutes

DIRECTIONS: For each of the following questions, select the choice which best answers the question or completes the statement.

1. Of the following, the one that is *not* a meaning of ⅔ is

   (A) 1 of the 3 equal parts of 2
   (B) 2 of the 3 equal parts of 1
   (C) 2 divided by 3
   (D) a ratio of 2 to 3
   (E) 4 of the 6 equal parts of 2

2. If the average weight of boys of John's age and height is 105 lbs. and if John weighs 110% of average, then John weighs

   (A) 110 lbs.   (B) 110.5 lbs.
   (C) 106.05 lbs.   (D) 126 lbs.
             (E) 115½ lbs.

3. On a house plan on which 2 inches represents 5 feet, the length of a room measures 7½ inches. The actual length of the room is

   (A) 12½ feet   (B) 15¾ feet
   (C) 17½ feet   (D) 18¾ feet
             (E) 13¾ feet

Questions 4-7 are to be answered with reference to the following diagram.

The figure shown in the diagram is made of pieces of plastic, each piece half a centimeter thick and one centimeter wide.

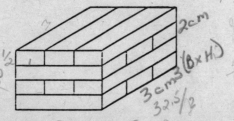

4. What is the volume of the figure?

   (A) 12 cu cm
   (B) 18 cu cm
   (C) 27 cu cm
   (D) 36 cu cm
   (E) Cannot be determined from the given information

5. How many pieces are touched by at least 8 other pieces?

   (A) 1   (B) 2
   (C) 3   (D) 4
             (E) 5

6. If all the pieces had been cut from one strip of plastic, how long a piece of ½ cm × 1 cm material would have been required?

   (A) 15 cm
   (B) 18 cm
   (C) 27 cm
   (D) 12 cm
   (E) 36 cm

7. What is the total surface in square centimeters of all the pieces?

   (A) 10
   (B) 18
   (C) 72
   (D) 120
   (E) 42

Questions 8-12 are to be answered with reference to the graph-chart below.

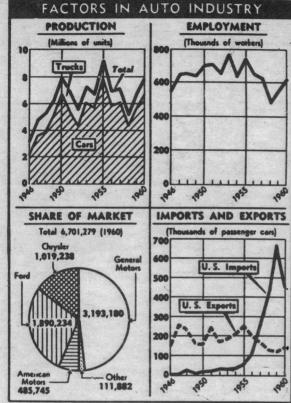

FACTORS IN AUTO INDUSTRY

PRODUCTION
(Millions of units)

Trucks   Total

Cars

EMPLOYMENT
(Thousnds of workers)

SHARE OF MARKET
Total 6,701,279 (1960)

Chrysler
1,019,238

Ford

General
Motors

3,193,180

1,890,234

American
Motors
485,745

Other
111,882

IMPORTS AND EXPORTS
(Thousands of passenger cars)

U.S. Imports

U.S. Exports

8. The number of auto workers in 1960 was about what per cent of the peak year of employment?

(A) 55%
(B) 70%
(C) 80%
(D) 88%
(E) 95%

9. These auto industry graphs and charts will not be able to tell you the following for the 1946-1960 period:

(A) how employment in one year compared with employment in another year
(B) the percent of production that trucks have constituted
(C) the breakdown of the Chrysler Company types of cars which have been sold
(D) the number of U.S.-made passenger cars marketed abroad
(E) how many passenger cars were produced

10. In 1960, the exports of cars made up approximately what part of the import-export total?

(A) one-eighth
(B) one-seventh
(C) one-fourth
(D) one-third
(E) one-half

11. General Motors and Ford combined have about what per cent of the entire market?

(A) 50%
(B) 60%
(C) 75%
(D) 85%
(E) 90%

12. The years in which the number of passenger car imports and exports were a) about the same and b) farthest apart were

(A) 1955 and 1950
(B) 1957 and 1959
(C) 1946 and 1957
(D) 1960 and 1959
(E) 1960 and 1957

13. ABCD is a parallelogram, and DE = EC

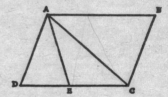

What is the ratio of triangle ADE to the area of the parallelogram?

(A) 1:2
(B) 1:3
(C) 2:5
(D) 1:4
(E) cannot be determined from the given information

14. If pencils are bought at 35 cents per dozen and sold at 3 for 10 cents the total profit on 5½ dozen is

(A) 25 cents
(B) 27½ cents
(C) 28½ cents
(D) 31½ cents
(E) 35 cents

15. Of the following, the one which may be used correctly to compute $26 \times 3\frac{1}{2}$ is

    (A) $(26 \times 30) + (26 \times \frac{1}{2})$
    (B) $(20 \times 3) + (6 \times 3\frac{1}{2})$
    (C) $(20 \times 3\frac{1}{2}) + (6 \times 3)$
    (D) $(20 \times 3) + (26 \times \frac{1}{2}) + (6 \times 3\frac{1}{2})$
    (E) $(26 \times \frac{1}{2}) + (20 \times 3) + (6 \times 3)$

16. It costs 31 cents a square foot to lay linoleum. To lay 20 square yards of linoleum it will cost

    (A) $16.20
    (B) $18.60
    (C) $62.80
    (D) $62.00
    (E) $55.80

Questions 17-21 are to be answered with reference to the following explanation and table.

Ten judges were asked to judge the relative sweetness of five compounds (A, B, C, D, and E) by the method of paired comparisons. In judging each of the possible pairs they were required to state unequivocally which of the two compounds was the sweeter—a judgment of equality or no difference was not permitted.

The results of their judgments are summarized in the table below. In studying the table, note that each cell entry shows the number of comparisons in which the "row" compound was judged to be sweeter than the "column" compound.

	A	B	C	D	E
A		5	8	10	2
B	5		3	9	6
C	2	7		7	8
D	0	1	3		4
E	8	4	2	6	

17. How many comparisons did each judge make?

    (A) 5
    (B) 10
    (C) 15
    (D) 20
    (E) 25

18. Which compound was judged to be sweetest?

    (A) A
    (B) B

(C) C
(D) D
(E) E

19. Which compound was judged to be least sweet?

    (A) A
    (B) B
    (C) C
    (D) D
    (E) E

20. Which of the following statements is most nearly correct?

    (A) There was almost perfect agreement among the ten judges.
    (B) The clearest discrimination was between B and C.
    (C) The judges were not expert in discriminating sweetnesses.
    (D) Compound D was most clearly discriminated from the other four compounds.
    (E) Compounds C and E were judged to have the same sweetness.

21. Between which two compounds was the discrimination least consistent?

    (A) A and D
    (B) B and E
    (C) C and E
    (D) C and D
    (E) A and B

22. A piece of wood 35 feet, 6 inches long was used to make 4 shelves of equal length. The length of each shelf was

    (A) 9 feet, 1½ inches
    (B) 8 feet, 10½ inches
    (C) 7 feet, 10½ inches
    (D) 7 feet, 1½ inches
    (E) 6 feet, 8½ inches

23. A class punch ball team won 2 games and lost 10. The fraction of its games won is correctly expressed as

    (A) 1/6
    (B) 1/5
    (C) 4/5
    (D) 5/6
    (E) 1/10

24. 10 to the fifth power may correctly be expressed as

   (A) 10×5
   (B) 5^{10}
   (C) $5\sqrt{10}$
  —(D) $10 \times 10 \times 10 \times 10 \times 10$
   (E) $10^{10} \div 10^{2}$

25. The total cost of 3½ pounds of meat at $1.10 a pound and 20 oranges at $.60 a dozen will be

   (A) $4.65
  —(B) $4.85
   (C) $5.05
   (D) $4.45
   (E) none of these

Questions 26-28 are to be answered with reference to the following number system:

The following symbols are used in the same fashion as Roman numerals are used.

1	I	ꞁ
5	V	∩
10	X	𝟡
50	L	ᚏ
100	C	ᚊ
500	D	☉
1000	M	ꝏ

IV = 4

For example, $9|\cap = 14$.

Thousands are indicated by drawing a line over the symbol. For example, $\overline{\cap} = 5000$.

✓26. $\overline{9}\,0\,ᚏ$ equals ?

   (A) 1915
   (B) 10,315
   (C) 10,915
  —(D) 10,150
   (E) 11,050

27. $4(10^{4}) + 5(10^{3}) + 4(100)$ is represented by

   (A) ꝏ 𝟶𝟶𝟶𝟶 ∩
   (B) $\overline{9999}$ ᚏ∩
  —(C) ∩ᚏ 𝟶𝟶𝟶𝟶
   (D) $\overline{9990}$ᚏ
   (E) $\overline{9ᚏ}$·𝟬∩∩

28. Select the correct expression for $\overline{\text{ꝏ ᚊ}}$ ꞁꞁꞁꞁ

   (A) $1{,}000{,}000 + 100 + 2{,}000 + 100{,}000 + 2$
   (B) $2(10^{6}) + 2(10^{4}) + 10 + 1{,}000 + 2$
   (C) $2(100) + 2(10^{3}) + 5(10) + 10(1000{,}000) + 2$
  —(D) $10^{6} + 50(10{,}000) + 2{,}000 + 2$
   (E) $100 \times 10^{5} + 5 \times 10^{5} + 20 \times 10^{2} + 2 \times 10^{1}$

29. The total number of eighths in two wholes and three fourths is

   (A) 11
   (B) 14
   (C) 19
  —(D) 22
   (E) 24

30. The difference between one hundred five thousand eighty-four and ninety-three thousand seven hundred nine is

   (A) 37,215
   (B) 12,131
   (C) 56,294
   (D) 56,375
  —(E) 11,375

31. A recipe for a cake calls for 2½ cups of milk and 3 cups of flour. With this recipe, a cake was baked using 14 cups of flour. How many cups of milk were required?

   (A) 10⅓
   (B) 10¾
   (C) 11
   (D) 11⅗
  — (E) 11⅔

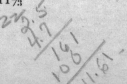

Questions 32-34 are to be answered with reference to the following explanation and diagram.

A cube may be rotated about any one of its three axes, a, b, or c. The rotation of the cube 90° about "a" in the direction of the arrow may be denoted by a; the rotation of the cube 90° about "b" in the direction of the arrow by b; and rotation of the cube 90° about "c" in the direction of the arrow by c.

If operation a is performed twice, the whole operation may be indicated as a^2; if three times, as a^3; etc. Similarly, the same holds for b and c. If operation b is performed, and then c, the result is bc.

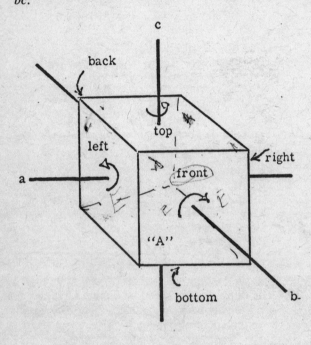

32. After the operation a^3b, where is face "A"?

   (A) back
   (B) bottom
   (C) left
   (D) top
   (E) right

33. Where was the face which is on the bottom after the operation bc before the operation?

   (A) back
   (B) left
   (C) right
   (D) top
   (E) bottom

34. Which operation leaves the cube in the same position as it is after $a^2b^2c^2$?

   (A) $(bc)^2$
   (B) b^3c^3
   (C) c^4
   (D) c^3ba^3
   (E) $(ab)^3$

35. What would be the marked price of an article if the cost was $12.60 and the gain was 10% of the selling price?

   (A) $13.66
   (B) $13.86
   (C) $11.34
   (D) $12.48
   (E) $14.00

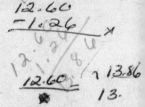

36. A certain type of board is sold only in lengths of multiples of 2 feet from 6 ft. to 24 ft. A builder needs a large quantity of this type of board in 5½ foot lengths. For minimum waste, the lengths to be ordered should be

   (A) 6 ft.
   (B) 12 ft.
   (C) 24 ft.
   (D) 22 ft.
   (E) 18 ft.

37. The tiles in the floor of a bathroom are 15/16 inch squares. The cement between the tiles is 1/16 inch. There are 3240 individual tiles in this floor. The area of the floor is

   (A) 225 sq. yds.
   (B) 2.5 sq. yds.
   (C) 250 sq. ft.
   (D) 22.5 sq. yds.
   (E) 225 sq. ft.

38. A group of 15 children received the following scores in a reading test: 36 36 30 30 30 29 27 27 27 26 26 26 26 18 13. What was the median score?

   (A) 25.4
   (B) 26
   (C) 27
   (D) 30
   (E) 24.5

Questions 39-43 are to be answered with reference to the following diagram and explanation.

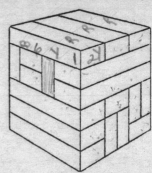

The 6-inch cube shown in the diagram is made up of pieces each 1 inch thick, 2 inches wide, and 6 inches long. Each block is painted in three colors, red, blue, and yellow according to its position as shown in the diagram. The top side of each block is red. The bottom side of each piece is blue, and the vertical sides are yellow.

39. How many 1 × 2 × 6 blocks are there in the 6-inch cube?
    (A) 15
    —(B) 18
    (C) 27
    (D) 36
    (E) 24

40. How many square inches of block are painted blue?
    (A) 150
    (B) 316
    (C) 210
    (D) 256
    —(E) 180

41. What is the largest number of plane surfaces of other blocks touched by the plane surfaces of any one block?
    (A) 8
    —(B) 11
    (C) 13
    (D) 15
    (E) 16

42. How many square inches of blue surface are touching red surfaces?
    (A) 94
    (B) 108
    —(C) 144
    (D) 196
    (E) 216

43. Which arrangement of the blocks, forming a 6-inch cube, painted in the fashion described in the paragraph, would require the smallest possible area of yellow paint?
    (A) all blocks laid with a 2 × 6 side horizontal
    (B) all blocks laid with a 1 × 6 side horizontal
    (C) all blocks laid with a 1 × 2 end horizontal
    (D) all blocks laid with a 1 × 2 side vertical
    (E) the arrangement makes no difference

44. Of the following the one that is *not* equivalent to 376 is
    (A) (3 × 100) + (6 × 10) + 16
    (B) (2 × 100) + (17 × 10) + 6
    (C) (3 × 100) + (7 × 10) + 6
    —(D) (2 × 100) + (16 × 10) + 6
    (E) (2 × 100) + (7 × 10) + 106

45. A man bought a TV set that was listed at $160. He was given successive discounts of 20% and 10%. The price he paid was
    (A) $112.00
    —(B) $115.20
    (C) $119.60
    (D) $129.60
    (E) $118.20

46. The total length of fencing needed to enclose a rectangular area 46 feet by 34 feet is
    (A) 26 yards 1 foot
    (B) 26⅔ yards
    (C) 52 yards 2 feet
    —(D) 53⅓ yards
    (E) 37⅔ yards

47. Mr. Jones' income for a year is $15,000. He pays 15% of this in federal taxes and 10% of the remainder for state taxes. How much is left?
    (A) $12,750
    (B) $ 9,750
    (C) $14,125
    (D) $13,500
    —(E) $11,475

Questions 48-53 are to be answered with reference to the graph below.

48. The decade in which there was the greatest variation in the price of silver is

(A) 1920-30
(B) 1930-40
(C) 1940-50
(D) 1950-60
(E) not the kind of information given

49. The price of silver in 1934 was about what fraction of the price in 1931?

(A) 1/2
(B) 3/4
(C) 1/1
(D) 2/1
(E) 4/3

50. Which of the following is *false*, according to the chart?

(A) The price of silver was higher in 1947 than in 1937.

(B) There was a sharp drop in the price of silver between 1920 and 1921.

(C) Silver prices between 1943 and 1945 averaged $0.45 per pound.

(D) The price of silver in 1960 was higher than that in any year from 1921 through 1931.

(E) The three years with the three highest silver prices were 1920, 1935, 1946.

51. The price was most steady during the period

(A) 1915-1917
(B) 1929-1931
(C) 1935-1937
(D) 1943-1945
(E) 1954-1956

52. The graph indicates that the price of silver, since 1940, has

(A) risen slightly
(B) risen sharply
(C) fallen slightly
(D) fallen sharply
(E) remained about the same

53. A year during which the price was approximately the same as the year immediately preceding was

(A) 1919
(B) 1929
(C) 1935
(D) 1944
(E) 1951

VERBAL ABILITY PART

39 questions - 20 minutes

TEST IV. ANTONYMS

TIME: 5 Minutes

DIRECTIONS: For each question in this test, select the appropriate letter preceding the word that is opposite in meaning to the capitalized word.

1. PALLIATE *RELIEVE THE SYMPTOMS EOUT curing*
   - (A) apologize
   - (B) hesitate
   - (C) wait impatiently
   - (D) decide finally
   - (E) cure completely

2. CONSONANT *BEING IN AGREEMENT / HARSH INSOUND*
   - (A) insuperable
   - (B) dissonant
   - (C) nonexistent
   - (D) clear
   - (E) abundant

3. CONCISE *EXPRESSING IN BREIF FORM*
   - (A) wordy
   - (B) mundane
   - (C) ignorant
   - (D) sturdy
   - (E) wrong

4. FECUND *FERTILE*
   - (A) sinister
   - (B) pure
   - (C) young
   - (D) barren
   - (E) beneficial

5. FORTUITOUS *OCCURRING BY CHANCE*
   - (A) unfortunate
   - (B) stupid
   - (C) designed
   - (D) fearful
   - (E) pious

6. SATURNINE *OF OR PERTAINING TO THE PLANET SATURN GLOOMY & HEAVY*
   - (A) earthy
   - (B) cheerful
   - (C) complicated
   - (D) maudlin
   - (E) honest

7. FRANGIBLE *EASILY BROKEN, FRAGILE*
   - (A) argumentative
   - (B) docile
   - (C) insincere
   - (D) indestructible
   - (E) inedible

8. LETHARGY *APATHY*
   - (A) acidity
   - (B) prodigy
   - (C) rigidity
   - (D) alertness
   - (E) corpulence

9. ENDEMIC *PECULIAR TO A PARTICULAR COUNTRY OR PEOPLE*
   - (A) decorative
   - (B) frustrating
   - (C) terrorizing
   - (D) dry
   - (E) universal

10. COMPENDIOUS *CONCISE, STATING BREIFLY*
    - (A) profound
    - (B) inflated
    - (C) simple
    - (D) ambiguous
    - (E) vague

11. ASSUAGE *TO MAKE LESS HARSH SEVERE ; TO CALM OR*
    - (A) cleanse
    - (B) sway
    - (C) aggravate
    - (D) bless
    - (E) advance

12. PRATE *TO TALK IDLEY) CHATTER*
    - (A) remark casually
    - (B) laugh raucously
    - (C) talk meaningfully
    - (D) weep copiously
    - (E) whisper fearfully

13. CAVIL *TO RAISE TRIVIAL OBJECTIONS*
    - (A) dishonest behavior
    - (D) small price
    - (B) frequent occurrence
    - (E) light burden
    - (C) serious complaint

14. TYRO *A BEGINNER, A NOVICE*
    - (A) promulgate effectively
    - (E) play freely
    - (B) possess rightfully
    - (C) eradicate completely
    - (D) protect skillfully

TEST V. VERBAL ANALOGIES

TIME: 7 Minutes

DIRECTIONS: In these test questions each of the two CAPI-TALIZED words have a certain relationship to each other. Following the capitalized words are other pairs of words, each designated by a letter. Select the lettered pair wherein the words are related in the same way as the two CAPITALIZED words are related to each other.

1. ERRORS : INEXPERIENCE ::
   (A) skill : mistakes
   (B) training : economy
   (C) success : victory
   (D) news : publication
   (E) losses : carelessness

2. CAUCASIAN : SAXON ::
   (A) lamp : stove
   (B) hammer : nail
   (C) furniture : chair
   (D) carriage : horse
   (E) city : house

3. CLOTH : TEXTURE ::
   (A) wool : silk
   (B) book : text
   (C) wood : grain
   (D) linen : flax
   (E) paper : weight

4. CHILD : FAMILY
   (A) flower : bunch
   (B) bird : set
   (C) calf : herd
   (D) fish : brace
   (E) deer : gang

5. ACORN : OAK ::
   (A) fig : bush
   (B) flower : stalk
   (C) seed : nut
   (D) bulb : tulip
   (E) leaf : limb

6. SORROW : DEATH ::
   (A) laugh : cry
   (B) plum : peach
   (C) happiness : birth
   (D) fear : hate
   (E) confusion : anger

7. TEPID : HOT ::
   (A) pat : slap
   (B) winter : summer
   (C) topple : tumble
   (D) bing : bang
   (E) storm : rain

8. HYPOTHESIS : PROBLEM ::
   (A) forecast : warning
   (B) prognosis : condition
   (C) cause : worry
   (D) effect : solution
   (E) preparation : conclusion

9. OCTAVO : BINDING ::
   (A) pica : printing
   (B) music : octave
   (C) day : week
   (D) pamphlet : book
   (E) ruler : artist

10. GOVERNMENT : EXILE ::
    (A) police : arrest
    (B) judge : convict
    (C) constitution : amendment
    (D) church : excommunicate
    (E) society : reform

11. RIBS : UMBRELLA ::
    (A) rafter : roof
    (B) hub : wheel
    (C) crank : engine
    (D) trunk : tree
    (E) wall : fence

12. PEDAL : BICYCLE ::
    (A) run : race
    (B) climb : hill
    (C) wind : clock
    (D) switch : motor
    (E) twist : cork

TEST VI. SENTENCE COMPLETIONS

TIME: 8 Minutes

DIRECTIONS: Each of the completion questions in this test consists of an incomplete sentence. Each sentence is followed by a series of lettered words, one of which best completes the sentence. Select the word that best completes the meaning of each sentence, and mark the letter of that word opposite that sentence.

1. Even when his reputation was in _____, almost everyone was willing to admit that he had genius.

   (A) dialogue
   (B) retaliation
   (C) eclipse
   (D) differentiation
   (E) rebuttal

2. How many of the books published each year in the United States make a(n) _____ contribution toward improving men's _____ with each other?

   (A) conservational . . . reservations
   (B) standardized . . . customs
   (C) referential . . . rudeness
   (D) squalid . . . generalities
   (E) significant . . . relationships

3. No one can say for sure how _____ the awards have been.

   (A) determined
   (B) effective
   (C) reducible
   (D) effervescent
   (E) inborn

4. For fifty years, only such women and the few intellectuals who shared his _____ scorn read Stendhal.

   (A) reverberating
   (B) explicit
   (C) sensational
   (D) sensuous
   (E) retreating

5. The _____ of the chronic balance of payments deficits which have _____ the U.S. Treasury Department under three Presidents is very real.

   (A) temptation . . . reviled
   (B) understanding . . . menaced
   (C) impact . . . underestimated
   (D) dilemma . . . plagued
   (E) strengthening . . . deceived

6. The fact that a business has _____ does not create an _____ on it to give away its prosperity.

   (A) prospered . . . imperative
   (B) halted . . . insensitivity
   (C) incorporated . . . indecision
   (D) supplemented . . . obligation
   (E) accumulated . . . aspect

7. When I watch drivers slam their cars to a halt, take corners _____ on two wheels, and blunder wildly over construction potholes and railroad crossings, I consider it a _____ to automotive design that cars don't shake apart far sooner.

   (A) gradually . . . curiosity
   (B) sensibly . . . blessing
   (C) gracefully . . . misfortune
   (D) habitually . . . tribute
   (E) religiously . . . verdict

8. On the ground, liquid hydrogen must be stored in large stainless steel tanks with double walls filled with _____ and evacuated to a high vacuum.

   (A) velocity   (B) visibility
   (C) sufficiency   (D) elasticity
           (E) insulation

9. The second act, which jumps forward to the late 1930's, a much less interesting period to _____, is nevertheless the more effective of the two.
   - (A) caricature
   - (B) instigate
   - (C) stem
   - (D) concentrate
   - (E) validate

10. It is true that some of the most interesting novels of our age are in many ways closer to poetry than they are to old-fashioned _____, and the examination of _____ and imagery is by now a standard academic approach to fiction.
    - (A) expression . . . styles
    - (B) realism . . . symbolism
    - (C) romances . . . character
    - (D) manners . . . truth
    - (E) prose . . . images

11. Britain, for the present, is deeply _____ in economic troubles, and the economic future, heavily _____, looks uncertain.
    - (A) engrossed . . . responsive
    - (B) ingrained . . . skeptical
    - (C) saturated . . . enveloped
    - (D) mired . . . mortgaged
    - (E) perplexed . . . obligated

12. Ontology is the word now used in place of metaphysics, on the grounds that it is less _____ and supernatural.
    - (A) theological
    - (B) applicable
    - (C) reliable
    - (D) philosophical
    - (E) approximate

13. The "loop" is a cheap, highly effective _____ device perfected in America and widely distributed throughout India.
    - (A) validating
    - (B) restraining
    - (C) participating
    - (D) contraceptive
    - (E) reactionary

END OF PART
If you finish before the allotted time is up, work on this part only. When time is up, proceed directly to the next part and do not return to this part.

DATA SUFFICIENCY PART

16 questions- 15 minutes

TEST VII. DATA SUFFICIENCY

TIME: 15 minutes

DIRECTIONS: Each question below is followed by two numbered facts. Decide whether the data given is sufficient for answering the question. Sometimes the two facts do not give enough information to answer the question. Sometimes the two facts give just enough data to answer the question. And sometimes one of the facts alone is sufficient to answer the question. Read each question and the two facts that follow it; then mark your answer on the answer sheet that follows.
Mark "A" if statement 1 alone is sufficient to answer the question, but statement 2 alone is not sufficient.
Mark "B" if statement 2 alone is sufficient to answer the question, but statement 1 alone is not sufficient.
Mark "C" if both statements together are needed to answer the question, but neither statement alone is sufficient.
Mark "D" if either statement by itself is sufficient to answer the question asked.
Mark "E" if not enough facts are given to answer the question.

Note: *In the data sufficiency problems which follow, the diagrams are generalized illustrations and are not necessarily drawn to scale.*

1. How many dimes does Jack have in his pocket?

   (1) He has 64¢ in coins in his pocket.
   (2) Five of his coins are nickels.

2.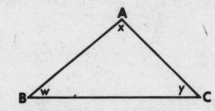

   What is the value of w in the above triangle?

   (1) AB = AC
   (2) Angle x = 50°

3. Which of the integers a, b, c, d, and e are odd numbers?

   (1) a, b, c, d, and e are consecutive integers.
   (2) c is an even integer.

4. Is a^2 an integer?

   (1) a is a negative whole number.
   (2) $4a^2$ is an integer.

5. What is the distance from point A to point C?

   (1) The distance from point A to point B is 8".
   (2) The distance from point B to point C is 4".

6. Are two triangles congruent?

(1) They are both equilateral triangles.
(2) They both have equal bases and equal heights.

7.

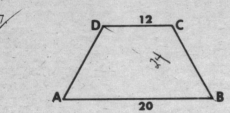

Find the area of the above trapezoid.

(1) The diagonal from D to B equals 24.
(2) The trapezoid is isosceles.

8. There are 82 students in a certain school who attend class A or class B or both. How many attend each class?

(1) 50 students attend class A only.
(2) 32 students attend class B.

9. What is the value of x?

(1) $3x - 2y = 14$
(2) $2w + 3x = 20$

10. Find the fourth consecutive even number.

(1) The sum of the last two numbers is 26.
(2) The sum of the first two numbers is 18.

11. What are the dimensions of a certain rectangle?

(1) The perimeter of the rectangle is 14.
(2) The diagonal of the rectangle is 5.

12.

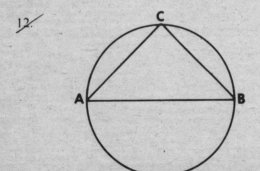

In the figure above, find the number of degrees in inscribed angle ACB.

(1) Inscribed angle ABC = 60°.
(2) AB is the diameter of the circle.

13. Is x > y?

(1) $8x = 6y$
(2) $x = y + 4$

14.

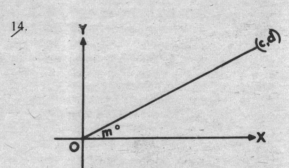

On the graph above, what is the value of m?

(1) $c = d$
(2) $c = 4$

15. What is the maximum age of any one woman, if the average of the three women's ages is 26 years?

(1) No one of them is greater than 34.
(2) No one of them is less than 22.

16.

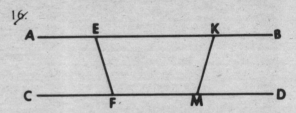

In the figure above, AB ∥ CD. Is EF shorter in length than KM?

(1) Angle BKM = 130° and angle EFM = 120°
(2) Angle KMF = 130° and angle EKB = 50°

READING AND GRAMMAR PART

50 Questions 35 Minutes

TEST VIII . READING COMPREHENSION

TIME: 20 Minutes

DIRECTIONS: Below each of the following passages, you will find questions or incomplete statements about the passage. Each statement or question is followed by lettered words or expressions. Select the word or expression that most satisfactorily completes each statement or answers each question in accordance with the meaning of the passage. Write the letter of that word or expression on your answer paper.

As the world's population grows, the part played by man in influencing plant life becomes more and more important. In old and densely populated countries, as in central Europe, man determines almost wholly what shall grow and what shall not grow. In such regions, the influence of man on plant life is in large measure a beneficial one. Laws, often centuries old, protect plants of economic value and preserve soil fertility. In newly settled countries the situation is unfortunately quite the reverse. The pioneer's life is too strenuous a one for him to think of posterity.

Some years ago Mt. Mitchell, the highest summit east of the Mississippi, was covered with a magnificent forest. A lumber company was given full rights to fell the trees. Those not cut down were crushed. The mountain was left a wasted area where fire would rage and erosion would complete the destruction. There was no stopping the devastating foresting of the company, for the contract had been given. Under a more enlightened civilization this could not have happened. The denuding of Mt. Mitchell is a minor chapter in the destruction of lands in the United States; and this country is by

no means the only or chief sufferer. China, India, Egypt, and East Africa all have their thousands of square miles of waste land, the result of man's indifference to the future.

Deforestation, grazing, and poor farming are the chief causes of the destruction of land fertility. Wasteful cutting of timber is the first step. Grazing then follows lumbering in bringing about ruin. The Caribbean slopes of northern Venezuela are barren wastes owing first to ruthless cutting of forests and then to destructive grazing. Hordes of goats have roamed these slopes until only a few thorny acacias and cacti remain. Erosion completed the devastation. What is there illustrated on a small scale is the story of vast areas in China and India, countries where famines are of regular occurrence.

Man is not wholly to blame, for Nature is often merciless. In parts of India and China, plant life, when left undisturbed by man, cannot cope with either the disastrous floods of wet seasons or the destructive winds of the dry season. Man has learned much; prudent land management has been the policy of the Chinese people since 2700 B. C., but even they have not learned enough.

When the American forestry service was in its infancy, it met with much opposition from legislators who loudly claimed that the protected land would in one season yield a crop of cabbages of more value than all the timber on it. Herein lay the fallacy, that one season's crop is all that need be thought of. Nature, through the years, adjusts crops to the soil and to the climate. Forests usually occur where precipitation exceeds evaporation. If the reverse is true, grasslands are found; and where evaporation is still greater, desert or scrub vegetation alone survives. The phytogeographic map of a country is very similar to the climatic map based on rainfall, evaporation, and temperature. Man ignores this natural adjustment of crops and strives for one "bumper" crop in a single season; he may produce it, but "year in and year out the yield of the grassland is certain, that of the planted fields, never."

Man is learning; he sprays his trees with insecticides and fungicides; he imports ladybugs to destroy aphids; he irrigates, fertilizes, and rotates his crops; but he is still indifferent to many of the consequences of his short-sighted policies. The great dust storms of the western United States are proof of this indifference.

In spite of the evidence to be had from this country, the people of other countries, still in the pioneer stage, farm as wastefully as did our own pioneers. In the interiors of Central and South American Republics, natives fell superb forest trees and leave them to rot in order to obtain virgin soil for cultivation. Where the land is hillside, it readily washes and after one or two seasons is unfit for crops. So the frontier farmer pushes back into the primeval forest, moving his hut as he goes, and fells more monarchs to lay bare another patch of ground for his plantings to support his family. Valuable timber which will require a century to replace is destroyed and the land laid waste to produce what could be supplied for a pittance.

How badly man can err in his handling of land is shown by the draining of extensive swamp areas, which to the uninformed would seem to be a very good thing to do. One of the first effects of the drainage is the lowering of the water-table, which may bring about the death of the dominant species and leave to another species the possession of the soil, even when the difference in water level is little more than an inch. Frequently, bog country will yield marketable crops of cranberries and

blueberries but, if drained, neither these nor any other economic plant will grow on the fallow soil. Swamps and marshes have their drawbacks but also their virtues. When drained they may leave waste land, the surface of which rapidly erodes to be then blown away in dust blizzards disastrous to both man and wild beasts.

1. The best title for this passage is
   (A) How to Increase Soil Productivity
   (B) Conservation of Natural Resources
   (C) Man's Effect on Soil
   (D) Soil Conditions and Plant Growth

2. A policy of good management is sometimes upset by
   (A) the indifference of man
   (B) centuries-old laws
   (C) floods and winds
   (D) grazing animals

3. Areas in which the total amounts of rain and snow falling on the ground are greater than that which is evaporated will support
   (A) forests   (C) scrub vegetation
   (B) grasslands   (D) no plants

4. Pioneers do not have a long range view on soil problems since they
   (A) are not protected by laws
   (B) live under adverse conditions
   (C) use poor methods of farming
   (D) must protect themselves from famine

5. Phytogeographic maps are those that show
   (A) areas of grassland
   (B) areas of bumper crops
   (C) areas of similar climate
   (D) areas of similar plants

6. The basic cause of frequent famines in China and India is probably due to
   (A) allowing animals to roam wild
   (B) drainage of swamps
   (C) over-grazing of the land
   (D) destruction of forests

7. With a growing world population, the increased need for soil for food production may be met by
   (A) draining unproductive swamp areas
   (B) legislating against excess lumbering
   (C) trying to raise bumper crops each year
   (D) irrigating desert areas

8. What is meant by "the yield of the grassland is certain; that of the planted field, never" is that

(A) it is impossible to get more than one bumper crop from any one cultivated area

(B) crops, planted in former grassland, will not give good yields

(C) through the indifference of man, dust blizzards have occurred in former grasslands

(D) if man does not interfere, plants will grow in the most suitable environment

9. The first act of prudent land management might be to
   (A) prohibit drainage of swamps
   (B) use irrigation and crop rotation in planted areas
   (C) increase use of fertilizers
   (D) prohibit excessive forest lumbering

10. The results of good land management may usually be found in
    (A) heavily populated areas
    (B) areas not given over to grazing
    (C) underdeveloped areas
    (D) ancient civilizations

Regarding physical changes that have been and are now taking place on the surface of the earth, the sea and its shores have been the scene of the greatest stability. The dry land has seen the rise, the decline, and even the disappearance, of vast hordes of various types and forms within times comparatively recent, geologically speaking; but life in the sea is today virtually what it was when many of the forms now extinct on land had not yet been evolved. Also, it may be parenthetically stated here, the marine habitat has been biologically the most important in the evolution and development of life on this planet. Its rhythmic influence can still be traced in those animals whose ancestors have long since left that realm to abide far from their primary haunts. For it is now generally held as an accepted fact that the shore area of an ancient sea was the birthplace of life.

Still, despite the primitive conditions still maintained in the sea, its shore inhabitants show an amazing diversity, while their adaptive characters are perhaps not exceeded in refinement by those that distinguish the dwellers of dry land. Why is this diversity manifest? We must look for an answer into the physical factors obtaining in that extremely slender zone surrounding the continents, marked by the rise and fall of the tides.

It will be noticed by the most casual observer that on any given seashore the area exposed between the tide marks may be roughly divided into a number of levels each characterized by a certain assemblage of animals. Thus, in proceeding from high- to low-water mark, new forms constantly become predominant while other forms gradually drop out. Now, provided that the character of the substratum does not change, these differences in the types of animals are determined almost exclusively by the duration of time that the individual forms may remain exposed to the air without harm. Indeed, so regularly does the tidal rhythm act on certain animals (the barnacles, for instance), that certain species have come to require a definite period of exposure in order to maintain themselves, and will die out if kept continuously submerged. Although there are some forms that actually require periodic exposure, the number of species inhabiting the shore that are able to endure exposure every twelve hours, when the tide falls, is comparatively few.

With the alternate rise and fall of the tides, the successive areas of the tidal zone are subjected to force of wave-impact. In certain regions the waves often break with considerable force. Consequently, wave-shock has had a profound influence on the structure and habits of shore animals. It is characteristic of most shore animals that they shun definitely exposed places, and seek shelter in nooks and crannies and such refuges as are offered under stones and seaweed; particularly is this true of those forms living on rock and other firm foundations. Many of these have a marked capacity to cling closely to the substratum; some, such as anemones and certain snails, although without the grasping organs of higher animals, have special powers of adhesion; others, such as sponges and sea squirts, remain permanently fixed, and if torn loose from their base are incapable of forming a new attachment. But perhaps the most significant method of solving the problem presented by the surf has been in the adaptation of body-form to minimize friction. This is strikingly displayed in the fact that seashore animals are essentially flattened forms. Thus, in the typically shore forms the sponges are of the encrusting type, the non-burrowing worms are leaflike, the snails and other mollusks are squat forms and are without the spines and other ornate extensions such as are often produced on the shells of many mollusks in deeper and quieter waters. The same influence is no less marked in the case of the crustaceans; the flattening is either lateral, as in the amphipods, or dorso-ventral, as in the isopods and crabs.

In sandy regions, because of the unstable nature of substratum, no such means of attachment as indicated in the foregoing paragraph will suffice to maintain the animals in their almost ceaseless battle with the billows. Most of them must perforce depend on their ability quickly to penetrate into the sand for safety. Some forms endowed with less celerity, such as the sand dollars, are so constructed that their bodies offer no more resistance to wave impact than does a flat pebble.

Temperature, also, is a not inconsiderable factor among those physical forces constantly operating to produce a diversity of forms among seashore animals. At a comparatively shallow depth in the sea, there is small fluctuation of temperatures; and life there exists in surroundings of serene stability; but as the shore is approached, the influence of the sun becomes more and more manifest and the variation is greater. This variation becomes greatest between the tide marks where, because of the very shallow depths and the fresh water from the land, this area is subjected to wide changes in both temperature and salinity.

Nor is a highly competitive mode of life without its bearing on structure as well as habits. In this phase of their struggle for existence, the animals of both the sea and the shore have become possessed of weapons for offense and defense that are correspondingly varied.

Although the life in the sea has been generally considered and treated as separate and distinct from the more familiar life on land, that supposition has no real basis in fact. Life on this planet is one vast unit, depending for its existence chiefly on the same sources of supply. That portion of animal life living in the sea, notwithstanding its strangeness and unfamiliarity, may be considered as but the aquatic fringe of the life on land. It is supported largely by materials washed into the sea, which are no longer available for the support of land animals. Perhaps we have been misled in these considerations of sea life because of the fact that approximately three times as many major *types* of animals inhabit salt water as live on the land: of the major types of animals no fewer than ten are exclusively marine, that is to say, nearly half again as many as land-dwelling types together. A further interesting fact is that despite the greater variety in the form and structure of sea animals about three-fourths of all known *kinds* of animals live on the land, while only one-fourth lives in the sea.

In this connection it is noteworthy that sea life becomes scarcer with increasing distance from land; toward the middle of the oceans it disappears almost completely. For example, the central south Pacific is a region more barren than is any desert area on land. Indeed, no life of any kind has been found in the surface water, and there seems to be none on the bottom.

Sea animals are largest and most abundant on those shores receiving the most copious rainfall. Particularly is this true on the most rugged and colder coasts where it may be assumed that the material from the land finds its way to the sea unaltered and in greater quantities.

11. The best title for this passage is
    (A) Between the Tides   (C) The Tides
    (B) Seashore Life   (D) The Seashore

12. Of the following adaptations, the one that would enable an organism to live on a sandy beach is
    (A) the ability to move rapidly
    (B) the ability to burrow deeply
    (C) a flattened shape
    (D) spiny extensions of the shell

13. The absence of living things in mid-ocean might be due to
    (A) lack of rainfall in mid-ocean
    (B) the distance from material washed into the sea
    (C) larger animals feeding on smaller ones which must live near the land
    (D) insufficient dissolved oxygen

14. A greater variety of living things exist on a rocky shore than on a sandy beach because
    (A) rocks offer a better foothold than sand
    (B) sandy areas are continually being washed by the surf
    (C) temperature changes are less drastic in rocky areas
    (D) the water in rock pools is less salty

15. Organisms found living at the high-tide mark are adapted to
    (A) maintain themselves in the air for a long time
    (B) offer no resistance to wave impact
    (C) remain permanently fixed to the substratum
    (D) burrow in the ground

16. The author holds that living things in the sea represent the aquatic fringe of life on land. This is so because
    (A) there are relatively fewer marine forms of animals than there are land-living forms
    (B) there is greater variety among land-living forms
    (C) marine animals ultimately depend upon material from the land
    (D) there are three times as many kinds of animals on land than there are in the sea

17. A biologist walking along the shore at the low-tide line would not easily find many live animals since
    (A) their flattened shapes make them indistinguishable
    (B) they are washed back and forth by the waves
    (C) they burrow deeply
    (D) they move rapidly

18. The intent of the author in the next to the last paragraph is to show that

    (A) the temperature and salinity of the sea determine the variety among shore animals
    (B) marine animals are vastly different from terrestrial organisms
    (C) colder areas can support more living things than warm areas
    (D) marine forms have the same problems as terrestrial animals

19. A scientist wishing to study a great variety of living things would do well to hunt for them
    (A) in shallow waters
    (B) on a rocky seashore
    (C) on a sandy seashore
    (D) on any shore between the tide lines

20. The most primitive forms of living things in the evolutionary scale are to be found in the sea because
    (A) the influence of the sea is found in land animals
    (B) the sea is relatively stable
    (C) many forms have become extinct on land
    (D) land animals are supposed to have evolved from sea organisms

END OF TEST

Go on to the next Test in the Examination, just as you would do on the actual exam. Check your answers when you have completed the entire Examination. The correct answers for this Test, and all the other Tests, are assembled at the conclusion of this Examination.

TEST IX. ENGLISH USAGE

TIME: 8 Minutes

DIRECTIONS: This is a test of standard written English. The rules may differ from everyday spoken English. Many of the following sentences contain grammar, usage, word choice, and idiom that would be incorrect in written composition. Some sentences are correct. No sentence has more than one error. Any error in a sentence will be underlined and lettered; all other parts of the sentence are correct and cannot be changed. If the sentence has an error, choose the underlined part that is incorrect, and mark that letter on your answer sheet. If there is no error, mark E on your answer sheet.

1. When the members of the committee are at odds; when
          A   B
   they are in the process of offering their resignations,
                                 C
   problems become indissoluble. No error.
                D   E

2. Further acquaintance with the memoirs of Elizabeth
      A
   Barrett Browning and Robert Browning enable us to ap-
                                B
   preciate the depth of influence that two people of talent
           C
   can have on one another. No error.
            D   E

3. When the reviews appeared in the morning papers, we
                         A
   saw that everybody but Carolyn and him had received
           B   C
   averse notices. No error.
     D   E

4. An inexperienced liar, Mary explained her absence from
   school with an incredulous tale of daring in which she
            A   B
   played the role of the heroine. No error.
        C   D   E

5. Irregardless of what people say, I must repeat that these
      A   B
   are the facts concerning the requirements for the position.
             C   D
   No error.
    E

6. There is no objection to him joining the party if he is
   <u>A</u>   <u>B</u>   <u>C</u>
   willing to fit in with the plans of the group. No error.
             <u>D</u>   <u>E</u>

7. If you saw the number of pancakes he consumed at break-
            <u>A</u>   <u>B</u>   <u>C</u>
   fast this morning, you would have understood why he is
                         <u>D</u>
   so overweight. No error.
                  <u>E</u>

8. Ceremonies were opened by a drum and bugle corps of
                 <u>A</u>   <u>B</u>
   Chinese school children parading up Mott Street in col-
          <u>C</u>   <u>D</u>
   orful uniforms. No error.
                   <u>E</u>

9. Neither the Brontë sisters nor their brother Branwell are
   <u>A</u>   <u>B</u>   <u>C</u>
   remembered as healthy or happy. No error.
                 <u>D</u>   <u>E</u>

10. When my commanding officer first looked up from his
             <u>A</u>   <u>B</u>
    desk, he took Lieutenant Baxter to be I. No error.
         <u>C</u>   <u>D</u> <u>E</u>

11. Such a habit is not only dangerous to the individual's
                    <u>A</u>   <u>B</u>
    health but a man will find it a serious drain on his
                          <u>C</u>   <u>D</u>
    finances. No error.
              <u>E</u>

12. She saw that there was nothing else she could do; the
                            <u>A</u>   <u>B</u>
    room was clean like it had never been before. No error.
               <u>C</u>   <u>D</u>   <u>E</u>

13. The teacher was justly annoyed by him walking in late
                     <u>A</u>   <u>B</u>   <u>C</u>
    and disturbing the class. No error.
        <u>D</u>   <u>E</u>

14. Each of the nurses were scrupulously careful about per-
                      <u>A</u>   <u>B</u>   <u>C</u>
    sonal cleanliness. No error.
          <u>D</u>   <u>E</u>

15. I enjoy eating in good restaurants and to go to the the-
      <u>A</u>   <u>B</u>   <u>C</u>
    ater afterwards. No error.
         <u>D</u>   <u>E</u>

END OF TEST

TEST X. ENGLISH USAGE

TIME: 7 Minutes

DIRECTIONS: *This is a test of standard written English. The rules may differ from everyday spoken English. Many of the following sentences contain grammar, usage, word choice, and idiom that would be incorrect in written composition. Some sentences are correct. No sentence has more than one error. Any error in a sentence will be underlined and lettered; all other parts of the sentence are correct and cannot be changed. If the sentence has an error, choose the underlined part that is incorrect, and mark that letter on your answer sheet. If there is no error, mark E on your answer sheet.*

1. He had a chance to invest <u>wisely</u>, establish <u>his</u> position,
                  A   B
  and <u>displaying</u> his ability <u>as</u> an executive. <u>No error.</u>
         C   D   E

2. <u>Inspecting</u> <u>Robert's</u> report card, his mother noted that
    A   B
  he had <u>received</u> high ratings in Latin and <u>History. No</u>
          C   D
  <u>error.</u>
   E

3. When one buys tickets in <u>advance</u>, there is no guaranty
                         A
  sure that <u>you</u> will be free <u>to attend</u> the play on the night
          B   C
  of the <u>performance.</u> <u>No error.</u>
        D   E

4. His brother, the <u>captain</u> of the <u>squad</u> scored <u>many points.</u>
   A   B   C   D
  <u>No error.</u>
    E

5. People who are <u>too</u> credulous are <u>likely</u> <u>to be deceived</u> <u>by</u>
            A   B   C   D
  unscrupulous individuals. <u>No error.</u>
                    E

6. Due to <u>his being hospitalized,</u> the <u>star</u> halfback was
     A   B   C
  <u>unable to play</u> in the championship game. <u>No error.</u>
     D   E

7. Lifeguards <u>have been known</u> to <u>effect</u> rescues <u>even</u> <u>during</u>
                 A   B   C   D
tumultuous storms. <u>No error.</u>
                        E

8. The <u>mayor</u> <u>expressed</u> concern about the large <u>amount of</u>
        A   B   C
people injured at street <u>crossings.</u> <u>No error.</u>
                         D   E

9. "<u>Leave</u> us <u>face</u> the fact that <u>we're</u> in <u>trouble!</u>" he
       A   B   C   D
shouted. <u>No error.</u>
          E

10. Jones seems <u>slow</u> on the track, but you will find few
             A
boys <u>quicker</u> <u>than</u> <u>him</u> on the basketball court. <u>No error.</u>
     B   C   D   E

11. We had <u>swam</u> <u>across</u> the lake <u>before</u> the sun <u>rose.</u>
          A   B   C   D
<u>No error.</u>
 E

12. The <u>loud noise</u> of the cars and trucks <u>annoys</u> those <u>who</u>
        A   B   C
<u>live near the road.</u> <u>No error.</u>
      D   E

13. I know that you <u>will enjoy</u> <u>receiving</u> flowers that <u>smell</u>
               A   B   C
<u>so sweetly.</u> <u>No error.</u>
     D   E

14. He is at least ten years <u>older</u> <u>then</u> <u>she</u> <u>is.</u> <u>No error.</u>
               A   B   C D   E

15. I <u>found one of them</u> books that <u>tell</u> you how to build a
      A   B   C
<u>model airplane.</u> <u>No error.</u>
   D   E

END OF PART

PRACTICAL BUSINESS JUDGMENT

30 questions - 25 Minutes

DIRECTIONS: In testing your aptitude for business, they will ask you to evaluate a Situation and a Decision. You will be quizzed on goals, assumptions, conclusions, information, predictions, problems, options, and opinions. First, you will read a comprehensive analysis of a business situation; and then you will take two subtests based on your analysis: Data Application Quiz, and Data Evaluation Quiz.

Business Situation The Shareholders vs. the Entrepreneur.

Rise and Decline of the Company. Six years ago Peter Williams formed an unusual enterprise. His company creates unique electronic toys, but does not sell them through retail outlets. Instead, Peter Williams creates a prototype toy and then takes it to toy companies. A firm which sees market potential for the idea contracts with Williams for its full development. Williams then receives a substantial fee, which is in actuality an advance against royalty.

Early in the history of Williams' business, he found that he needed investment money for personnel expansion and expensive electronic equipment. He contacted a group of five men who had banded together to search for venture capital projects. They bought one-third of the company stock for $100,000.

At first, everyone was pleased. Business went up from $151,000 in the second year of existence to $896,000 in the fourth year. The only problem was that the company never seemed to make any money. The costs of contracts usually were greater than contract fees. When the investors became concerned, Williams admitted that he perhaps had underestimated costs, but that anticipated royalties would make up the deficit and produce a substantial profit.

Williams sought no further investment, but kept the company solvent by bank loans and what he called "bouncing," that is, by paying the costs of one contract with the fees of the next. This did not make outside suppliers too happy, as some of them had to wait up to six months to get paid. Nonetheless, the company staggered on, and Williams was even able to add to his staff until there were 22 employees.

However, in the fifth year, business fell off sharply to $304,000. The sixth year was even worse; Williams only got one contract for $136,000.

The investors' grumbles, meanwhile, have increased to a roar. They point out that the overall debt of the company, including their outlay, is close to a quarter of a million dollars. Royalties, which they expected to produce a flood of cash by this time, are hardly a trickle. They are suspicious that Peter Williams' creativity has run dry.

Two Propositions. They suggest two alternatives. The first is that the company discontinue business after completion of the one remaining contract in the house. In this way, debts will eventually be paid. After that, all shareholders, including Williams, will possibly receive very substantial dividends from future royalty revenue.

The second alternative is that Peter Williams assign to them the royalties from the ten most potential contracts. For these considerations, they will surrender their shares. The advantages to Williams, they claim, are many. He would be rid of disgruntled shareholders who are looking for any legal excuse to force him out. He would then own all the shares and would be free to dictate policy unopposed. Very possibly he might be able to make more royalty money from the five contracts remaining to him than by sharing in the total fifteen contracts.

Decision. Peter Williams thinks over the alternatives for one month. Then he turns both down.

It is true, he admits, that relations between him and the investors have become very acrimonious. Board meetings are far from pleasant and usually end in shouting matches.

However, he does not feel that he has run out of creative ideas. To the contrary, he points out that he has been making prototypes right along, and he is sure that they will eventually result in contracts.

He attributes the business slowdown to a general decline in the toy industry. This, in turn, is due to an acute recession throughout the nation. But national business indicators seem to predict a sharp upturn in the economy in the very near future.

He has initiated many economies. He has reduced the staff to only five people, including himself. He has cut his own salary in half. He has sublet two of the three floors of his rented premises.

He feels that the royalties will soon produce considerable funds. He regrets having the investors unhappy, but he reminds them that he is the majority shareholder; as such, he can dictate policy as long as he stays within the law and makes full and frequent disclosure of the company's financial position to them.

TEST XI. DATA APPLICATION

DIRECTIONS: Based on your understanding of the Business Situation, answer the following questions testing your comprehension of the information supplied in the passage. For each question, select the choice which best answers the question or completes the statement.

1. Peter Williams' company is basically a

   (A) retail business (D) manufacturer
   (B) wholesaler (E) middleman operation
   (C) service firm

2. When the venture capital group invested, the company's worth was estimated at

   (A) $100,000 (D) $151,000
   (B) $300,000 (E) $896,000
   (C) $ 33,000

3. Peter Williams hopes to make up losses by

   (A) securing further investment
   (B) income from future royalties
   (C) bank loans
   (D) "bouncing"
   (E) reducing his salary

4. The company's deficits seem to be the result of

   (A) incorrect estimation of contract costs
   (B) Williams' high salary
   (C) overstaffing
   (D) a lack of business
   (E) a national recession

5. "Bouncing" is a system by which Peter Williams

   (A) overdraws the company's bank account
   (B) contracts with two companies to make the same toy
   (C) makes bank loans by using future royalties as collateral
   (D) sublets part of the business premises
   (E) pays the costs of one contract with the fees of a subsequent one

6. Williams attributes the sharp decline in business to the

   (A) lack of interest in the kinds of toys he makes

   (B) desire of toy companies to develop their own products
   (C) lack of toy company funds to develop new toys
   (D) company's lack of electronic equipment
   (E) national recession

7. Excluding the shareholders' investment, the company's deficit is more nearly

   (A) $ 96,000
   (B) $150,000
   (C) $236,000
   (D) $280,000
   (E) $500,000

8. One of the investors' suggestions is that the company

   (A) discontinue business
   (B) declare bankruptcy
   (C) seek further investment
   (D) assign them royalties from all completed projects
   (E) let Williams buy back their shares

9. One of the things the investors would like is

   (A) Williams' resignation
   (B) a further cut in staff
   (C) Williams to sublet all of the business premises
   (D) future royalties from certain projects
   (E) Williams to stop making prototypes

10. The reason that Peter Williams is able to turn down the two alternatives offered by the investors is that

   (A) he has initiated internal economies
   (B) he can prove he is still creative
   (C) the company is not technically bankrupt
   (D) he is the majority shareholder
   (E) there will be an upturn in the national economy

TEST XII. DATA EVALUATION

DIRECTIONS: Based on your analysis of the Situation, classify each of the following conclusions in one of five categories. Check:
(A) *if the conclusion is a MAJOR OBJECTIVE in making the decision; that is, the outcome or result sought by the decision maker.*
(B) *if the conclusion is a MAJOR FACTOR in arriving at the decision; that is a consideration, explicitly mentioned in the passage that is basic in determining the decision.*
(C) *if the conclusion is a MINOR FACTOR in making the decision; that is, a secondary consideration that affects the criteria tangentially, relating to a Major Factor rather than to an Objective.*
(D) *if the conclusion is a MAJOR ASSUMPTION made in deliberating; that is a supposition or projection made by the decision maker before weighing the variables.*
(E) *if the conclusion is an UNIMPORTANT ISSUE in getting to the point; that is a factor that is insignificant or not immediately relevant to the situation.*

11. Coming to terms with stockholders' dissatisfaction.

12. Recent reduction of staff.

13. William's desire to remain in business.

14. Unpleasant board meetings.

15. Lack of substantial royalties so far.

16. Williams is a majority stockholder.

17. Purchase of expensive electronic equipment.

18. Assuring stockholders that business will grow.

19. Propositions made by stockholders.

20. The company has been kept solvent by bank loans and "bouncing".

21. There has been a general decline in the toy industry.

22. Financial position of Williams' company.

23. Williams' company receives income in the form of an advance against royalties.

24. Quality of Williams' toys.

25. Legality of Williams' operation.

26. Economies have been made in Williams' company.

END OF EXAMINATION

CORRECT ANSWERS FOR VERISIMILAR EXAMINATION II.

(Please make every effort to answer the questions on your own before look-
ing at these answers. You'll make faster progress by following this rule.)

TEST I. READING QUESTIONS

1.A	5.C	9.D	13.E	17.D	21.D	25.A
2.E	6.A	10.E	14.A	18.D	22.B	26.D
3.D	7.B	11.C	15.A	19.E	23.E	27.E
4.E	8.B	12.B	16.B	20.E	24.C	

TEST II. DATA INTERPRETATION

1.C	2.E	3.D	4.B	5.C	6.A

TEST II. EXPLANATORY ANSWERS

1. **(C)** All corporations had a profit of 22 billion. Manufacturing concerns had a profit of 10
billion. The difference is 12 billion.

2. **(E)** From 1962 to 1963 there was a drop in
the Per Cent of National Income for All Corporations as well as for Manufacturing Corporations.

3. **(D)** It was 10 billion for All Corporations.
All Corporations had 6% of the National Income.

$$\frac{10 \text{ billion}}{X} = \frac{6\%}{100\%}$$

X = approx. 170 billion.

4. **(B)** In 1948, All Corporations had a 20 billion dollar profit. This was 9% of the National
Income. In 1952, All Corporations had the same
20 billion dollar profit. This was 7% of the National Income. It is clear, then, that the National
Income increased, but did not double, in 1952.

5. **(C)** The *average* income means the income
of one of the thousands of Manufacturing Corporations. There is no mathematical possibility that an
average corporation exceeded 4% of the National
Income.

6. **(A)** Corporations made twice the profit in
1948 than they did in 1946. Since there were
twice as many corporations, the profit remained
the same.

TEST III. PROBLEM SOLVING

1.E	8.C	15.E	22.B	29.D	36.D	43.A	50.E
2.E	9.C	16.E	23.A	30.E	37.B	44.D	51.D
3.D	10.C	17.B	24.D	31.E	38.C	45.B	52.B
4.B	11.C	18.A	25.B	32.C	39.B	46.D	53.D
5.B	12.B	19.D	26.D	33.C	40.E	47.E	
6.E	13.D	20.D	27.C	34.C	41.B	48.A	
7.D	14.B	21.E	28.D	35.E	42.C	49.E	

TEST III. EXPLANATORY ANSWERS

1. **(E)** 4 of the 6 equal parts of 2 means $\frac{4}{6} \times 2$, or $\frac{4}{3}$.

2. **(E)** 110% of 105 is 1.1×105, or 115.5

3. **(D)** This is a proportion: 2 inches: 7½ inches = 5 feet: x, so x = 18¾ feet.

4. **(B)** The horizontal edges are each 3 cm. long, and the vertical edges are 2 cm. long. Therefore, the volume is $3 \times 3 \times 2$, or 18 cc.

5. **(B)** The only pieces that touch eight other pieces are the shaded ones in this diagram:

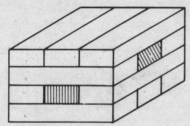

6. **(E)** In order to have a volume of 18 cc., the piece of material must be ½ cm. × 1 cm. × 36 cm.

7. **(D)** Each piece has two faces which are 1 cm. × ½ cm., or ½ sq. cm., two faces which are 1 cm. × 3 cm., or 3 sq. cm., and two faces which are ½ cm. × 3 cm., or 1½ sq. cm. The surface area of each piece is therefore 10 sq. cm. Since there are 12 such pieces, the total area is 120 sq. cm.

8. **(C)** The employment in the peak year was about 750,000, while the employment in 1960 was about 600,000. 600,000 is about 80% of 750,000.

9. **(C)** The only mention of Chrysler cars is their total production, not a breakdown of their types of cars.

10. **(C)** In 1960, the U.S. exported about 150,000 cars, and imported 450,000. 150,000 is about ¼ of the total, 600,000.

11. **(C)** General Motors had a little under 50%, and Ford had a little over 25%, so their sum was about 75%.

12. **(B)** In 1957, both were about 200,000 while in 1959, imports were close to 700,000, while exports fell nearly to 100,000.

13. **(D)** The area of triangle ADE equals the area of triangle AEC, since they have the same base and altitude. The area of triangle ABC equals that of triangle ADC, since the diagonal of a parallelogram divides it equally.

14. **(B)** At 3 for 10¢, one dozen pencils cost 40¢, so the profit on each dozen is 5¢. With 5½ dozen, the profit is 27½¢.

15. **(E)** $26 \times 3\frac{1}{2} = (26 \times 3) + (26 \times \frac{1}{2})$ by the distributive law. $26 \times 3 = (20 \times 3) + (6 \times 3)$ by the distributive law. Therefore, $26 \times 3\frac{1}{2} = (26 \times \frac{1}{2}) + (20 \times 3) + (6 \times 3)$.

16. **(E)** 20 square yards equals 180 square feet. At 31¢ per square foot, it will cost $55.80.

17. **(B)** Each compound is compared with all the others, giving 20, but since each comparison has been counted twice, we divide by 2 to give 10.

18. **(A)** A was judged sweeter 25 times.

19. **(D)** D was judged sweeter only 8 times.

20. **(D)** The other compounds were judged sweeter 25, 23, 24, and 20 times, while D was judged sweeter only 8 times.

21. **(E)** 5 judges called A sweeter, and 5 called B sweeter.

22. **(B)** 35 feet, 6 inches equals 426 inches. One-fourth of this is 106½ inches, or 8 feet, 10½ inches.

23. **(A)** Out of 12 total games, two were won. Thus, the fraction is 2/12, or 1/6.

24. **(D)** 10^5 is defined as $10 \times 10 \times 10 \times 10 \times 10$, or 100,000. $10 \times 5 = 50$; $5^{10} = 25^5$; $5\sqrt{10}$ is between 1 and 2; and $10^{10} \div 10^2 = 10^8$.

25. **(B)** $3\frac{1}{2} \times \$1.10 = \$3.85$. At 60¢ a dozen, one orange costs 5¢, and 20 cost \$1.00. The total is \$4.85.

26. **(D)** $\overline{\varphi}\int \int_{\circ}^{\circ} = \text{XCL} = 10,150$.

27. **(C)** $4(10^4) + 5(10^3) + 4(100) = 45,400 =$

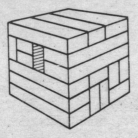

28. **(D)** $\text{SQII II} = 1,502,002 = 10^6 + 50(10,000) + 2,000 + 2$.

29. **(D)** $2\frac{3}{4} \div \frac{1}{8} = \frac{11}{4} \div \frac{1}{8} = \frac{11}{4} \times 8 = 22$

30. **(E)** $105,084 - 93,709 = 11,375$.

31. **(E)** This is a proportion → $2\frac{1}{2} : 3 = x : 14$; $x = \frac{35}{3}$, or $11\frac{2}{3}$.

32. **(C)** After a^3, "A" is on the bottom. After this, then b; "A" moves to the left.

33. **(C)** Starting on the right, b brings the face in question to the bottom, and c then leaves it in the same position.

34. **(C)** $a^2b^2c^2$ returns the cube to its original position, and so does c^4.

35. **(E)** If the gain was 10% of the selling price, then \$12.60 was 90% so 100% was equal to \$14.00.

36. **(D)** There will be no waste if the lengths are multiples of 5½ feet. This occurs between 6 and 24 only for 22 feet.

37. **(B)** Each tile, including half of the cement around it, has an area of 1 square inch. 3240 square inches equals 22.5 square feet, or 2.5 square yards.

38. **(C)** A median score is the middle score when all scores are arranged in ascending or descending order. This is 27 here.

39. **(B)** The volume of the large cube is 6^3, or 216 cubic inches. Each $1'' \times 2'' \times 6''$ block has a volume of 12 cubic inches. Dividing, there are 18 cubes.

40. **(E)** 12 blocks have their $2'' \times 6''$ faces painted blue. 6 more have their $1'' \times 6''$ faces painted blue. The total area of blue is 180 sq. in.

41. **(B)** The shaded block touches 11 other blocks.

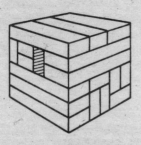

38. **(C)** A median score is the middle score when all scores are arranged in ascending or descending order. This is 27 here.

39. **(B)** The volume of the large cube is 6^3, or 216 cubic inches. Each $1'' \times 2'' \times 6''$ block has a volume of 12 cubic inches. Dividing, there are 18 cubes.

40. **(E)** 12 blocks have their $2'' \times 6''$ faces painted blue. 6 more have their $1'' \times 6''$ faces painted blue. The total area of blue is 180 sq. in.

41. **(B)** The shaded block touches 11 other blocks.

42. **(C)** All the blue surface touches red surface, except for the 36 square inches on the bottom of the cube. Since 180 square inches are blue (see #40), 144 of these touch red surfaces.

43. **(A)** It is required to have the least possible vertical area. This is obtained when the 2″ × 6″ side is horizontal, leaving only 1″ × 2″ and 1″ × 6″ sides to be vertical.

44. **(D)** (2 × 100) + (16 × 10) + 6 = 200 + 160 + 6 = 366.

45. **(B)** After the 20% discount, the price was $128. After the 10% discount, the price was $115.20.

46. **(D)** The perimeter of a 46′ × 34′ rectangle is 160 feet, which equals 53⅓ yards.

47. **(E)** After the 15% deduction, $12,750 is left. After the 10% is deducted from $12,750, $11,475 is left. Note that you cannot simply deduct 25% from the $15,000.

48. **(A)** In 1920, the price was almost $1.40 per pound, while in 1930, the price was only about $0.30.

49. **(E)** In 1934, the price was about 40¢ per pound, and in 1931 it was about 30¢. 40¢ is 4/3 of 30¢. Do not be fooled by the appearance of the graph, which suggests that the answer should be 2/1. This effect is produced by making the first level $0.20, instead of $0.00.

50. **(E)** 1920 was the highest year, but it is obvious that silver prices were higher in 1919 than in 1935 or 1946.

51. **(D)** In the 1943-45 period, the price of silver was almost constant.

52. **(B)** The graph clearly indicates the sharp rise from 1940.

53. **(D)** In 1943, and also in 1944, the price was about $0.45.

TEST IV. ANTONYMS

1.E	3.A	5.C	7.D	9.E	11.C	13.C
2.B	4.D	6.B	8.D	10.B	12.C	14.A

TEST V. VERBAL ANALOGIES

1.E	3.C	5.D	7.A	9.A	11.A
2.C	4.C	6.C	8.B	10.D	12.C

TEST VI. SENTENCE COMPLETIONS

1.C	3.B	5.D	7.D	9.A	11.D	13.D
2.E	4.D	6.A	8.E	10.B	12.A	

TEST VII. DATA SUFFICIENCY

1.E	3.C	5.E	7.C	9.D	11.C	13.C	15.D
2.C	4.A	6.C	8.E	10.B	12.B	14.A	16.A

TEST VII. EXPLANATORY ANSWERS

1. (E)

   It is impossible to determine from information given.

2. (C)

   By statement (1)

   if $AB = AC$, then $\angle W = \angle Y$

   By statement (2)

   if $\angle x = 50$, then $\angle W + \angle Y = 130$.

   Hence both are $65°$.

3. (C)

   Using both statements, if c is an even integer, then b and d must be odd.

4. (A)

   By statement (1) if a is a whole number, then its square is also a whole number.

5. (E)

   To do the problem the points would have to be collinear and a definite direction given for each.

6. (C)

   Equilateral triangles having equal bases are congruent by the side, side, side postulate.

7. (C)

   To find the area of a trapezoid, the height and both bases are needed. The diagram gives the bases as 12 and 20. The altitude can be found by using both statements and applying the Pythagorean theorem.

   $$c^2 = a^2 + b^2$$
   $$24^2 = a^2 + 16^2$$
   $$576 = a^2 + 256$$
   $$320 = a^2$$
   $$\sqrt{320} = a$$

8. (E)

   Impossible to determine from information given.

9. (D)

   Since a numerical answer was not asked for, x can be solved in terms of y in statement (1), and in terms of w in statement (2).

10. (B)

    By statement (2)

    Let x = the first number
    $x + 2$ = the second number
    $2x + 2 = 18$
    $2x = 16$
    $x = 8$

    Hence 14 equals the fourth number.

11. (C)

    To find the dimensions of a rectangle, the length and the width require two equations. By statement (1)

    $$2l + 2w = 14$$

    By statement (2)

    $$l^2 + w^2 = 5^2$$

    Using both statements, the length and the width of the rectangle can now be determined.

12. (B)

    By statement (2) $\angle ACB$ is identified as an angle inscribed in a semicircle, hence $\angle ACB = 90°$.

13. (C)

    To determine if x is greater than Y requires two equations. Statement (1) is an equation, and statement (2) is an equation.

14. (A)

    By statement (1), the coordinates are equal. When the coordinates are equal, then the $m < m = 45°$.

15. **(D)**

If the average of 3 ages is 26, then the total of the 3 ages is 78. By statement (2) if 2 satisfy the minimum 22, their total is 44. Subtracting this total from 78, the maximum age for one is 34. Statement (1) specifies the maximum age to be 34.

16. **(A)**

The smallest line that can be drawn between 2 parallel lines is a perpendicular. Comparing the sizes of other lines drawn between parallels is accomplished by comparing the angles they form with either parallel line. The greater the angle, the larger the line. Statement (1) shows the angle measurement of both lines.

TEST VIII. READING COMPREHENSION

1.C	5.D	9.D	13.B	17.D
2.C	6.D	10.A	14.B	18.D
3.A	7.B	11.B	15.A	19.D
4.B	8.D	12.A	16.C	20.B

TEST IX. ENGLISH USAGE

1.B	4.A	7.A	10.D	13.B
2.D	5.A	8.E	11.C	14.A
3.D	6.B	9.C	12.C	15.C

TEST X. ENGLISH USAGE

1.C	4.C	7.E	10.D	13.D
2.D	5.E	8.C	11.A	14.C
3.B	6.A	9.A	12.E	15.B

TEST XI. TEST XII. DATA APPLICATION AND EVALUATION

1.C	5.E	9.D	13.B	17.E	21.D	24.E
2.B	6.E	10.D	14.C	18.A	22.B	25.D
3.B	7.B	11.A	15.C	19.B	23.D	26.C
4.A	8.A	12.C	16.D	20.C		

TEST XI. TEST XII. EXPLANATORY ANSWERS

1. **(C)** Basically, Peter Williams' company is a service firm, its service being the creation of new products for toy companies.

2. **(B)** Since the investors bought one-third of the company's stock for $100,000, the total value must be $300,000.

3. **(B)** Williams states that the royalties will soon produce considerable funds. It is true that he has reduced his own salary, but this is a stopgap method of reducing present operating costs and would not make up a quarter-million dollar deficit. He did not mention getting bank loans or seeking more investment money. "Bouncing" cannot reduce losses.

4. **(A)** Contract-cost overruns have certainly been the major factor in creating the large deficit. We do not know what Williams' salary is, but the investors did not object to it so we can assume it is not too high. Williams has pared down his staff, but they too did not seem to bother the investors. The recession and the resulting lack of

business are unfortunate for the company, but the deficit existed prior to the decline; it merely grew during the bad times.

5. **(E)** "Bouncing" is defined in the story.

6. **(E)** So stated.

7. **(B)** We are told that the company's deficit, which includes the investors' money, is nearly a quarter of a million dollars. The investors put in $100,000. Therefore, when we subtract that figure, the result is under $150,000.

8. **(A)** So stated. The investors do not go so far as to suggest bankruptcy proceedings, nor do they recommend more investment or that Williams buy back their shares. They want royalties only from some of the completed projects, not all.

9. **(D)** The investors want the royalties from ten of the fifteen completed projects.

10. **(D)** Williams tells the investors bluntly that policy is in his hands because he is the majority shareholder.

LETTER CODE FOR EVALUATING DATA

(A) means that the Conclusion is a Major Objective;
(B) means that the Conclusion is a Major Factor;
(C) means that the Conclusion is a Minor Factor;
(D) means that the Conclusion is a Major Assumption;
(E) means that the Conclusion is an Unimportant Issue.

11. **(A)** The decision maker in this passage is Williams. The decision he must make is to accept or reject the shareholders' demands. The objective is to come to terms with stockholder dissatisfaction.

12. **(C)** The recent reduction of staff is a minor factor that relates to the major factor of the financial position of Williams' company.

13. **(B)** Williams' desire to remain in business is a major factor in his decision.

14. **(C)** Unpleasant board meetings are a minor factor that resulted in the major factor of propositions being made by the stockholders.

15. **(C)** Lack of substantial royalties is a minor factor that relates to the major factor of shareholder dissatisfaction and to the financial position of the company.

16. **(D)** It is assumed that Williams is a majority stockholder.

17. **(E)** The purchase of expensive electronic equipment is not related to the present decision.

18. **(A)** Assuring stockholders that business will grow is a major objective.

19. **(B)** The propositions made by the shareholders are a major factor in necessitating the decision made by Williams.

20. **(C)** The way the company has been kept solvent relates to the general financial position of Williams' company.

21. **(D)** The general decline in the toy industry is an assumption.

22. **(B)** The financial position of Williams' company is a major factor in the arousal of shareholder dissatisfaction.

23. **(D)** It is assumed that Williams' company receives income as an advance against royalty.

24. **(E)** The quality of Williams' toys is undisputed and not a factor.

25. **(D)** The legality of Williams' operation is assumed.

26. **(C)** Economies have been made which relate to the financial position of the company.

GRADUATE MANAGEMENT ADMISSION TEST

III. A VERISIMILAR EXAM

Based on all the information available before going to press we have constructed this examination to give you a comprehensive and authoritative view of what's in store for you. To avoid any misunderstanding, we must emphasize that this test has never been given before. We devised it specially to provide a final opportunity of employing all you've learned in a situation that closely simulates the real thing.

The time allowed for the entire examination is 3½ hours.

ANALYSIS AND TIMETABLE: III. VERISIMILAR EXAMINATION

The timetable below is both an index to your practice test and a preview of the actual exam. In constructing this examination, we have analyzed every available announcement and official statement about the exam and thus predict that this is what you may face.

It is well known that examiners like to experiment with various types of questions, so the test you take may be slightly different in form or content. However, we feel certain that if you have mastered each subject covered here, you will be well on your way to scoring high.

SUBJECT TESTED	Time Allowed
READING RECALL	35 minutes
DATA INTERPRETATION & PROBLEM SOLVING	75 minutes
VERBAL ABILITY	20 minutes
DATA SUFFICIENCY	15 minutes
READING COMPREHENSION	20 minutes
ENGLISH USAGE	15 minutes
PRACTICAL BUSINESS JUDGMENT	25 minutes

READING RECALL

4 passages-27 questions

TEST I. READING PASSAGES

TIME: 15 Minutes

DIRECTIONS: This is a test to determine your ability to remember main ideas and significant details. You are to read the four passages that follow in a period of 15 minutes altogether. It is suggested that you divide your time equally among the four passages. When the time is up, you will be asked to recall certain ideas and facts about the four passages. You will not be able to refer back to the passages after 15 minutes.

PASSAGE 1

That guessing is not always random is scarcely contestable. What is, perhaps, of more interest is the contention that the type of correction for guessing often made in aptitude tests of the multiple-choice variety is inadequate. Evidence has been offered in support of the thesis that guesses have a better than random probability of being right and that therefore "It can pay to guess." The implication seems to be that guessing in this context is a mild form of delinquency and is not sufficiently penalized by applying the usual correction formula. Two points arise and need clarification. The first has to do with item uniqueness, while the second involves more fundamental considerations.

To illustrate the argument, we may use the synonym-type questions of a typical aptitude test. In answering such questions, it can hardly be denied that on balance it pays to guess when in doubt. Two sorts of reasons account for this. First, the subject may have good grounds for rejecting some of the choices, either because he knows their meanings and is sure that they are not synonymous with the word specified, or because they are the wrong part of speech, or for some similar reason. If only one of the distractors is of this form, then a subject's chance of hitting the right answer is not $1/n$ but $1/(n-1)$, and so on. Secondly, as is widely recognized, there is a continuum between ignorance and certainty which may favor guessing in certain circumstances. In vocabulary tests this influence will favor guessing unless the distractors have been specially chosen to mislead the unwary. However, the broad as-

sertion that this influence must favor guessing overlooks the factor of item uniqueness. If we choose items carefully, we can easily demonstrate that guessing raises or lowers scores, or leaves them unaffected.

The following multi-choice item is a good example:

CONDIGN means the same as
BLAME, MEET, PEPPERY, PRAISEWORTHY, SLANDER.

Unless the subject actually knows the right answer he is more likely to choose one of the distractors. The main point of the argument is that it is possible to produce items of this kind and to engineer the distribution of guessing probabilities in any way that takes the fancy. It is a matter of interest to examine why this should be so.

In this particular example we have engineered the situation by:

(*a*) Using a word that is in any case little known.

(*b*) Using a target word that has a far more common meaning than the alternative meaning that corresponds to CONDIGN.

(*c*) Choosing distractors that are plausible. For example, CONDIGN has about it a similar ring to CONDEMN, and so may easily be thought akin to any word involving value judgments.

(*d*) Confusing the subject still further by not giving clues as to whether he should be looking for a verb, adjective or noun. Only PEPPERY and PRAISEWORTHY are clearly adjectives; BLAME and SLANDER can operate as nouns or verbs; while

MEET in its common form is a verb, although it is as an adjective that it provides a synonym for CONDIGN.

An experiment was recently carried out in which a vocabulary test was presented to subjects who were also asked to give, with each response, an assessment of their own feelings of confidence or doubt. The subjects—forty in number—were all adults with a good educational background. The CONDIGN item was added to the end. The null hypothesis was that each word on the CONDIGN item would be chosen an equal number of times, and that any observed differences would merely be chance variations. The prediction was that those who "guess"—those who express some "doubt" or are "very doubtful"—on this item would tend to choose one of the distractors rather than the target alternative; in other words, less than 20 per cent of the subjects would choose MEET.

All the subjects were doubtful about the CONDIGN item, and the following results were obtained.

NUMBER OF SUBJECTS CHOOSING TARGET WORD
AND DISTRACTORS

Meet	*Distractors*
1	39

PASSAGE 2

The origin of continental nuclei has long been a puzzle. Theories advanced so far have generally failed to explain the first step in continent growth, or have been subject to serious objections. It is the purpose of this article to examine the possible role of the impact of large meteorites or asteroids in the production of continental nuclei.

Unfortunately, the geological evolution of the Earth's surface has had an obliterating effect on the original composition and structure of the continents to such an extent that further terrestrial investigations have small chance of arriving at an unambiguous answer to the question of continental origin. Paradoxically, clues to the origin and early history of the surface features of the Earth may be found on the Moon and planets, rather than on the Earth, because some of these bodies appear to have had a much less active geological history. As a result, relatively primitive surface features are preserved for study and analysis.

In the case of both the Moon and Mars, it is generally concluded from the appearance of their heavily cratered surfaces that they have been subjected to bombardment by large meteoroids during their geological history. Likewise, it would appear a reasonable hypothesis that the Earth has also been subjected to meteoroid bombardment in the past, and that very large bodies struck the Earth early in its geological history.

The largest crater on the Moon listed by Baldwin has a diameter of 285 km. However, if we accept the hypothesis of formation of some of the mare basins by impact, the maximum lunar impact crater diameter[1] is probably as large as 650 km. Based on a lunar analogy, one might expect several impact craters of at least 500 km diameter to have been formed on Earth. By applying Baldwin's[1] equation, the depth of such a crater should be about 20 km. Baldwin admits that his equation gives excessive depths for large craters so that the actual depth should be somewhat smaller. Based on the measured depth of smaller lunar craters, a depth of 10 km is probably a conservative estimate for the depth of a 500 km impact crater. Baldwin's equation gives the depth of the zone of brecciation for such a crater as about 75 km. The plasticity of the Earth's mantle at the depth makes it impossible to speak of "brecciation" in the usual sense. However, local stresses may be temporarily sustained at that depth, as shown by the existence of deep-focus earthquakes. Thus, short-term effects might be expected to a depth of more than 50 km in the mantle.

Even without knowing the precise effects, there is little doubt that the formation of a 500-km crater would be a major geological event. Numerous authors have considered the geological implications of such an event. Donn *et al.* have, for example, called on the impact of continent-size bodies of sialic composition to form the original continents. Two major difficulties inherent in this concept are the lack of any known sialic meteorites, and the high probability that the energy of impact would result in a wide dissemination of sialic material, rather than its concentration at the point of impact.

Gilvarry, on the other hand, called on meteoroid impact to explain the production of ocean basins. The major difficulties with this model are that the morphology of most of the ocean basins is not consistent with impact, and that the origin and growth of continents is not adequately explained.

We agree with Donn *et al.* that the impact of large meteorites or asteroids may have caused continent formation, but would rather think in terms of the localized addition of energy to the system, rather than in terms of the addition of actual sialic material.

PASSAGE 3

The communists' preoccupation with economic growth and their whole attitude toward economic progress have been shaped by Marx's theory of long-run development of human society. This theory places economic development at the centre of the entire social philosophy and it is impossible to study the Marxists' political, social and economic views without referring to it. Without the knowledge of this theory it is difficult to understand the communists' dogmatic belief in the superiority of their system, whatever are the observable facts, and their faith in the final victory over capitalism. Economic development has to lead, sooner or later, to socialism and communism and it is necessary to build socialism and, later, communism to make future economic growth possible. This principle is valid for all countries without an exception. They all have to proceed along the same path although they may be placed at different points of it at present. Such is the logic of history.

This theory, which is usually referred to as "historical materialism," "the materialistic conception of history," or "Marx's historical determinism," is believed by the Marxists to be useful not only as the explanation of the past and the present but also as the basis for the prediction of the future course of history. As the final judgment on any prophecy has to be made in the light of the subsequent events, it is interesting to compare the developments since the theory was presented by Marx with the pattern which could have been expected on the basis of Marx's prediction. The purpose of this paper is to outline briefly such a comparison and to discuss the communist explanation of the disparity which has appeared between the actual and the predicted course of events. The paper does not attempt to evaluate the philosophical aspects of the theory, its materialism, onesidedness and methodological oversimplification. Similarly, the value of the theory as a summary of the past historical events preceding the time when it was presented by Marx and its merits and weaknesses as one of numerous "stages of growth" theories are not discussed.

Marx's theory accepts as its basis that man's life is a conscious struggle with the natural environment, the struggle which takes the form of production as "life involves, before everything else, eating and drinking, a habitation, clothing, and many other things." The process of production is the interaction between man and nature and it takes the form of social labour. Man has to improve his instruments of production in order to master the natural environment but "the development of these instruments follows a definite sequence" as "each new improvement and invention can be made only on the basis of those that have preceded it, and must rest upon gradually accumulated production experience, the labour skills and knowledge of the people . . ." Production is carried on as a social process, because "in the process of producing material wealth, people, whether they like it or not, find themselves in some way linked with one another and the labour of each producer becomes a part of the social labour." These relationships among men are called the "relations of production." They exist independently of human consciousness and this gives them their materialistic character. They are determined by the level of development and the nature of productive forces.

PASSAGE 4

According to Hegel, a conflict between a thesis and its antithesis produces a synthesis which partakes of the natures of both. The general councils of the Church which so far number twenty-one may serve as an illustration of this philosophy. To start from not very far away in the past, the Council of Trent (1545-63) was a reaction to the Lutheran revolt. The first Ecumenical Council of the Vatican (1869-70) was held in the shadow of the French Revolution of 1789, of the revolutions in 1848 and of the rationalist movement. The First Session of the Second Ecumenical Council of the Vatican (1963) was against the atheistic movement, mainly represented by communism, the new scientific irreligious trends and the fact that "The World was too strong for a divided Christianity." The Second Session of this Council, which began on September 29, 1963, and culminated in Pope Paul's visit to the Holy Land in January 1964, is mainly a unitive Council, to try to bring together the various churches in Christendom and to try to have dialogues with other religions for a united stand against disruptive forces in the world. This is the meaning of "ecumenism" in its Christian sense and in its wider and world-wide sense. Islam is only concerned with the latter sense. The thaw which is taking place at the Vatican, a new synthesis, may be regarded as a prelude to a wider thaw with the world religions through continuous dialogue with Islam, Judaism, and other religions.

The dialogue with Islam has a long history. In its beginning, the conflict between Christianity and Islam was violent. One could cite here the Muslim conquests in the seventh and eighth centuries, the Crusades, the Inquisition in Spain, religious persecution and the missionary movements. But throughout this long period there were sometimes peaceful and more rational dialogues and debates. Peter the Venerable in the twelfth century, for instance, wrote in his first book of *Adversus Nefandum Sectum Saracenorum* (against the unspeakable sect of the Saracens) as follows, addressing Muslims: "It appears odd and perhaps is actually so that a man so removed from you by great distance, speaking another language, and having a profession and customs and a manner of life so different from your own, should write from the furthest West to men who live in the countries of the Orient, and should direct his attacks against a people whom he has never seen, and that he assails you not with weapons, as Christians have often done, but by word, not by force but with reasons, not with hate but with love." Peter then pleads with the Saracens to enter into discussion. He was indignant that the Latins were living in ignorance of a religion so widespread as Islam. A century later, Roger Bacon condemned the method of the crusade and wanted to see the intellectuals taking part in discussions. He gave an illustration from the King of Tartary, who gathered before him people of differing beliefs in order that he might thereby come to a knowledge of the truth. This reminds us of Akbar, the Mughal emperor of India. Raymund Lull appealed in 1312 to Frederick III of Sicily to make representations to the King of Tunis whereby Christians versed in the literature and language of the Arabs might be sent to Tunis, and learned doctors from among the Saracens of Tunis might be invited to Sicily where they could enter into discussion with Christians. He also said, referring to the Crusades, that the Holy Land would never be conquered except by love and prayer. Thomas Aquinas wrote his book *Summa Contra Gentiles* in order to use reason and discussion, especially with Muslims in Spain.

But what has been the attitude of the Muslims to all such approaches? It is one which stems from the Prophet's example given in his dealings with Christians and Jews in Arabia. He used to enjoin his followers not to enter into polemics with their adversaries, but to content themselves with saying to them that they (the Muslims) neither believed nor disbelieved what the others claimed in their Scriptures, but only believed in what was contained in the Quran. A verse in the Quran says: "Our Lord, we believe in what thou hast revealed and we follow the Apostle." Another verse says: "O followers of the Bible! Come to an equitable proposition between us and you that we shall not serve any but God and that we shall not associate anyone with Him, and that some of us shall not take others for Lords besides God: but if they [the Scriptuaries] turn back, then say: bear witness that we are muslims." A third verse says: "And do not dispute with the people of the Scriptures except by what is best, except those of them who act unjustly, and say: We believe in that which has been revealed to us and revealed to you, and our God and your God is one, and to him do we submit."

END OF SECTION

If you finish before the allotted time is up, work on this part only.
When time is up, proceed directly to the next part and do not
return to this part.

TEST I. READING QUESTIONS

TIME: 20 minutes

DIRECTIONS: Answer the following questions in accordance with the contents of the preceding passages. You are not to turn back to the passages.

QUESTIONS ON PASSAGE 1

1. The author of the article believes that

   (A) guessing is always haphazard in nature
   (B) deducting a certain amount of credit for every wrong guess is reasonable and logical
   (C) in a five-choice multiple-choice question, it is safe to assume that if one guesses, he will be correct approximately 20% of the time
   (D) there should be more severe penalties for guessing on multiple-choice tests than the penalties usually invoked
   (E) there is a definite correlation between moral delinquency and the tendency to guess on tests

2. The writer is obviously

   (A) opposed to aptitude tests for college entrance but not for graduate school admission
   (B) in disagreement with established practices of penalizing for guessing
   (C) in favor of vocabulary tests to prognosticate success in college
   (D) of the opinion that the essay-type question has greater validity than the multiple-choice question
   (E) interested in developing a test which will tolerate no guessing

3. A multiple-choice vocabulary question

   (A) should never require an opposite meaning as the correct choice
   (B) should have at least one choice which is obviously incorrect
   (C) should, at times, have two correct choices

   (D) should always have a synonym and an antonym among its choices
   (E) should have choices all of which seem possible to many candidates, at first glance

4. The antonym of "condign" is

   (A) unconditional   (B) untidy
   (C) insincere   (D) undeserved
             (E) interesting

5. Assuming that we wished to add a "distractor" sixth-choice for the five-choice "condign" question given, we would use

   (A) petite   (B) indigenous
   (C) destroyed   (D) blatant
             (E) durable

6. The results of the test in which subjects were asked to give their feelings afterwards, show that _____ percent actually chose the correct answer.

   (A) 2.5   (B) 16.1
   (C) 20   (D) 39.8
             (E) 78.2

7. If we are dealing with a five-choice multiple-choice question, *n* in 1/n would be

   (A) 1
   (B) 2
   (C) 3
   (D) 4
   (E) 5

S1361

QUESTIONS ON PASSAGE 2

8. A mare basin is

    (A) an area where animal life flourished at one time
    (B) a formula for determining the relationship between the depth and width of craters
    (C) a valley that is filled in when a spatial body has impact with the moon or the earth
    (D) a planetoid (small planet) created when a meteorite, upon striking the moon, breaks off a part of the moon
    (E) a dark spot on the moon, once supposed to be a sea, now a plain

9. A lunar crater, at the time it was formed, was approximately

    (A) half as wide as it is today
    (B) twice as wide as it is today
    (C) as wide as it is today
    (D) four times as wide as it is today
    (E) one-fourth as wide as it is today

10. When man reaches the moon and explores its surface, the widest crater that he will be able to find will measure about

    (A) 1 mile across
    (B) 15 miles across
    (C) 95 miles across
    (D) 180 miles across
    (E) 1,200 miles across

11. The writer does *not* believe that

    (A) an asteroid is larger than a meteorite

    (B) material from space, upon hitting the earth, was eventually distributed
    (C) oceans were formerly craters
    (D) the earth, at one time, had craters
    (E) tremendous meteorites, in early times, fell upon our planet

12. The article is primarily concerned with

    (A) the origin of continents
    (B) the craters on the moon
    (C) differences of opinion among authoritative geologists
    (D) the relationship between asteroids and meteorites
    (E) planetary surface features

13. Sialic material refers to

    (A) the broken rock resulting from the impact of a meteorite against the earth
    (B) material that exists on planets other than the earth
    (C) a composite of rocks typical of continental areas of the earth
    (D) the lining of craters
    (E) material that is man-made to simulate materials that existed far back in geological history

14. In order to research how our continents came about, geologists would do well to devote the greater part of their study to

    (A) asteroids and meteorites
    (B) the earth
    (C) the sun
    (D) planetoids
    (E) other planets and the moon

QUESTIONS ON PASSAGE 3

15. The author indicates that the typical communist

    (A) is more interested in the success of communism than in the welfare of his own family
    (B) no longer adheres to the economic and/or philosophic principles set down by Marx
    (C) has the same fundamental interests as the non-communist
    (D) is afraid to express his true beliefs for fear of punishment
    (E) has an authoritative—if not arrogant—opinion about the advantages of communism over capitalism

16. A primary feature of Marxism is the stress on

    (A) studying the lessons of history to formulate plans for the eventual victory of communism over capitalism
    (B) the development and management of the material wealth of a government or community
    (C) the need to move ahead with the implementation of the communist philosophy by violent means
    (D) the eventual compromise between communism and the Western world
    (E) the improvement of educational practices and the provision of educational opportunities for all

17. That a state of communism is to be preceded by socialism is

    (A) contrary to Marxist theory
    (B) considered by Marx to be just as feasible as the converse
    (C) a phase of "relations of production"
    (D) the doctrine of historical determinism

    (E) not the concern of advocates of the communist philosophy

18. The writer states or implies that

    (A) one cannot accurately appraise a proposed social or political philosophy until the results have been seen
    (B) there is essentially no difference in practice between the communistic and the democratic form of government
    (C) in the final analysis, man is an animal who cannot be guided by moral considerations
    (D) the great majority of individuals are not intelligent enough to govern themselves—a dictator must always be present to make decisions for them
    (E) there is no reason to feel that communistic countries and nations with other forms of government cannot exist in peace

19. The writer's attitude toward the Communist Revolution is one of

    (A) righteous indignation
    (B) unnecessary oversimplification
    (C) hardheaded materialism
    (D) studied indifference
    (E) scholarly objectivity

20. The selection does *not*

    (A) refer to the importance of wealth in communistic philosophy
    (B) explain what the productive process involves
    (C) appraise the materialist conception of history
    (D) deal with nations other than those which are now communistic
    (E) quote Marx directly

QUESTIONS ON PASSAGE 4

21. The "rationalist movement" refers to

    (A) the procedure of fixing allowances of food and other goods in time of scarcity
    (B) the reorganization of religion in accordance with up-to-date methods and practices

    (C) the removal of radicals not only in scientific procedures but also in society as well
    (D) the explanation of behavior on grounds ostensibly rational but not in accord with the actual motives
    (E) the reliance upon reason alone, independently of authority or of revelation

22. The leaders of Islam

    (A) have traditionally been averse to religious discussions with the Catholics
    (B) are agreeable to combining their religion with that of the Christians, since there are many features in common, provided certain specified beliefs can be retained by each religion
    (C) are planning ecumenical councils of their own
    (D) have had a continuously friendly relationship with the Christians
    (E) were responsible for conducting the Spanish Inquisition

23. The work, *Adversus Nefandum Sectum Saracenorum,*

    (A) urged a final victory, bloody if necessary, over the followers of Islam
    (B) favored talks with the Saracens in order to arrive at a peaceful settlement of their differences
    (C) presented ideas that could be employed in the conversion of the Muslims
    (D) commended the religious beliefs of the Islamites
    (E) suggested a cultural and professional interchange between the Christians and the Muslims

24. Synonyms for *Muslim* and *Quran* are

    (A) Mussel and Querin
    (B) Muslin and Quorum
    (C) Islam and Queries
    (D) Mohammedan and Koran
    (E) Clay and Cura

25. A major function of the ecumenical councils has been

    (A) to discuss religious persecution and missionary movements
    (B) to determine how to rid the world of evils such as poverty, disease, and war
    (C) to find common ground with the churches other than Catholic
    (D) to arrive at the most efficient means of eliminating atheism
    (E) to plan procedures for converting the rest of the world to Catholicism

26. That the learned men of both Christianity and Islam should meet to iron out their differences was a proposal of a(n)

    (A) apostle
    (B) monk
    (C) general
    (D) pope
    (E) scientist

27. The article does not make reference to a part of the following area:

    (A) the Iberian peninsula
    (B) Italy
    (C) Northern Africa
    (D) the United States
    (E) South Asia

END OF PART
If you finish before the allotted time is up, work on this part only.
When time is up, proceed directly to the next part and do not
return to this part.

QUANTITATIVE PART

55 questions- 68 minutes

TEST II. DATA INTERPRETATION

TIME: 15 Minutes

DIRECTIONS: Read each question in this test carefully. Answer each one on the basis of the following table. Select the best answer among the given choices.

VALUE OF PROPERTY STOLEN— 1963 and 1964
LARCENY

CATEGORY	1963		1964	
	Number of Offenses	Value of Stolen Property	Number of Offenses	Value of Stolen Property
Pocket - picking	20	$ 1,950	10	$ 950
Purse - snatching	175	5,750	120	12,050
Shoplifting	155	7,950	225	17,350
Automobile thefts	1040	127,050	860	108,000
Thefts of automobile accessories	1135	34,950	970	24,400
Bicycle thefts	355	8,250	240	6,350
All other thefts	1375	187,150	1300	153,150

1. Of the total number of larcenies reported for 1963, automobile thefts accounted for, most nearly,
   (A) 5%   (B) 15%   (C) 25%
   (D) 50%   (E) 75%

2. The largest percentage decrease in the value of the stolen property from 1963 to 1964 was in the category of
   (A) bicycle thefts
   (B) automobile thefts
   (C) thefts of automobile accessories
   (D) pocket-picking
   (E) all other thefts

3. In 1964 the average amount of each theft was lowest for the category of
   (A) pocket-picking
   (B) purse-snatching
   (C) thefts of automobile accessories
   (D) shoplifting
   (E) bicycle thefts

4. The category which had the largest numerical reduction in the number of offenses from 1963 to 1964 was
   (A) pocket-picking
   (B) automobile thefts
   (C) thefts of automobile accessories
   (D) bicycle thefts
   (E) all other thefts

5. When the categories are ranked, for each year, according to the number of offenses committed in each category (largest number to rank first), the number of categories which will have the same rank in 1963 as in 1964 is
   (A) 3   (B) 4   (C) 5
   (D) 6   (E) 7

6. For the two years combined (1963 and 1964), the average value of property stolen by pocket-picking was approximately
   (A) $25   (B) $30   (C) $150
   (D) $97   (E) $74

Answer questions solely on the basis of the
following table.

Number of Persons Receiving Public Assistance and Cost of Public Assistance in 1961 and 1962

Category of Assistance	Monthly average number receiving assistance during		Total Cost for Year in Millions of Dollars		Cost Paid by New York City for Year in Millions of Dollars	
	1961	1962	1961	1962	1961	1962
H R	36,097	38,263	$19.2	$17.4	$9.7	$8.7
V A	6,632	5,972	2.5	1.6	1.3	.8
O A A	32,545	31,804	33.7	29.7	6.5	5.0
M A A	13,992	11,782	13.2	21.3	3.3	5.3
A D C	212,795	228,795	108.3	121.4	27.5	31.3

7. Assume that the *total* cost of the Home Relief program decreases by 10% each year for the next three years after 1962. Then the total cost of the Home Relief program for 1965 will be, most nearly,
   (A) $11.5 million   (C) $12.7 million
   (B) $14.1 million   (D) $14.5 million
        (E) $36.0 million

8. The category for which New York City paid the smallest percentage of the total cost was
   (A) O A A in 1961   (C) V A in 1961
   (B) A D C in 1961   (D) O A A in 1962
        (E) A D C in 1962

9. The *monthly* cost to the city for each person receiving MAA during 1962 was, most nearly,
   (A) $18 more than in 1961
   (B) $26 less than in 1961
   (C) $20 more than in 1961
   (D) $67 more than in 1961
   (E) $18 less than in 1961

10. Assume that 40% of the number of persons receiving ADC in 1961 were adults caring for minor children, but the city's contribution towards maintaining these adults was only 36% of its total contribution to the ADC program in 1961, then the amount paid by the city for each adult per month in 1961 is, most nearly,
    (A) $10 (B) $14 (C) $31 (D) $36
         (E) $107

11. Assume that 10% of the persons receiving OAA in 1962 will be transferred to MAA in 1963, and 6% of the persons receiving MAA in 1962 will no longer need any public assistance in 1963, then the percentage change from 1962 to 1963 in the monthly average number receiving MAA would be, most nearly,

    (A) an increase of 4%
    (B) an increase of 27%
    (C) a decrease of 6%
    (D) an increase of 21%

END OF TEST

Go on to the next Test in the Examination, just as you would do on the actual exam. Check your answers when you have completed the entire Examination. The correct answers for this Test, and all the other Tests, are assembled at the conclusion of this Examination.

TEST III. PROBLEM SOLVING

TIME: 48 minutes

DIRECTIONS: For each of the following questions, select the choice which best answers the question or completes the statement.

1. Which one of these quantities is the smallest?

   (A) ⅘   (B) ⅞
   (C) .76   (D) 5/7
   (E) 9/11

DO YOUR FIGURING HERE

2. A girl earns twice as much in December as in each of the other months. What part of her entire year's earnings does she earn in December?

   (A) 2/11
   (B) 2/13
   (C) 3/14
   (D) ⅙
   (E) ½

3. If $x = -1$, then $3x^3 + 2x^2 + x + 1 =$

   (A) -1
   (B) 1
   (C) -5
   (D) 5
   (E) 2

4. How many twelfths of a pound are equal to 83⅓% of a pound?

   (A) 5
   (B) 10
   (C) 12
   (D) 14
   (E) 16

5. An equilateral triangle 3 inches on a side is cut up into smaller equilateral triangles one inch on a side. What is the greatest number of such triangles that can be formed?

   (A) 3
   (B) 6
   (C) 9
   (D) 12
   (E) 15

GO ON TO THE NEXT PAGE

S1346

6. If $\dfrac{a}{b} = \dfrac{3}{5}$, then $15a =$

   (A) 3b
   (B) 5b
   (C) 6b
   (D) 9b
   (E) 15b

7. A square 5 units on a side has one vertex at the point (1, 1). Which one of the following points *cannot* be diagonally opposite vertex?

   (A) (6, 6)
   (B) (− 4, 6)
   (C) (− 4, − 4)
   (D) (6, − 4)
   (E) (4, − 6)

8. Five equal squares are placed side by side to make a single rectangle whose perimeter is 372 inches. Find the number of square inches in the area of one of these squares.

   (A) 72
   (B) 324
   (C) 900
   (D) 961
   (E) 984

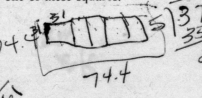
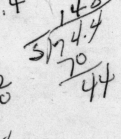

9. Which is the smallest of the following numbers?

   (A) $\sqrt{3}$

   (B) $\dfrac{1}{\sqrt{3}}$

   (C) $\dfrac{\sqrt{3}}{3}$

   (D) ⅓

   (E) $\dfrac{1}{3\sqrt{3}}$

10. In the figure, what percent of the area of rectangle PQRS is shaded?

   (A) 20

   (B) 25

   (C) 30

   (D) 33⅓

   (E) 40

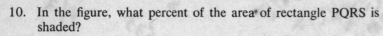
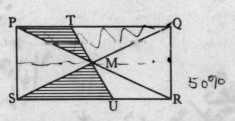

GO ON TO THE NEXT PAGE

11. ⅙ of an audience consisted of boys and ⅓ of it consisted of girls. What percent of the audience consisted of children?

(A) 66⅔
(B) 50
(C) 37½
(D) 40
(E) 33⅓

12. One wheel has a diameter of 30 inches and a second wheel has a diameter of 20 inches. The first wheel traveled a certain distance in 240 revolutions. In how many revolutions did the second wheel travel the same distance?

(A) 120
(B) 160
(C) 360
(D) 420
(E) 480

13. If x and y are two different real numbers and $rx = ry$, then $r =$

(A) 0
(B) 1
(C) $\dfrac{x}{y}$
(D) $\dfrac{y}{x}$
(E) $x - y$

14. If $\dfrac{m}{n} = \dfrac{5}{6}$, then what is $3m + 2n$?

(A) 0
(B) 2
(C) 7
(D) 10
(E) cannot be determined from the information given.

15. If $x > 1$, which of the following increase(s) as x increase(s)?

I. $x - \dfrac{1}{x}$

II. $\dfrac{1}{x^2 - x}$

III. $4x^3 - 2x^2$

(A) only I
(B) only II
(C) only III
(D) only I and III
(E) I, II, and III

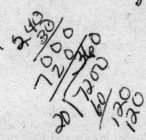

GO ON TO THE NEXT PAGE

16. In the figure, PQRS is a parallelogram, and ST = TV = VR. What is the ratio of the area of triangle SPT to the area of the parallelogram?

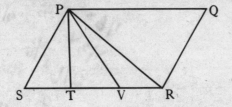

(A) ⅙

(B) ⅕

(C) ⅓

(D) 2/7

(E) cannot be determined from the information given

DO YOUR FIGURING HERE

17. One angle of a triangle is 82°. The other two angles are in the ratio 2:5. Find the number of degrees in the smallest angle of the triangle.

(A) 14
(B) 25
(C) 28
(D) 38
(E) 82

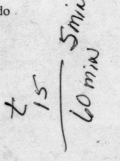

18. If a boy can mow a lawn in t minutes, what part can he do in 15 minutes?

(A) t — 15

(B) $\dfrac{t}{15}$

(C) 15t

(D) 15 — t

(E) $\dfrac{15}{t}$

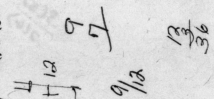

19. A typist uses lengthwise a sheet of paper 9 inches by 12 inches. She leaves a 1-inch margin on each side and a 1½ inch margin on top and bottom. What fractional part of the page is used for typing?

(A) 21/22
(B) 7/12
(C) 5/9
(D) ¾
(E) 5/12

20. It takes a boy 9 seconds to run a distance of 132 feet. What is his speed in miles per hour?

(A) 8
(B) 9
(C) 10
(D) 11
(E) 12

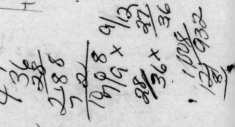

GO ON TO THE NEXT PAGE

21. A rectangular sign is cut down by 10% of its height and 30% of its width. What percent of the original area remains?

    (A) 30
    (B) 37
    (C) 57
    (D) 70
    (E) 63

DO YOUR FIGURING HERE

22. How many of the numbers between 100 and 300 begin or end with 2?

    (A) 20
    (B) 40
    (C) 180
    (D) 100
    (E) 110

23. If Mary knows that y is an integer greater than 2 and less than 7 and John knows that y is an integer greater than 5 and less than 10, then Mary and John may correctly conclude that

    (A) y can be exactly determined
    (B) y may be either of 2 values
    (C) y may be any of 3 values
    (D) y may be any of 4 values
    (E) there is no value of y satisfying these conditions

24. The area of a square is $49 x^2$ What is the length of a diagonal of the square?

    (A) 7x
    (B) $7x \sqrt{2}$
    (C) 14x
    (D) $7x^2$
    (E) $\dfrac{7x}{\sqrt{2}}$

25. In the figure, MNOP is a square of area 1, Q is the mid-point of MN, and R is the mid-point of NO. What is the ratio of the area of triangle PQR to the area of the square?

    (A) ¼
    (B) ⅓
    (C) ¹⁄₁₆
    (D) ⅜
    (E) ½

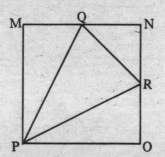

26. If a rectangle is 4 feet by 12 feet, how many two-inch tiles would have to be put around the outside edge to completely frame the rectangle?

(A) 32
(B) 36
(C) 192
(D) 196
(E) 200

DO YOUR FIGURING HERE

27. One-tenth is what part of three-fourths?

(A) $^{40}\!/_3$
(B) $^3\!/_{40}$
(C) $^{15}\!/_2$
(D) $\frac{1}{8}$
(E) $^2\!/_{15}$

28. The area of square PQRS is 49. What are the coordinates of Q?

(A) $\dfrac{(7\sqrt{2},\ 0)}{2}$

(B) $(0,\ \dfrac{7}{2}\sqrt{2})$

(C) $(0, 7)$

(D) $(7, 0)$

(E) $(0, 7\sqrt{2})$

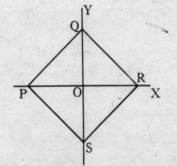

29. Village A has a population of 6800, which is decreasing at a rate of 120 per year. Village B has a population of 4200, which is increasing at a rate of 80 per year. In how many years will the population of the two villages be equal?

(A) 9
(B) 11
(C) 13
(D) 14
(E) 16

30. The average of 8 numbers is 6; the average of 6 other numbers is 8. What is the average of all 14 numbers?

(A) 6
(B) $6^6\!/_7$
(C) 7
(D) $7^2\!/_7$
(E) $8^1\!/_7$

GO ON TO THE NEXT PAGE

1. If x is between 0 and 1, which of the following increases as x increases?

   I. $1 - x^2$
   II. $x - 1$
   III. $\dfrac{1}{x^2}$

   (A) I and II
   (B) II and III
   (C) I and III
   (D) II only
   (E) I only

32. In the formula $T = 2\sqrt{\dfrac{L}{g}}$, g is a constant.

    By what number must L be multiplied so that T will be multiplied by 3?

    (A) 3
    (B) 6
    (C) 9
    (D) 12
    (E) $\sqrt{3}$

33. Three circles are tangent externally to each other and have radii of 2 inches, 3 inches, and 4 inches respectively. How many inches are in the perimeter of the triangle formed by joining the centers of the three circles?

    (A) 9
    (B) 12
    (C) 15
    (D) 18
    (E) 21

34. If a circle of radius 10 inches has its radius decreased 3 inches, what percent is its area decreased?

    (A) 9
    (B) 49
    (C) 51
    (D) 70
    (E) 91

35. If a hat cost $4.20 after a 40% discount, what was its original price?

    (A) $2.52
    (B) $4.60
    (C) $5.33
    (D) $7.00
    (E) $10.50

TEST IV. DATA INTERPRETATION

TIME: 12 Minutes

DIRECTIONS: All the questions in this test refer to the following chart. Read each question carefully and answer it on the basis of the chart. Select the best of the choices given and mark the correct space on the answer sheet.

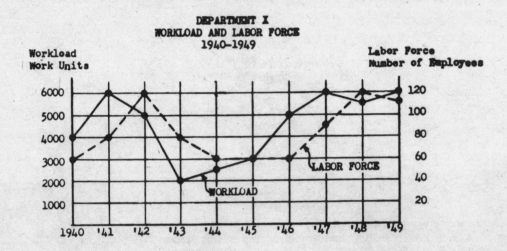

DEPARTMENT X
WORKLOAD AND LABOR FORCE
1940–1949

1. The one of the following years for which average employee production was LOWEST was

(A) 1941   (B) 1943   (C) 1945
(D) 1947   (E) 1949

2. The average annual employee production for the ten year period was, in terms of work units, most nearly

(A) 30   (B) 50   (C) 70
(D) 80   (E) 90

3. On the basis of the chart, it can be deduced that personnel needs for the coming year are budgeted on the basis of

(A) workload for the current year
(B) expected workload for the coming year
(C) no set plan
(D) average workload over the five years immediately preceding the period
(E) expected workload for the five coming years

4. "The chart indicates that the operation is carefully programmed and that the labor force has been used properly." This opinion is

(A) supported by the chart; the organization has been able to meet emergency situations requiring much additional work without commensurate increases in staff
(B) not supported by the chart; the irregular work load shows a complete absence of planning
(C) supported by the chart; the similar shapes of the "Workload" and "Labor Force" curves show that these important factors are closely related
(D) not supported by the chart; poor planning with respect to labor requirements is obvious from the chart
(E) supported by the chart; the average number of units of work performed in any 5 year period during the 10 years shows sufficient regularity to indicate a definite trend.

5. "The chart indicates that the department may be organized in such a way as to require a permanent minimum staff which is too large for the type of operation indicated." This opinion is

(A) supported by the chart; there is indica-tion that the operation calls for an ir-reducible minimum number of employees and application of the most favorable work production records show this to be too high for normal operation

(B) not supported by the chart; the absence of any sort of regularity makes it impos-sible to express any opinion with any degree of certainty

(C) supported by the chart; the expected close relationship between workload and labor force is displaced somewhat, a phenome-non which usually occurs as a result of a fixed minimum requirement

(D) not supported by the chart; the violent movement of the "Labor Force" curve makes it evident that no minimum require-ments are in effect

(E) supported by the chart; calculation shows that the average number of employees was 84 with an average variation of 17.8 thus indicating that the minimum number of 60 persons was too high for efficient operation.

DIRECTIONS: Read each test question carefully. Each one refers to the following graph, and is to be answered solely on that basis. Select the best answer among the given choices and blacken the proper space on the answer sheet.

Note: Hourly figures represent total number of occurrences in the immediately preceding hour.

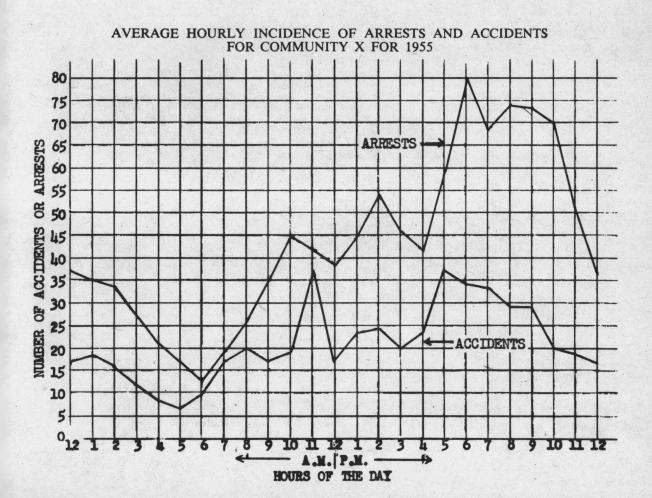

AVERAGE HOURLY INCIDENCE OF ARRESTS AND ACCIDENTS FOR COMMUNITY X FOR 1955

6. According to the above graph, the *least* average hour-to-hour variation, during the following time periods, was in the number of
   (A) arrests during the 4 p.m. through 8 p.m. period
   (B) accidents during the 12 noon through 4 p.m. period
   (C) arrests during the 8 p.m. through 12 midnight period
   (D) accidents during the 8 a.m. through 12 noon period.

7. According to the above graph, of all the accidents occurring from 12 noon through midnight, the percentage which occurred from 12 noon through 4 p.m. was most nearly
   (A) 26%
   (B) 30%
   (C) 34%
   (D) 38%.

8. According to this graph, of the following hours of the day, the hour which shows the highest ratio of arrests to accidents is
   (A) 2 p.m.
   (B) 6 p.m.
   (C) 8 p.m.
   (D) 10 p.m.

9. On the basis of the graph
   (A) an equal number of accidents was recorded daily at 8 a.m. and 3 p.m.
   (B) on any given day, during the year covered, there were more arrests recorded at 2 p.m. than at 10 a.m.
   (C) the number of accidents entered in the first 12 o'clock column must always equal the number of accidents in the last 12 o'clock column
   (D) the wide variation in the number of arrests makes statistical interpretation of the figures unreliable.

END OF PART
*If you finish before the allotted time is up, work on this part only.
When time is up, proceed directly to the next part and do not
return to this part.*

VERBAL ABILITY PART

TEST V. ANTONYMS

TIME: 5 Minutes

DIRECTIONS: For each question in this test, select the appropriate letter preceding the word that is opposite in meaning to the capitalized word.

1. IMMUTABLE:

   (A) erudite   (B) abject
   (C) changeable   (D) fantastic
          (E) aura

2. DUCTILE:

   (A) feted   (B) alluvial
   (C) stubborn   (D) abnormal
          (E) belabor

3. FASTIDIOUS:

   (A) factitious   (B) absurd
   (C) indifferent   (D) sloppy
          (E) chary

4. TEMERITY:

   (A) affinity   (B) cherubim
   (C) humility   (D) degenerate
          (E) celerity

5. ITINERANT:

   (A) animosity   (B) metaphor
   (C) perpetrator   (D) resident
          (E) cerebrum

6. TACITURN:

   (A) malevolent   (B) loquacious
   (C) paltry   (D) opaque
          (E) morbid

7. NEFARIOUS:

   (A) grotesque   (B) virtuous
   (C) jovial   (D) pious
          (E) cerement

8. OBSEQUIOUS:

   (A) harbinger   (B) bold
   (C) heredity   (D) quaff
          (E) falchion

9. OSTENTATION:

   (A) emulsion   (B) languid
   (C) modesty   (D) kilogram
          (E) bey

10. CONTENTION:

   (A) equation   (B) oblivion
   (C) guild   (D) pacification
          (E) bream

11. IMPUTATION:

   (A) assiduous   (B) radiant
   (C) challis   (D) raiment
          (E) vindication

12. BENIGN:

   (A) cavenne   (B) relevant
   (C) robot   (D) malevolent
          (E) precarious

13. COHERENT:

   (A) perspicacious   (B) zephyr
   (C) weal   (D) chaotic
          (E) changeling

14. DEPREDATION:

   (A) plethoric   (B) gloss
   (C) restoration   (D) usher
          (E) trochal

TEST VI. VERBAL ANALOGIES

TIME: 7 Minutes

*DIRECTIONS: In these test questions each of the two CAPI-
TALIZED words have a certain relationship to each other.
Following the capitalized words are other pairs of words, each
designated by a letter. Select the lettered pair wherein the words
are related in the same way as the two CAPITALIZED words are
related to each other.*

1. ADVERSITY : HAPPINESS ::
   (A) fear : misfortune
   (B) solace : adversity
   (C) vehemence : serenity
   (D) troublesome : petulance
   (E) graduation : felicitation

2. MARACAS : RHYTHM ::
   (A) flute : base
   (B) xylophone : percussion
   (C) drum : harmony
   (D) violin : concert
   (E) piano : octave

3. FEATHERS : PLUCK ::
   (A) goose : duck
   (B) garment : weave
   (C) car : drive
   (D) wool : shear
   (E) duck : down

4. MODESTY : ARROGANCE ::
   (A) debility : strength
   (B) cause : purpose
   (C) passion : emotion
   (D) finance : Wall Street
   (E) practice : perfection

5. BLOW : HORN ::
   (A) switch : tracks
   (B) turn on : lights
   (C) go over : map
   (D) accelerate : engine
   (E) tune : radio

6. BAY : SEA ::
   (A) mountain : valley
   (B) plain : forest
   (C) peninsula : land
   (D) cape : reef
   (E) island : sound

7. DECEMBER : WINTER ::
   (A) April : showers
   (B) September : summer
   (C) June : fall
   (D) March : spring
   (E) February : autumn

8. NECKLACE : ADORNMENT ::
   (A) medal : decoration
   (B) bronze : medal
   (C) scarf : dress
   (D) window : house
   (E) pearl : diamond

9. LIQUOR : ALCOHOLISM ::
   (A) pill : dope
   (B) tranquilizer : emotions
   (C) perfume : smell
   (D) candy : overweight
   (E) atomizer : sinusitis

10. INTERRUPT : SPEAK ::
    (A) shout : yell
    (B) intrude : enter
    (C) interfere : assist
    (D) telephone : telegraph
    (E) concede : defend

11. ENCOURAGE : RESTRICT ::
    (A) gain : succeed
    (B) deprive : supply
    (C) see : believe
    (D) detain : deny
    (E) finish : complete

12. SETTING : STONE ::
    (A) pen : paper
    (B) glass : window
    (C) socket : bulb
    (D) ring : finger
    (E) locket : chain

TEST VII. SENTENCE COMPLETIONS

TIME: 8 Minutes

DIRECTIONS: Each of the completion questions in this test consists of an incomplete sentence. Each sentence is followed by a series of lettered words, one of which best completes the sentence. Select the word that best completes the meaning of each sentence, and mark the letter of that word opposite that sentence.

1. The admiration the Senator earns is _____ by his _____ instinct for getting onto the front pages.
   (A) concocted . . . proverbial
   (B) evolved . . . haughty
   (C) belied . . . aggressive
   (D) engendered . . . unerring
   (E) transcended . . . dogged

2. The accelerated growth of public employment _____ the dramatic expansion of budgets and programs.
   (A) parallels
   (B) contains
   (C) revolves
   (D) escapes
   (E) populates

3. So great is the intensity of Shakespeare's dramatic language that the audience becomes _____ and sees messages and equivocations everywhere, until the play becomes an apocalypse of _____ and fall.
   (A) stunned . . . rise
   (B) hallucinated . . . temptation
   (C) aroused . . . doubt
   (D) dulled . . . zeal
   (E) weary . . . disgust

4. Not every _____ mansion, church, battle site, theater, or other public hall can be preserved.
   (A) novel
   (B) structured
   (C) comparative
   (D) unknown
   (E) venerable

5. Man is still a _____ in the labor market.
   (A) glut
   (B) possibility
   (C) commodity
   (D) resumption
   (E) provision

6. As we moved on to Melford shortly after noon on Saturday, the clear air and the rolling _____ made one wonder whether this festival would lead all others, at least in altitude.
   (A) stones
   (B) hovels
   (C) skyline
   (D) oaks
   (E) terrain

7. Witness the long waiting list for the overworked psychiatrists and psychologists and the twentieth-century _____ for lying on the couch talking about oneself and the neuroses that have resulted from a too intense _____ with oneself.
   (A) wish . . . inspection
   (B) process . . . tirade
   (C) plan . . . understanding
   (D) fad . . . preoccupation
   (E) garb . . . implication

8. The book will be _____ by every Western student of the USSR, and it will be a thrilling adventure for any reader.
   (A) skimmed
   (B) perused
   (C) rejected
   (D) blasphemed
   (E) borrowed

S1583

9. With this realization, the people suddenly found themselves left with _____ moral values and little ethical _____.

   (A) obsolete . . . perspective
   (B) established . . . grasp
   (C) portentous . . . insinuation
   (D) extreme . . . judgment
   (E) continued . . . pronouncement

10. There is a notion abroad that history has gotten away from us; that our lives are beyond control; that there are no points of _____ which mean anything any more.
    (A) conference   (B) inference
    (C) prudence   (D) incidence
              (E) reference

11. I cannot honestly number myself among the pious and I have frequently had the experience of being _____ among the unholy.

(A) regenerated   (B) deteriorated
(C) compiled   (D) consigned
              (E) inflamed

12. These avant-garde thinkers believe that the major peace movements are ineffective because the thinking that underlies these movements is old-fashioned, confused, _____, and out-of-step with the findings of _____ science.
    (A) stimulating . . . natural
    (B) delusionary . . . behavioral
    (C) loaded . . . true
    (D) uncertain . . . physical
    (E) blatant . . . scholastic

13. Today, we who read Latin return far more often to the exuberance of Apuleius than to the carefully molded _____ of Cicero.
    (A) literature   (B) redundancies
    (C) objects   (D) piracies
              (E) platitudes

END OF PART
If you finish before the allotted time is up, work on this part only.
When time is up, proceed directly to the next part and do not
return to this part.

DATA SUFFICIENCY PART

15 questions - 15 minutes

TEST VIII. DATA SUFFICIENCY

TIME: 15 Minutes

DIRECTIONS: Each question below is followed by two numbered facts. Decide whether the data given is sufficient for answering the question. Sometimes the two facts do not give enough information to answer the question. Sometimes the two facts give just enough data to answer the question. And sometimes one of the facts alone is sufficient to answer the question. Read each question and the two facts that follow it; then mark your answer on the answer sheet that follows.

Mark "A" if statement 1 alone is sufficient to answer the question, but statement 2 alone is not sufficient.

Mark "B" if statement 2 alone is sufficient to answer the question, but statement 1 alone is not sufficient.

Mark "C" if both statements together are needed to answer the question, but neither statement alone is sufficient.

Mark "D" if either statement by itself is sufficient to answer the question asked.

Mark "E" if not enough facts are given to answer the question.

1. How much did a man earn in 1962?
   (1) He earned $6500 in 1963 which is 12½% more than he earned in 1962.
   (2) His wife (who earned half the amount he earned) and he earned $8666.62 together in 1962.

2. A merchant has gone bankrupt. How much will his creditors receive?
   (1) With debts of $43,250, he will pay off 15 cents on the dollar.
   (2) His total loss is $125,000.

3. What is a student's over-all average?
   (1) He receives 90 in English, 84 in Algebra, 75 in French, and 76 in Music.
   (2) The subjects have the following weights: English 4, Algebra 3, French 3, and Music 1.

4. How long will it take two pipes to empty or fill a tank that is ¾ full?
   (1) Pipe A can fill the tank in 12 minutes.
   (2) Pipe B can empty it in 8 minutes.

5. What is the average of the walking speeds of two men?
   (1) One man travels at four miles an hour?
   (2) The other man completes 60 miles.

6. A desk has a marked price of $100. Discounts of 20% and 25% are allowed. What is the cost of the desk to the dealer?
   (1) The dealer's profit is 30% of the selling price.
   (2) The dealer's cost of doing business is 10% of the selling price.

7. How many letters can two typists complete in one day?
   (1) A working day consists of six hours and thirty minutes.
   (2) Four typists can type 600 letters in three days.

8. What time is it on a certain watch?
   (1) The minute hand is at 6.
   (2) The hour hand is halfway between 9 and 10.

9. How much pie did the fourth man eat?
   (1) The first three men ate ¼, ²⁄₇, and ³⁄₁₁ of the pie respectively.
   (2) Together the four men ate the whole pie.

10. How long is a bridge that crosses a river which is 760 feet wide?
    (1) One bank of the river holds ⅛ of the bridge.
    (2) The other bank holds ⅙ of the bridge.

11. What is the non-voting population of a certain European country?
    (1) Only males over 20 years of age are permitted to vote.
    (2) The country has a total population of 5,362,486.

12. Was Pericles a famous historian of ancient Greece?
    (1) Pericles is the greatest Greek historian.
    (2) Pericles lived in Greece (490-429 B.C.).

13. What tax is to be paid on $60,000 worth of land?
    (1) The tax rate is $2.56 per $1000.
    (2) The land is assessed at 20% of its value.

14. What is the annual interest which a bank will pay on a principal of $10,000?
    (1) The interest is paid every six months.
    (2) The interest rate is 4%.

15. A wine merchant wishes to reduce the price of his wine on hand by adding water. How many gallons of water must he add to reduce the price from $1.50 a gallon to $1.20 a gallon?
    (1) He has 32 gallons of wine on hand.
    (2) The wine originally contained 14% alcohol.

END OF PART
If you finish before the allotted time is up, work on this part only.
When time is up, proceed directly to the next part and do not return to this part.

READING AND GRAMMAR PART

TEST IX. READING COMPREHENSION

TIME: 20 Minutes

DIRECTIONS: Below each of the following passages, you will find questions or incomplete statements about the passage. Each statement or question is followed by lettered words or expressions. Select the word or expression that most satisfactorily completes each statement or answers each question in accordance with the meaning of the passage. Write the letter of that word or expression on your answer paper.

Recent scientific discoveries are throwing new light on the basic nature of viruses and on the possible nature of cancer, genes and even life itself. These discoveries are providing evidence for relationships among these four subjects which indicate that one may be dependent upon another to an extent not fully appreciated heretofore. Too often one works and thinks within too narrow a range and hence fails to recognize the significance of certain facts for other areas. Sometimes the important new ideas and subsequent fundamental discoveries come from the borderline areas between two well-established fields of investigation. This will result in the synthesis of new ideas regarding viruses, cancer, genes and life. These ideas in turn will result in the doing of new experiments which may provide the basis for fundamental discoveries in these fields.

There is no doubt that of the four topics, life is the one most people would consider to be of the greatest importance. However, life means different things to different people and it is in reality difficult to define just what we mean by life. There is no difficulty in recognizing an agent as living so long as we contemplate structures like a man, a dog or even a bacterium, and at the other extreme a piece of iron or glass or an atom of hydrogen or a molecule of water. The ability to grow or reproduce and to change or mutate has long been regarded as a special property characteristic of living agents along with the ability to respond to external stimuli. These are properties not shared by bits of iron or glass or even by a molecule of hemoglobin. Now if viruses had not been discovered, all would have been well. The organisms of the biologist would have ranged from the largest of animals all the way down to the smallest of the bacteria which are about 200 millimicra. There would have been a definite break with respect to size; the largest molecules known to the chemist were less than 20 millimicra in size. Thus life and living agents would have been represented by those structures which possessed the ability to reproduce themselves and to mutate and were about ten times larger than the largest known molecule. This would have provided a comfortable area of separation between living and non-living things.

Then came the discovery of the viruses. These infectious, disease-producing agents are characterized by their small size, by their ability to grow or reproduce within specific living cells, and by their ability to change or mutate during reproduction. This was enough to convince most people that viruses were merely still smaller living organisms. When the sizes of different viruses were determined, it was found that some were actually smaller than certain protein molecules. When the first virus was isolated in the form of a crystallizable material it was found to be a nucleoprotein. It was found to possess all the usual properties associated with protein molecules yet was larger than any molecule previously described. Here was a molecule that possessed the ability to reproduce itself and to mutate. The distinction between living and non-living things seemed to be tottering. The gap in size between 20 and 200 millimicra has been filled in completely by the viruses, with some actual overlapping at both ends. Some large viruses are larger than some living organisms, and some small viruses are actuallly smaller than certain protein molecules.

Let us consider the relationship between genes and viruses since both are related to life. Both genes and viruses seem to be nucleoproteins and both reproduce only within specific living cells. Both possess the ability to mutate. Although viruses generally reproduce many times within a given cell, some situations are known in which they appear to reproduce only once with each cell division. Genes usually reproduce once with each cell division, but here also the rate can be changed. Actually the similarities between genes and viruses are so remarkable that viruses were referred to as "naked genes" or "genes on the loose."

Despite the fact that today viruses are known to cause cancer in animals and in certain plants, there exists a great reluctance to accept viruses as being of importance in human cancer. Basic biological phenomena generally do not differ strikingly as one goes from one species to another. It should be recognized that cancer is a biological problem and not a problem that is unique for man. Cancer originates when a normal cell suddenly becomes a cancer cell which multiplies widely and without apparent restraint. Cancer may originate in many differrent kinds of cells, but the cancer cell usually continues to carry certain traits of the cell of origin. The transformation of a normal cell into a cancer cell may have more than one kind of cause, but there is good reason to consider the relationships that exist between viruses and cancer.

Since there is no evidence that human cancer, as generally experienced, is infectious, many persons believe that because viruses are infectious agents they cannot possibly be of importance in human cancer. However, viruses can mutate and examples are known in which a virus that never kills its host can mutate to form a new strain of virus that always kills its host. It does not seem unreasonable to assume that an innocuous latent virus might mutate to form a strain that causes cancer. Certainly the experimental evidence now available is consistent with the idea that viruses as we know them today, could be the causative agents of most, if not all cancer, including cancer in man.

1. People were convinced that viruses were small living organism, because viruses
   (A) are disease-producing
   (B) reproduce within living cells
   (C) could be grown on artificial media
   (D) consist of nucleoproteins

2. Scientists very often do not apply the facts learned in one subject area to a related field of investigation because
   (A) the borderline areas are too close to both to give separate facts
   (B) scientists work in a very narrow range of experimentation
   (C) new ideas are synthesized only as a result of new experimentation
   (D) fundamental discoveries are based upon finding close relationships in related sciences

3. Before the discovery of viruses, it might have been possible to distinguish living things from non-living things by the fact that
   (A) animate objects can mutate
   (B) non-living substances cannot reproduce themselves
   (C) responses to external stimuli are characteristic of living things
   (D) living things were greater than 20 millimicra in size

4. The size of viruses is presently known to be
   (A) between 20 and 200 millimicra
   (B) smaller than any bacterium
   (C) larger than any protein molecule
   (D) larger than most nucleoproteins

5. That genes and viruses seem to be related might be shown by the fact that
   (A) both are ultra-microscopic
   (B) each can mutate but once in a cell
   (C) each reproduces but once in a cell
   (D) both appear to have the same chemical structure

6. Viruses were called "genes on the loose" because they
   (A) are able to reproduce very freely
   (B) like genes, seem to be able to mutate
   (C) seemed to be genes without cells
   (D) can loosen genes from cells

7. Cancer should be considered to be a biological problem rather than a medical one because
   (A) viruses are known to cause cancers in animals
   (B) at present, human cancer is not believed to be contagious
   (C) there are many known causes for the transformation of a normal cell to a cancer cell
   (D) results of experiments on plants and animals do not vary greatly from species to species

8. The possibility that a virus causes human cancer is indicated by
   (A) the fact that viruses have been known to mutate
   (B) the fact that a cancer-immune individual may lose his immunity
   (C) the fact that reproduction of human cancer cells might be due to a genetic factor
   (D) the fact that man is host to many viruses

9. The best title for this passage is
   (A) New Light on the Cause of Cancer
   (B) The Newest Theory on the Nature of Viruses
   (C) Viruses, Genes, Cancer and Life
   (D) On the Nature of Life

10. According to the passage, cancer cells are
    (A) similar to the cell of origin
    (B) mutations of viruses
    (C) unable to reproduce
    (D) among the smallest cells known
    (E) present in small amounts in all individuals

An action of apparent social significance among animals is that of migration. But several different factors are at work causing such migrations. These may be concerned with food–getting, with temperature, salinity, pressure and light changes; with the action of sex hormones and probably other combinations of these factors.

The great aggregations of small crustaceans, such as copepods found at the surface of the ocean, swarms of insects about a light, or the masses of unicellular organisms making up a part of the plankton in the lakes and oceans, are all examples of nonsocial aggregations of organisms brought together because of the presence or absence of certain factors in their environment, such as air currents, water currents, food or the lack of it, oxygen or carbon dioxide, or some other contributing causes.

Insects make long migrations, most of which seem due to the urge for food. The migrations of the locust, both in this country and elsewhere, are well known. While fish, such as salmon, return to the same stream where they grew up, such return migrations are rare in insects, the only known instance being in the monarch butterfly. This is apparently due to the fact that it is long-lived and has the power of strong flight. The mass migrations of the Rocky Mountain and the African species of locust seem attributable to the need for food. Locusts live, eat, sun themselves and migrate in groups. It has been suggested that their social life is in response to the two fundamental instincts, aggregation and imitation.

Migrations of fish have been studied carefully by many investigators. Typically the migrations are from deep to shallow waters, as in the herring, mackerel and many other marine fish. Fresh-water fish in general exhibit this type of migration in the spawning season. Spawning habits of many fish show a change in habitat from salt to fresh water. Among these are the shad, salmon, alewife and others. In the North American and European eels, long migrations take place at the breeding season. All these migrations are obviously not brought about by a quest for food, for the salmon and many other fish feed only sparingly during the spawning season, but are undoubtedly brought about by metabolic changes in the animal initiated by the interaction of sex hormones. If this thesis holds, then here is the beginning of social life.

Bird migrations have long been a matter of study. The reasons for the migration of the golden plover from the Arctic regions to the tip of South America and return in a single year are not fully explainable. Several theories have been advanced, although none have been fully proved. The reproductive "instinct," food scarcity, temperature and light changes, the metabolic changes brought about by the activity of the sex hormones and the length of the day, all have been suggested, and ultimately several may prove to be factors. Aside from other findings, it is interesting to note that bird migrations take place year after year on about the same dates. Recent studies in the biochemistry of metabolism, showing that there is a seasonal cycle in the blood sugar that has a definite relation to activity and food, seem to be among the most promising leads.

In mammals the seasonal migrations that take place, such as those of the deer, which travel from the high mountains in summer to the valleys in winter, or the migration of the caribou in the northern areas of Canada, are based on the factor of temperature which regulates the food supply. Another mystery is the migration of the lemming, a small ratlike animal found in Scandinavia and Canada. The lemming population varies greatly from year to year, and, at times when it greatly increases, a migration occurs in which hordes of lemmings march across the country, swimming rivers and even plunging into the ocean if it bars their way. This again cannot be purely social association of animals. The horde is usually made up entirely of males, as the females seldom migrate.

11. The migration of the lemmings cannot be considered one of social association since
    (A) only males migrate
    (B) migrations occur only with population increases
    (C) it is probably due to the absence of some factor in the environment
    (D) the migrants do not return

12. Animals which apparently migrate in quest of food are the
    (A) fish   (C) mammals
    (B) birds   (D) insects

13. A characteristic of migration is the return of the migrants to their former home areas. This is, however, not true of the
    (A) birds   (C) mammals
    (B) insects   (D) fish

14. The reproductive instinct is probably not a factor in the actual migration of
    (A) shad   (C) golden plover
    (B) lemming   (D) monarch butterfly

15. In paragraph 1, several probable factors causing migrations are given. None of these seem to explain the migrations of
    (A) lemming   (C) salmon
    (B) caribou   (D) locusts

16. The reasons for the migrations of birds may ultimately be determined by scientists working in the field of
    (A) population studies
    (B) ecology
    (C) metabolism chemistry
    (D) reproduction

17. According to the passage, the reproductive process seems to be a known factor in the migration of many
    (A) fish   (B) insects
    (C) mammals   (D) birds

18. Animals which migrate back and forth between the same general areas are
    (A) locusts and salmon
    (B) salmon and golden plover
    (C) golden plover and lemming
    (D) monarch butterfly and caribou

19. The shortest distance covered by any migrating group is taken by
    (A) insects   (C) birds
    (B) fish   (D) mammals

20. The main purpose of the passage is to
    (A) show how a natural event effects change in different species
    (B) present a new theory in regard to biological evolution
    (C) teach the reader how to evaluate a natural phenomenon
    (D) describe a phenomenon that has not yet been satisfactorily explained
    (E) show how species behave similarly under the same conditions

21. Return migrations are usually associated with animals that
    (A) make long migrations
    (B) are long-lived
    (C) migrate to spawn
    (D) make short migrations

END OF TEST

Go on to the next Test in the Examination, just as you would do on the actual exam. Check your answers when you have completed the entire Examination. The correct answers for this Test, and all the other Tests, are assembled at the conclusion of this Examination.

TEST X. ENGLISH USAGE

TIME: 15 Minutes

DIRECTIONS: This is a test of standard written English. The rules may differ from everyday spoken English. Many of the following sentences contain grammar, usage, word choice, and idiom that would be incorrect in written composition. Some sentences are correct. No sentence has more than one error. Any error in a sentence will be underlined and lettered; all other parts of the sentence are correct and cannot be changed. If the sentence has an error, choose the underlined part that is incorrect, and mark that letter on your answer sheet. If there is no error, mark E on your answer sheet.

1. What affect the law will have on our drivers and how it
       A   B   C
   will affect our lives remain to be seen. No error.
                     D   E

2. If I was you, I should be careful of who my friends are.
       A   B   C   D
   No error.
    E

3. Merrihew, who I never thought was even in the running,
            A   B
   not only won handily but also broke a record. No error.
            C   D   E

4. Although his story had aspects of truth about it, I
        A   B
   couldn't hardly believe what he said. No error.
       C   D   E

5. I would gladly have attended your wedding if you invited
               A   B   C   D
   me. No error.
       E

6. Whoever the gods wish to destroy, they first make mad.
       A   B   C   D
   No error.
    E

7. <u>Drawing</u> up the plan <u>promised</u> <u>to be</u> a <u>years'</u> work.
     A   B   C   D
   <u>No error.</u>
    E

8. There are <u>less</u> tramps on the <u>Bowery</u> since the <u>elevated</u>
       A   B   C
   structure was <u>razed.</u> <u>No error.</u>
        D   E

9. <u>Uncle Jack has</u> <u>expressed</u> the belief that lilacs <u>smell more</u>
       A   B   C
   <u>sweetly</u> than roses. <u>No error.</u>
    D   E

10. I <u>shall vote for</u> <u>whichsoever</u> is, in my opinion, <u>best</u>
      A   B   C
    <u>qualified.</u> <u>No error.</u>
     D   E

11. He is always polite not only to his supervisors and

    <u>colleagues</u> but to <u>anyone</u> else he thinks <u>is deserving</u> of
      A   B   C
    <u>kindly</u> consideration. <u>No error.</u>
     D   E

12. I <u>don't</u> understand your <u>fondness</u> for <u>them;</u> I can't stand
      A   B   C
    <u>the both</u> of them. <u>No error.</u>
     D   E

13. A <u>torrential</u> downpour, <u>in addition to</u> long stretches of
      A   B
    road construction that made it necessary to slow down

    to fifteen miles an hour, <u>have</u> so delayed us that we shall
               C
    not be able to be <u>on hand</u> for the ceremony. <u>No error.</u>
           D   E

14. The teacher, <u>along with</u> a <u>committee</u> of bright students,
         A   B   C
    have compiled a <u>reading list.</u> <u>No error.</u>
     C   D   E

15. We buy <u>only</u> purple plums, <u>since</u> we like <u>those kind</u> best.
      A B   C   D
    <u>No error.</u>
     E

16. It was he, not I, who became nauseous because of the
    $\overline{A}$ $\overline{B}$ $\overline{C}$
    boat's motion. No error.
    $\overline{D}$ $\overline{E}$

17. Although Richard graduated high school with honors, he
                        $\overline{A}$ $\overline{B}$
    failed three subjects as a college freshman. No error.
    $\overline{C}$ $\overline{D}$ $\overline{E}$

18. If you have read "A Tale of Two Cities," you know that
          $\overline{A}$ $\overline{B}$
    Jerry Cruncher was aggravated by his wife's praying.
                        $\overline{C}$ $\overline{D}$
    No error.
    $\overline{E}$

19. If he would have come when I asked him, he might not
          $\overline{A}$ $\overline{B}$ $\overline{C}$
    have made the error. No error.
                  $\overline{D}$ $\overline{E}$

20. They invited my whole family to the cookout—my father,
          $\overline{A}$ $\overline{B}$ $\overline{C}$
    my mother, my sister and I. No error.
                        $\overline{D}$ $\overline{E}$

21. Why should these newcomers to the club have the same
                        $\overline{A}$ $\overline{B}$
    privileges as we older members? No error.
    $\overline{C}$ $\overline{D}$ $\overline{E}$

22. Being that I arrived first, I helped the hostess prepare
    $\overline{A}$ $\overline{B}$ $\overline{C}$
    the hors d'oeuvres. No error.
        $\overline{D}$ $\overline{E}$

23. Such a large amount of pupils in the room is bound to
    $\overline{A}$ $\overline{B}$ $\overline{C}$
    cause confusion. No error.
          $\overline{D}$ $\overline{E}$

24. Saying only that she was a friend of Mary's, she left
    $\overline{A}$ $\overline{B}$ $\overline{C}$ $\overline{D}$
    without giving her name. No error.
                                $\overline{E}$

25. Because they were unaware of his interest in the build-
                        $\overline{A}$
    ing, they did not understand why he felt so bad about it's
                                                $\overline{B}$ $\overline{C}$
    being condemned. No error.
        $\overline{D}$ $\overline{E}$

END OF PART

PRACTICAL BUSINESS JUDGMENT

30 questions- 25 Minutes

DIRECTIONS: In testing your aptitude for business, they will ask you to evaluate a Situation and a Decision. You will be quizzed on goals, assumptions, conclusions, information, predictions, problems, options, and opinions. First, you will read a comprehensive analysis of a business situation; and then you will take two sub-tests based on your analysis: Data Application Quiz, and Data Evaluation Quiz.

Business Situation The Amateur Printer.

The Business. Mary and Robert Johnson run a flower-and-vegetable seed business, which Robert inherited from his father who started it in 1926. Although confined to the state of Colorado, the business has made over $200,000 in sales revenue during each of the past three years. The Johnsons have netted a profit of about $30,000 per annum after corporate taxes have been paid.

Only 25% of the volume comes from retail stores. The remainder is the result of direct-mail campaigns. The company's "special customer" list, comprised of people who have ordered one or more times, produces most of the direct-mail revenue. The average order is $15.20, and the average customer purchases seeds for five years. This high company loyalty speaks well for the Johnsons and the quality of their products.

The Printing Press. Robert Johnson has always been fascinated by printing presses. Indeed, the most interesting part of the business to him is the creation of the catalog. Not only does he write it, he also designs it and works closely with the printer in producing it.

Now he has an opportunity to buy a press of his own. He reasons that now production would be in his absolute control. Four years ago, his printer was hit with a strike while producing the Johnson catalog. The spring issue went out two weeks late—a disaster in a business in which timing is so important. Sales volume dropped $39,000 that year. Johnson believes that ownership of a press would prevent this from happening again.

There would be a saving in money as well, even though he would have to pay in the neighborhood of $4,000 a year for a part-time pressman. Printing costs at present run $40,000 a year. After carefully investigating prices of paper and inks, Johnson figures that his printing costs would drop to $16,000, excluding the compensation for his moonlighting pressman. The offset press costs $18,000. He reasons that he will make up the price of the machine in one year.

Mary's Objections. Mary opposes the purchase. First of all, she believes that owning a press is impractical. She points out that Robert hasn't figured into his calculations how much more time he would have to devote to printing. Even with the part-time pressman, Robert would still have to be highly involved in the printing process, much more than he is now. She is sure that this activity would take him away from the more important duties of overseeing the selection of seeds, managing the cash flow, and making sure that orders get out quickly and accurately.

Furthermore, she says, mechanical breakdowns are inevitable. Even though home printing is Robert's hobby, there is a big difference between running a small hand-cranked press and the maintenance of a commercial high-speed press. Robert is a good amateur but not a professional printer. She also doubts that the quality of the catalog will be as good as it has been in the past.

Decision. Robert considers Mary's objections carefully and decides to postpone making a decision for six months.

TEST XI. DATA APPLICATION

DIRECTIONS: Based on your understanding of the Business Situation, answer the following questions testing your comprehension of the information supplied in the passage. For each question, select the choice which best answers the question or completes the statement. When you understand the data and interpret it correctly, you will be better prepared to evaluate Data, as required by the second part of this test.

1. In the past three years, the Johnson Seed Company has produced an average profit when compared with sales revenue of about

    (A) 5%
    (B) 10%
    (C) 15%
    (D) 30%
    (E) 50%

2. The volume of sales revenue resulting from direct mail has for the past three years averaged about

    (A) $ 30,000
    (B) $ 40,000
    (C) $ 150,000
    (D) $ 200,000
    (E) $ 230,000

3. One reason Robert Johnson wishes to buy a press is that

    (A) his printer has gone out of business
    (B) his spring catalogs have often gone out late
    (C) he could have another business on the side
    (D) he would avoid delays caused by strikes of printing plants
    (E) he believes it will increase sales volume

4. Even though a part-time printer would have to be paid, Robert estimates he could reduce his yearly printing costs by

    (A) $ 16,000
    (B) $ 20,000
    (C) $ 22,000
    (D) $ 36,000
    (E) $ 40,000

5. The business of the Johnsons is

    (A) seasonal
    (B) spread throughout the year
    (C) varied throughout the year as far as sales are concerned
    (D) dropping off
    (E) countrywide

6. According to Mary, Robert's calculations have not included the

    (A) costs of paper
    (B) compensation for the part-time pressman
    (C) cost of the printing press
    (D) price of ink
    (E) cost of his own time

7. According to Mary, an important function performed by Robert is

    (A) the supervision of a part-time pressman
    (B) order processing
    (C) reducing the number of names on the expensive "special customer" list
    (D) working closely with an outside printer
    (E) settling strikes of outside suppliers

8. One of Mary's objections to purchasing a printing press is that she believes

   (A) Robert does not have personal contact with customers
   (B) the sales volume has been on a plateau for three years
   (C) Robert spends too much time now working on the catalog
   (D) Robert has had too little experience in direct mail
   (E) Robert is not competent in running a high-speed press

9. Mary implies that the possible purchase of a press is

   (A) a practical and reasonable idea.

   (B) due to the fact that Robert is bored with the seed business
   (C) due to sentiment on Robert's part
   (D) foolish because the company cannot afford the purchase price
   (E) the result of panic due to a drop in sales

10. Mary seems to believe that the quality of the catalog

   (A) will drop if the press is purchased
   (B) is of less importance than prompt delivery
   (C) will be better when Robert controls the printing
   (D) will remain the same if they buy the press
   (E) has never been of a high standard

END OF TEST

Go on to the next Test in the Examination, just as you would do on the actual exam. Check your answers when you have completed the entire Examination. The correct answers for this Test, and all the other Tests, are assembled at the conclusion of this Examination.

TEST XII. DATA EVALUATION

DIRECTIONS: Based on your analysis of the Situation, classify each of the following conclusions in one of five categories. Check:

(A) if the conclusion is a MAJOR OBJECTIVE in making the decision; that is, the outcome or result sought by the decision maker.

(B) if the conclusion is a MAJOR FACTOR in arriving at the decision; that is a consideration, explicitly mentioned in the passage that is basic in determining the decision.

(C) if the conclusion is a MINOR FACTOR in making the decision; that is, a secondary consideration that affects the criteria tangentially, relating to a Major Factor rather than to an Objective.

(D) if the conclusion is a MAJOR ASSUMPTION made in deliberating; that is a supposition or projection made by the decision maker before weighing the variables.

(E) if the conclusion is an UNIMPORTANT ISSUE in getting to the point; that is a factor that is insignificant or not immediately relevant to the situation.

11. Possible drop in quality of catalog.

12. Absolute control of production.

13. Expansion of sales revenue.

14. Mailing catalog on most advantageous date.

15. Printing cost reduction.

16. Making up cost of purchase of printing press within one year.

17. Increase profit.

18. Strike at outside printer's plant.

19. Failure to estimate cost of increased time Robert would have to spend on printing press.

20. Robert's fascination with printing.

21. 75% of sales revenue from direct mail.

22. Business confined to one state.

23. Hiring of part-time pressman.

24. Managing cash flow.

25. Robert's knowledge of printing.

26. Robert's belief in his ability to handle big printing presses.

27. Robert's experience in designing catalogs.

28. Inevitability of mechanical breakdowns.

29. Drop of revenue due to late mailing of catalog.

30. Loyalty of customers to company.

END OF EXAMINATION

CORRECT ANSWERS FOR VERISIMILAR EXAMINATION III.

(Please make every effort to answer the questions on your own before look-
ing at these answers. You'll make faster progress by following this rule.)

TEST I. READING QUESTIONS

1.D	5.B	9.B	13.C	17.D	21.E	25.C
2.B	6.A	10.D	14.E	18.A	22.A	26.E
3.E	7.E	11.C	15.E	19.E	23.B	27.D
4.D	8.E	12.A	16.B	20.C	24.D	

TEST II. DATA INTERPRETATION

1.C	3.C	5.C	7.C	9.A	11.D
2.D	4.B	6.D	8.D	10.A	

TEST III. PROBLEM SOLVING

1.D	6.D	11.B	16.A	21.E	26.D	31.D
2.B	7.E	12.C	17.C	22.E	27.E	32.C
3.A	8.D	13.A	18.E	23.A	28.B	33.D
4.B	9.E	14.E	19.B	24.B	29.C	34.C
5.C	10.B	15.D	20.C	25.D	30.B	35.D

TEST III. EXPLANATORY ANSWERS

1. **(D)** $\frac{4}{5} = .8$

$$\frac{7}{9} = 9\overline{)7.00} \quad .78$$

$$\frac{5}{7} = 7\overline{)5.00} \quad .71$$

$$\frac{9}{11} = 11\overline{)9.00} \quad .82$$

Thus $\frac{5}{7}$ is the smallest quantity.

2. **(B)** Let $x =$ amount earned each month

$2x =$ amount earned in December

Then $11x + 2x = 13x$ (entire earnings)

$$\frac{2x}{13x} = \frac{2}{13}$$

3. **(A)** $3x^3 + 2x^2 + x + 1$
$= 3(-1)^3 + 2(-1)^2 + (-1) + 1$
$= 3(-1) + 2(1) - 1 + 1$
$= -3 + 2 + 0$
$= -1$

4. **(B)** $\dfrac{x}{12} = \dfrac{83\frac{1}{3}}{100} = \dfrac{250}{300}$

or $\dfrac{x}{12} = \dfrac{25}{30} = \dfrac{5}{6}$

$6x = 60$

$x = 10$

5. **(C)** Since the ratio of the sides is 3 : 1, the ratio of the areas is 9 : 1.

The subdivision into 9 △ is shown

157

6. **(D)** $\dfrac{a}{b} = \dfrac{3}{5}$

   $5a = 3b$

   Multiply both sides by 3.

   $15a = 9b$

7. **(E)** The opposite vertices may be any of the number pairs $(1 \pm 5, 1 \pm 5)$ or $(6,6)$, $(-4, -4)$, $(-4, 6)$, $(6, -4)$
   Thus $(4, -6)$ is not possible.

8. **(D)**

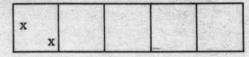

   Perimeter of rectangle $= x + 5x + x + 5x$
   Thus $12x = 372$

   $x = 31$

   Area of square $= 31^2 = 961$

9. **(E)** $\sqrt{3} = 1.73$ (approx.)

   $\dfrac{1}{\sqrt{3}} = \dfrac{\sqrt{3}}{3} = \dfrac{1.73}{3} = .57$

   $\dfrac{\sqrt{3}}{3} = \dfrac{1.73}{3} = 5.7$

   $\frac{1}{3} = .3333\ldots\ldots$

   $\dfrac{1}{3\sqrt{3}} = \dfrac{\sqrt{3}}{3.3} = \dfrac{\sqrt{3}}{9} = \dfrac{1.73}{9} = .19$

   Thus the smallest is $\dfrac{1}{3\sqrt{3}}$

10. **(B)**

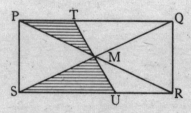

   Since $\triangle TQM \cong \triangle SMU$, it follows that the shaded area $= \triangle PTM + \triangle TQM = \triangle PMQ$. But $\triangle PMQ = \frac{1}{2} \triangle PQS = \frac{1}{4}$ PQRS, $\frac{1}{4} = 25\%$

11. **(B)** Let x = number of people in audience
    then $\frac{1}{6}x$ = no. of boys

    $\frac{1}{3}x$ = no. of girls

    $\frac{1}{6}x + \frac{1}{3}x = \frac{1}{6}x + \frac{2}{6}x = \frac{3}{6}x =$
    $\frac{1}{2}x$ = no. of children

    $\frac{1}{2} = 50\%$

12. **(C)** The number of revolutions is inversely proportional to size of wheel.

    Thus $\dfrac{30}{20} = \dfrac{n}{240}$

    Where n = no. of revolutions for 2nd wheel,

    $2n = 720$

    $n = 360$

13. **(A)** r cannot equal any number other than zero, for, if we divided by r, x would equal y. Since $x \neq y$, it follows that $r = 0$

14. **(E)** $\dfrac{m}{n} = \dfrac{5}{6}$

    $6m = 5n$

    $6m - 5n = 0$

    However, it is not possible to determine from this the value of $3m + 2n$.

15. **(D)** I. As x increases, $\dfrac{1}{x}$ decreases and

    $x - \dfrac{1}{x}$ increases.

    II. $\dfrac{1}{x^2 - x} = \dfrac{1}{x(x-1)}$ As x increases, both x and $(x-1)$ increase, and $\dfrac{1}{x(x-1)}$ decreases.

    III. $4x^3 - 2x^2 = 2x^2(2x-1)$. As x increases, both $2x^2$ and $(2x-1)$ increase, and their product increases. Therefore, I and III increase.

16. **(A)** $\triangle SPT = \frac{1}{3} \triangle PSR$ since they have common altitude and the base $ST = \frac{1}{3}SR$. But $\triangle PSR = \frac{1}{2}$ P PQRS.
    Hence $\triangle SPT = \frac{1}{3} \cdot \frac{1}{2}$ P $= \frac{1}{6}$ P

17. **(C)** Let the other two angles be $2x$ and $5x$.
    Thus, $2x + 5x + 82 = 180$

    $7x = 98$

    $x = 14$

    $2x = 28$

    $5x = 70$

    Smallest angle $= 28°$

18. **(E)** His rate is $\dfrac{1}{t}$ of the lawn per minute.

    Hence, in 15 minutes, he will do

    $15 \cdot \dfrac{1}{t} = \dfrac{15}{t}$ of the lawn

19. **(B)** Typing space is $12 - 3 = 9$ inches long and $9 - 2 = 7$ inches wide. Part used $= \dfrac{9 \times 7}{9 \times 12} = \dfrac{7}{12}$

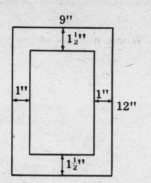

20. **(C)** 132 feet in 9 seconds
    $= 132 \times 400$ feet in $9 \times 400 = 3600$ seconds (1hr.)

    $= \dfrac{132 \times 10}{132}$ miles per hr.

    $= 10$ miles per hr.

21. **(E)** Let the original sign be 10 by 10.

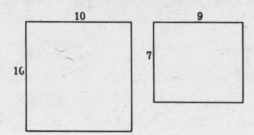

    Then the new sign is 9 by 7
    $\dfrac{63}{100} = 63\%$

22. **(E)** All the numbers from 200 to 299 begin with 2. There are 100 of these. Then all numbers like 102, 112, ——, 192 end with 2. There are ten of these.
    Hence, there are 110 such numbers.

23. **(A)** If $2 < y < 7$ and $5 < y < 10$, then $5 < y < 7$ (intersection of 2 sets). Since y is an integer, it must be 6.

24. **(B)** If the area is $49x^2$, the side of the square is 7x. Therefore, the diagonal of the square must be the hypotenuse of a right isosceles triangle of leg 7x.

    Hence diagonal $= 7x \sqrt{2}$

25. **(D)** Since $MP = 1$ and $MQ = \frac{1}{2}$, the area of $\triangle PMQ = $ area of $\triangle POR = \frac{1}{2} \cdot 1 \cdot \frac{1}{2} = \frac{1}{4}$

    The area of $\triangle QNR = \frac{1}{2} \cdot \frac{1}{2} \cdot \frac{1}{2} = \frac{1}{8}$
    Area of $\triangle PQR = 1 - 2(\frac{1}{4}) - \frac{1}{8} = 1 - \frac{5}{8} = \frac{3}{8}$

26. **(D)** 72 tiles along each length. 24 tiles along each width. $2 \times 96 = 192$ tiles along perimeter. But 4 more are needed for the corners of the frame.

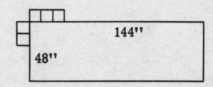

    Hence, 196 tiles are needed.

27. **(E)** $\dfrac{1}{10} = x \quad \dfrac{3}{4} = \dfrac{3x}{4}$
    Cross-multiplying, we obtain
    $30x = 4$
    $x = \frac{2}{15}$

28. **(B)** Since $QR = 7$, and QOR is a right, isosceles triangle, $OQ = \dfrac{7}{\sqrt{2}} = \dfrac{7\sqrt{2}}{2}$
    Hence, coordinates of Q are $(0, \frac{7}{2}\sqrt{2})$

29. **(C)** Let $x = $ no. of years for 2 populations to be equal
    Then $6800 - 120x = 4200 + 80x$
    $\qquad\qquad 2600 = 200x$
    $\qquad\qquad\quad x = 13$

30. **(B)** $8 \times 6 = 48$
    $6 \times 8 = \frac{48}{96}$ (sum of all 14 numbers)
    Average $= \frac{96}{14} = 6\frac{6}{7}$

31. **(D)**
    I. As x increases, $(1 - x^2)$ decreases.
    II. As x increases, $(x - 1)$ increases.
    III. As x increases, $\frac{1}{x^2}$ decreases.

    Hence, II only increases.

32. **(C)** $T = 2\pi \sqrt{\dfrac{L}{g}}$

    In order for T to be tripled, L must be multiplied by 9, since the square root of this factor will be 3.

33. **(D)** The line of center of two tangent circles passes through the point of tangency.
    Hence, perimeter of $\triangle = (2 + 3) + (3 + 4) + (4 + 2) = 5 + 7 + 6 = 18$

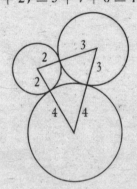

34. **(C)** Area of outer circle $= 100\pi$
    Area of inner circle $= 49\pi$
    Decrease in area $= 51\pi$
    % decrease $= \dfrac{51\pi}{100\pi} = 51\%$

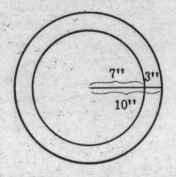

35. **(D)** Let x = original price.
    Then $.60x = \$\ 4.20$
    or $\quad 6x = \$42.00$
    $x = \$\ 7.00$

TEST IV. DATA INTERPRETATION

1.B	3.A	5.A	7.B	9.C
2.B	4.C	6.B	8.D	

TEST V. ANTONYMS

1.C	3.D	5.D	7.B	9.C	11.E	13.D
2.C	4.C	6.B	8.B	10.D	12.D	14.C

TEST VI. VERBAL ANALOGIES

1.C	3.D	5.B	7.D	9.D	11.B
2.B	4.A	6.C	8.A	10.B	12.C

TEST VII. SENTENCE COMPLETIONS

1.D	3.B	5.C	7.D	9.A	11.D	13.E
2.A	4.E	6.E	8.B	10.E	12.B	

TEST VIII. DATA SUFFICIENCY

1.D	3.C	5.E	7.B	9.C	11.E	13.C	15.A
2.A	4.C	6.C	8.B	10.C	12.C	14.E	

TEST VIII. EXPLANATORY ANSWERS

1. (D) According to Statement 1, he earned 87½% of $6500 in 1962 = $5777.77. According to Statement 2, he earned ⅔ of $8666.67 in 1962 = $5777.77.

2. (A) $43,250 × .15 will be the sum that creditors will receive.

3. (C) (90 × 4 + 84 × 3 + 75 × 3 + 76 × 1) ÷ 11 will give the student's over-all average.

4. (C) Pipe A will fill $\frac{1}{12}$ of the tank in one minute. Pipe B will empty $\frac{1}{8}$ of the tank in one minute. Together, in one minute, A and B will empty $\frac{1}{8} - \frac{1}{12} = \frac{1}{24}$ of the tank. The time required to empty ¾ or $\frac{18}{24}$ of the tank, can now be determined (18 minutes).

5. (E) To arrive at the average rate, it would be necessary to know how many miles per hour *each* man walked.

6. (C) The double discount will bring the selling price down to $60. Since the dealer's profit is 30% of this (from Statement 1), he has bought the desk for $60 × .7 = $42. His cost of doing business is $60 × 10% = $6 (from Statement 2). The cost of the desk to him is $42 minus $6 = $36.

7. (B) The length of the working day is irrelevant in this solution. From Statement 2 we can determine that the two typists can type 300 letters in three days—therefore, 100 letters in one day.

8. (B) If the hour hand is exactly half-way between 9 and 10, the minute hand must be on the 30—it's half-past nine.

9. (C) From Statement 1 we know that the first three men ate $\frac{249}{308}$ of the pie. From Statement 2 we learn that the fourth man ate the rest of the pie $= \frac{59}{308}$.

10. (C) Let x = the length of the bridge. Then, $\frac{1}{5} x + \frac{1}{6} x + 760$ feet = x.

11. (E) To solve, it is necessary to know the number of males over 20.

12. (C) Statement 1 tells us that Pericles was a historian. Statement 2 tells us that he lived in ancient times.

13. (C) The tax to be paid is arrived at as follows: $2.56 × 60 × .20

14. (E) The bank's compounding practice is required for solution.

15. (A) The wine will lose 30¢ worth of quality per gallon—that is, $\frac{1}{5}$ of the original quality. In other words, $\frac{1}{5}$ of each gallon of wine will be replaced by $\frac{1}{5}$ gallon of water. Therefore, $3\frac{2}{5}$ will be the total number of gallons of water to be added.

TEST IX. READING COMPREHENSION

1.B	4.A	7.D	10.A	13.B	16.C	19.D
2.B	5.D	8.A	11.A	14.B	17.A	20.A
3.D	6.B	9.C	12.D	15.A	18.B	21.B

TEST X. ENGLISH USAGE

1.A	6.A	11.E	16.C	21.E
2.A	7.D	12.D	17.A	22.A
3.E	8.A	13.C	18.C	23.B
4.C	9.D	14.C	19.A	24.E
5.D	10.E	15.D	20.D	25.C

TEST XI. TEST XII. DATA APPLICATION AND DATA EVALUATION

1.C	6.E	11.C	16.D	21.C	26.D
2.C	7.B	12.A	17.A	22.E	27.C
3.D	8.E	13.E	18.C	23.C	28.D
4.B	9.C	14.A	19.C	24.C	29.B
5.A	10.A	15.B	20.B	25.C	30.E

TEST XI. TEST XII. EXPLANATORY ANSWERS

1. **(C)** It is stated that the Johnsons make $30,000 on an average annual sales revenue of $200,000.

2. **(C)** It is stated that 25% of the $200,000 sales revenue comes from retail outlets, and the rest (75%) from direct mail.

3. **(D)** It is stated that Robert wishes to own his own press so he can avoid the sharp drop in sales that resulted from a late mailing of his catalog, caused by a strike at his printers. **(B)** is wrong; we have only been told about one late mailing. **(C)** is wrong; Robert apparently has no desire to have an additional business. It is never mentioned that acquisition of a press will help increase sales volume, so **(E)** is wrong. We are not told that his printer is out of business; thus **(A)** is incorrect.

4. **(B)** His present printing cost is $40,000. If he owned his own press, he would have to pay $16,000 for paper and ink and $4,000 for a part-time pressman, making a total of $20,000, or a reduction of $20,000.

5. **(A)** It is a seasonal business, of course, dealing in seeds which must be planted at a certain time. That is the reason why sales volume dropped sharply when the Johnson catalog was mailed only two weeks late. **(D)** is incorrect; we are told that the company made over $200,000 in sales revenue during each of the past three years. **(E)** is wrong; the business is confined to the state of Colorado.

6. **(E)** Mary points out that Robert has not figured into his calculations how much more time he will now have to spend in the printing process, which will take time away from other duties. Robert did enter all the other possible answers into his estimates.

7. **(B)** Order processing is listed by Mary as being more important than printing.

8. **(E)** Mary is strong in her objection that Robert is only a gifted amateur when it comes to printing, not a professional pressman.

9. **(C)** She calls it his hobby. **(B)** is wrong; we are not told that Robert is bored with the business. **(A)** is also incorrect; she does not think that buying the press is practical. **(D)** is wrong because the purchase price of the press does not seem to be a concern. Sales have been about $200,000 for each of the past three years; therefore **(E)** is wrong.

10. **(A)** So stated. That does not mean she believes the catalog is of no importance, **(B)**, or that it has never been of a high standard, **(E)**; we are not told her opinions on these.

LETTER CODE FOR EVALUATING DATA

(A) means that the Conclusion is a Major Objective;
(B) means that the Conclusion is a Major Factor;
(C) means that the Conclusion is a Minor Factor;
(D) means that the Conclusion is a Major Assumption;
(E) means that the Conclusion is an Unimportant Issue.

11. **(C)** That there may be a possible drop in the quality of the catalog is a minor factor.

12. **(A)** It is Robert's aim to be able to control production so that he can avoid outside delays.

13. **(E)** Increased sales revenue resulting from his ownership of a printing press does not seem to enter into Robert's calculations.

14. **(A)** The date on which the catalog is mailed is of critical importance; having this date assured is a major objective.

15. **(B)** Reduction of printing costs is a major factor since it directly influences the major objective of increasing profit.

16. **(D)** Making up the price of the printing press within one year is an assumption on Robert's part, which can only be proved if he actually buys the press and tries it for a year.

17. **(A)** Robert wishes to increase profits by lowering printing costs.

18. **(C)** The strike at the printing plant is a minor factor that led to a major factor of delaying the catalog mailing.

19. **(C)** Failure to correctly estimate costs of his time devoted to printing should a press be purchased is a minor factor that obviously leads him to postpone making a decision. It bears directly on the major factor to reduce printing costs, which in turn leads to the major objective of increasing profits.

20. **(B)** Robert's fascination with printing seems to be a major factor in his desire to own a press.

21. **(C)** A minor factor since printing is an essential part of direct mail and the reduction of printing costs is a major factor.

22. **(E)** The geographic extent of the Johnsons' business plays no part in the considerations of whether or not to buy a press.

23. **(C)** The fact that a part-time pressman must be hired is a minor factor in the financial considerations.

24. **(C)** Managing cash flow enters into the situation when Mary points out that time devoted to the press might reflect adversely on this important chore. Robert must have taken this argument into account when he decided to postpone purchasing the press for at least six months.

25. **(C)** A minor factor; Robert would not be considering buying a printing press unless he had a knowledge of printing.

26. **(D)** Robert's ability or inability to handle a large high-speed press are only assumptions.

27. **(C)** Robert's catalog design work is a minor factor that illustrates his fascination with printing and his belief that he can handle the whole printing process.

28. **(D)** It is probable that a press will break down from time to time, but this must still be classified as an assumption.

29. **(B)** This is a major factor leading to the major objective of certainty in mailing at the right time.

30. **(E)** Customer loyalty plays no part in the considerations.

AFTER TAKING EXAMINATION III.

Use the following Check List to establish areas
that require the greatest application on your part. One check (√)
after the item means moderately weak; two checks (√ √) means
seriously weak.

AREA OF WEAKNESS	CHECK BELOW	AREA OF WEAKNESS	CHECK BELOW
READING RECALL		DATA SUFFICIENCY	
DATA INTERPRETATION		DATA APPLICATION	
PROBLEM SOLVING		DATA EVALUATION	
ANTONYMS		READING COMPREHENSION	
VERBAL ANALOGIES		ENGLISH USAGE	
SENTENCE COMPLETIONS			

When you have strengthened yourself sufficiently
where strengthening is necessary, take the other Examination
in the book. Again place yourself under strict testing conditions.
We have every confidence that you will do better on the following
Exam than you did on this one, if you've followed our suggestions
for eliminating "soft spots." Now, please get to work.

PART THREE

A Practical Course of Self-Instruction

3

TOP SCORES ON VOCABULARY TESTS

Although questions on vocabulary may not actually appear on your test, it is advisable to practice with the kind of material you have in this chapter. Words and their meanings are quite important in pushing up your score on tests of reading, comprehension, effective writing and correct usage. By broadening your vocabulary, you will definitely improve your marks in these and similar subjects.

INCREASE YOUR VOCABULARY

How is your vocabulary? Do you know the meanings of just about every word you come upon in your reading—or do you find several words that stump you? You must increase your vocabulary if you want to read with understanding. Following are six steps that you can take in order to build up your word power:

(a) Read as much as you have the time for. Don't confine yourself to one type of reading either. Read all kinds of newspapers, magazines, books. Seek variety in what you read—different newspapers, several types of magazines, all types of books (novels, poetry, essays, plays, etc.). If you get into the habit of reading widely, your vocabulary will grow by leaps and bounds. You'll learn the meanings of words *by context*. That means that, very often, even though you may not know the meaning of a certain word in a sentence, the other words that you are familiar with will help you get the meaning of the hard word.

(b) Take vocabulary tests. There are many practice books which have word tests. We suggest one of these: *2300 Steps to Word Power* — (Arco Publishing Co.). These tests are fun to take—and they will build up your vocabulary fast.

(c) Listen to lectures, discussions, and talks by people who speak well. There are some worthwhile TV programs that have excellent speakers. Listen to these people—you'll learn a great many words.

(d) Use a dictionary. Whenever you don't know the meaning of a word, make a note of it. Then, when you get to a dictionary, look up the meaning of the word. Keep your own little notebook—call it "New Words." In a month or two, you will have added a great many words to your vocabulary. If you do not have a dictionary at home, you should buy one. A good dictionary is not expensive. Any one of the following is highly recommended:

Standard College Dictionary (Funk and Wagnalls)

Seventh New Collegiate Dictionary (Merriam-Webster)

American College Dictionary (Random House)

You'll never regret buying a good dictionary for your home.

(e) Play word games. Have you ever played Anagrams or Scrabble? They're really interesting. Buy one of these at a stationery store. They are quite inexpensive but effective in building up your vocabulary. Crossword puzzles will teach you new words also. Practically every daily newspaper has a crossword puzzle.

(f) Learn stems, prefixes, and suffixes.

BASIC LETTER COMBINATIONS

One of the most efficient ways in which you can build up your vocabulary is by a systematic study of the basic word and letter combinations which make up the greater part of the English language.

Etymology is the science of the formation of words, and this somewhat frightening-sounding science can be of great help to you in learning new words and identifying words which may be unfamiliar to you. You will also find that the progress you make in studying the following pages will help to improve your spelling.

A great many of the words which we use every day have come into our language from the Latin and Greek. In the process of being absorbed into English, they appear as parts of words, many of which are related in meaning to each other.

For your convenience, this material is presented in easy-to-study form. Latin and Greek syllables and letter-combinations have been categorized into three groups:

1. *Prefixes:* letter combinations which appear at the beginning of a word.

2. *Suffixes:* letter combinations which appear at the end of a word.

3. *Roots or stems:* which carry the basic meaning and are combined with each other and with prefixes and suffixes to create other words with related meanings.

With the prefixes and suffixes, which you should study first, we have given examples of word formation with meanings, and additional examples. If you find any unfamiliar words among the samples, consult your dictionary to look up their meanings.

The list of roots or stems is accompanied by words in which the letter combinations appear. Here again, use the dictionary to look up any words which are not clear in your mind.

Remember that this section is not meant for easy reading. It is a guide to a program of study that will prove invaluable if you do your part. Do not try to swallow too much at one time. If you can put in a half-hour every day, your study will yield better results.

After you have done your preliminary work and have gotten a better idea of how words are formed in English, schedule the various vocabulary tests and quizzes we have provided in this chapter. They cover a wide variety of the vocabulary questions commonly encountered on examinations. They are short quizzes, not meant to be taken all at one time. Space them out. Adhere closely to the directions which differ for the different test types. Keep an honest record of your scores. Study your mistakes. Look them up in your dictionary. Concentrate closely on each quiz . . . and watch your scores improve.

ETYMOLOGY

A KEY TO WORD RECOGNITION

PREFIXES

PREFIX	MEANING	EXAMPLE
ab, a	away from	absent, amoral
ad, ac, ag, at	to	advent, accrue, aggressive, attract
an	without	anarchy
ante	before	antedate
anti	against	antipathy
bene	well	beneficent
bi	two	bicameral
circum	around	circumspect
com, con, col	together	commit confound, collate
contra	against	contraband
de	from, down	descend
dis, di	apart	distract, divert
ex, e	out	exit, emit
extra	beyond	extracurricular
in, im, il, ir, un	not	inept, impossible, illicit
inter	between	interpose
intra, intro, in	within	intramural, introspective

PREFIX	MEANING	EXAMPLE
mal	bad	malcontent
mis	wrong	misnomer
non	not	nonentity
ob	against	obstacle
per	through	permeate
peri	around	periscope
poly	many	polytheism
post	after	post-mortem
pre	before	premonition
pro	forward	propose
re	again	review
se	apart	seduce
semi	half	semicircle
sub	under	subvert
super	above	superimpose
sui	self	suicide
trans	across	transpose
vice	instead of	vice-president

SUFFIXES

SUFFIX	MEANING	EXAMPLE
able, ible	capable of being	capable, reversible
age	state of	storage
ance	relating to	reliance
ary	relating to	dictionary
ate	act	confiscate
ation	action	radiation
cy	quality	democracy

SUFFIX	MEANING	EXAMPLE
ence	relating to	confidence
er	one who	adviser
ic	pertaining to	democratic
ious	full of	rebellious
ize	to make like	harmonize
ment	result	filament
ty	condition	sanity

LATIN AND GREEK STEMS

STEM	MEANING	EXAMPLE
ag, ac	do	agenda, action
agr	farm	agriculture
aqua	water	aqueous
cad, cas	fall	cadence, casual
cant	sing	chant
cap, cep	take	captive, accept
capit	head	capital
cede	go	precede
celer	speed	celerity
cide, cis	kill, cut	suicide, incision
clud, clus	close	include, inclusion
cur, curs	run	incur, incursion
dict	say	diction
duct	lead	induce
fact, fect	make	factory, perfect
fer, lat	carry	refer, dilate
fring, fract	break	infringe, fracture
frater	brother	fraternal
fund, fus	pour	refund, confuse
greg	group	gregarious
gress, grad	move forward	progress, degrade
homo	man	homicide
ject	throw	reject
jud	right	judicial
junct	join	conjunction
lect, leg	read, choose	collect, legend
loq, loc	speak	loquacious, interlocutory
manu	hand	manuscript
mand	order	remand
mar	sea	maritime
mater	mother	maternal
med	middle	intermediary
min	lessen	diminution
mis, mit	send	remit, dismiss
mort	death	mortician
mote, mov	move	remote, remove
naut	sailor	astronaut
nom	name	nomenclature
pater	father	paternity
ped, pod	foot	pedal, podiatrist
pend	hang	depend
plic	fold	implicate
port	carry	portable
pos, pon	put	depose, component
reg, rect	rule	regicide, direct
rupt	break	eruption
scrib, scrip	write	inscribe, conscription
anthrop	man	anthropology

STEM	MEANING	EXAMPLE
arch	chief, rule	archbishop
astron	star	astronomy
auto	self	automatic
biblio	book	bibliophile
bio	life	biology
chrome	color	chromosome
chron	time	chronology
cosmo	world	cosmic
crat	rule	autocrat
dent, dont	tooth	dental, indent
eu	well, happy	eugenics
gamos	marriage	monogamous
ge	earth	geology
gen	origin, people	progenitor
graph	write	graphic
gyn	women	gynecologist
homo	same	homogeneous
hydr	water	dehydrate
logy	study of	psychology
meter	measure	thermometer
micro	small	microscope
mono	one	monotony
onomy	science	astronomy
onym	name	synonym
pathos	feeling	pathology
philo	love	philosophy
phobia	fear	hydrophobia
phone	sound	telephone
pseudo	false	pseudonym
psych	mind	psychic
scope	see	telescope
soph	wisdom	sophomore
tele	far off	telepathic
theo	god	theology
thermo	heat	thermostat
sec	cut	dissect
sed	remain	sedentary
sequ	follow	sequential
spect	look	inspect
spir	breathe	conspire
stat	stand	status
tact, tang	touch	tactile, tangible
ten	hold	retentive
term	end	terminal
vent	come	prevent
vict	conquer	evict
vid, vis	see	video, revise
voc	call	convocation
volv	roll	devolve

SKILL WITH VERBAL ANALOGIES

This is an interesting variation of the vocabulary question, often encountered on intelligence tests. It tests your understanding of word meanings and your ability to grasp relationships between words and ideas. We expect this kind of question on your test, so you can be sure that this chapter is worthwhile. But even more important is the practice in mental agility which will carry over to better results with all the other questions on the test.

IN addition to their simple meanings, words carry subtle shades of implication that depend in some degree upon the relationship they bear to other words. There are various classifications of relationship, such as similarity (synonyms) and opposition (antonyms). The careful student will examine each word in these analogy questions for the exact shade of meaning indicated.

The ability to detect the exact nature of the relationship between words is a function of your intelligence. In a sense, the verbal analogy test is a vocabulary test. But it is also a test of your ability to analyze meanings, think things out and to see the relationships between ideas and words, and avoid confusion of ideas. In mathematics, this type of situation is expressed as a ratio and proportion problem: $3:5 = 6:X$. Sometimes verbal analogies are written in this mathematical form:

CLOCK: TIME—THERMOMETER: (A) hour (B) degrees (C) temperature (D) climate (E) weather.

Or the question may be put:

CLOCK is to TIME as THERMOMETER is to (A) hour (B) degrees (C) temperature (D) climate (E) weather.

The problem is to determine which of the lettered words has the same relationship to thermometer as time has to clock.

The best way of determining the correct answer is to provide the word or phrase which shows the relationship between these words. In the example above, the word is measures. However, this may not be enough. The analogy must be correct in exact meaning. Climate or weather would not be exact enough. Temperature, of course, is the correct answer.

You will find that many of the choices you have to select from have some relationship to the third word. You must select the one with a relationship most closely approximating the relationship between the first two words.

What the Analogy Question Measures

The analogy question tests your ability to see a relationship between words and to apply this relationship to other words. Although the verbal analogy test is, to some degree, an indicator of your vocabulary, it is essentially a test of your ability to think things out. In other words, analogy questions will spotlight your ability to think clearly—your ability to sidestep confusion of ideas. In mathematics, this type of situation is expressed as a proportion problem—for example, $3:5 :: 6:X$. Verbal analogy questions, are written in this mathematical form.

Three Forms of the Analogy Question

Type 1. Example:

From the four (or five) pairs of words which follow, you are to select the pair which is related in the same way as the words of the first pair.

SPELLING : PUNCTUATION :: (A) pajamas : fatigue (B) powder : shaving (C) bandage : cut (D) biology : physics

SPELLING and *PUNCTUATION* are elements of the mechanics of English; *BIOLOGY* and *PHYSICS* are two of the subjects that make up the field of science. The other choices do not possess this PART : PART relationship. Therefore, (D) is the correct choice.

Type 2. Example:

Another popular form is the type in which two words are followed by a third word. The latter is related to one word in a group of choices in the same way that the first two words are related.

WINTER is to SUMMER as COLD is to
(A) wet (B) future (C) warm (D) freezing
WINTER and *SUMMER* bear an opposite relationship. *COLD* and *WARM* have the same type of opposite relationship. Therefore, (C) is the correct answer.

Type 3. Example:

Still another analogy form is that in which *one* of the four relationship elements is not specified. From choices offered—regardless of the position—you are to select the one choice which completes the relationship with the other three items.

SUBMARINE : FISH as (A) kite (B) limousine (C) feather (D) chirp : BIRD
Both a *SUBMARINE* and a *FISH* are found in the water; both a *KITE* and *BIRD* are customarily seen in the air. (A), consequently, is the correct answer.

This third type is used in the Miller Analogy Test, considered one of the most reliable and valid tests for selection of graduate students in universities, and high-level personnel in government, industry, and business.

Kinds of Relationship

In analogy questions, the relationship between the first two words may be one of several kinds. Following are relationship possibilities.

1. *Purpose Relationship*
GLOVE : BALL :: (A) hook : fish (B) winter : weather (C) game : pennant (D) stadium : seats

2. *Cause and Effect Relationship*
RACE : FATIGUE :: (A) track : athlete (B) ant : bug (C) fast : hunger (D) walking : running

3. *Part : Whole Relationship*
SNAKE : REPTILE :: (A) patch : thread (B) removal : snow (C) struggle : wrestle (D) hand : clock

4. *Part : Part Relationship*
GILL : FIN : (A) tube : antenna (B) instrument : violin (C) sea : fish (D) salad : supper

5. *Action to Object Relationship*
KICK : FOOTBALL :: (A) kill : bomb (B) break : pieces (C) question : team (D) smoke : pipe

6. *Object to Action Relationship*
STEAK : BROIL :: (A) bread : bake (B) food : sell (C) wine : pour (D) sugar: spill

7. *Synonym Relationship*
ENORMOUS : HUGE :: (A) rogue : rock (B) muddy : unclear (C) purse : kitchen (D) black : white

8. *Antonym Relationship*
   PURITY : EVIL :: (A) suavity : bluntness (B) north : climate (C) angel : horns (D) boldness : victory

9. *Place Relationship*
   MIAMI : FLORIDA :: (A) Chicago : United States (B) New York : Albany (C) United States : Chicago (D) Albany : New York

10. *Degree Relationship*
    WARM : HOT :: (A) glue : paste (B) climate : weather (C) fried egg : boiled egg (D) bright : genius

11. *Characteristic Relationship*
    IGNORANCE : POVERTY :: (A) blood : wound (B) money : dollar (C) schools : elevators (D) education : stupidity

12. *Sequence Relationship*
    SPRING : SUMMER :: (A) Thursday : Wednesday (B) Wednesday : Monday (C) Monday : Sunday (D) Wednesday : Thursday

13. *Grammatical Relationship*
    RESTORE : CLIMB :: (A) segregation : seem (B) into : nymph (C) tearoom : although (D) overpower : seethe

14. *Numerical Relationship*
    4 : 12 :: (A) 10 : 16 (B) 9 : 27 (C) 3 : 4 (D) 12 : 6

15. *Association Relationship*
    DEVIL : WRONG :: (A) color : sidewalk (B) slipper : state (C) ink : writing (D) picture : bed

Correct Answers

(You'll learn more by writing your own answers before comparing them with these.)

1. A	5. D	9. D	13. D
2. C	6. A	10. D	14. B
3. D	7. B	11. A	15. C
4. A	8. A	12. D	

Note 1: In many analogy questions, the incorrect choices may relate in some way to the first two words. Don't let this association mislead you. For example, in Number 4 above (PART : PART RELATIONSHIP example), the correct answer is (A) tube : antenna. The choice (C) sea : fish is incorrect, although these two latter words are associated in a general sense with the first two words (gill : fin).

Note 2: Very often, the relationship of the first two words may apply to more than *one* of the choices given. In such a case, you must "narrow down" the initial relationship in order to get the correct choice. For example, in Number 6 above (OBJECT : ACTION RELATIONSHIP), a STEAK is something that you BROIL. Now let us consider the choices: BREAD is something that you BAKE; FOOD is something that you SELL; WINE is something that you POUR; and SUGAR is something that you (can) SPILL. Thus far, each choice seems correct. Let us now "narrow down" the relationship: a STEAK is something that you BROIL with *heat.* The only choice that fulfils this *complete* relationship is (A) BREAD — something that you BAKE with *heat.* It follows that (A) is the correct choice.

Two Important Steps to Analogy Success

Step One—Determine the relationship between the first two words.

Step Two—Find the same relationship among the choices which follow the first two words.

NOW LET US APPLY THESE TWO STEPS

1. *Determining the relationship.*

Directions: Each question consists of two words which have some relationship to each other. From the five following pairs of words, select the one which is related in the same way as the words of the first pair:

ARC : CIRCLE :: (A) segment : cube (B) angle : triangle (C) tangent : circumference (D) circle : cube (E) cube : square

An arc is part of a circle, just as an angle is part of a triangle. The other choices do not bear this PART : WHOLE relationship. Therefore, (B) is correct.

With the foregoing line of reasoning, you probably eliminated choice (A) immediately. Choice (B) seemed correct. Did you give it *final* acceptance without considering the remaining choices? In this analogy question, choice (B), as it turned out, was the correct choice. However, let us change the question slightly:

ARC : CIRCLE :: (A) segment : cube
(B) angle : triangle (C) tangent : circumference (D) circle : cube (E) line: square

Note that the (E) choice has been changed. (E)— not (B)— is now the correct answer. REASON: An arc is *any* part of the drawn circle. Likewise, a line is *any* part of the drawn square. However, an angle is *not* any part of the drawn triangle. The correct answer is, therefore, (E) line : square.

This illustration should caution you not to "jump to conclusions." Consider *all* choices carefully before you reach your conclusion.

2. *Use the word that shows the relationship.*

The best way of determining the correct answer to an analogy question is to *provide the word or phrase* which shows the relationship that exists between the first two words. Let us illustrate with the following analogy question:

CLOCK : TIME :: (A) hour : latitude
(B) thermometer : temperature (C) weather : climate (D) tide : moon

The problem here is to determine which choice has the same relationship that *clock* has to *time*. Let us, now, provide the word or phrase which shows the relationship between *clock* and *time*. The word is *measures*. Choice B, then, is the correct answer since a thermometer *measures* temperature.

You will find that many of the choices which you are given have some relationship to the opening pair. You must be sure to select *that* choice which bears a relationship most closely approximating the relationship between the opening two words.

ANALYSIS OF ANALOGY PITFALLS

DIRECTIONS: In each of the following questions the FIRST TWO words in capital letters go together in some way. Find how they are related. Then write the correct letter to show which one of the last five words goes with the THIRD word in capital letters in the same way that the second word in capital letters goes with the first.

The important rule to remember in answering an analogy question is to determine the specific relationship of the first two words of the analogy, and then choose the word given in the alternatives bearing a similar relationship to the third member of the analogy.

It is also important to point out some of the more important pitfalls involved in answering this type of question. Let us take some sample questions:

I.   FOOD is to HUNGER as SLEEP is to
(A) night   (B) dream
(C) weariness   (D) health
(E) rest

Obviously, all of the words are related to sleep in some way. None of them except weariness bears the same relationship to sleep as hunger does to food. Before answering one of these questions, then, we must fix in our minds the relationship that the first two words of the analogy bear to each other.

(A) although one sleeps at night, it is not the night that is relieved by sleep.
(B) sleep is certainly related to dream because people dream when they sleep. But again, it is not dreams that are relieved by sleep.
(C) food relieves hunger and sleep relieves weariness. Therefore weariness is correct.
(D) sleep is productive, in part, of health, but this is not the relationship that we are seeking.
(E) sleep results in rest but food does, not result in hunger.

II. CUP is to DRINK as PLATE is to
(A) supper   (B) fork
(C) dine   (D) earthenware
(E) silver

What is the relationship between cup (noun) and drink (verb)?

It is obvious that one DRINKS from a cup.
What does one do from a plate in the same manner that one drinks from a cup?

It becomes apparent that of the five choices offered, (C) dine, is the only one which bears a similar relationship, since one dines from a plate.

A closer analogy would have been one EATS from a plate, but since this word is not offered, the best of the five choices is DINE.

Notice that all of the remaining choices bear some relationship to the word plate but not the same that cup bears to drink.

(A) supper is related to plate since one's supper may be eaten from a plate. Supper, however, is a noun, and the part of speech required is a verb.

(B) fork is related to plate since both are eating utensils, but this is not the relationship required, so it must be eliminated.

(C) earthenware is related to plate since many plates are made of earthenware, but this also is not the relationship called for.

(D) silver is related to plate since in one sense they are synonyms. There is also a relationship established in the word "silver-plated," but neither of these is the relationship required.

III. GUILLOTINE is to DECAPITATE as RAZOR is to
(A) beard   (B) hair
(C) shave   (D) cut
(E) steel

This is the type of analogy which deals with the use, purpose or function of an object or instrument.

The purpose of a guillotine is to decapitate.

What is a razor used for?

It is obvious that the most important use of the razor is to shave, so (C) is the correct answer.

Notice the relationships of the remaining choices:

(A) razor is related to beard, since it is used to cut beards, but it is not the relation-

ship required. Also, the sense of the analogy calls for a verb, not a noun.

(B) razor is related to hair, since it cuts hair, but hair is not the purpose of razor.

(C) cut is one of the uses of a razor, but it is not its primary function. Relatively it is not as important as shave.

(E) steel is related to razor in the sense that some razors are made of steel, but since steel is not the function of a razor, it must be eliminated as incorrect.

IV. ADDER is to SNAKE as CROCODILE is to
(A) ruminant   (B) marsh
(C) reptile   (D) carnivore
(E) rapacious

This is a type of analogy question frequently met on examinations. The candidate must learn to distinguish between a specific and a general. In many cases it is a question of comparing a specie of an animal, plant, tree, bird, etc. to its broader classification.

An adder is a kind or type of snake.

Snake is a general term including many different species, of which adder is only one.

In the same way, which of the five choices is the general classification under which the specie crocodile can be classified?

(A) a ruminant is an animal that chews the cud, as a goat or a sheep. A crocodile is not a ruminant.

(B) a marsh is a tract of low, miry land. It has no connection with types of crocodiles.

(C) reptile is a broad classification of animals including the crocodile. It has the same relation to crocodile as adder has to snake, and is therefore the correct choice.

(D) a carnivore is a mammalian animal which lives on flesh for food. The crocodile is not of this type.

(E) rapacious is an adjective meaning subsisting on prey or animals seized by violence." Since rapacious is not a type of crocodile, it could not possibly be the correct choice.

V. BREAKABLE is to FRANGIBLE as GUL-LIBLE is to

(A) credulous   (B) deceptive
(C) capable   (D) lurid
(E) marine

This is an analogy formed by comparing two adjectives.

They are synonymous since they have the same meanings.

Inasmuch as the first words of the analogy are adjectives the second pair must also be adjectives.

Gullible is an exact synonym of credulous and is therefore the most correct choice.

None of the other choices bears any resemblance in meaning to gullible.

ANALOGY TEST

DIRECTIONS: In these test questions each of the two CAPI-TALIZED words have a certain relationship to each other. Following the capitalized words are other pairs of words, each designated by a letter. Select the lettered pair wherein the words are related in the same way as the two CAPITALIZED words are related to each other.

EXPLANATIONS OF KEY POINTS BEHIND THESE QUESTIONS ARE GIVEN WITH THE ANSWERS WHICH FOLLOW THE QUESTIONS

1. INTIMIDATE : FEAR ::
   (A) maintain : satisfaction
   (B) astonish : wonder
   (C) sooth : concern
   (D) feed : hunger
   (E) awaken : tiredness

2. STOVE : KITCHEN ::
   (A) window : bedroom
   (B) sink : bathroom
   (C) television : living room
   (D) trunk : attic
   (E) pot : pan

3. CELEBRATE : MARRIAGE ::
   (A) announce : birthday
   (B) report : injury
   (C) lament : bereavement
   (D) face : penalty
   (E) kiss : groom

4. MARGARINE : BUTTER ::
   (A) cream : milk
   (B) lace : cotton
   (C) nylon : silk
   (D) egg : chicken
   (E) oak : acorn

5. NEGLIGENT : REQUIREMENT ::
   (A) careful : position (B) remiss : duty
   (C) cautious : injury (D) cogent : task
   (E) easy : hard

6. GAZELLE : SWIFT ::
   (A) horse : slow (B) wolf : sly
   (C) swan : graceful (D) elephant : gray
   (E) lion : tame

7. IGNOMINY : DISLOYALTY ::
   (A) fame : heroism
   (B) castigation : praise
   (C) death : victory
   (D) approbation : consecration
   (E) derelict : martyr

8. SATURNINE : MERCURIAL ::
   (A) Saturn : Venus
   (B) Appenines : Alps
   (C) redundant : wordy
   (D) allegro : adagio
   (E) heavenly : starry

9. ORANGE : MARMALADE ::
   (A) potato : vegetable (B) jelly : jam
   (C) tomato : ketchup (D) cake : picnic
   (E) sandwich : ham

10. BANISH : APOSTATE ::
    (A) reward : traitor
    (B) request : assistance
    (C) remove : result
    (D) avoid : truce (E) welcome : ally

11. CIRCLE : SPHERE ::
    (A) square : triangle
    (B) balloon : jet plane
    (C) heaven : hell (D) wheel : orange
    (E) pill : drop

12. OPEN : SECRETIVE ::
    (A) mystery : detective
    (B) tunnel : toll
    (C) forthright : snide
    (D) better : best
    (E) gun : mask

13. AFFIRM : HINT ::
    (A) say : deny (B) assert : convince
    (C) confirm : reject
    (D) charge : insinuate
    (E) state : relate

14. THROW : BALL ::
    (A) kill : bullet   (B) shoot : gun
    (C) question : answer (D) hit : run
    (E) stab : knife

15. SPEEDY : GREYHOUND ::
    (A) innocent : lamb
    (B) animate : animal
    (C) voracious : tiger (D) clever : fox
    (E) sluggish : sloth

16. TRIANGLE : PYRAMID ::
    (A) cone : circle (B) corner : angle
    (C) tube : cylinder
    (D) pentagon : quadrilateral
    (E) square : box

17. IMPEACH : DISMISS ::
    (A) arraign : convict
    (B) exonerate : charge
    (C) imprison : jail (D) plant : reap
    (E) president : Johnson

18. EMULATE : MIMIC ::
    (A) slander : defame
    (B) praise : flatter
    (C) aggravate : promote
    (D) complain : condemn
    (E) express : imply.

19. HAND : NAIL ::
    (A) paw : claw
    (B) foot : toe
    (C) head : hair
    (D) ear : nose
    (E) jaw : tooth

20. SQUARE : DIAMOND ::
    (A) cube : sugar
    (B) circle : ellipse
    (C) innocence : jewelry
    (D) rectangle : square
    (E) prizefight : baseball

21. WOODSMAN : AXE ::
    (A) mechanic : wrench
    (B) soldier : gun
    (C) draftsman : ruler
    (D) doctor : prescription
    (E) carpenter : saw

22. BIGOTRY : HATRED ::
    (A) sweetness : bitterness
    (B) segregation : integration
    (C) equality : government
    (D) sugar : grain
    (E) fanaticism : intolerance

23. ASSIST : SAVE ::
    (A) agree : oppose
    (B) rely : descry
    (C) hurt : aid
    (D) declare : deny
    (E) request : command

24. 2 : 5 ::
    (A) 5 : 7   (B) 6 : 17
    (C) 6 : 15   (D) 5 : 14
    (E) 21 : 51

25. DOUBLEHEADER : TRIDENT ::
    (A) twin : troika
    (B) ballgame : three bagger
    (C) chewing gum : toothpaste
    (D) freak : zoo
    (E) two : square

26. BOUQUET : FLOWER ::
    (A) key : door   (B) air : balloon
    (C) skin : body   (D) chain : link
    (E) eye : pigment

27. LETTER : WORD ::
    (A) club : people
    (B) homework : school
    (C) page : book
    (D) product : factory
    (E) picture : crayon

28. 36 : 4 ::
    (A) 3 : 27   (B) 9 : 1   (C) 12 : 4
    (D) 12 : 4   (E) 5 : 2

29. GERM : DISEASE ::
    (A) trichinosis : pork
    (B) men : woman
    (C) doctor : medicine
    (D) war : destruction
    (E) biologist : cell

30. WAVE : CREST ::
    (A) pinnacle : nadir
    (B) mountain : peak
    (C) sea : ocean
    (D) breaker : swimming
    (E) island : archipelago

Correct Answers For The Foregoing Questions

(Check your answers with these that we provide. You should find considerable correspondence between them. If not, you'd better go back and find out why. On the next page we have provided concise clarifications of basic points behind the key answers. Please go over them carefully because they may be quite useful in helping you pick up extra points on the exam.)

Answer Sheet	Answer Sheet	SCORE

SCORE

%

NO. CORRECT *19*

NO. OF QUESTIONS ON THIS TEST

EXPLANATORY ANSWERS

Elucidation, clarification, explication and a little help with the fundamental facts covered in the Previous Test. These are the points and principles likely to crop up in the form of questions on future tests.

1. **(B)** To intimidate is to inspire fear; to astonish is to inspire wonder.

2. **(B)** A stove is an essential part of a kitchen; a sink is an essential part of a bathroom.

3. **(C)** You happily celebrate a marriage; you sorrowfully lament a bereavement.

4. **(C)** Margarine is a manufactured substitute for butter; nylon is a manufactured substitute for silk.

5. **(B)** A person may be negligent in meeting a requirement; he may similarly be remiss in performing his duty.

6. **(C)** A gazelle is known to be swift; a swan is known to be graceful.

7. **(A)** One falls into ignominy if he shows disloyalty; one gains fame if he shows heroism.

8. **(D)** Saturnine and mercurial are antonyms; so are allegro and adagio.

9. **(C)** Marmalade is made from oranges; ketchup is made from tomatoes.

10. **(E)** An apostate is banished (sent away); an ally is welcomed (brought in).

11. **(D)** All four are round: circle, sphere, wheel, and orange.

12. **(C)** Open is the opposite of secretive; forthright is the opposite of snide.

13. **(D)** When you affirm, you are direct—when you hint, you are indirect; when you charge, you are direct—when you insinuate, you are indirect.

14. **(B)** One throws a ball and one shoots a gun.

15. **(E)** A greyhound is proverbially speedy; on the other hand, a sloth is proverbially sluggish.

16. **(E)** A triangle is a three-sided plane figure—a pyramid is a three-sided solid figure; a square is a four-sided plane figure—a box is a four-sided solid figure.

17. **(A)** To impeach is to charge or challenge—if the impeachment proceedings are successful, the charged person is dismissed; to arraign is to call into court as a result of accusation—if the accusation is proved correct, the arraigned person is convicted.

18. **(B)** To emulate is to do things similar to what another person does—to mimic is to do exactly what another person does; to praise is to speak well of another person—to flatter is to praise excessively. Moreover, all four words indicate a favorable attitude toward some person.

19. **(A)** For people the horny sheaths at the end of the hand are called nails; for animals the horny sheaths at the end of the paws are called claws.

20. **(B)** A diamond is a partially "compressed" square; an ellipse is a partially "compressed" circle.

21. **(E)** A woodsman cuts with an axe; a carpenter cuts with a saw.

22. **(E)** Bigotry breeds hatred; fanaticism breeds intolerance.

23. **(E)** When you assist, you help—when you save, you help a great deal; when you request, you ask—when you command, you are very strong in what you ask for.

24. **(C)** 2½ times 2 = 5; 2½ times 6 = 15.

25. **(A)** A doubleheader has two parts—a trident has three teeth; a twin is two of a kind—a troika is a vehicle drawn by three horses.

26. **(D)** A flower is part of a bouquet; a link is part of a chain.

27. **(C)** Letters make up a word; pages make up a book.

28. **(B)** 36 = 9 times 4; 9 = 9 times 1.

29. **(D)** A germ often causes disease; a war often causes destruction.

30. **(B)** The top of the wave is the crest; the top of the mountain is the peak.

TOP SCORES ON READING TESTS

In the following pages you'll find every proven technique for succeeding with the reading comprehension question, the pitfall of many a test-taker. These methods have worked beautifully for thousands of ambitious people and they are certain to help you. They are well worth all the time you can afford to devote to them.

Students must be able to read the paragraphs quickly, and still be able to answer questions correctly. The more correct answers you can give, the better your score will be. But if there are twenty paragraphs, and you are able to finish only ten because you read slowly, obviously, you are going to get a score of 50 percent, even if you answer all the questions correctly. On the other hand, if you finish all the paragraphs but can only answer half of the questions correctly, you will still get only 50 percent. Your goal, then, is to build up enough speed to finish all the paragraphs, and at the same time give as many correct answers as possible.

Our goal is to help you reach your goal—and then some. We want you to get the best score possible on any test of reading comprehension; and we also want you to be able to read with enough speed and understanding so that your studying time is cut in half, and your pleasure reading time is multiplied.

You *can* upgrade your reading ability—but you must have a plan—a procedure—a method. First,

let us understand that there are two aspects of success in reading interpretation:

1. READING SPEED
   and
2. UNDERSTANDING WHAT YOU READ.

But these two aspects are not separate. As a matter of fact, they are totally dependent on each other. You can improve your speed by improving your comprehension—and then your comprehension will improve further because you have improved your speed. What you are improving, therefore, is your *speed of comprehension*. Your eyes and your mind must work together. As your mind begins to look for ideas rather than words, your eyes will begin to obey your mind. Your eyes will start to skim over words, looking for the ideas your mind is telling them to search for. Good reading is good thinking—and a good thinker will be a good reader. Speed and comprehension work together.

For convenience, however, let us divide our discussion into two parts—increasing reading speed and improving reading comprehension.

Increasing Reading Speed

A great many people read very slowly and with little comprehension, yet are completely unaware of just how badly they do read. Some people pronounce the words to themselves as they read, saying each word almost as distinctly as though reading aloud; or they think each one separately.

The reason for this is that many people have not gone quite far enough in their "learning to read" process. When you were first taught to read, you learned the sounds of each letter. Then you learned that if you put the letters together, they would make words. But that is where many people stop. Reading, to them, is reading words. But try reading a sentence out loud, saying each word as

though it were a separate unit. How does it sound? Pretty meaningless! A more mature reader will put words together to make phrases. And the most mature reader will put phrases together to make ideas. A writer uses words to state ideas—and that is what a good reader looks for—those ideas. This will affect the way his eyes work. Let's see how.

HOW YOUR EYES WORK IN READING

As you learn to read phrases and thoughts, you will find that your eyes are increasing their *span*. This means that your eyes are seeing several words at a time as you are reading, not just one.

Your eyes work as a camera does. When you want to take a picture, you hold the camera still and snap the shutter. If you move the camera, the picture will blur. When you read, your eyes take pictures of words—and, like a camera, when they are "photographing," they are standing still. Each time your eyes "picture" words in a line of print, they stop—and each stop is called a *fixation*. Watch someone read, and you will see how his eyes make very quick stops across the line. You know he has finished a line when you see his eyes sweep back to the beginning of the next line.

EYE SPAN AND FIXATION

The more words your eyes take in with one fixation, the larger the eye span. And the larger the eye span, the fewer stops your eyes will have to make across the line. Thus, you will be reading faster.

For example, let's divide a sentence the way a slow, word-by-word reader would:

You/ will/ find/ that/ you/ can/ read/ faster/ if/ you/ per/ mit/ your/ eyes/ to/ see/ large/ thought/ units/.

The reader's eyes have made at least nine stops on each line.

This is the way a fast reader would divide the same sentence:

You will find that/ you can read faster/ if/ you permit/ your eyes to see/ large thought/ units.

This reader's eyes have stopped only three times on each line, so of course he will be able to read much faster. Also, reading thought units will enable him to grasp the meaning more effectively. Now here are some exercises to help you increase your eye span.

EXERCISES FOR INCREASING EYE-SPAN

1.

```
0...............0...............0...............0
0...............0...............0...............0
0...............0...............0...............0
0...............0...............0...............0
0...............0...............0...............0
0...............0...............0...............0
```

In the above "paragraph," the dots stand for letters and each 0 is one eye fixation. "Read" a line, forcing your eyes to shift from 0 to 0. When you finish the first line, let your eyes swing back to the next line. Try to get an even rhythm. Now you can feel what your eyes should be doing as they read a line in four fixations. Is this different from the way they usually feel when you read? Keep practicing this "paragraph" until it feels comfortable, and then try to read a line of print in the same way. You can make up your own "paragraph" with only three fixations and practice.

2. Here is a list of three-word phrases, with a line drawn down the center. Focus your eyes on the line, and look at the three words at once. Remember, only *one* fixation. Do not read each word separately. If you have trouble at first, read the phrases through once in your usual way, and then practice the one fixation.

at the store
day and night
box of candy
come with me
in the house
bring my paper
time to finish
make every effort
all the questions
read very fast

3. Choose a newspaper column on a subject that interests you, and read it through. Then draw two vertical lines equally distant from each other down the center. Reread the column fixating on first one vertical line, then the next—two fixations per line. When you get very good at this, try drawing just one line down the center and fixating once. You can practice this daily.

VOCALIZING CAN SLOW YOU DOWN

Some readers move their lips or whisper while they read "silently." This habit is called vocalizing. It is caused by the fact that your earliest reading was done aloud, and the habit of hearing each word as you read it, persists.

It would be physically impossible for you to speak at the rate of speed at which a good reader can read—say 350 words per minute. And if you could, no one could understand you. If you read only as fast as you can talk, you will never be a fast reader.

Obviously, then, you must stop vocalizing. Your

lips and vocal cords must not be permitted to interfere in the exchange of ideas between eyes and mind. Even if you are not obviously vocalizing, you may be subvocalizing. Your lips are not moving, your vocal cords are not involved, but you are hearing each word as you read it. This is as much a deterrent to reading speed as actual vocalizing. Most people *do* subvocalize.

HOW TO STOP VOCALIZING

1. Put your fingers on your lips. Make sure your lips do not move as you read. If they do, put a pencil or a rubber eraser between your teeth. Then read. If you start to vocalize, the pencil will drop out. If you are reading in public you might be embarrassed to appear with a pencil in your mouth. In that case, just clench your teeth hard—and keep reading.

2. Only *you* will know if you are subvocalizing—and be honest with yourself. If you are subvocalizing (and you probably are) try this exercise. Before you start to read, repeat these nonsense syllables to yourself for 30 seconds: da-rum, da-rum, da-rum, da-rum, etc. Now begin to read and continue to repeat da-rum as you read. If you are doing this, then you cannot subvocalize what you are reading. At first you will find this extremely difficult to do, but if you keep practicing, soon you will find that there is a direct connection between written word and thought—with no intervening vocalizing.

VARY YOUR READING SPEED

One should adjust his reading speed to what he is reading. Some paragraphs will be easier for you than others, possibly because you are more interested in the subject matter, or know something about it. Other paragraphs, particularly those that deal with factual or technical material, may have to be read more slowly.

Flexibility should be employed so that the reader will change his speed from paragraph to paragraph—even from sentence to sentence, just as a driver would vary his driving speed depending on where he is driving. Some passages are open highways while others are crowded city thoroughfares.

For example, read the following passage:

It was a sunny Sunday afternoon in December. Some people were at the movies; some were out walking; and some were at home listening to the radio. Suddenly an announcement was broadcast—and the United States was plunged into war.

On December 7, 1941, the Japanese Air Force attacked Pearl Harbor, destroying battleships, aircraft carriers, planes, and a strategic military base, leaving the United States without the military arsenals needed for anti-aircraft activity and civilian protecton.

Which of these paragraphs is the "highway"? Which is the crowded city thoroughfare? Where can you breeze through? Where will you need to slow down to absorb every detail. You're right! The first paragraph is a simple introduction. A glance should suffice. The second paragraph is fact-packed, so you will need to slow down.

OTHER PHYSICAL FACTORS

Don't neglect the obvious reading aids. Good eyesight is essential. When was your last eye checkup? If glasses were prescribed, are you using them? Make sure that you are physically comfortable, sitting erect wlth head slightly inclined. You should have good direct and indirect light, with the direct light coming from behind you and slightly above your shoulder. Hold your reading matter at your own best reading distance so that you don't have to stoop or squint.

FORCE YOURSELF TO FASTER READING

Now that you know the elements that make for fast reading, you must continue to force yourself to read as quickly as you can. Use a stop-watch to time yourself. You can figure your rate of speed by dividing the number of words on a page into the number of seconds it took you to read it, and then multiplying by 60. This will give you your rate in words-per-minute. Since no one rate of speed is possible for all reading material, your rate will vary. But an average reading speed of 350 words-per-minute should be possible for uncomplicated, interesting, straightforward material. If you are already reading that fast, then try for 500 words-per-minute. You should be able to answer correctly at least 80 per cent of the questions following a reading passage.

Practice reading quickly. Move your eyes rapidly across the line of type, skimming it. Don't permit your eyes to stop for individual words. Proceed quickly through the paragraph without backtracking. If you think you don't understand what you are reading, then reread two or three times—but always read quickly. You will be amazed to discover how much you actually do understand.

Improving Reading Comprehension

Many readers are afraid of not understanding what they read quickly. But the old idea that slow readers make up for their slowness by better comprehension of what they read has been proven untrue. Your ability to comprehend what you read will keep pace with your increase in speed. You will absorb as many ideas per page as before, and get many more ideas per unit of reading time.

It has been demonstrated that those who read quickly also read best. This is probably due to the fact that heavier concentration is required for rapid reading; and concentration is what enables a reader to grasp important ideas contained in the reading material.

GETTING THE MAIN IDEA

A good paragraph generally has one central thought—and that thought is usually stated in one sentence. That sentence, the *topic sentence,* is often the first sentence of the paragraph, but it is sometimes buried in the middle, or it can be at the end. Your main task is to locate that sentence and absorb the thought it contains while reading the paragraph. The correct interpretation of the paragraph is based on that thought *as it is stated,* and not on your personal opinion, prejudice, or preference about that thought.

Here are several examples of paragraphs. Read them quickly and see if you can pick out the topic sentence. It is the key sentence. The rest of the paragraph either supports or illustrates it. The answers follow the paragraphs.

1. Pigeon fanciers are firmly convinced that modern inventions can never replace the carrier pigeon. "A pigeon gets through when everything else fails," they say. In World War II, one pigeon flew twenty miles in twenty minutes to cancel the bombing of a town. Radios may get out of order and telephone lines may get fouled up, but the pigeon is always ready to take off with a message.

2. When a piece of paper burns, it is completely changed. The ash that is left behind does not look like the original piece of paper. When dull-red rust appears on a piece of tinware, it is quite different from the gleaming tin. The tarnish that forms on silverware is a new substance unlike the silver itself. Animal tissue is unlike the vegetable substance from which it is made. A change in which the original substance is turned into a different substance is called a chemical change.

3. A child who stays up too late is often too tired to be successful in school. A child who is allowed to eat anything he wishes may have bad teeth and even suffer from malnutrition. Children who are rude and disorderly often suffer pangs of guilt. Children who are disciplined are happy children. They blossom in an atmosphere where they know exactly what is expected of them. This provides them with a sense of order, a feeling of security.

Answers: In paragraph 1, the first sentence is the topic sentence. In paragraph 2, the last sentence is the topic sentence. In paragraph 3, it is the fourth sentence—"Children who are disciplined. . . . .".

If a selection consists of two or more paragraphs, the correct interpretation is based on the central idea of the entire passage. The ability to grasp the central idea of a passage can be acquired by practice—practice that will also increase the speed with which you read.

Reading for a Purpose—The Survey Method

Many readers don't know what they are looking for when they read. They plunge into a page full of words, and often that is what they end up with —just words. It's like walking into a supermarket without having made a list of what you want to buy. You wander aimlessly up and down the aisles and end up with a basketful of cookies and fruit and pickles—and nothing for a main dish.

It is extremely important to have a purpose in mind *before* you start to read—to make a "list" before you start shopping. Good readers use the *survey* method. By "survey" we mean a quick over-view of what you are going to read before you actually start reading. It is like looking at a road map before you start on a trip. If you know in what direction you are going, you are apt to get there sooner, and more efficiently. This is what you do.

1. Read the title. Think about what the selection will probably be about. What kind of information can you expect to obtain? Gear your mind to look for the central thought.

2. Think about the kind of vocabulary you will meet. Will it be technical? Are you familiar with the subject, or will you have to prepare yourself to meet many new words? After a quick glance, you may decide to skip this selection and go back to it later. (Remember, on a timed reading test you want to give yourself a chance to sample *all* the selections. The one at the end may be easier for you than the one in the middle, but you won't know if you never get to the end.) The difficulty of the vocabulary may be the deciding factor.

3. If there are subheadings, read them. They can provide a skeleton outline of the selection.

4. Read the first sentence of each paragraph. It usually contains the most important ideas in the selection. The topic sentence is more often found in the beginning of a paragraph than in any other position.

5. READ THE QUESTIONS BASED ON THE SELECTION. The questions are there to test whether or not you understand the most important ideas in the selection. If you read them first, they will steer you through your reading in the most effective way possible. Now you really know what to look for! In any kind of reading, whether on test or in texts, always look at the questions first (unless you are directed not to do so).

The survey method can be applied to all kinds of reading, particularly textbook reading. In addition to the above, you should include the following in your textbook survey:

(a) Read the preface quickly. It states the author's purpose in writing the book.

(b) Look at the publication date (on the copyright page). This can tell you if the information is up-to-date.

(c) Look through the table of contents. See what the author has included, and the order in which it appears. Some tables of contents can serve as an outline for the book.

(d) If there are chapter or part summaries, read through them quickly. They'll give you a forecast of what's to come.

(e) Look at illustrations, maps, graphs, etc. These are meant to help you visualize essential information. Remember, one picture can be worth a thousand words.

Increase Your Vocabulary

In order to understand what you are reading, you must know the meaning of the words that are used. Very often you can guess at the meaning from the rest of the sentence, but that method is not completely reliable. The sentence itself is important for determining which of the word's several meanings is intended, but you usually have to have some idea of the word itself.

How can you build a larger vocabulary? You could sit down with a long list of words and try to memorize it, or perhaps go through the diction- ary page by page. This would be very time consuming—and very boring! Memorizing words is probably the *least* successful way of building a vocabulary.

Words are best remembered when they are understood and used, when they are part of your own experience. Here are some ways in which you can do this.

1. Learn a little etymology. You already know a lot, because approximately 70 per cent of the words we use consist of roots and prefixes de-

rived from Latin and Greek. There are 84 roots and 44 prefixes that are the mainstay of our language. If you learn those you will have a clue to the meaning of thousands of words. For example, the Latin root *voc* (meaning "to call") appears in the words advocate, vocation, irrevocable, vociferous, etc. The root *port* (meaning "to carry") is found in the words report, export, support, porter, etc.

Learn to look for the roots of words, and for familiar parts of words you meet.

2. Read—everything, anything. Even signs and posters sometimes have new words in them. Try to find at least one new word every day.

3. Use the dictionary—frequently and extensively. Look up the meaning of a word you don't know, and see if you can identify its root.

4. Play word games—like Anagrams, Scrabble. And do Crossword Puzzles.

5. Listen to people who speak well. Don't be afraid to ask them the meaning of a word they use that is unfamiliar to you. They'll be flattered.

6. Make a personal word list of your new words. Make it on index cards so that you can play a "flash-card" game with yourself.

7. Look for special word meanings in special subject areas. Since most reading comprehension passages deal with science, literature, or social studies, a weakness in the vocabulary used in these subjects can put you at a great disadvantage. Be sure you know the meaning of the terms that are frequently used.

8. Use the new words you learn each day. Don't save them for a rainy day—by then they may be lost. When you talk or write, try to use as many new words as you can. A word used is a word remembered!

Cues and Clues For Readers

Examination points may be unnecessarily lost by ignoring the author's hints as to what *he* thinks is most important. Be on the lookout for such phrases as "Note that . . ." "Of importance is . . ." "Don't overlook . . ." These give clues to what the writer is stressing. Beware of negatives and all-inclusive statements. They are often put in to trip you up. Words like *always, never, all, only, every, absolutely, completely, none, entirely, no,* can sometimes turn a reasonable statement into an untrue statement. For example look at the following sentence:

When you get caught in the rain, you catch cold.
True? Of course. Now look at this sentence:
When you get caught in the rain, you *always* catch cold.
Different, isn't it? Not *always* true.

PUNCTUATION

Other hints which you should also watch for are those given by punctuation. Here are a few points to keep in mind:

1. QUOTATION MARKS—When a statement is quoted, it may not necessarily represent the author's opinion, or the main thought of the passage. Be sure you make this distinction if it is called for.

2. EXCLAMATION POINT—This mark is often used to indicate an *emphatic* or *ironical* comment. It's the author's way of saying, "This is important!"

3. COMMAS—Watch those commas. They can change the meaning of a sentence. For example:

As I left the room, in order to go to school John called me.

As I left the room in order to go to school, John called me.

In each sentence, a different person is going to school.

4. PARENTHESES—These are often used to set off a part of the sentence that is not absolutely necessary to the sentence. But don't ignore them in reading comprehension tests. Sometimes they give vital information. For example:

Shakespeare (whose life spanned the sixteenth and seventeenth centuries) was a great dramatist.

5. COLON—Often used to emphasize a sequence in thought between two independent sentences. For example:

Science plays an important role in our civilization: thus we should all study physics, chemistry, and biology.

6. ELLIPSES—Three dots often found in quoted material which indicates that there has been an omission of material from the original quotation. Often the material omitted is not important, but a good, critical reader should be aware of the omission.

A Systematic Plan

You can't sit down the night before a test in reading comprehension and "cram" for it. The only way you can build up your reading skill is to practice systematically. The gains you make will show up not only in an increased score on a reading comprehension test, but also in your reading for study and pleasure.

Trying to change reading habits that you have had for a long time can be difficult and discouraging. Do not attempt to apply *all* of the suggestions we have given to *all* your reading *all* at once. Try to follow a program like the one below.

1. Set aside 15 minutes a day to practice new reading techniques.

2. Start off with a short, easy-to-read article for a magazine or newspaper—and time yourself. At the end of your practice session, time yourself on another short article, and keep a record of both times.

3. Select a news story. Read it first, and then practice an eye-span exercise. Work towards reducing your eye fixations to no more than two for a line, the width of a newspaper column.

4. Read an editorial, book review, or movie or drama review in a literate magazine or newspaper. This type of article always expresses the author's (or the paper's) point of view and is therefore good practice for searching out the main idea. After you read, see whether you can write a good title for the article and jot down in one sentence the author's main idea. Also, you can try making up a question based on the article with five alternate answers (the kind you find on reading comprehension tests). This is excellent practice for determining main ideas, and you can use the questions to test your friends.

5. Find one new word and write the sentence in which it appears. Guess at its meaning from the context. Then look up the definition in a dictionary and try to make up a sentence of your own, using the word. Then try to use the word in your conversation at least twice the following day.

If you follow this program daily, you will soon find that you can extend to more and more reading the skills you are building, and your reading comprehension test score will show the great gains you have made.

Sample Questions Analyzed

Here is a sample question followed by an analysis. Try to understand the process of arriving at the correct answer.

(Reading Passage)

"Too often, indeed, have scurrilous and offensive allegations by underworld creatures been sufficient to blast the career of irreproachable and incorruptible executives who, because of their efforts to serve the people honestly and faithfully, incurred the enmity of powerful political forces and lost their positions."

Judging from the contents of the preceding paragraph, you might best conclude that

(A) the larger majority of executives are irreproachable and incorruptible

(B) criminals blast executives with machine guns and kill their careers

(C) political forces are always clashing with government executives

(D) underworld creatures make scurrilous and offensive allegations against incorruptible executives

(E) false statements by criminals sometimes cause honest officials the loss of their positions or the ruin of their careers.

Analysis of Choices

(A) This statement is probably true, and you may agree with it—*but* it is not stated in the paragraph. Remember, no personal opinions. Just deal with the facts.

(B) This is ridiculous and far-fetched.

(C) This choice is not stated in the paragraph at all. The catch-word "always" makes this choice entirely invalid.

(D) This is stated in the paragraph, and is true. However, in the paragraph the qualifying words "too often" are used, which limit the scope of the statement. Also, this choice does not quite summarize the entire central thought of the passage—it is too narrow. We must look further.

(E) This choice is open to no exceptions and accurately sums up the entire central thought of the paragraph. It is the best conclusion that could be drawn in the light of the five choices given.

STEPS TO BETTER READING COMPREHENSION SCORES

Here are five success steps to use when working out any reading comprehension question. If you apply them calmly, you should come up with the right answer most of the time.

1. Survey Selection

Read the entire selection quickly to get the general sense and main idea.

2. Survey Stems

Read the stem of each question (Don't look at the five possible choices of answers yet).

3. Reread Selectively

Reread the selection, concentrating on the parts which seem to be related to the questions.

4. Concentrate on Each Question

Now look at the first question with its five possible answers and eliminate any answer which is far-fetched, ridiculous, irrelevant, false, or impossible. Cross out the answers you have eliminated. You should be left with two or three answers that seem possible.

5. Shuttle Back to Selection

Reread only the part of the selection that applies to the question, and make your decision as to the correct choice based on these considerations:

(a) A choice must be based on fact actually given or definitely understood (and not on your personal opinion or prejudice.) Some questions require making a judgment—and this judgment also must be based on the facts as given.

(b) In questions involving the central thought of the passage (for example: "The best title for this selection . . .") the choice must accurately reflect the entire thought—not too narrow, and not too general.

(c) Remember, some choices have trick expressions or catch-words in them which sometimes destroy the validity of a seemingly acceptable answer. These include expressions like *under all circumstances, at all times, never, always, under no conditions, absolutely, completely, entirely, every, no.* Watch for these carefully.

USING "SUCCESS STEPS" ON A PRACTICE QUESTION

Now let us take an actual exam-type question and apply the five success steps as well as our question analysis skills for a demonstration analysis.

(Reading Passage)

Vacations were once the prerogative of the privileged few, even as late as the 19th century. Now they are considered the right of all, except for such unfortunate masses as, for example, the bulk of China's and India's population, for whom life, save for sleep and brief periods of rest, is uninterrupted toil.

They are more necessary now than once because the average life is less well-rounded and has become increasingly departmentalized. I suppose the idea of vacations, as we conceive it, must be incomprehensible to primitive peoples. Rest of some kind has of course always been a part of the rhythm of human life, but earlier ages did not find it necessary to organize it in the way that modern man has done. Holidays, feast days, were sufficient.

With modern man's increasing tensions, with the stultifying quality of so much of his work, this break in the year's routine became steadily more necessary. Vacations became mandatory for the purpose of renewal and repair. And so it came about that in the United States, the most self-indulgent of nations, the tensest and most departmentalized, vacations have come to take a predominant place in domestic conversation.

1. The title below that best expresses the ideas of this passage is:
    A. Vacation Preferences
    B. Vacations: the Topic of Conversation
    C. Vacations in Perspective
    D. The Well-Organized Vacation
    E. Renewal, Refreshment and Repair

2. We need vacations now more than ever before because we have
    A. a more carefree nature
    B. much more free time
    C. little diversity in our work
    D. no emotional stability
    E. a higher standard of living

3. It is implied in the passage that the lives of Americans are very
    A. habitual   C. patriotic
    B. ennobling   D. varied
              E. independent

4. As used in the passage, the word "prerogative" (line 1) most nearly means
    A. habit   C. request
    B. distinction   D. demand
            E. hope

STEP-BY-STEP EXPLANATIONS

STEP 1—We read the selection through quickly to get the general sense.

STEP 2—*We read the stem of each question.*

STEP 3—*We reread the passage selectively* and note that the answer to Question 1 involves the entire selection; the answer to Question 2 is in the first sentence of paragraph 2; the answer to Question 3 lies in paragraph 3; and the answer to Question 4 is in the beginning of paragraph 1.

STEP 4—*Concentrate on each question.* We now consider Question 1 and the five answer choices. We bear in mind that the selection has to do with vacations and man's growing need for them, so that the title we select must reflect that idea. We can eliminate Choice A—the selection does not deal with vacation preferences. Choice B—vaca-

tions as a topic of conversation—should also be eliminated as this is a lesser detail and not the whole main idea. Choice C looks like a possibility, but there may be a better choice, so we will look further. Choice D is completely irrelevant, for the passage does not in any way deal with the organization of a vacation. Choice E, while reflecting part of the idea of the passage, does not encompass the historical scope. Therefore, we go back to Choice C, which is direct and all-inclusive, and the best of the five possible choices.

Explanation of Question

We concentrate on Question 2 and its five possible answers. We remember that first reading indicated that the answer to this question is in the beginning of paragraph 2, so we reread just that part of the selection, which deals with the necessity or need of vacations. Choice A is irrelevant and ridiculous, and we eliminate it. Choice B may be a true statement, but it does not pertain to the *need* for vacations. Choice C looks like a good possibility, because a less well-rounded life that is increasingly departmentalized indicates little diversity—but better to check further. We eliminate Choice D immediately because of the word "no," one of our trick expressions. Choice E, like Choice B, does not refer to need. So we return to Choice C as the best possible answer.

Explanation of Question

We concentrate on Question 3 with its five possible answers, remembering that the answer is to be found in paragraph 3—so we go directly to that paragraph. The word "implied" in the stem of the question tells us that we may not find a direct answer but will have to do some thinking. The paragraph tells us that much work is stultifying, that there is much routine, and that vacations are necessary for renewal and repair. We can conclude, then, that life is pretty dull and we will look at the choices to find a word that is synonymous with "dull." Choice A is certainly a possibility, but we look quickly at the remaining choices just to be sure, and discover that there is no other possible choice; B, C, and E are irrelevant, and D is the exact opposite. Choice A is our answer.

Explanation of Question

Concentrating on Question 4 we find that it calls for the definition of a word which is located in line 1, so we go to that portion of the paragraph. Word definitions can often be answered by a careful reading of the sentence in which the word appears, and often the following sentence as well. If we read the sentence in which "prerogative" appears and look at the five possible answers, any one of them might be correct. However, if we read the first part of the second sentence in paragraph 1, we see the clue word *now*. In other words, at this time, as contrasted with the past, vacations are the right of all instead of the right of a few. We can thus conclude that the word "prerogative" is synonymous with the word "right." We look at the five possible choices in this light. We can eliminate A and E immediately since they are in no way synonymous with "right."

Choice C, while a possible synonym, is really too mild a word if we substitute it in the sentence. Choices B and D are possible, with Choice D seeming to be the most likely. But if we substitute it in the sentence for the word prerogative, it does not make as much sense as does Choice B, for vacations were not actually a demand of the privileged few—but more a distinction. Since the stem of our question asks for the nearest meaning, we can be most comfortable in choosing B.

STEP 5—*Shuttle back to the selection*. We check to see that we have answered each question and marked the answer in accordance with the directions specified at the beginning of the examination.

If you follow the outlined procedure for answering reading comprehension questions, you will find that you are answering questions correctly and quickly. Most passages will require at least two readings—one for general sense and one for answering the questions. The important thing is to know where to spot the answers, and to remain calm and collected when examining the possible choices. Don't panic—you can be pretty sure that if a question is hard for you it will be hard for everyone else, too.

BUSINESS DEFINITIONS

This is some of the language you're likely to see on your examination. You may not need to know all the words in this carefully prepared glossary, but if even a few appear, you'll be that much ahead of your competitors. Perhaps the greater benefit from this list is the frame of mind it can create for you. Without reading a lot of technical text you'll steep yourself in just the right atmosphere for high test marks.

A GLOSSARY FOR TEST TAKERS

ABATEMENT. A deduction or allowance, as, a discount given for prompt payment.

ACCOUNT. A detailed statement of items affecting property or claims, listed respectively as Debits or Credits, and showing excess of Debits or Credits in form of a balance. Sufficient explanatory matter should be given to set forth the complete history of the account. There need not be both Debits and Credits, nor more than one of either of these. If Debits and Credits, or both are made frequently, the account is active. Items held in suspense awaiting future classification or allocation may be charged or credited to an adjustment account. When desirable to keep a separate accounting for specific shipments of goods, it is known as an Adventure Account. If more than one party is interested in such shipment, it is a joint venture account.

Asset Accounts record value owned.

Book Accounts are kept in books, and show in formal manner the details regarding transactions between parties. To be of legal effect the entries must be original, not transferred or posted.

Capital Accounts show the amounts invested in an enterprise either net, as in case of the Capital Accounts of proprietors, partners, and stockholders shown on the liability side of Balance Sheets; or gross, as in case of the Asset Accounts which show both owned and borrowed Capital invested.

Cash Accounts set forth receipts and disbursements of cash as well as balance on hand at beginning and end of period.

Clearing Accounts are employed to collect items preliminary to their allocation to a more detailed classification of the accounts, or preliminary to the determination of the accounts to which such items properly belong.

Contingent Accounts are those which list liabilities or assets dependent for their validity upon some event which may or may not occur.

Contra Accounts are those which offset each other.

Controlling Accounts are those which summarize and afford an independent check upon detailed accounts of a given class which are usually kept in a subordinate ledger. The controlling accounts are kept in the General Ledger. The balance of the controlling account equals the aggregate of the balances of the detailed accounts when all postings affecting these accounts are completed.

Current Accounts are open or running accounts not balanced or stated.

S1528

Deficiency Accounts supplement statements of affairs of an insolvent enterprise, showing what items comprise the deficiency of assets subject to lien for payment of unsecured creditors.

Depreciation Accounts are expense accounts which are charged periodically with the amounts credited to the respective Depreciation Reserve Accounts.

Depreciation Reserve Accounts are credited periodically with the amounts charged to contra depreciation expense accounts. Depreciation Reserve Accounts are valuation accounts because they supplement or evaluate the asset accounts for the ultimate replacement of which they are intended.

Discount Accounts are: accounts which are either charged with discounts allowed to customers or credited with discounts secured from creditors; or accounts which are charged with amounts paid to have Notes Discounted; or accounts which are carried unamortized differences between par of Bonds sold and the amounts realized at time of sale, such amounts realized being less than the par of the Bonds.

Dividend Accounts are credited with amounts declared payable as dividends by boards of directors. These accounts are charged for amounts disbursed in payment, the charge being made either at time checks are sent out and for full amount of dividend, or for the amounts of the individual checks as they are returned for payment.

Impersonal Accounts record expenses and revenues, assets and liabilities, but do not make reference to persons in their titles.

Income Accounts show sources and amounts of operating revenues, expenses incurred for operations, sources and amounts of non-operating revenues, fixed charges, net income and disposition thereof.

Investment Accounts record property owned but not used for operating purposes.

Liability Accounts record value owed.

Merchandise Accounts are charged with cost of buying goods and crediting with sales, thus exhibiting Gross Profit when opening and closing inventories are taken into consideration.

Nominal Accounts are those which, during the accounting period, record changes which affect proprietorship favorably or unfavorably.

Open Accounts are those not balanced or closed.

Personal Accounts are those with individuals, usually customers and creditors.

Profit and Loss Account is an account into which all earnings and expenses are closed.

Real Accounts record Assets and Liabilities.

Revenue Accounts are equivalent to nominal accounts, showing income and expense.

Sales Accounts are rendered by agents to principals in explanation of consigned goods sold.

Sinking Fund Accounts record periodic installments paid into sinking funds and interest accretions added thereto.

Surplus Accounts record accretions to capital from profits.

ACCOUNTING. The science of accounts, their construction, classification and interpretation.

ACCRUE. Accumulation of wealth or liabilities based on passage of time.

ACCRUED EXPENSE. A liability representing expense that has accrued but is not yet due and payable. It is in reality postpaid expense, and therefore the opposite of prepaid expense, which is an asset.

ACCRUED INCOME. Income that has accrued but is not yet due. It is in reality postpaid income, and therefore the opposite of prepaid income, which is a liability.

AGENT. One possessing authority to act for another to a more or less limited extent.

ALLOCATION. Determination of the proper distribution of a given sum among a series of accounts.

AMORTIZATION. Extinction of a debt by systematic application of installments to a sinking fund, or reduction of premiums or discount incurred on sale or purchase of bonds by application of the effective interest rate.

ANNUITY. A sum of money payable periodically in installments.

APPRECIATION. Increase in value of assets.

ASSET. Wealth owned. Assets may be classified in various ways. From the point of view of ease of liquidation they are Quick or Fixed in varying degrees.

AUDIT. Verification of the accuracy of account books by examination of supporting vouchers, making tests of postings and computations and determining whether all entries are made according to correct accounting principles making sure that there are no omissions.

BALANCE. The excess of the sum of the items on one side of an account over the sum of the items on the other side.

BALANCE SHEET. A schedule of Assets and Liabilities so classified and arranged as to enable an intelligent study to be made of the important financial ratios existing between different classes of assets, between different classes of liabilities and between assets and liabilities; also to enable one to observe the origin of the equity existing in the assets and to determine to whom it belongs.

BOND. A bond is a written promise under seal to pay a certain sum of money at a specified time. Bonds bear interest at a fixed rate, usually payable semiannually. Bonds may be sold either above or below par, in which case the coupon rate of interest differs from the effective rate when the bonds are sold below par and higher when bonds are sold above par.

BURDEN. Elements of production cost which, not being directly allocable to output, must be distributed on more or less arbitrary basis.

CAPITAL. In accounting, capital is excess of assets over liabilities of a given enterprise.

Fixed Capital consists of wealth in form of land, buildings, machinery, furniture and fixtures, etc.

Floating Capital is capital which can be readily converted into cash.

Nominal Capital is the authorized capital stock of a corporation.

Paid-Up Capital is the amount of capital stock issued and fully paid.

Working Capital is the excess of current assets over current liabilities.

CASH. All forms of exchange media which by custom are received in settlement of debts.

CHARGES. Items debited in accounts.

CHECK OR CHECQUE. See Draft.

COLLATERAL SECURITY. Personal property transferred by the owner to another to secure the carrying out of an obligation.

CONSIGNEE. An agent who receives shipments of goods from his principal to be sold on commission basis, title to goods remaining in the principal or consignor.

CONSIGNMENT. A shipment of goods to another and held by him for account of the principal or consignor.

CONSIGNOR. One who ships goods to an agent or factor who holds them for account of the principal or consignor.

CONSOLIDATION. Unification or affiliation of enterprises engaged in competitive or supplementary undertakings.

CONTINGENT. That which depends upon some happening or occurence; doubtful, conditional.

CORPORATION. An artificial person created by law to carry out a certain purpose or purposes.

COST. Cost is the outlay, usually measured in terms of money, necessary to buy or to produce a commodity. The two elements of Cost are Prime Cost and Overhead or Burden. Prime Cost is the outlay on direct labor and raw materials necessary to produce a commodity. Burden includes all elements of Cost other than direct labor and raw materials.

COST ACCOUNTING. Determination, by means of applying accounting principles, of the elements of Cost entering into the production of a commodity or service.

CREDITOR. One who gives credit in business matters; one to whom money is due.

DEBT. An obligation to pay money or that which one owes to another.

DEBTOR. One who owes money.

DEFERRED ASSET OR CHARGE. See Prepaid Expense.

DEFERRED CREDIT & INCOME OR LIABILITY. See Prepaid Income.

DEFICIENCY. Insufficiency of assets to discharge debts or other obligations.

DEPRECIATION. Decline in value of assets resulting from one or more of the following:

1. Wear and tear.
2. Tenure of holding.

3. Permanency or steadiness of industry.
4. Exhaustion of raw materials.
5. Obsolescence.
6. Accidents.
7. Fluctuations in trade.
8. Inadequacy.

DISBURSEMENTS. Cash payments.

DISCOUNT. Deduction from a listed or named figure, usually computed on a percentage basis.

DIVIDEND. Division of profits among stockholders on a pro rata basis.

DRAFT. A draft or bill of exchange is defined by Uniform Negotiable Instrument Law as, "an unconditional order in writing addressed by one person to another, signed by the person giving it, requiring the person to whom it is addressed to pay on demand or at a fixed or determinable future time a certain sum in money to order or to bearer."

DRAWEE. The person against whom a draft is drawn and who becomes primarily liable upon acceptance.

DRAWER. The maker of a draft or bill of exchange.

ENTRY. Written description of a business transaction or adjustment made in books of accounts.

ESTATE. A right of ownership in property.

FIXED ASSETS. Those assets which are not readily convertible into cash and in the usual routine of business are not so converted.

FRANCHISE. A privilege or liberty given by the Government to certain individuals.

GOOD WILL. Present right to receive expected future superprofits, superprofits being the amount by which future profits are expected to exceed all economic expenditure incident to its production.

IMPREST SYSTEM. Plan used to account for petty cash disbursements whereby the cashier is at intervals reimbursed for the amount disbursed by him through a check drawn to Cash and charged to the accounts against which such disbursements were made.

INCOME. A flow of benefits from wealth over a period of time.

INTEREST. Expense or income resulting from use of wealth over a period of time.

INVENTORY. An itemized list of goods giving amounts and prices.

INVOICE. A statement issued by a seller of goods to the purchaser giving details regarding quantities, prices and terms of payment.

JOURNAL. The book of original entry in double entry bookkeeping.

Cash Journal is a combination cash book and journal, containing columns for both cash and non-cash transactions.

Purchases Journal records purchases made and the names of persons credited therefor.

Sales Journal records sales and the names of persons charged therefor.

LEDGER. A ledger is the book in which transactions are classified according to function. When subordinate ledgers are used, the General Ledger becomes a digest of details kept in subordinate ledgers, as well as the record of all usual ledger accounts.

Accounts Receivable Ledger contains a record of all transactions affecting trade debtors.

Accounts Payable Ledger contains a record of all transactions affecting trade creditors.

LIABILITY. A debt.

Capital Liabilities are those which are incurred in the acquisition of permanent assets, and which are usually in form on bonded indebtedness having a maturity date removed more than a year.

Contingent Liability are those which may or may not become definite obligations, depending upon some event.

Current Liability are those which will fall due within a period of a year.

Deferred Liability are income received but not yet due; see Prepaid Income.

Fixed Liability are those in form of bonds or long term notes.

NOTES PAYABLE. The sum of all notes and acceptances upon which a concern is primarily liable as maker, endorser or acceptor.

NOTES RECEIVABLE. The sum of all notes and acceptances upon which others are liable to the holding concern.

NOTES RECEIVABLE DISCOUNTED. Contingent Liability for all notes receivable discounted at bank but not yet liquidated by the makers.

OVERDRAFT. A debit balance in a deposit account which should normally have a credit balance.

POSTING. Transferring items from journals to ledgers, and making the necessary cross-references in folio columns.

PREMIUM ON BONDS. Amount above par at which bonds are bought or sold.

PREPAID EXPENSE. An asset representing expenditures for services not yet rendered. Also known as Deferred Charge or Deferred Asset.

PREPAID INCOME. Income received for services not yet rendered. It is therefore a liability. Also known as Deferred Credit or Deferred Liability.

PROFIT. Increase in net worth resulting from business operations.

PROPRIETORSHIP. Equity in assets over and above liability.

QUICK ASSETS. Assets that can ordinarily be readily converted into cash without involving heavy loss.

RESERVE. A segregation of surplus, or a retention of revenues equivalent to losses in asset values. In the former case it is a reserve of surplus, in the latter case, a valuation reserve.

RESERVE FUND. An amount set aside in form of cash or investments for general or special purposes.

REVENUE. Income from all sources.

SINKING FUND. An amount set aside in form of cash or investments for the purpose of liquidating some liability.

STATEMENT. To set forth in systematic form all data with reference to some phase of a business undertaking. To present essential details, subordinate schedules are frequently appended. A statement of Assets and Liabilities.

Balance Sheets set forth the status of a business as of a given date.
Consolidated Balance Sheets set forth the status of affiliated businesses as of a given time.

Consolidated Income Statements set forth the results of operations of affiliated enterprises over a period.

Income Statements set forth the result of operations over a period.

Statement of Affairs set forth the status of an insolvent business as of a given time, the arrangement being such as to show both book value of assets, what they are expected to realize and gross liabilities, how they are expected to rank.

STOCK. Share issued by a corporation, evidenced by formal certificates representing ownership therein. The total amount of such shares is known as the Capital Stock of the corporation.

Common Stock is that upon which dividends are paid only after dividend requirements on preferred stock and interest requirements on bonds are met.

Donated Stock is stock of a corporation which has been given back to be sold at a discount, usually to afford working capital in cases where the stock was originally issued in payment for fixed assets.

Guaranteed Stock is that which is guaranteed as to principal or interest or both by some other corporation or corporations.

Inactive Stock is that which is seldom traded on the exchange.

Preferred Stock is that which has prior rights over common stock either as to dividends or assets or both. Various provisions are found relative to the voting power, as for example, the preferred stock may be given control of the corporation if dividends thereon remain unpaid for two consecutive years. In case of cumulative preferred stock, unpaid dividends become a lien upon profits of following years.

Treasury Stock is that which has been returned to the treasury of the issuing corporation.

Unissued Stock is the excess of Authorized over Issued Stock.

STOCK BONUSES. Gifts of stock offered to furnish incentive to investors to buy some other security of the issuing company.

STOCK RIGHTS. Privileges extended to stockholders to subscribe to new stock at a price below the market value of outstanding stock.

STOCK SUBSCRIPTIONS. Agreements to purchase the stock of a corporation. They become effective only when ratified by the corporation, unless accepted by a trustee in behalf of the corporation.

SURPLUS. In case of corporations having only par value stock, surplus ordinarily measures excess of net worth or proprietorship over par value of stock outstanding.

Capital Surplus is that derived from extraordinary sources, as sale of stock at premium or sale of fixed assets at a profit.

Surplus from Operations is that derived from undertakings from the carrying out of which the business was established.

TRIAL BALANCE. A list of balances of all General Ledger accounts made to determine the correctness of postings from books of original entry as well as the correctness of the work of determining these balances.

TURNOVER. Rapidity of replacement of capital invested in inventories, accounts receivable, etc.

VOUCHER. Any document which serves as proof of a transaction.

VOUCHER SYSTEM. A scheme of accounting under which distribution of all expenditures is made on vouchers preliminary to their entry in the voucher register.

WORK IN PROCESS. Materials in process of manufacture, partly finished goods including all material, labor and overhead costs incurred on those goods up to the time of taking inventory.

GRADUATE MANAGEMENT ADMISSION TEST

BUSINESS PRACTICES QUIZ

This rather specialized field is another one of the subjects for which the candidate is expected to have an "aptitude." The following series of examination type questions and answers are designed to provide systematic preparation for test questions likely to be found on your exam.

BUSINESS TEST I.

DIRECTIONS: For each of the following questions, select the choice which best answers the question or completes the statement.

1. What term is applied to the valuation fixed for purposes of taxation?

   (A) market value
   (B) assessed valuation
   (C) cash value
   (D) exchange value
   (E) reproduction value

2. What is the single discount equivalent to the series 30%, 10%, and 5%?

   (A) 38.5%
   (B) 40.15%
   (C) 41%
   (D) 45%
   (E) none of these

3. In gathering data on a neighborhood in which a residence is to be appraised, which of the following factors is least significant for this purpose?

   (A) average size of families in area
   (B) physical or structural aspects of neighborhoods
   (C) nuisances or economic influences
   (D) shopping facilities
   (E) transportation facilities

4. The cost price of an article is $8.50. The selling price is to be computed so that a profit of 25% will be made on the selling price. What is the selling price?

   (A) $9.78
   (B) $10.36
   (C) $11.33
   (D) $12.05
   (E) none of these

5. In defining an appraisal, which of the following definitions would be most accurate?

   (A) a statement of absolute value
   (B) a professional guess of market value
   (C) a judgment on the quality of that which is being appraised
   (D) an estimate of the public's opinion of the value
   (E) an indeterminate but useful evaluation of property

6. A machine costing $8,500 will have a scrap value of $300. Machines of this class have a working-hour average life of 25,000 hours. What will be the depreciation charge at the end of the first year if the machine is operated a total of 1500 hours?

   (A) $492.00
   (B) $600.00
   (C) $548.50
   (D) $398.00
   (E) none of these

S2004

198

7. In determining depreciation, one of the factors involved is functional obsolescence. Which among the following conditions would be considered functional obsolescence?

   (A) wear and tear from use
   (B) negligent maintenance
   (C) misplacement of improvements
   (D) poor architectural design
   (E) damage by termites

8. Under the straight-line method of depreciation, what will be the depreciation charge at the end of each year for an asset costing $3,000 and having an estimated life of 20 years and an estimate scrap value of $200?

   (A) $140.00
   (B) $130.00
   (C) $145.50
   (D) $150.00
   (E) none of these

9. Which of the following properties would most likely have the highest capitalization rate?

   (A) a business property in a busy area
   (B) a new residence in a new development
   (C) an apartment house in an undesirable area
   (D) a business property on a heavily traveled highway
   (E) a new residence in an old neighborhood

10. Which of the following would most probably *not* be charged against gross income from a rented property?

    (A) collection losses
    (B) improvement costs
    (C) management costs
    (D) insurance
    (E) maintenance costs

11. What is the net price of an article listed at $3,500, with discounts of 20%, 12.5%, 5%, and 2%?

    (A) $2,290.85
    (B) $2,295.45
    (C) $2,270.75
    (D) $2,280.95
    (E) none of these

12. Among the following, which is generally considered to be the first necessary thing to determine in estimating the value of a piece of land?

    (A) its highest and best use

    (B) its adaptability to several purposes
    (C) its size
    (D) the cost of surrounding land
    (E) the probable income which can be derived from it

13. What would a business be worth which shows a profit of $365 a month and is earning 7% on the total investment?

    (A) $59,437.67
    (B) $62,571.43
    (C) $5,214.28
    (D) $64,188.50
    (E) none of these

14. Which of the following factors would be least important in the appraisal of land intended for industrial purposes?

    (A) availability of railroads
    (B) character of subsoil
    (C) the plottage value
    (D) the topography of the land
    (E) climatic conditions in area where land is located

15. What is the interest on $3,120.50 from November 1, 1952, to May 1, 1954, at 5.5% per annum? (Consider a year as 12 months of 30 days each.)

    (A) $249.74
    (B) $263.45
    (C) $251.89
    (D) $257.44
    (E) none of these

16. In determining the depreciation of a building by the straight-line method, which among the following factors is most important?

    (A) location of building
    (B) architectural design of building
    (C) cost of replacing the building
    (D) estimated economic life of building
    (E) annual income of building

17. *A* leases a storeroom to *B* on a percentage basis. The lease calls for a minimum monthly rent of $200 and 5% on the gross yearly business over $60,000. How much rent would *A* receive yearly from *B* if *B* did a gross business of $90,000?

    (A) $3,850.00
    (B) $3,725.50
    (C) $4,000.00
    (D) $3,900.00
    (E) none of these

18. Which of the following distinguishes an open mortgage from a closed mortgage?

    (A) an open mortgage is one which cannot be paid off before maturity
    (B) an open mortgage can be paid off at anytime
    (C) an open mortgage can be paid off anytime before or at maturity
    (D) an open mortgage allows anyone to assume the indebtedness
    (E) an open mortgage relieves the mortgagor of certain responsibilities

19. What is the simple interest on $6,500 for 4 years, 8 months and 15 days at 6%? (Consider a year as 12 months of 30 days each.)

    (A) $1,846.50
    (B) $1,836.25
    (C) $1,856.25
    (D) $1,936.40
    (E) none of these

20. Which of the following is the most accurate definition of an amortization?

    (A) the liquidation of a financial obligation on an installment basis
    (B) the meeting of all financial obligation in a business transaction
    (C) a seizure and sale of the property of a delinquent mortgagor
    (D) the liquidation of a business concern
    (E) a financial obligation incurred by borrowing money at an agreed interest rate

21. The commission for selling a certain article was 5% of the first $5,000 and 2.5% for all over that amount. The salesman received a commission of $305. What did the article sell for?

    (A) $7,200
    (B) $7,400
    (C) $7,000
    (D) $7,500
    (E) none of these

22. Which of the following best describes unearned increment?

    (A) value received above the cost of goods or service rendered
    (B) value added to land for which owner is in no way responsible
    (C) value added to land by minimal improvements
    (D) money received at selling in excess of original value
    (E) value received by owners of agricultural land in year of exceptional yield

23. Which of the following is the best statement of the purpose of a sinking fund?

    (A) to offset damage caused by casualties
    (B) to build up a reserve for future improvements
    (C) to compensate for a property's depreciation
    (D) to compensate for a reduction in income
    (E) to reduce the capitalization rate of a property

24. A broker receives half the first month's rent for leasing an apartment and 6% of each month's rent thereafter for collecting the rent of $75 per month. What would be his total commission after 12 months?

    (A) $85.50
    (B) $87.20
    (C) $87.00
    (D) $79.00
    (E) none of these

25. The economic life of a building would be at an end under which of the following conditions?

    (A) when repair costs would exceed the income
    (B) when the directional growth of the area is turned away from it
    (C) when the buildings facilities become obsolete
    (D) when the capitalization rate becomes high
    (E) when the building's income fails to justify its existence

26. An article has a list price of $125. Trade discounts on this article are 20%, 10%, and 8-1/3%. What is the net price of the article?

    (A) $77.12
    (B) $82.50
    (C) $85.22
    (D) $79.50
    (E) none of these

27. Among the following assets, which would most likely be considered a capital asset by tax laws?

    (A) a copyright
    (B) stock in trade
    (C) property held for sale to customers
    (D) shares of stock in a corporation
    (E) real property used in business

28. The cost price of an article is $16.80. The selling price is to be computed to render a 35% profit of the cost. What is the selling price?

    (A) $22.68
    (B) $25.85
    (C) $22.40
    (D) $21.44
    (E) none of these

29. Among the following, which is the best example of a short-term capital gain?

    (A) a delivery truck sold at a profit within a year of its purchase
    (B) a gift of corporation stock which is resold within six months of receipt
    (C) a house held by a real estate dealer for sale, the value of which has increased before purchase
    (D) a pleasure car sold for more than was paid for it within 4 months of the original purchase
    (E) none of these

30. If a distributor buys an article listing at $480 from a manufacturer, terms 2/10, net 25, and honors the invoice within five days of the date of the invoice, how much does he remit to the manufacturer? (The amount of the invoice is net.)

    (A) $360.00
    (B) $350.40
    (C) $352.90
    (D) $354.00
    (E) none of these

31. What was the purchase price of a machine whose depreciation charges are $0.30 per working hour, has a scrap value of $200, and a working-hour average life of 22,000 hours?

    (A) $6,600.00
    (B) $6,900.00
    (C) $6,800.00
    (D) $10,000.00
    (E) none of these

32. In determining gain or loss on the sale of property, purchase price can be compared with selling price. For tax purposes, however, which one of the following is compared with selling price?

    (A) the cost of the property
    (B) the cost of the property plus improvements
    (C) the purchase price less damages
    (D) the adjusted basis of the property
    (E) none of these

33. What is a business worth whose income is $685 a month and which is earning 12% on the total investment?

    (A) $72,480.00
    (B) $54,500.00
    (C) $68,500.00
    (D) $61,484.50
    (E) $65,397.00

34. Which of the following properties is not subject to depreciation?

    (A) land
    (B) automotive equipment
    (C) buildings
    (D) manufacturing machinery
    (E) none of these

35. For rental of certain machines, a company was charged as follows: $25 for each of four units, $40 for each of six units, $50 for each of two units. The agent who handled the transaction paid out $24 for repairs to the machines before they were rented. The agent was to receive 3% of the gross rentals as commission. How much was the net amount paid to the owner of the machines?

    (A) $440.00
    (B) $426.80
    (C) $453.20
    (D) $398.75
    (E) $402.80

ANSWER SHEETS AND CORRECT ANSWERS APPEAR ON THE FOLLOWING PAGE.

CONSOLIDATE YOUR KEY ANSWERS HERE

Answer Sheet

	A	B	C	D	E
1					
2					
3					
4					
5					
6					
7					
8					
9					
10					
11					
12					

Answer Sheet

	A	B	C	D	E
13					
14					
15					
16					
17					
18					
19					
20					
21					
22					
23					
24					

Answer Sheet

	A	B	C	D	E
25					
26					
27					
28					
29					
30					
31					
32					
33					
34					
35					

CORRECT ANSWERS FOR BUSINESS PRACTICES QUIZ

1. B	10. B	19. B	28. A
2. B	11. D	20. A	29. D
3. A	12. A	21. A	30. E
4. C	13. B	22. B	31. C
5. D	14. E	23. C	32. D
6. A	15. D	24. C	33. C
7. D	16. D	25. E	34. A
8. A	17. D	26. B	35. E
9. C	18. C	27. D	

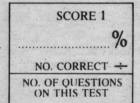

SCORE 1

.... %

NO. CORRECT ÷

NO. OF QUESTIONS
ON THIS TEST

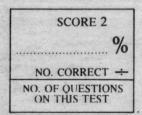

SCORE 2

.... %

NO. CORRECT ÷

NO. OF QUESTIONS
ON THIS TEST

SCORE 3

.... %

NO. CORRECT ÷

NO. OF QUESTIONS
ON THIS TEST

BUSINESS TEST II.

DIRECTIONS: For each of the following questions, select the choice which best answers the question or completes the statement.

Correct key answers to all these test questions will be found at the end of the test.

A FAIR SAMPLING OF THE QUESTIONS YOU'LL BE ASKED

1. Which one of the following industries is least affected by the business cycle?
   (A) Automobile manufacture
   (B) Food processing
   (C) Construction industry
   (D) Shipbuilding
   (E) Iron and Steel production

2. To sell a stock short means to
   (A) sell a low-priced stock
   (B) sell a stock after only a short time
   (C) sell a stock that one does not own
   (D) buy a stock, then sell it within a week
   (E) buy a stock on short notice

3. Often in financial statement analysis the current ratio is used. This ratio is
   (A) current assets divided by current liabilities
   (B) current liabilities divided by current assets
   (C) current assets, less inventory divided by current liabilities
   (D) current assets, less current liabilities divided by working capital
   (E) current assets, less prepaid expenses divided by current liabilities

4. The way to determine inventory turnover for a firm is computed by
   (A) dividing the cost of goods sold by the average inventory
   (B) dividing the cost of goods sold by the ending inventory
   (C) dividing total sales by average inventory
   (D) dividing total sales by ending inventory
   (E) dividing total sales by beginning inventory

5. Gross National Product is defined as
   (A) total goods produced
   (B) total goods and services produced
   (C) total goods and services produced, less taxes
   (D) Net National Product plus dividends
   (E) Net National Product plus investments

6. The Federal Reserve can do all of the following *except*
   (A) set the discount rate
   (B) open market operations
   (C) set the reserve requirements
   (D) set margin requirements
   (E) set the prime rate

7. If a stock is selling at $60 and the annual dividend is $2 per share, what is the yield?
   (A) 3.5 percent
   (B) 3.6 percent
   (C) 3.3 percent
   (D) 3.7 percent
   (E) 3.2 percent

8. The mode is
   (A) the arithmetic average of the distribution
   (B) the geometric average of the distribution
   (C) the score with the greatest frequency of the distribution
   (D) another name for the median
   (E) none of the above

9. Which one of the following is *not* true about a normal distribution?
   (A) It is represented by a bell-shaped curve.
   (B) It has one mode.
   (C) The mode and the mean are equal.
   (D) The mean and the median are equal.
   (E) It has two modes.

10. The order of payment of bonds, preferred stock and common stock, in case of bankruptcy, is
    (A) bonds, common stocks and, lastly, preferred stocks
    (B) bonds, then common and preferred stocks, equally
    (C) bonds, common stocks and preferred stocks, all equally
    (D) bonds, preferred stocks and, lastly, common stocks
    (E) preferred stocks, bonds and, lastly, common stocks

Questions 11 to 15 refer to the graph below.

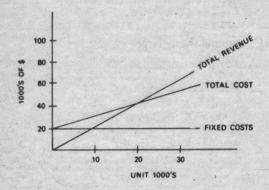

11. What is the breakeven point in dollars?
    (A) $60
    (B) $60,000
    (C) $40
    (D) $40,000
    (E) $80,000

12. What is the breakeven point in units?
    (A) 20 units
    (B) 200 units
    (C) 20,000 units
    (D) 15,000 units
    (E) 150 units

13. At the breakeven point, how much is total variable cost?
    (A) $20,000
    (B) $25,000
    (C) $40,000
    (D) $35,000
    (E) $30,000

14. What would total revenue equal at an output of 30,000 units?
    (A) $80,000
    (B) $65,000
    (C) $60,000
    (D) $55,000
    (E) $70,000

15. At what level of production do total revenues equal fixed costs?
    (A) 20,000 units
    (B) 15,000 units
    (C) zero production
    (D) 10,000 units
    (E) cannot be determined from the above chart

16. Leverage is successful when
    (A) the rate of return on all invested capital exceeds the cost of borrowed funds
    (B) common stockholders receive additional dividends
    (C) the rate of return on all invested capital equals the cost of borrowed funds
    (D) the rate of return on all invested capital exceeds the capitalization rate
    (E) interest rates are going up

17. Which one of the following would *not* be a reason to lease rather than buy real estate?
    (A) Liquidity problems
    (B) Uncertainty of the desirability of the location
    (C) Extensive use of the address in advertising
    (D) Refusal to tie up necessary capital
    (E) Both (A) and (B)

18. If a firm's demand curve is completely horizontal, then the firm faces a
    (A) perfectly elastic demand
    (B) perfectly inelastic demand
    (C) semi-elastic demand
    (D) semi-inelastic demand
    (E) demand curve with elasticity equal to one-half

19. If a company earned $1,000,000 last year and has a price earnings ratio of twenty with 500,000 shares outstanding, what should its stock be selling at?
    (A) $20.00
    (B) $25.50
    (C) $38.50
    (D) $41.50
    (E) $40.00

20. All of the following are likely to provide funds for the mortgage market *except*
    (A) mutual savings banks
    (B) insurance companies
    (C) pension funds
    (D) commercial banks
    (E) mutual funds

21. The relatively recent commercial use of the jet has benefited which product most?
    (A) Automobiles
    (B) Shoes
    (C) Petroleum
    (D) Oranges
    (E) Steel

22. The standard deviation is
    (A) similar to the median
    (B) one-half the mode
    (C) a measure of dispersion
    (D) an average
    (E) one-third the mean

23. The distribution is used when
    (A) sample size is small
    (B) the population standard deviation is not known
    (C) sample size is large
    (D) population mean is not known
    (E) both (A) and (B) pertain

Questions 24 to 26 refer to the graphs below.

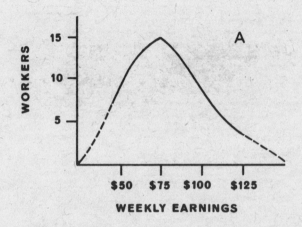

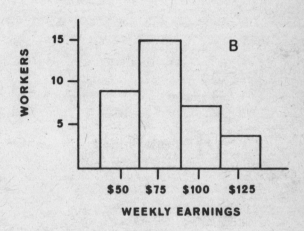

24. Graph A is a(n)
    (A) histogram
    (B) frequency polygon
    (C) pictograph
    (D) normal distribution
    (E) ogive curve

25. Graph B is a(n)
    (A) histogram
    (B) frequency polygon
    (C) lorenz curve
    (D) normal distribution
    (E) ogive curve

26. The mode in graph A is
    (A) $50
    (B) $60
    (C) $75
    (D) $100
    (E) $25

27. Gross National Product differs from Net National Product by
    (A) corporate earnings
    (B) savings
    (C) investments
    (D) dividends
    (E) depreciation

28. National Income differs from Net National Product by
    (A) depreciation
    (B) income taxes
    (C) indirect business taxes
    (D) direct business taxes
    (E) savings

29. During deflationary times your dollar buys
    (A) more
    (B) less
    (C) an amount of goods equal to that of the previous year
    (D) more goods but fewer services
    (E) fewer goods but more services

Questions 30 to 32 refer to the table below.

LEVELS	DISPOSABLE INCOME	CONSUMPTION EXPENDITURES
1	$4,000	$4,000
2	$5,000	$4,800
3	$6,000	$5,400

30. What is the propensity to save for level 1?
    (A) 95 percent
    (B) 99.7 percent
    (C) 000 percent
    (D) 100 percent
    (E) 96.7 percent

31. What is the propensity to consume for level 2?
    (A) 95 percent
    (B) 96 percent
    (C) 4 percent
    (D) 5 percent
    (E) cannot be determined from the table

32. If a person goes from level 2 to level 3, his propensity to save will increase by
    (A) 25 percent
    (B) 10 percent
    (C) 250 percent
    (D) 200 percent
    (E) 100 percent

33. If a reduction in price increases revenue, then the demand curve is said to be
    (A) elastic
    (B) inelastic
    (C) unitary
    (D) either elastic or inelastic
    (E) not determinable from given information

34. During a recession, the Federal Reserve would probably do all of the following *except*
    (A) lower the discount rate
    (B) lower reserve requirements
    (C) buy bonds through its open market operations
    (D) lower margin requirements
    (E) lower the prime rate

35. An oligopoly in industry occurs where there are (is)
    (A) few sellers
    (B) few buyers
    (C) one seller
    (D) one buyer
    (E) both few sellers and few buyers

36. The mortgage market is very sensitive to
    (A) a drop in deposits at commercial banks
    (B) a drop in deposits at savings and loan associations as well as in mutual savings banks
    (C) the stock market
    (D) the yield on common stocks
    (E) a drop in pension fund assets

37. Insurance is used for all of the following *except*
    (A) protection against loss
    (B) savings
    (C) protect the family in case of death of the breadwinner
    (D) income tax reduction
    (E) an asset that can be pledged for a loan

38. If a bond is presently yielding 5 percent and its annual interest payment is $2.50, what is the bond selling at?
    (A) $25.00
    (B) $37.50
    (C) $50.00
    (D) $51.75
    (E) $26.67

39. Current assets minus current liabilities equals
    (A) working capital
    (B) total capital
    (C) cost of goods sold
    (D) current value of the firm
    (E) book value of the firm

40. All of the following are frequent demands made by labor unions *except*
    (A) higher wages
    (B) pension funds
    (C) job security
    (D) longer vacations
    (E) a seat on the Board of Directors

41. Which one of the following is *not* indicative that a study must be made of the material handling practices?
    (A) Delicate parts frequently damaged in transit
    (B) Materials being unloaded by hand
    (C) Poorly labeled pallets or tote boxes
    (D) Poor employee morale
    (E) Workers employed to remove scrap manually

42. All of the following are effects of good material handling *except*
    (A) lower handling costs
    (B) decrease in non productive time
    (C) reduced fatigue
    (D) reduced cost
    (E) increased labor costs

43. The duties of the material handling department include all of the following *except*
    (A) making surveys of handling efficiency
    (B) designing new equipment
    (C) recommending new installations
    (D) recommending new products
    (E) follow-up on the effectiveness of new installations

44. A good layout of an industrial plant brings all of the following benefits *except*
    (A) easier maintenance
    (B) better service to customers
    (C) better quality of product
    (D) reduced capital investment
    (E) increased wages

45. All of the following are duties of the maintenance department *except*
    (A) making emergency repairs
    (B) maintaining a written work-order system
    (C) inspecting plant and equipment
    (D) suggesting ways of increasing safety
    (E) suggesting ways of improving productivity

46. All of the following are incentive pay plans *except*
    (A) straight salary
    (B) Halsey 50-50 plan
    (C) 100 percent bonus plan
    (D) straight piece work
    (E) straight piece work with guaranteed base

47. For management, the following are objectives of wage incentives:
    I. Lower unit costs
    II. Improved cost control
    III. Increased worker morale

(A) I only
(B) II only
(C) I and II only
(D) I and III only
(E) I, II and III

48. If the cost of living went up 20 percent from 1950–1960 and monetary wages remained constant, what happened to real wages?
    (A) remained constant
    (B) increased 20 percent
    (C) decreased 20 percent
    (D) decreased 18 percent
    (E) cannot be determined

49. All of the following are job evaluation criteria *except*
    (A) ranking
    (B) classification
    (C) point rating
    (D) factor comparison
    (E) need of the worker

50. It is generally recognized that the "father" of scientific management is
    (A) John Maynard Keynes
    (B) Frank Gilbreth
    (C) A.D.H. Kaplan
    (D) Frederick Winslow Taylor
    (E) Peter F. Drucker

ANSWER KEY FOR SAMPLE BUSINESS TEST

In order to help you pinpoint your weaknesses, the specific area of each question is indicated in parentheses after the answer. Refer to textbooks and other study material wherever you have an incorrect answer.

Area Code

ACCOUNTING	= A	ECONOMICS	= E
FINANCE	= F	LAW	= L
MARKETING	= MK	REAL ESTATE	= R
MANAGEMENT	= MG	TRANSPORTATION	= T
STATISTICS	= S	INSURANCE	= I

1. B(E)	14. C(F)	26. C(S)	38. C(F)
2. C(F)	15. D(F)	27. E(E)	39. A(A)
3. A(F)	16. A(F)	28. C(E)	40. E(MG)
4. A(A)	17. C(R)	29. A(E)	41. D(MG)
5. B(E)	18. A(E)	30. C(E)	42. E(MG)
6. E(F)	19. E(F)	31. B(E)	43. D(MG)
7. C(F)	20. E(R)	32. C(E)	44. E(MG)
8. C(S)	21. D(T)	33. A(E)	45. E(MG)
9. E(S)	22. C(S)	34. E(F)	46. A(MG)
10. D(F)	23. E(S)	35. A(E)	47. E(MG)
11. D(F)	24. B(S)	36. B(R)	48. C(F)
12. C(F)	25. A(S)	37. D(I)	49. E(MG)
13. A(F)			50. D(MG)

SCORE 1	SCORE 2	SCORE 3
.... %	.... %	.... %
NO. CORRECT	NO. CORRECT	NO. CORRECT
NO. OF QUESTIONS ON THIS TEST	NO. OF QUESTIONS ON THIS TEST	NO. OF QUESTIONS ON THIS TEST

PART FOUR

Extra Practice With Subjects
Likely to Give You Trouble

4

Practice Using Answer Sheets

Alter numbers to match the practice and drill questions in each part of the book.
Make only ONE mark for each answer. Additional and stray marks may be counted as mistakes.
In making corrections, erase errors COMPLETELY. Make glossy black marks.

1 A B C D E	1 A B C D E	1 A B C D E	1 A B C D E	1 A B C D E
2 A B C D E	2 A B C D E	2 A B C D E	2 A B C D E	2 A B C D E
3 A B C D E	3 A B C D E	3 A B C D E	3 A B C D E	3 A B C D E
4 A B C D E	4 A B C D E	4 A B C D E	4 A B C D E	4 A B C D E
5 A B C D E	5 A B C D E	5 A B C D E	5 A B C D E	5 A B C D E
6 A B C D E	6 A B C D E	6 A B C D E	6 A B C D E	6 A B C D E
7 A B C D E	7 A B C D E	7 A B C D E	7 A B C D E	7 A B C D E
8 A B C D E	8 A B C D E	8 A B C D E	8 A B C D E	8 A B C D E
9 A B C D E	9 A B C D E	9 A B C D E	9 A B C D E	9 A B C D E
0 A B C D E	0 A B C D E	0 A B C D E	0 A B C D E	0 A B C D E

1 A B C D E	1 A B C D E	1 A B C D E	1 A B C D E	1 A B C D E
2 A B C D E	2 A B C D E	2 A B C D E	2 A B C D E	2 A B C D E
3 A B C D E	3 A B C D E	3 A B C D E	3 A B C D E	3 A B C D E
4 A B C D E	4 A B C D E	4 A B C D E	4 A B C D E	4 A B C D E
5 A B C D E	5 A B C D E	5 A B C D E	5 A B C D E	5 A B C D E
6 A B C D E	6 A B C D E	6 A B C D E	6 A B C D E	6 A B C D E
7 A B C D E	7 A B C D E	7 A B C D E	7 A B C D E	7 A B C D E
8 A B C D E	8 A B C D E	8 A B C D E	8 A B C D E	8 A B C D E
9 A B C D E	9 A B C D E	9 A B C D E	9 A B C D E	9 A B C D E
0 A B C D E	0 A B C D E	0 A B C D E	0 A B C D E	0 A B C D E

1 A B C D E	7 A B C D E	13 A B C D E	19 A B C D E	25 A B C D E
2 A B C D E	8 A B C D E	14 A B C D E	20 A B C D E	26 A B C D E
3 A B C D E	9 A B C D E	15 A B C D E	21 A B C D E	27 A B C D E
4 A B C D E	10 A B C D E	16 A B C D E	22 A B C D E	28 A B C D E
5 A B C D E	11 A B C D E	17 A B C D E	23 A B C D E	29 A B C D E
6 A B C D E	12 A B C D E	18 A B C D E	24 A B C D E	30 A B C D E

TEAR OUT ALONG THIS LINE AND MARK YOUR ANSWERS AS INSTRUCTED IN THE TEXT

APTITUDE FOR BUSINESS

The questions in this chapter are provided as practice for the kind of questions you will be asked to answer on your test. Do them all carefully yourself and then compare your answers with those given at the end of the chapter. These questions have been scientifically designed to bring out all the tricks and difficulties you may expect to encounter on your test. When you have practiced with them you will be better able to cope with the actual test questions.

AN OVERVIEW OF THIS NEW KIND OF QUESTION

This new kind of question confronts you with an actual business problem. It requires you to consider a situation and arrive at a decision. You will read the arguments for and against certain solutions. You will sort out facts, discard superficial issues, and finally get to the heart of the matter. In this test, the conclusion is not as important as the process by which you arrive at it. You will evaluate and classify data into various categories. You will be quizzed on your understanding of the situation and on your grasp of its significance.

The whole test consists of three parts: a Business Situation (problem, company and people involved, financial data, alternatives, and possible solutions); a Data Application Quiz to see whether you have understood and interpreted the information correctly; and a Data Evaluation Quiz in which you are asked to evaluate the data.

At the end of each test, you will find the key answers to the questions in the quizzes, together with explanations of the answers. The structure of the whole test can be seen at a glance from the following paragraphs which give all the directions required.

TEST I. APTITUDE FOR BUSINESS

TIME: 20 Minutes

DIRECTIONS: In testing your aptitude for business, they will ask you to evaluate a Situation and a Decision. You will be quizzed on goals, assumptions, conclusions, information, predictions, problems, options, and opinions. First, you will read a comprehensive analysis of a business situation; and then you will take two sub-tests based on your analysis: Data Application Quiz, and Data Evaluation Quiz.

Business Situation I.
The Billionaire's Autobiography? To Publish or Not To Publish.

The Problem. Handborn, Inc., a major publisher, is offered the autobiography of a fabulous and mysterious business tycoon. However, there is a question as to whether or not the offer is genuine, and whether this is the kind of book Handborn should publish. If the autobiography is truly the billionaire's life story, a great deal of money can be made. The logical step would be to approach the billionaire directly to ascertain if he did indeed write the book, but the go-between warns that if this is done, Handborn will be turned down. Should the publisher make a contract with the go-between?

The Company. Handborn, Inc., is one of the world's largest publishers. A great part of its sales revenue is derived from scientific textbooks and magazines. Its trade book division, which publishes novels and general non-fiction, is a recently organized branch of the eighty-year-old company. This division has been unprofitable through most of its existence, although high hopes are held for it.

The Proposal Under Consideration. Peter Handborn, who has been president for two years, listens carefully to a proposal made by John Robinson, head of the trade book division, at an executive editorial meeting where major projects are approved or turned down. Robinson states that William Milton, a Handborn author of four novels and three non-fiction books, has established contact with Lawrence Magnerson, a brilliant business tycoon. The eccentric Magnerson, has tentatively agreed to allow Handborn to publish his autobiography, provided that Milton does the actual writing based on taped interviews between the author and the business executive. Magnerson has shunned interviews and any public contact for almost two decades. He has become a "man of mystery," although his fabulous business deals have been national news.

The Terms. Milton is to receive $100,000 as an advance against royalties. Magnerson is to receive $250,000 as an advance against royalties. The royalty will be 15% of the price of the book. Handborn also must share on a fifty-fifty basis all subsidiary revenue, such as would result from the publication of excerpts in magazines, etc., with Milton and Magnerson. According to Milton, the billionaire will only deal with him and no one else.

Possible Subsidiary Deals. Robinson asserts that such a book would be a coup for Handborn. Robinson has had informal contacts with *National*, a news magazine with a very large circulation; Twinights, a major book club; and Vale, a very large paperback publisher. Representatives of these firms have expressed strong interest in the Magnerson autobiography. Payments to Handborn from these companies would be substantial and would probably pay for the printing of the book. Robinson predicts that 100,000 copies of the Handborn edition would be sold, adding that this figure is probably low. An excellent profit could be realized.

Is It Really Magnerson's Story? Robinson is questioned on the authenticity of Milton's tale in light of Magnerson's obvious distaste for the public spotlight. Robinson says he considers Milton to be completely honest, an opinion he has formed over years of acquaintance with the writer. But why, Robinson is asked, cannot Handborn deal with Magnerson directly? He replies that Magnerson apparently wishes to keep his contacts with the outside world to a bare minimum. According to Milton, the billionaire would scuttle the deal if Handborn attempted to meet with him.

Proof of Authenticity. Robinson produces a handwritten agreement, signed "Lawrence Magnerson," which authorizes Milton as his sole agent. The note has been checked by a leading handwriting expert who, after checking samples of Magnerson's writing of 20 years ago, has declared it to be authentic.

Options. Peter Handborn considers the matter carefully. On the negative side, there is some doubt as to whether the manuscript is indeed Magnerson's. Moreover, this is not the type of book that Handborn would ordinarily publish. It smacks a little of sensationalism which might reflect upon the conservative, solid image of Handborn, Inc.

On the other hand, as Robinson said, publication certainly would be a coup. Profits are almost guaranteed. Robinson seems to have taken adequate precautions concerning the validity of Milton's story.

Alternatives. Peter Handborn thinks about contacting Magnerson directly or through the tycoon's executives or friends. This he rejects because Magnerson might call off the deal and go to another publisher. He defers the decision until further proof of authenticity is forthcoming. Too much delay might result in the book going to another publisher.

Decision. He finally decides to publish without reaching Magnerson directly, persuaded by the available documents and the confidence inspired by Mr. Milton. Despite misgivings and the problems involved, Peter Handborn approves the project.

DATA APPLICATION. QUIZ I.

DIRECTIONS: Based on your understanding of the Business Situation, answer the following questions testing your comprehension of the information supplied in the passage. For each question, select the choice which best answers the question or completes the statement. When you understand the data and interpret it correctly, you will be better prepared to evaluate Data, as required by the second part of this test.

Explanations of the key points behind these questions appear with the answers at the end of this test. The explanatory answers provide the kind of background that will enable you to answer test questions with facility and confidence.

1. Which of the following would be the strongest factor in persuading Peter Handborn to publish Magnerson's autobiography?

   (A) He desires to make the book division profitable.

   (B) He would like to enhance Handborn's public image.

   (C) He would like to develop a new line of books.

   (D) He desires the opportunity to develop good subsidiary relationships with other companies.

   (E) He desires to solidify his position as president.

2. Robinson's belief in Milton's integrity is based on

   (A) Milton's record as an author of several books for Handborn

   (B) Robinson's opinion after working with Milton for several years

   (C) Milton's producing an agreement between himself and Magnerson

   (D) Milton's receipt of a minor part of the total royalty advance

   (E) Milton coming to Handborn rather than to another publisher with a stronger trade book division

3. It was decided that Magnerson could not be approached directly by Handborn because

   (A) Milton wouldn't allow it

   (B) Robinson strongly opposed it

   (C) Magnerson might feel that Handborn doubted the authenticity of the manuscript

   (D) it would be difficult to establish contact with the recluse

   (E) Magnerson might then refuse to allow the book to be published by Handborn

4. What are the terms of the subsidiary rights of the proposal being considered by Handborn, Inc.?

   (A) Fifty percent of revenue from this market must be given to Milton and Magnerson.

   (B) The author and the tycoon would receive all the money.

   (C) The total revenue from this source would be in excess of a million dollars.

   (D) More than half would be given directly to Magnerson.

   (E) The revenue given to Magnerson and Milton would be counted as part of the advance against royalties.

S3329

5. Concern over the possibility that Magnerson's autobiography is not authentic arises because

   (A) the only proof is the agreement between Milton and Magnerson
   (B) the figure that Magnerson asks as an advance is surprisingly low
   (C) the tone of the autobiography does not sound authentic
   (D) Handborn has never dealt with an intermediary before
   (E) Magnerson has long avoided publicity concerning himself

6. Robinson believes that subsidiary rights contracts would

   (A) be the main source of revenue
   (B) be difficult to negotiate
   (C) probably cover the printing costs of the book
   (D) be dangerous to accept because of the possibility that the manuscript might not be authentic
   (E) not be desirable since they might hurt the sales of the Handborn edition

7. The agreement between Magnerson and Milton states that

   (A) only Handborn should be the publisher
   (B) the manuscript will be edited from taped interviews
   (C) Milton is Magnerson's sole agent
   (D) the terms of the agreement will be kept secret
   (E) Milton is to receive an advance of $100,000

8. Robinson believes that the sales of the Handborn edition of the book

   (A) would be less than 50,000 copies
   (B) would be more than a million copies
   (C) should not be a factor in deciding whether to publish the book or not
   (D) would be about 100,000 copies at a conservative estimate
   (E) cannot be estimated

9. One reason Handborn, Inc. might consider publishing Magnerson's autobiography is that

   (A) Magnerson's life is the kind of subject that falls within the general Handborn publishing program
   (B) Magnerson is an enigma whose mystery is fascinating to the public
   (C) Magnerson will contribute a substantial amount toward publication costs
   (D) Magnerson has been the subject of several successful books
   (E) Magnerson owns the companies that would pay for the subsidiary rights

10. Handborn derives most of its income from

    (A) specialized magazines
    (B) novels and general non-fiction
    (C) elementary school textbooks
    (D) scientific and technical textbooks and magazines
    (E) subsidiary rights

END OF QUIZ

Go on to the Data Evaluation Quiz next, just as you would do on the actual exam. Check your answers when you have completed the entire Test.

DATA EVALUATION. QUIZ I.

DIRECTIONS: Based on your analysis of the Situation, classify each of the following conclusions in one of five categories. Check:
- *(A) if the conclusion is a MAJOR OBJECTIVE in making the decision; that is, the outcome or result sought by the decision maker.*
- *(B) if the conclusion is a MAJOR FACTOR in arriving at the decision; that is a consideration, explicitly mentioned in the passage that is basic in determining the decision.*
- *(C) if the conclusion is a MINOR FACTOR in making the decision; that is, a secondary consideration that affects the criteria tangentially, relating to a Major Factor rather than to an Objective.*
- *(D) if the conclusion is a MAJOR ASSUMPTION made in deliberating; that is a supposition or projection made by the decision maker before weighing the variables.*
- *(E) if the conclusion is an UNIMPORTANT ISSUE in getting to the point; that is a factor that is insignificant or not immediately relevant to the situation.*

11. The trade division will realize a profit from the Magnerson book.

12. The company can pay the advance.

13. The subsidiary rights would bring in substantial revenue.

14. Milton might not be telling the truth.

15. Handborn would sell at least 100,000 copies.

16. The public is interested in Magnerson.

17. Magnerson's handwriting on the agreement seems to be authentic.

18. The trade division has been unprofitable.

19. If Handborn circumvents Milton and contacts Magnerson directly, the deal might be called off.

20. Delay might mean that Magnerson's autobiography might be published by another company.

21. Handborn has great marketing skill in scientific and technical books .

22. The book might not be authentic.

23. A national magazine, a book club, and a paperback book publisher may publish all or part of the book.

24. Handborn's image might be damaged if it were to publish the autobiography.

25. Publication of the book would be a coup for Handborn.

26. William Milton is an established author.

27. Handborn is one of the world's largest publishers.

28. The handwriting expert compared the signed agreement with samples of Magnerson's handwriting of twenty years ago.

29. The autobiography is not the kind of book that Handborn usually publishes.

30. The advances against royalties are high.

CONSOLIDATE YOUR KEY ANSWERS HERE

To assist you in scoring yourself we have provided Correct Answers alongside your Answer Sheet. May we therefore suggest that while you are doing the test you cover the Correct Answers with a sheet of white paper.....to avoid temptation and to arrive at an accurate estimate of your ability and progress.

Make only ONE mark for each answer. Additional and stray marks may be counted as mistakes.

CORRECT ANSWERS FOR TEST I

(Check your answers with these that we provide. You should find considerable correspondence between them. If not, you'd better go back and find out why. On the next page we have provided concise clarifications of basic points behind the key answers. Please go over them carefully because they may be quite useful in helping you pick up extra points on the exam.)

1.A	6.C	11.A	16.D	21.E	26.C
2.B	7.C	12.D	17.B	22.B	27.E
3.E	8.D	13.B	18.C	23.D	28.C
4.A	9.B	14.B	19.B	24.C	29.C
5.E	10.D	15.B	20.D	25.B	30.E

TEST I. EXPLANATORY ANSWERS

Elucidation, clarification, explication and a little help with the fundamental facts covered in the Previous Test. These are the points and principles likely to crop up in the form of questions on future tests.

1. **(A)** The trade book division has been unprofitable. Magnerson's story might very well put it into the black. None of the other answers are given.

2. **(B)** Robinson specifically states that his belief in Milton's honesty has been developed over years of working with him.

3. **(E)** Robinson states that Magnerson might very well call the whole thing off if Handborn approached him directly.
(B) is nearly right, but it cannot be said that Robinson "strongly" opposed this possible move.

4. **(A)** The agreement states that Magnerson and Milton get half of the subsidiary revenues. What the figure will be is unknown. Magnerson's share is also unknown. The subsidiary revenue has nothing to do with the advance against royalties.

5. **(E)** Magnerson has been avoiding the public spotlight for years. To suddenly allow his autobiography to be published seems out of character.

6. **(C)** Robinson has stated that he is sure the subsidiary rights income would be very substantial and probably would cover printing costs.

7. **(C)** The agreement is between Milton and Magnerson only and does not involve Handborn. The agreement was signed and is judged to be genuine by the handwriting expert.

8. **(D)** Robinson states that at least 100,000 copies would be sold. This is a conservative guess, but he does not commit himself to any other figure.

9. **(B)** The mystery of Magnerson fascinates the general public.

10. **(D)** So stated in the first paragraph.

LETTER CODE FOR EVALUATING DATA

(A) means that the Conclusion is a Major Objective;
(B) means that the Conclusion is a Major Factor;
(C) means that the Conclusion is a Minor Factor;
(D) means that the Conclusion is a Major Assumption;
(E) means that the Conclusion is an Unimportant Issue.

11. **(A)** To make a profit is a major objective.

12. **(D)** It is assumed the company has the resources to pay the advance.

13. **(B)** Certainly the subsidiary revenues play a large part in getting an affirmative decision.

14. **(B)** The possibility that Milton might not be telling the truth is a major consideration.

15. **(B)** The potential sales of the book is a major factor.

16. **(D)** An assumption certainly, since no one at Handborn has conducted a survey to find out if the public is interested in Magnerson.

17. **(B)** Magnerson's signature seems to establish the credibility of Milton's story.

18. **(C)** A minor factor. The trade division's unprofitability is mentioned at the very beginning, but not after that. Peter Handborn doesn't seem to think about it.

19. **(B)** A strong factor. No one seems to want to do anything that might ruin the deal.

20. **(D)** It's highly possible that another company would publish the Magnerson autobiography, but this is still an assumption.

21. **(E)** Handborn's marketing ability in other fields has nothing to do with deciding to publish Magnerson.

22. **(B)** The authenticity of the book was an important point, discussed at length.

23. **(D)** An assumption, even though Robinson had spoken to the other companies concerning subsidiary rights.

24. **(C)** Peter Handborn is slightly concerned that Handborn's image might be damaged by publishing such a sensational book, but that does not bother him long.

25. **(B)** The fact that the book would be a coup and thus bring publicity to Handborn is certainly a strong motivator.

26. **(C)** A very minor factor, if at all. Milton's name certainly would carry some weight, but he would be far outshadowed by Magnerson.

27. **(E)** Handborn is one of the world's largest publishers, but Peter Handborn does not even think about this.

28. **(C)** A factor relating to Milton's honesty.

29. **(C)** A minor factor not related to profits but to the decision to publish.

30. **(E)** The book promises great revenues, so there is no concern about quickly recouping the big advances.

DATA QUIZ
.... %
NO. CORRECT ÷
NO. OF QUESTIONS ON THIS TEST

SCORE TEST I
.... %
NO. CORRECT ÷
NO. OF QUESTIONS ON THIS TEST

JUDGMENT QUIZ
.... %
NO. CORRECT ÷
NO. OF QUESTIONS ON THIS TEST

TEST II. APTITUDE FOR BUSINESS

TIME: 20 Minutes

DIRECTIONS: In testing your aptitude for business, they will ask you to evaluate a Situation and a Decision. You will be quizzed on goals, assumptions, conclusions, information, predictions, problems, options, and opinions. First, you will read a comprehensive analysis of a business situation; and then you will take two sub-tests based on your analysis: Data Application Quiz, and Data Evaluation Quiz.

Business Situation II.   The Billionaire's Autobiography?
A Whistle Is Blown. What Can Be Salvaged from the Wreckage?

The Problem: A billionaire's autobiography turns out to be a fake. It can't be published, since the putative writer and subject states that he doesn't know a thing about it and never heard of William Milton to whom the book was allegedly dictated. Naturally, he threatens suit if the book is published. Having paid large sums of money, expending a great deal of time in preparing the project, and incurring a bad name for gullibility, what can Handborn now do to recoup its losses?

Recapitulation. After Peter Handborn approves the project, John Robinson sends Milton two contracts, one for him and one for Magnerson. The contracts are returned promptly, duly signed. Then two checks are sent to Milton. The first, for $50,000, is made out to Milton and represents half of the royalty advance he is to receive. He will get the balance upon acceptance of the manuscript by Handborn. A $250,000 check made out to Magnerson is also sent, covering his entire advance against royalties.

Four months later, Milton delivers a portion of the manuscript. He also states that Magnerson has changed his mind about the advance. Now the eccentric tycoon demands a total advance of one million dollars!

This is a blow indeed. But it is softened somewhat by the knowledge that Handborn has signed substantial subsidiary rights contracts with *National* magazine, Twinights Book Club, and Vale Paperback Company. After long consultation with John Robinson, Peter Handborn gives permission to increase the advance, but he limits this to a total of $650,000 or $400,000 additional.

Two weeks later, Milton informs Handborn that he has spoken to Magnerson and persuaded the billionaire to accept the new terms. A revised contract is sent to Milton and returned with Magnerson's signature. A check for $400,000 is sent to Milton.

Handborn's comptroller is dubious. Why, he asks, would a man of Magnerson's enormous wealth, in the highest tax bracket, bargain for new terms?

S3329

Other Handborn executives agree that it is strange, but then Magnerson certainly is not the usual author.

A month later, the Handborn comptroller reveals that the Magnerson checks have been deposited in a foreign bank by a woman. The checks are endorsed "Hannah Magnerson." Milton is asked about this. He states that Magnerson, like God, moves in mysterious ways, and therefore there's no need for alarm.

Subsequently, Milton turns in the rest of the manuscript. He also delivers tapes on which he has recorded the conversations between himself and Magnerson.

Robinson and his editors are elated after reading the manuscript. They are sure they have an excellent book. It is pithy, humorous in parts, and reveals much about leading public figures. The manuscript is accepted, and Milton is given his final advance payment of $50,000.

Magnerson Threatens Suit. As soon as Handborn publicly announces the forthcoming publication, a letter is received from Magnerson's lawyer, stating that the book must be a complete fabrication since Magnerson has never met Milton, nor has he had any communication with him. Legal action is threatened.

The letter does not cause consternation at Handborn. They reason that Magnerson might be getting cold feet because of his revelations concerning public figures. Then again, there has been some conflict among executives in the Magnerson industrial empire. This letter could be a result of that struggle. Also, there is the verification of Magnerson's signature by the handwriting expert. Lastly, Robinson asks three people who know Magnerson personally to listen to the tapes. All three agree it is the voice of the billionaire.

Evidence of Fraud. Confidence in the project starts to fade, though, when the comptroller informs Peter Handborn that the Magnerson money has been withdrawn from the foreign bank by the mysterious "Hannah Magnerson." The government of the country in which the bank is located is most concerned since it suspects that fraud is involved. No one knows where "Hannah" took the money. Furthermore, a description of the woman sounds very much like Milton's wife.

Peter Handborn and John Robinson have a conference with William Milton. The writer insists that the manuscript is 100% authentic and that he met with Magnerson on several occasions. He does admit, however, that "Hannah" is indeed his wife, but that Magnerson asked him to handle the money in this manner. He claims Magnerson ordered him to remove the cash from the foreign bank without divulging its present location.

Later investigation turns up several people who are willing to swear that they were with Milton on the dates he said he met with Magnerson . . . and none of these people remember meeting the billionaire.

Alternatives. It is obvious to Mr. Handborn that publication must be aborted. The advances against subsidiary rights must be returned at once.

But what can be done about recouping the money that Handborn, Inc., has invested in this project? William Milton can be prosecuted, of course, resulting in bad publicity for Handborn, Inc. But that does not mean that the advances will be returned. In fact, Peter Handborn doubts that the advance money will ever find its way back into the company's coffers. Yet the picture here is not entirely bleak since Handborn, Inc., is insured against fraud. They can recover $500,000.

That would leave a loss of $250,000 from the advances. Other costs (overhead, editorial charges, prepublication advertising, etc.) would increase this amount to a total of around $400,000.

John Robinson has an idea. Why not write an insider's story of the whole affair? This would be of great interest and might sell better than the ill-starred autobiography.

Peter Handborn considers the possibilities. The danger of publishing such a book is that it might expose the gullibility of the Handborn executives, including himself, and thus might harm the company's public image. How would this affect the company's relationships with the banks on which it, like any other major publisher, depends?

Decision. Peter Handborn approves Robinson's project. He reasons thus: Handborn, Inc., will receive some adverse publicity, despite any attempt it might make to keep the matter quiet. Why not make an asset out of a liability? Admit that the company executives, although cautious men, were completely fooled. Probably a great deal of sympathy might be engendered, for who has not been taken in by a con artist at some time? And quite possibly Handborn might recoup most or all of its losses.

Now, push forward! Test yourself and practice for your test with the carefully constructed quizzes that follow. Each one presents the kind of question you may expect on your test. And each question is at just the level of difficulty that may be expected.

DATA APPLICATION.   QUIZ II.

DIRECTIONS: Based on your understanding of the Business Situation, answer the following questions testing your comprehension of the information supplied in the passage. For each question, select the choice which best answers the question or completes the statement. When you understand the data and interpret it correctly, you will be better prepared to evaluate Data, as required by the second part of this test.

Explanations of the key points behind these questions appear with the answers at the end of this test. The explanatory answers provide the kind of background that will enable you to answer test questions with facility and confidence.

1. Partway through the project, before the entire manuscript was delivered,

   (A) Magnerson threatened to sue

   (B) Milton demanded more money for himself

   (C) the contract had to be renegotiated

   (D) the Magnerson money was withdrawn from the foreign bank

   (E) the Magnerson advance was increased to a million dollars

2. The main reason Handborn decided to increase the advance was that

   (A) prepublication orders for the book were enormous

   (B) Magnerson refused to finish the manuscript

   (C) the publishing company didn't think Milton was receiving enough for his work

   (D) substantial subsidiary rights contracts had been signed

   (E) the treasurer insisted on it

3. How was the advance to Magnerson handled by the Handborn Company?

   (A) Upon signing the contract, the company deposited a check for the full amount in a foreign bank.

   (B) Upon signing the contract, the company sent a check to Milton for one half the advance to Magnerson.

   (C) Upon signing the contract, the company held a check in escrow for the full advance to Magnerson.

   (D) Upon signing the contract, the company sent a check to Milton for the full advance to Magnerson.

   (E) Upon signing the contract, the company paid an advance to Magnerson which they limited to $650,000.

4. The woman who deposited the Magnerson checks was finally identified as

   (A) Milton's wife

   (B) Magnerson's wife

   (C) A Magnerson aide

   (D) Milton in disguise

   (E) A Handborn employee

5. The person who first voiced suspicion was

   (A) Peter Handborn
   (B) John Robinson
   (C) Magnerson's lawyer
   (D) a friend of Magnerson who listened to the tape recording
   (E) the Handborn comptroller

6. All of the following are reasons why the letter from Magnerson's lawyer did not raise much concern at Handborn except

   (A) Magnerson had possibly revealed too much about his relationships with certain public figures.
   (B) The handwriting expert had examined Magnerson's signatures carefully.
   (C) Qualified people had listened to the tapes of the interviews.
   (D) The letter could be the result of an executive conflict within the Magnerson industrial complex.
   (E) Milton had notified the company that Magnerson had asked him to conceal the whereabouts of the advance paid to the billionaire.

7. When John Robinson and his editors examined the complete manuscript, they came to the conclusion that it was

   (A) poor but would sell well
   (B) concise and entertaining
   (C) an obvious and crude fake
   (D) in need of extensive revision
   (E) technically well written but dull

8. After it was learned that the advance money had been withdrawn from a foreign bank, Peter Handborn met with William Milton. At this meeting, Milton

   (A) admitted the book was a fraud
   (B) denied that "Hannah" was his wife
   (C) stuck to his story that the manuscript was genuine
   (D) offered to return his advance
   (E) threatened a lawsuit for libel

9. One reason Handborn might NOT initiate legal proceedings against Milton is that

   (A) unfavorable publicity might result for Handborn, Inc.
   (B) the manuscript might be authentic after all
   (C) Magnerson would dislike the publicity
   (D) there is no ample proof of fraud
   (E) the money received from subsidiary rights would have to be returned

10. One consequence considered by Handborn should they publish a book revealing details of the fraud is that

   (A) readers would sympathize with the company
   (B) the company would lose even more money
   (C) the relationships with the banks might be improved
   (D) Magnerson might then publish his autobiography with Handborn, Inc.
   (E) the insurance company might refuse to pay money to cover damages

END OF QUIZ

Go on to the Data Evaluation Quiz next, just as you would do on the actual exam. Check your answers when you have completed the entire Test.

DATA EVALUATION.   QUIZ II.

DIRECTIONS: Based on your analysis of the Situation, classify each of the following conclusions in one of five categories. Check:

(A)   if the conclusion is a MAJOR OBJECTIVE in making the decision; that is, the outcome or result sought by the decision maker.

(B)   if the conclusion is a MAJOR FACTOR in arriving at the decision; that is a consideration, explicitly mentioned in the passage that is basic in determining the decision.

(C)   if the conclusion is a MINOR FACTOR in making the decision; that is, a secondary consideration that affects the criteria tangentially, relating to a Major Factor rather than to an Objective.

(D)   if the conclusion is a MAJOR ASSUMPTION made in deliberating; that is a supposition or projection made by the decision maker before weighing the variables.

(E)   if the conclusion is an UNIMPORTANT ISSUE in getting to the point; that is a factor that is insignificant or not immediately relevant to the situation.

11. Handborn, Inc., has invested a great deal of money in the project.

12. Handborn, Inc., must extricate itself from the "fraud" situation as quickly as possible.

13. Either Milton or Magnerson renegotiated the contract.

14. The advance money given to Milton may not be recovered.

15. Substantial subsidiary rights contracts have been signed.

16. There is an executive struggle going on within the Magnerson organization.

17. The manuscript is a fake.

18. Handborn hopes to recoup some or all of its losses.

19. Handborn, Inc., is insured against fraud.

20. If a book about the hoax is published, it is almost certain to be a best-seller.

21. The letter from Magnerson's lawyer is genuine.

22. It is important that Handborn, Inc., maintain good relations with banks.

23. Some people are willing to swear that Milton did not meet with Magnerson on the dates he claimed he did.

24. Magnerson might have had second thoughts and now wishes to avoid exposing his relationships with public figures.

25. It is desirable that Handborn, Inc., maintain good relations with the company that insured it against fraud.

26. One alternative is to keep the affair quiet.

27. William Milton's reputation is at stake.

28. The government of the country in which the bank was located is most concerned.

29. Handborn, Inc., can recover part of the amount of the advance from the insurance company.

30. If Milton has indeed perpetrated a fraud, he can go to jail.

CONSOLIDATE YOUR KEY ANSWERS HERE

To assist you in scoring yourself we have provided Correct Answers alongside your Answer Sheet. May we therefore suggest that while you are doing the test you cover the Correct Answers with a sheet of white paper.....to avoid temptation and to arrive at an accurate estimate of your ability and progress.

Make only ONE mark for each answer. Additional and stray marks may be counted as mistakes.

	A B C D E		A B C D E		A B C D E		A B C D E		A B C D E		A B C D E		A B C D E		A B C D E
1		2		3		4		5		6		7		8	
9		10		11		12		13		14		15		16	
17		18		19		20		21		22		23		24	
25		26		27		28		29		30		31		32	

CORRECT ANSWERS FOR TEST II

(Check your answers with these that we provide. You should find considerable correspondence between them. If not, you'd better go back and find out why. On the next page we have provided concise clarifications of basic points behind the key answers. Please go over them carefully because they may be quite useful in helping you pick up extra points on the exam.)

1.C	6.E	11.B	16.C	21.D	26.C
2.D	7.B	12.A	17.E	22.C	27.E
3.D	8.C	13.E	18.A	23.B	28.E
4.A	9.A	14.D	19.D	24.E	29.B
5.E	10.A	15.E	20.B	25.E	30.E

TEST II. EXPLANATORY ANSWERS

Elucidation, clarification, explication and a little help with the fundamental facts covered in the Previous Test. These are the points and principles likely to crop up in the form of questions on future tests.

1. (C) is the only correct statement. (A), (B), and (E) are false. (D) is true, but happened after the entire manuscript was delivered.

2. (D) The subsidiary rights revenues were substantial, so there seemed to be no financial danger in agreeing to an increase in the royalty advance to Magnerson. (B) is nearly right, but not quite because Magnerson made no threat to withdraw publication, although the implication was there.

3. (D) This is the only correct statement of the five possible answers.

4. (A) Milton admitted his wife had deposited the Magnerson advance money.

5. (E) The Handborn comptroller wondered why a billionaire would feel he had to get more advance money. This happened long before the letter from Magnerson's lawyer.

6. (E) All the possible answers were true, but it was after the letter from the Magnerson lawyer that Milton asserted the billionaire had told him to hide his advance money.

7. (B) is the only correct statement.

8. (C) is the only correct statement.

9. (A) Peter Handborn is concerned about bad publicity for his company.

10. (A) (B) is possible, but not probable. (C) is wrong since Peter Handborn thinks that publication might prejudice his company's relationships with banks. (D) and (E) are not considered at all by Peter Handborn.

LETTER CODE FOR EVALUATING DATA

(A) *means that the Conclusion is a Major Objective;*
(B) *means that the Conclusion is a Major Factor;*
(C) *means that the Conclusion is a Minor Factor;*
(D) *means that the Conclusion is a Major Assumption;*
(E) *means that the Conclusion is an Unimportant Issue.*

11. (B) The money is paramount in Peter Handborn's mind.

12. (A) That is why Peter Handborn wishes to cancel publication immediately and return the subsidiary rights money.

13. (E) The renegotiated contract is of little interest. The company's more immediate need is to get out of the spiderweb.

14. (D) An assumption certainly. Peter Handborn presumably believes that Milton will risk going to prison because he will be a rich man when he gets out and collects his loot.

15. (E) The return of subsidiary rights money is hardly important in this dilemma.

16. (C) The struggle within the Magnerson organization has been mentioned as a fact, but this is of little interest to Peter Handborn as he considers what his company should do.

17. (E) By the time Peter Handborn thinks about what he must do, he is sure that the company has been the victim of a fraud.

18. (A) This is the main reason for adopting Robinson's idea to publish a book on the affair.

19. **(D)** A major assumption is the ability to collect some money from the insurance company.

20. **(B)** A major factor is the decision to publish an exposé.

21. **(D)** It is assumed the letter is genuine.

22. **(C)** It is stated that Handborn needs banks for financing.

23. **(B)** The fact that people have been found who say that Milton did not meet with Magnerson on the dates he said he did seems to be the clincher that the book is a fraud.

24. **(E)** Peter Handborn is not swayed by the possibility that Magnerson is squirming out of the deal because of potential libel suits.

25. **(E)** Peter Handborn wishes to be reimbursed by the insurance company.

26. **(C)** It is an alternative, but a weak one since it will be impossible to avoid some publicity.

27. **(E)** The fact that Milton's reputation is at stake is of no importance in light of Handborn's problems.

28. **(E)** What a foreign government thinks is of little concern to Handborn.

29. **(B)** As stated, Handborn can collect from the insurance company.

30. **(E)** William Milton in jail will not help Handborn at the moment.

DATA QUIZ	SCORE TEST II	JUDGMENT QUIZ
.... %	.... %	.... %
NO. CORRECT	NO. CORRECT	NO. CORRECT
NO. OF QUESTIONS ON THIS TEST	NO. OF QUESTIONS ON THIS TEST	NO. OF QUESTIONS ON THIS TEST

TEST III. APTITUDE FOR BUSINESS

TIME: 20 Minutes

DIRECTIONS: In testing your aptitude for business, they will ask you to evaluate a Situation and a Decision. You will be quizzed on goals, assumptions, conclusions, information, predictions, problems, options, and opinions. First, you will read a comprehensive analysis of a business situation; and then you will take two sub-tests based on your analysis: Data Application Quiz, and Data Evaluation Quiz.

Business Situation III.   What's To Be Done with the Trade Division?

The Problem.   Handborn, Inc. is a major publisher that specializes in scientific textbooks and magazines. A management consulting firm questions whether Handborn can make money from its trade book division. Cogent arguments are given for disbanding the division, based chiefly on its unprofitability and Handborn's lack of experience in this field. Peter Handborn believes there are valid arguments for its continued existence. He considers both sides of the question.

Recommendations of Management Consultant.

At the suggestion of the Board of Directors, Prudence, Inc., a management consulting firm, is called in to examine the structure of the entire company. After eight months of exhaustive study, it submits the following recommendations:

1) Handborn, Inc., should divest itself of certain technical magazines. These are no longer profitable since they are aimed at trades and crafts declining due to technological advance.

2) Handborn, Inc., has bought two companies within the last five years. They specialize in the home-study market. This is a rapidly growing area of the book field, and one that is likely to continue expanding. Many people find home-study courses desirable for polishing job skills and for keeping abreast of new developments. Prudence recommends that Handborn, Inc., seek further acquisitions in this segment of publishing.

3) Handborn, Inc., has a substantial base in the college text market. However, it is weak in providing special materials for the two-year community colleges which are cropping up everywhere. Prudence, the management consulting firm, suggests that a separate division be created for books for these schools. Again, this represents an opportunity for expansion.

4) Handborn, Inc., has been a major publisher in the elementary-high school field for only ten years. It has acquired several companies which operate independently. One division produces and sells textbooks, another audio-visual materials, a third scientific equipment, and another reading and skill tests. For

230 / *Graduate Management Admission Test*

the sake of efficiency, Prudence recommends that these divisions be merged. This would help to drive down costs, an important point, since these divisions have yielded little profit.

5) Finally, and most important, it is urged that the trade division be discontinued, and that its books be sold to other companies. Prudence points out that trade books represent the most hazardous area of book publishing. Handborn, Inc., has neither sufficient skill nor knowledge to exploit the field successfully.

Peter Handborn's Reactions. Peter Handborn considers the recommendations. He concurs that unprofitable technical magazines should be discontinued.

He also agrees that acquiring additional home-study companies would be desirable. The same holds true for "spinning off" a two-year college division out of the present college division.

He is more hesitant when it comes to the idea of combining the various divisions serving the elementary-high school field. He feels that the consultants have ignored some very important facts. Not all school products are sold in the same way, nor are they always purchased by the same customers. Textbooks are reached by contacting teachers and supervisors, and Handborn, Inc., maintains a large sales staff for just this purpose. On the other hand, audio-visual materials are usually sold by free-lance equipment dealers who work on a commission basis. They generally deal with audio-visual directors. Handborn decides this suggestion needs more study.

The Trade Book Situation.   He is most disturbed by the recommendation to sell the trade book division. He recognizes the validity of the argument that this publishing activity is off the Handborn trail.   Nonetheless, he feels that a solid trade book division is one of the best ways to build up a good public image. And the reputation gained via trade books pays off in the sales of textbooks and technical magazines.

The trade book division is relatively new in the history of the company. Although it still has to realize a profit, it hasn't had a fair chance in his opinion. More time is needed.

There is one more consideration that the consultants overlooked. Handborn trade books written for children and teen-agers have been most successful. Several of them have won awards and more than fifty percent have been in existence for at least five years—an excellent record in trade books. It is the only profitable part of the trade book division.

Perhaps the adult trade books could be sold to another company. But Peter Handborn doubts that any other publisher would want the adult books alone. Handborn, Inc., would probably have to sell all the trade books—juvenile as well as adult—and the Board of Directors would not stand for this.

Decision. Peter Handborn will oppose the sale or dissolution of the trade book division. He will study further the feasibility of merging the elementary-high school divisions. He will recommend adoption of the other Prudence suggestions at the next board meeting.

DATA APPLICATION. QUIZ III.

DIRECTIONS: Based on your understanding of the Business Situation, answer the following questions testing your comprehension of the information supplied in the passage. For each question, select the choice which best answers the question or completes the statement. When you understand the data and interpret it correctly, you will be better prepared to evaluate Data, as required by the second part of this test.

Explanations of the key points behind these questions appear with the answers at the end of this test. The explanatory answers provide the kind of background that will enable you to answer test questions with facility and confidence.

1. The recommendations regarding the trade book division originated with

   (A) Peter Handborn
   (B) the Board of Directors
   (C) executives of Handborn, Inc.
   (D) a Senate committee which is investigating monopoly
   (E) Prudence, Inc.

2. Prudence, Inc., sees a great potential in the home-study field because

   (A) text books are easily acquired in this field
   (B) no other company provides adequate texts
   (C) the federal government provides funds to ghetto youth to take job-training home-study courses
   (D) many people wish to up-date their job skills
   (E) less and less high school graduates go on to college

3. The management consulting team sees potential growth in which one of the following?

   (A) Texts for community colleges
   (B) Technical magazines for trades and crafts
   (C) Adult trade books
   (D) Juvenile trade books
   (E) Elementary-high school textbooks

4. Which of the following is one of the five recommendations made by Prudence, Inc.?

   (A) The juvenile trade book line should be retained while the adult trade book line should be sold.

   (B) Handborn, Inc. should sell some of its elementary-high school divisions.

   (C) New magazines should be started.

   (D) The elementary-high school divisions should be merged.

   (E) The college division should be dissolved.

5. Peter Handborn's view of the recommendations is that

   (A) none of them should be adopted
   (B) all of them should be put into action immediately
   (C) there are good suggestions concerning two-year colleges, magazines, and home-study courses
   (D) at least two divisions should be sold as quickly as possible
   (E) it doesn't matter if the trade book division makes a profit or not

6. The problem in merging the elementary-high school divisions is

   (A) there would be a foolish mixing of profitable and unprofitable divisions
   (B) the various Handborn divisions in this market do not sell in the same way
   (C) Handborn, Inc., should really get out of this field altogether
   (D) Handborn, Inc. is not the sole owner of some of the divisions
   (E) the divisions are located in different parts of the country

7. The main factor in Peter Handborn's deliberation over selling the trade book division is his belief that

(A) a solid trade book division is a creator of good public relations

(B) there is an enormous profit to be made in adult trade books

(C) the Magnerson-Milton affair has shown that Handborn, Inc. knows little about trade books

(D) the adult trade books should be separated from juveniles so the adult books would show a profit

(E) the trade book division has had ample time to show a profit

8. Regarding the recommendations of Prudence, Inc., Peter Handborn is most dubious about their suggestions concerning

(A) certain technical magazines

(B) the home-study market

(C) the college text market

(D) the adult trade book division

(E) the elementary-high school divisions

9. It can be inferred from the passage that Handborn, Inc. is a company that

(A) is much too hesitant about entering new and promising fields

(B) is well-diversified in the field of publishing

(C) is known primarily in the field of elementary texts

(D) sells most of its books by mail

(E) is well-established in the two-year community college field

10. Within the last five years, Handborn, Inc. has acquired two companies that specialize in

(A) trade books

(B) technical magazines

(C) elementary-high school materials

(D) materials for two-year community colleges

(E) materials for home-study and self-improvement

END OF QUIZ

Go on to the Data Evaluation Quiz next , just as you would do on the actual exam. Check your answers when you have completed the entire Test.

DATA EVALUATION. QUIZ III.

DIRECTIONS: Based on your analysis of the Situation, classify each of the following conclusions in one of five categories. Check:

(A) *if the conclusion is a MAJOR OBJECTIVE in making the decision; that is, the outcome or result sought by the decision maker.*

(B) *if the conclusion is a MAJOR FACTOR in arriving at the decision; that is a consideration, explicitly mentioned in the passage that is basic in determining the decision.*

(C) *if the conclusion is a MINOR FACTOR in making the decision; that is, a secondary consideration that affects the criteria tangentially, relating to a Major Factor rather than to an Objective.*

(D) *if the conclusion is a MAJOR ASSUMPTION made in deliberating; that is a supposition or projection made by the decision maker before weighing the variables.*

(E) *if the conclusion is an UNIMPORTANT ISSUE in getting to the point; that is a factor that is insignificant or not immediately relevant to the situation.*

11. Retaining the trade book division will be an assured benefit to the company.

12. Trade books can help create a good public image.

13. The trade book division has yet to realize a profit.

14. The consulting firm has recommended that the trade book division be discontinued.

15. A reputation gained through trade books helps to sell text books.

16. Trade books are an uncertain source of revenue.

17. Handborn's books for juveniles have won awards.

18. The Handborn company lacks experience in marketing trade books.

19. The trade book division is a relatively new division of Handborn.

20. Books for juveniles are the only profitable part of the trade book division.

21. The adult trade book line cannot be sold to another company without also selling the juvenile line.

22. The Board of Directors wouldn't approve the sale of the entire trade book division.

23. Handborn, Inc. has bought two companies within the past two years.

24. Handborn has a desire to make a profit from the trade book division.

25. Handborn, Inc. has the ability to sell the trade book division.

26. The retention of the juvenile trade book line is desirable.

27. Prudence, Inc. has the ability to make a reliable study.

CONSOLIDATE YOUR KEY ANSWERS HERE

To assist you in scoring yourself we have provided Correct Answers alongside your Answer Sheet. May we therefore suggest that while you are doing the test you cover the Correct Answers with a sheet of white paper.....to avoid temptation and to arrive at an accurate estimate of your ability and progress.

Make only ONE mark for each answer. Additional and stray marks may be counted as mistakes.

	A B C D E		A B C D E		A B C D E		A B C D E		A B C D E		A B C D E		A B C D E		A B C D E
1		2		3		4		5		6		7		8	
9		10		11		12		13		14		15		16	
17		18		19		20		21		22		23		24	
25		26		27		28		29		30		31		32	

CORRECT ANSWERS FOR TEST III

(Check your answers with these that we provide. You should find considerable correspondence between them. If not, you'd better go back and find out why. On the next page we have provided concise clarifications of basic points behind the key answers. Please go over them carefully because they may be quite useful in helping you pick up extra points on the exam.)

1.E	6.B	11.A	16.B	20.C	24.A
2.D	7.A	12.B	17.C	21.C	25.D
3.A	8.D	13.B	18.B	22.B	26.B
4.D	9.B	14.B	19.C	23.E	27.D
5.C	10.E	15.B			

TEST III. EXPLANATORY ANSWERS

Elucidation, clarification, explication and a little help with the fundamental facts covered in the Previous Test. These are the points and principles likely to crop up in the form of questions on future tests.

1. **(E)** The Board of Directors did not make the recommendations, but suggested that the consulting firm be hired. Peter Handborn is reacting to the consultants' report.

2. **(D)** Perhaps home study is the cheapest and best way to learn, but this is not mentioned, nor is any special federal program. The number of high school graduates going to college has no bearing upon home studies.

3. **(A)** Prudence, Inc., believes that the technical magazines, published for declining crafts, should be eliminated. The consulting team did not mention the growth potential of trade books, juvenile trade books, or elementary-high school textbooks.

4. **(D)** The merger of the separate elementary-high school divisions is recommended on the grounds of efficiency and economy. The management consultants believe that the entire trade book line should be sold. The management consultants realize that the college division is solidly based. The only change they would make would be to add a community college division. Peter Handborn is thinking about starting new magazines, but this idea did not come from the management consultants nor did the management consultants suggest selling any of the elementary-high school divisions.

5. **(C)** If you marked **(E)**, you were fairly close, but it would not be fair to say that he does not care whether the trade book division becomes profitable or not. He only wishes that it would be given more time to get into the black. All the other answers are completely false.

6. **(B)** There are some grounds for merging the elementary-high school divisions, and Peter Handborn does not turn the idea down completely. However, he is aware that the various divisions have different customers within the school-product market. A merger would probably decrease costs and increase efficiency. The mixing of profitable and unprofitable divisions did not come into his thinking at all, nor has there been any suggestion that Handborn, Inc., should divest itself of its elementary-high school lines.

7. **(A)** Peter Handborn is keenly aware that trade books enhance a company's public image. He does not reflect on whether or not enormous profits can be attained in the adult trade book field, nor would he probably agree with the contention that Handborn, Inc., knows little about trade books. **(D)** is wrong because the juvenile trade books are making money. Peter Handborn does not believe that the trade book division has had time enough to show a profit.

8. **(D)** Peter Handborn does not believe that another publisher will buy the unprofitable adult trade books without the profitable juvenile trade books.

9. **(B)** Handborn, Inc., is well-diversified as far as the publishing industry is concerned. It certainly does not show too much hesitation when it sees new opportunities; yet its posture is cautious and it does not enter new fields rashly. **(D)** and **(E)** are completely false.

10. **(E)** The two companies Handborn, Inc. has purchased specialize in the home-study market.

S3329

LETTER CODE FOR EVALUATING DATA

(A) means that the Conclusion is a Major Objective;
(B) means that the Conclusion is a Major Factor;
(C) means that the Conclusion is a Minor Factor;
(D) means that the Conclusion is a Major Assumption;
(E) means that the Conclusion is an Unimportant Issue.

11. **(A)** The decision of whether or not to retain the trade book division is based on the assumption that the trade book division will benefit the company, either directly through sales or indirectly through the enhancement of the company's image which will stimulate sales of texts.

12. **(B)** A major factor in deciding whether or not to retain the trade book division is the favorable image that the trade book line can create.

13. **(B)** A major consideration is the lack of profit from the trade book division.

14. **(B)** A major consideration mentioned in the passage is the recommendation of the consulting firm that the trade book division be discontinued.

15. **(B)** That the reputation gained through trade books may help sell texts is a consideration that Peter Handborn makes in his decision to retain the trade book division.

16. **(B)** One of the reasons Prudence, Inc. gives in its recommendation that the trade book line be discontinued is that trade books represent the most hazardous area of book publishing.

17. **(C)** The fact that Handborn's books for juveniles have won awards is a consideration that relates to the favorable image created by the trade book line.

18. **(B)** That Handborn, Inc. lacks experience in the trade book field is a major consideration pointed out by Prudence, Inc.

19. **(C)** That the trade book division is relatively new is related to Handborn, Inc.'s lack of experience in this field; hence the lack of profit in this area.

20. **(C)** The fact that the juvenile trade books are successful is incorporated in major considerations of profit and reputation to be gained through the trade book division.

21. **(C)** That adult trade books cannot be sold without selling the juvenile line is a factor that relates to the major considerations of profit and reputation.

22. **(B)** If the Board of Directors will not allow the selling of the trade book division in its entirety than that fact is a major consideration.

23. **(E)** The two companies Handborn, Inc. has bought have nothing to do with the decision regarding the trade book division.

24. **(A)** The desire to make a profit is a major objective.

25. **(D)** It is assumed that the trade book division could be sold if a decision to do so is made.

26. **(B)** The desirability of retaining the juvenile trade book line is a major consideration.

27. **(D)** The ability of Prudence, Inc. to make a reliable study is unquestioned.

DATA QUIZ .... %	SCORE TEST III .... %	JUDGMENT QUIZ .... %
NO. CORRECT	NO. CORRECT	NO. CORRECT
NO. OF QUESTIONS ON THIS TEST	NO. OF QUESTIONS ON THIS TEST	NO. OF QUESTIONS ON THIS TEST

TEST IV. APTITUDE FOR BUSINESS

TIME: 20 Minutes

DIRECTIONS: In testing your aptitude for business, they will ask you to evaluate a Situation and a Decision. You will be quizzed on goals, assumptions, conclusions, information, predictions, problems, options, and opinions. First, you will read a comprehensive analysis of a business situation; and then you will take two sub-tests based on your analysis: Data Application Quiz, and Data Evaluation Quiz.

Business Situation   Offer and Counteroffer.

Afsky's Offer. Hans Muller's Restaurant has been a landmark on Route 77 for 59 years. The present owner is the third Hans Muller to run the establishment. It is profitable and busy all year around.

Muller is approached by Afsky Limited, a large conglomerate that owns a number of widely diversified businesses. Recently, Afsky has bought a chain of motels and wishes to combine them with excellent restaurants. They have discovered that Muller owns a large lot next to his restaurant, which they see as a spot on a major highway upon which to build a motel. They offer to buy Muller out with an offer of $250,000 in cash for the restaurant and $50,000 for the lot.

The offer is intriguing at first to Muller. He is a widower and his children are now adults, married, and living far away. None of them are interested in carrying on the restuarant business. He himself has always dreamed of retiring to Florida.

However, the restaurateur thinks over the offer carefully. He is 55 years old, too young to become inactive. On the other hand, he feels too old to enter a new line of work or even to start a new restaurant in Florida. He has not tired of running his establishment and he enjoys the company of those steady customers he has known personally for years.

Also, a cash payment is not in his best interests. Taxes would eat up most of the money.

Muller's Counteroffer. He makes a counteroffer to Afsky. He wishes $50,000 in cash and $400,000 of Afsky stock.

He also wishes to remain as manager of the restaurant. He would like a ten-year employment contract at an annual salary of $25,000 plus three percent of the total revenue. Furthermore, at the end of five years, he would like to be able to sell his Afsky stock for not more than $50,000 a year. Afsky can receive full title to his lot.

238 / *Graduate Management Admission Test*

He points out to the conglomerate executives that they are newcomers to the restaurant business and liable to make mistakes that could result in heavy financial losses. By remaining as manager, he could save them from such a disaster. Furthermore, he adds, he has built personal good will and a friendly local clientele throughout the years. Afsky, by bringing in outsiders to run the place, would run the danger of losing the regular customers.

> Now, push forward! Test yourself and practice for your test with the carefully constructed quizzes that follow. Each one presents the kind of question you may expect on your test. And each question is at just the level of difficulty that may be expected.

DATA APPLICATION. QUIZ IV.

DIRECTIONS: Based on your understanding of the Business Situation, answer the following questions testing your comprehension of the information supplied in the passage. For each question, select the choice which best answers the question or completes the statement. When you understand the data and interpret it correctly, you will be better prepared to evaluate Data, as required by the second part of this test.

Explanations of the key points behind these questions appear with the answers at the end of this test. The explanatory answers provide the kind of background that will enable you to answer test questions with facility and confidence.

1. Hans Muller's Restaurant can be described as

   (A) a seasonal business, making most money during the winter when skiers visit the area
   (B) an old restaurant that is nearly bankrupt because of poor management
   (C) off the beaten path and does a marginal business
   (D) profitable
   (E) managed by the founder

2. Which of the following best describes Afsky, Ltd.?

   (A) It consists entirely of a motel chain.
   (B) It has been in the restaurant field for 59 years.
   (C) It is a widely diversified conglomerate.
   (D) It is a small local real-estate firm.
   (E) It wishes to avoid entering the restaurant business.

3. Which of the following does Afsky, Ltd. wish to buy?

   I. Muller's Restaurant
   II. A lot next to Muller's Restaurant
   III. A motel near Muller's Restaurant

   (A) I only
   (B) II only
   (C) I and II only
   (D) I and III only
   (E) I, II and III

4. Afsky, Ltd. believes that Muller's lot is desirable because

   (A) it is inexpensive
   (B) Muller wishes to go to Florida
   (C) it is on a busy highway
   (D) Muller's present customers will use the motel
   (E) there is not another motel for miles

5. Which of the following is included in Afsky's offer to Hans Muller?

   I. $250,000 in cash for the restaurant
   II. $25,000 annual salary for ten years
   III. $50,000 in cash for the lot

   (A) I only
   (B) II only
   (C) I and II only
   (D) I and III only
   (E) I, II and III

6. One reason Muller turns down Afsky's offer is that he

   (A) doesn't think he will be getting enough money
   (B) wants his sons to carry on the restaurant
   (C) would like to build the motel himself
   (D) doesn't want to retire
   (E) is opposed to letting Afsky, Ltd. start operations in this area

7. Which of the following is included in Muller's counteroffer?

    I. 3% of the restaurant's revenue
    II. $50,000 in cash
    III. 10-year employment contract

    (A) I only
    (B) II only
    (C) I and II only
    (D) I and III only
    (E) I, II and III

8. The reason Muller desires a great deal of stock and a relatively small amount in cash is that he

    (A) could live in comfort on the stock dividends
    (B) would have to pay a heavy tax if the settlement was in cash only
    (C) believes Afsky stock will greatly increase in value
    (D) could sell all the stock within five years
    (E) could put the stock in trust for his children

9. Which of the following are factors Muller thinks might affect Afsky adversely in running the restaurant?

    I. lack of restaurant management experience
    II. local resentment against a motel
    III. loss of present clientele

    (A) I only
    (B) II only
    (C) I and II only
    (D) I and III only
    (E) I, II and III

10. As part of his counteroffer, Hans Muller

    (A) wants a 5-year employment contract
    (B) wishes to continue managing the restaurant
    (C) proposes that he manage the motel
    (D) asks for a million dollars
    (E) would keep title to the lot

END OF QUIZ

Go on to the Data Evaluation Quiz next, just as you would do on the actual exam. Check your answers when you have completed the entire Test.

DATA EVALUATION. QUIZ IV.

DIRECTIONS: Based on your analysis of the Situation, classify each of the following conclusions in one of five categories. Check:

(A) *if the conclusion is a MAJOR OBJECTIVE in making the decision; that is, the outcome or result sought by the decision maker.*

(B) *if the conclusion is a MAJOR FACTOR in arriving at the decision; that is a consideration, explicitly mentioned in the passage that is basic in determining the decision.*

(C) *if the conclusion is a MINOR FACTOR in making the decision; that is, a secondary consideration that affects the criteria tangentially, relating to a Major Factor rather than to an Objective.*

(D) *if the conclusion is a MAJOR ASSUMPTION made in deliberating; that is a supposition or projection made by the decision maker before weighing the variables.*

(E) *if the conclusion is an UNIMPORTANT ISSUE in getting to the point; that is a factor that is insignificant or not immediately relevant to the situation.*

11. Making a deal for the restaurant and the lot .

12. Afsky's possible loss of regular restaurant customers.

13. Hans Muller's desire to remain in the restaurant business .

14. Muller's reluctance to retire .

15. Hans Muller's personal friendship with restaurant customers .

16. Afsky's ability to pay for the restaurant and lot .

17. Restaurant's 59-year existence .

18. Advantage of having motel on busy highway .

19. Hans Muller is too old to enter new line of work .

20. Hans Muller's enjoyment in running his restaurant.

21. Muller's children are not interested in running the restaurant .

22. Muller's disinclination to start a Florida restaurant .

23. Afsky shares as a good form of payment .

24. Afsky's desire to build a motel .

25. Afsky's desire to enter the restaurant business .

CONSOLIDATE YOUR KEY ANSWERS HERE

*To assist you in scoring yourself we have provided Correct
Answers alongside your Answer Sheet. May we therefore suggest
that while you are doing the test you cover the Correct Answers
with a sheet of white paper.....to avoid temptation and to arrive at
an accurate estimate of your ability and progress.*

Make only ONE mark for each answer. Additional and stray marks may be counted as mistakes.

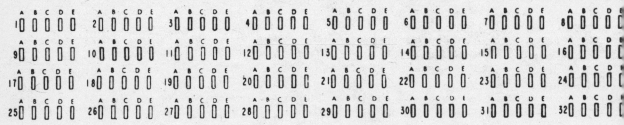

CORRECT ANSWERS FOR TEST IV.

*(Check your answers with these that we provide. You should find
considerable correspondence between them. If not, you'd better
go back and find out why. On the next page we have provided
concise clarifications of basic points behind the key answers.
Please go over them carefully because they may be quite useful in
helping you pick up extra points on the exam.)*

1.D	6.D	11.A	16.D	21.C
2.C	7.E	12.C	17.E	22.C
3.C	8.B	13.B	18.C	23.B
4.C	9.D	14.C	19.C	24.B
5.D	10.B	15.C	20.B	25.B

TEST IV. EXPLANATORY ANSWERS

Elucidation, clarification, explication and a little help with the fundamental facts covered in the Previous Test. These are the points and principles likely to crop up in the form of questions on future tests.

1. **(D)** It is stated that the restaurant is profitable. It is not seasonal, as **(A)** states, but busy all year round. It is certainly not near bankruptcy, as it says in **(B)**. **(C)** is wrong because it is stated that the restaurant is on a major highway, which is one of the reasons Afsky wants to build a motel next to the restaurant. **(E)** is also incorrect. Hans Muller is not the founder, but the "third Hans Muller to run the establishment."

2. **(C)** It is stated that Afsky, Ltd, is widely diversified. Thus, **(A)** and **(D)** are incorrect. **(B)** is wrong; Afsky is new to the restaurant business and wishes to build up its holdings in this field.

3. **(C)** Afsky wants to buy the restaurant and adjoining lot. It cannot buy a motel since there is none there; but it wishes to build one.

4. **(C)** Afsky believes that a motel on Route 77 would be desirable. **(A)** is wrong since we are not told whether or not $50,000 is a high price for the lot. Hans Muller does not wish to go to Florida yet, so **(B)** is incorrect. It is not stated if Muller's present customers would use the motel, but as they are local people, they probably would not. We are not told whether there is another motel in the area.

5. **(D)** Afsky offered $250,000 cash for the restaurant, and $50,000 cash for the lot. The annual salary was part of Muller's counteroffer.

6. **(D)** After thinking it over, Muller decides against retiring. His sons do not wish to carry on the restaurant. He is not necessarily against the price offered. He does not indicate any desire to build the motel himself, and he does not have any bias against Afsky coming into the area.

7. **(E)** Muller wants 3% of the restaurant's revenue, $50,000 in cash, and a 10-year employment contract.

8. **(B)** Taxes comprise the only reason Muller turns the cash offer down.

9. **(D)** Muller tells the Afsky people that they run a strong possibility of financial loss because they are inexperienced in restaurant management. Furthermore, he has a strong personal relationship with his customers which Afsky might lose. There seems to be no local resentment against a motel on the site.

10. **(B)** Muller definitely wishes to continue managing the restaurant. **(A)** is wrong since he wants a 10-year contract. **(C)** is wrong; he displays no interest in running the motel. **(D)** and **(E)** are wrong; he wants a total of $400,000, mostly in stock, and he is willing to give up title to the lot.

LETTER CODE FOR EVALUATING DATA

(A) means that the Conclusion is a Major Objective;
(B) means that the Conclusion is a Major Factor;
(C) means that the Conclusion is a Minor Factor;
(D) means that the Conclusion is a Major Assumption;
(E) means that the Conclusion is an Unimportant Issue.

11. **(A)** Making a deal is the main objective for both parties.

12. **(C)** Afsky's possible loss of regular customers is a minor factor.

13. **(B)** Muller's desire to remain in the restaurant business is a major factor in coming to an agreeable deal for the restaurant and lot.

14. **(C)** Muller's reluctance to retire is a minor factor in his offer to stay on as restaurant manager.

15. **(C)** Muller's personal friendship with his customers is a factor in his objective to remain as restaurant manager.

16. **(D)** Afsky's financial stability is a major assumption.

17. **(E)** The age of the restaurant is unimportant.

18. **(C)** The advantage of having a motel on Route 77 is a major factor in Afsky's desire to purchase.

19. **(C)** That Hans Muller feels too old is a minor factor relating to his reluctance to retire.

20. **(B)** Muller's enjoyment in running his restaurant must be a major factor, as it influences his counteroffer and his major objective of a satisfactory deal.

21. **(C)** The fact the Muller's children won't run the restaurant is a factor in Muller's decision to sell.

22. **(C)** Muller's disinclination to start all over again in Florida leads him to think about the major factors that influence his decision to stay.

23. **(B)** Shares of stock rather than a great deal of cash are part of Muller's considerations in forming his counteroffer.

24. **(B)** Building a motel is a major factor influencing Afsky's desire to make a deal for the restaurant and the adjoining lot.

25. **(B)** Afsky's entrance into the restaurant business must be termed a major factor in their desire to acquire Muller's restaurant.

DATA APPLICATION
.............................%
NO. CORRECT
NO. OF QUESTIONS ON THIS TEST

SCORE
.............................%
NO. CORRECT
NO. OF QUESTIONS ON THIS TEST

DATA EVALUATION
.............................%
NO. CORRECT
NO. OF QUESTIONS ON THIS TEST

MATH MADE SIMPLE

To help you learn to solve problems, references to earlier explanations are given in the form of a number which is enclosed in parentheses. If you go back to the original explanation, you will find it very easy to understand the problem at hand. Each chapter is followed by a short test. And each test is followed by the correct answers and clear-cut solutions to help you arrive at those answers.

FRACTIONS

1. A fraction is part of a unit, such as ½, ¾, etc.
   a. A fraction has a numerator and a denominator.
   Example: In the fraction ¾, 3 is the numerator, and 4 is the denominator.
   b. In any fraction, the numerator is being divided by the denominator.
   Example: The fraction $\frac{2}{7}$ indicates that 2 is being divided by 7.

2. A mixed number is an integer together with a fraction, such as $2\frac{3}{5}$, $7\frac{3}{8}$, etc. The integer is the integral part, and the fraction is the fractional part.

3. An improper fraction is one in which the numerator is greater than the denominator, such as $\frac{19}{6}$, $\frac{25}{4}$, etc.

4. To change a mixed number to an improper fraction:
   a. Multiply the denominator of the fraction by the integer.
   b. Add the numerator to this product.
   c. Place this sum over the denominator of the fraction.

   Illustration: Change $3\frac{4}{7}$ to an improper fraction.
   SOLUTION: $7 \times 3 = 21$ (4a)
   $21 + 4 = 25$ (4b)
   $3\frac{4}{7} = \frac{25}{7}$ (4c)
   Answer: $\frac{25}{7}$

5. To change an improper fraction to a mixed number:

   a. Divide the numerator by the denominator. The quotient, disregarding the remainder, is the integral part of the mixed number.
   b. Place the remainder, if any, over the denominator. This is the fractional part of the mixed number.

   Illustration: Change $\frac{36}{13}$ to a mixed number.

   SOLUTION: $13)\overline{36}$ (5a)
   with quotient 2, $\underline{26}$, 10 remainder
   $\frac{36}{13} = 2\frac{10}{13}$ (5b)
   Answer: $2\frac{10}{13}$

6. The numerator and denominator of a fraction may be changed by multiplying both by the same number, without affecting the value of the fraction.
   Example: The value of the fraction $\frac{2}{5}$ will not be altered if the numerator and the denominator are multiplied by 2, to result in $\frac{4}{10}$.

7. The numerator and the denominator of a fraction may be changed by dividing both by the same number, without affecting the value of the fraction.
   Example: The value of the fraction $\frac{3}{12}$ will not be altered if the numerator and denominator are divided by 3, to result in ¼.

8. As a final answer to a problem:
   a. Improper fractions should be changed to mixed numbers.
   b. Fractions should be reduced as far as possible.

ADDITION OF FRACTIONS

9. Fractions cannot be added unless the denominators are all the same. If they are, add all the numerators and place this sum over the common denominator. In the case of mixed numbers, follow the above rule for fractions and then add the integers.
   Example: The sum of $2\frac{3}{8}$, $3\frac{1}{8}$, and $\frac{5}{8}$ is $5\frac{9}{8}$ or $6\frac{1}{8}$. (8a). If the denominators are not the same, the fractions, in order to be added, must be converted to ones having the same denominator. In order to do this, it is first necessary to find the lowest common denominator.

10. The lowest common denominator (henceforth called the L.C.D.) is the lowest number which can be divided evenly by all the given denominators.
    If no two of the given denominators can be divided by the same number, then the L.C.D. is the product of all the denominators.
    Example: The L.C.D. of $\frac{1}{2}$, $\frac{1}{3}$, and $\frac{1}{5}$ is $2 \times 3 \times 5 = 30$.

11. To find the L.C.D. when two or more of the given denominators can be divided by the same number:
    a. Write down the denominators, separated a little from each other.
    b. Select the lowest number by which any two or more of these denominators can be divided evenly.
    c. Divide the denominators by this number, copying down those which cannot be divided evenly. Place this number to one side.
    d. Repeat this, placing each divisor to one side until there are no longer any denominators that can be divided evenly by any selected number.
    e. Multiply all the divisors to find the LCD.
    Illustration: Find the L.C.D. of $\frac{1}{5}$, $\frac{1}{7}$, $\frac{1}{10}$, and $\frac{1}{14}$.

    Solution: 2)5 7 10 14   (11a)
                            (11b)
         5)5 7 5 7   (11c)
                            (11b)
         7)1 7 1 7   (11c)
                            (11b)
            1 1 1 1   (11c)
         $7 \times 5 \times 2 = 70$ (11e)
    Answer: The L.C.D. is 70

12. Having learned how to find the L.C.D., we are now prepared to add fractions and mixed numbers when the denominators are not the same. The system presented here involves the drawing of a diagram which will be explained in the method that follows.
    To add fractions and mixed numbers:

    a. List them one under the other.
    b. Draw a diagram to add the fractions.
    c. Find the L.C.D. and write it in at (A).
    d. Ascertain the new numerators by dividing the L.C.D. by each denominator and multiplying this quotient by the old numerator. These new numerators are written in at (B).
    e. Add up the new numerators and place this sum over the L.C.D. (C/A in the diagram.)
    f. Reduce this fraction and change it to a mixed number if possible.
    g. Add this reduced fraction (or mixed number) to the sum of the whole numbers for the final answer.

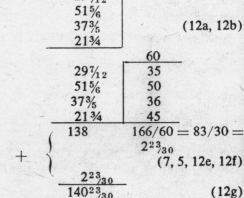

Illustration: Add $29\frac{7}{12}$, $51\frac{5}{6}$, $37\frac{3}{5}$, and $21\frac{3}{4}$.
SOLUTION:

                      60   (11, 12c)
    $29\frac{7}{12}$
    $51\frac{5}{6}$
    $37\frac{3}{5}$ (12a, 12b)
    $21\frac{3}{4}$

                      60
    $29\frac{7}{12}$ 35
    $51\frac{5}{6}$ 50
    $37\frac{3}{5}$ 36
    $21\frac{3}{4}$ 45
     138    $166/60 = 83/30 =$
                     $2\frac{23}{30}$
+   (7, 5, 12e, 12f)
    $2\frac{23}{30}$
   $140\frac{23}{30}$ (12g)

Answer: $140\frac{23}{30}$

Illustration: Subtract $16\frac{4}{5}$ from $29\frac{1}{3}$.
SOLUTION: $29\frac{1}{3} = \frac{88}{3}$, $16\frac{4}{5} = \frac{84}{5}$
                        (4, 14a)
    L.C.D. $= 15$ (10, 14b)
    $\frac{88}{3} - \frac{84}{5} = \frac{440}{15} - \frac{252}{15}$
                  (6, 12d, 14c)
    $= \frac{188}{15}$ (14d)
    $= 12\frac{8}{15}$ (14e, 5, 8a)

Answer: $12\frac{8}{15}$

SUBTRACTION OF FRACTIONS

13. a. More than two numbers may be added at the same time. In subtraction, however, only two numbers are involved. In subtraction, as in addition, the denominators must be the same.

    b. One must be careful to determine which term is first. The second term is always subtracted from the first, which should be the larger quantity.

To Subtract Fractions

14. a. Change the mixed numbers, if any, to improper fractions.
    b. Find the L.C.D.
    c. Change both fractions to ones having the L.C.D. as the denominator.
    d. Subtract the numerator of the second fraction from the numerator of the first, and place this difference over the L.C.D.
    e. Reduce if possible.

MULTIPLICATION OF FRACTIONS

15. a. To be multiplied, fractions need not have the same denominators.
    b. A whole number has the denominator 1 understood.

16. To Multiply Fractions:
    a. Change the mixed numbers, if any, to improper fractions.
    b. Multiply all the numerators, and place this product over the product of the denominators.
    c. Reduce, if possible.

Illustration: Multiply $\frac{2}{3} \times 2\frac{4}{7} \times \frac{5}{9}$.

SOLUTION: $2\frac{4}{7} = \frac{18}{7}$ (4, 16a)

    $\frac{2}{3} \times \frac{18}{7} \times \frac{5}{9} = \frac{180}{189}$ (16b)

    $= \frac{20}{21}$ (7, 8b, 16c)

Answer: $\frac{20}{21}$

17. When a whole number is multiplied by a mixed number.
    a. Multiply the whole number by the fractional part of the mixed number.
    b. Multiply the whole number by the integral part of the mixed number.
    c. Add both products.

Illustration: Multiply $23\frac{3}{4}$ by 95.

SOLUTION: $95 \times \frac{3}{4} = \frac{285}{4}$ (16, 17a)

          $= 71\frac{1}{4}$ (5)

    $95 \times 23 = 2185$ (17b

    $2185 + 71\frac{1}{4} = 2256\frac{1}{4}$ (17c)

Answer: $2256\frac{1}{4}$

18. Cancellation is a device to facilitate multiplication. To cancel means to divide a numerator and a denominator by the same number.
    Example: In the problem $\frac{4}{7} \times \frac{5}{6}$, the numerator 4 and the denominator 6 may be divided by 2.

$$\frac{\overset{2}{\cancel{4}}}{7} \times \frac{5}{\underset{3}{\cancel{6}}} = \frac{10}{21}$$

19. The word "of" is often used to mean "multiply."

    Example: $\frac{1}{2}$ of $\frac{1}{2} =$
        $\frac{1}{2} \times \frac{1}{2} = \frac{1}{4}$.

DIVISION OF FRACTIONS

20. In division, as in subtraction, only two terms are involved. It is very important to determine which term is first. If the problem reads, "$\frac{2}{3}$ divided by 5," then $\frac{2}{3}$ is the first term, and 5 is the second. If it reads, "How many times is $\frac{1}{2}$ contained in $\frac{1}{3}$?", then $\frac{1}{3}$ is first, and $\frac{1}{2}$ is second.

21. The reciprocal of a number is that number inverted.

    a. Since every whole number has the denominator 1 understood, the reciprocal of a whole number is a fraction having 1 as the numerator and the number itself as the denominator.
       Example: The reciprocal of 5 ($\frac{5}{1}$) is $\frac{1}{5}$.
    b. When a fraction is inverted, the numerator becomes the denominator and the denominator becomes the numerator.
    Example: The reciprocal of $\frac{3}{8}$ is $\frac{8}{3}$.
    Example: The reciprocal of $\frac{1}{3}$ is $\frac{3}{1}$, or simply 3.

22. To divide fractions:
    a. Change all the mixed numbers, if any, to improper fractions.
    b. Invert the second fraction and multiply.
    c. Reduce, if possible.

    Illustration: Divide $\frac{2}{3}$ by $2\frac{1}{4}$
    SOLUTION: $2\frac{1}{4} = \frac{9}{4}$ (22a, 4)
    $$\frac{2}{3} \div \frac{9}{4} = \frac{2}{3} \times \frac{4}{9}$$
    $$= \frac{8}{27} \quad (22b, 16)$$
    Answer: $\frac{8}{27}$

23. A mixed fraction is one that has a fraction as the numerator, or as the denominator, or as both.

    Example: $\dfrac{\frac{2}{3}}{5}$ is a mixed fraction.

24. To clear a mixed fraction:
    a. Divide the numerator by the denominator.
    b. Reduce, if possible.
    (The longer line indicates the point of division.)

Illustration: Clear $\dfrac{\frac{3}{7}}{\frac{5}{14}}$
SOLUTION: $\frac{3}{7} \div \frac{5}{14} = \frac{3}{7} \times \frac{14}{5} = \frac{42}{35}$
$$\quad (24a)$$
$$= \frac{6}{5} \quad (7)$$
$$= 1\frac{1}{5} \quad (24b, 8a)$$
Answer: $1\frac{1}{5}$

25. Fractions—General Facts.
    a. If two fractions have the same denominator, the one with the larger numerator is the greater fraction.
    Example: $\frac{3}{7}$ is greater than $\frac{2}{7}$.
    b. If two fractions have the same numerator, the one with the larger denominator is the smaller fraction.
    Example: $\frac{5}{12}$ is smaller than $\frac{5}{11}$.

26. In a fractional problem, the whole is 1, which may be expressed by a fraction in which the numerator and the denominator are the same number.
    Example: If the problem involves $\frac{1}{8}$ of a quantity, then the whole quantity is $\frac{8}{8}$, or 1.

PRACTICE PROBLEMS IN FRACTIONS

1. Find the L.C.D. of $\frac{1}{8}$, $\frac{1}{7}$, $\frac{1}{6}$, and $\frac{1}{10}$. (a) 800 (b) 860 (c) 840 (d) 830.
2. Add $16\frac{3}{8}$, $4\frac{4}{5}$, $12\frac{3}{4}$, and $23\frac{5}{6}$. (a) $57\frac{91}{120}$ (b) $57\frac{1}{4}$ (c) 58 (d) 59.
3. Subtract $27\frac{5}{14}$ from $43\frac{1}{6}$. (a) 15 (b) 16 (c) $15\frac{8}{21}$ (d) $15\frac{17}{21}$.
4. Multiply $17\frac{5}{8}$ by 128. (a) 2200 (b) 2305 (c) 2356 (d) 2256.
5. What is the sum of $12\frac{1}{6} - 2\frac{3}{8} - 7\frac{2}{3} + 19\frac{3}{4}$. (a) 21 (b) $21\frac{7}{8}$ (c) $21\frac{1}{8}$ (d) 22.
6. By how much does $\dfrac{6}{\frac{7}{8}}$ exceed $\dfrac{\frac{6}{7}}{8}$? (a) 1 (b) 8 (c) $6\frac{1}{4}$ (d) $6\frac{3}{4}$.
7. During one week, a man traveled $3\frac{1}{2}$, $1\frac{1}{4}$, $1\frac{1}{6}$, and $2\frac{3}{8}$ miles. The next week he traveled $\frac{1}{4}$, $\frac{3}{8}$, $\frac{9}{16}$, $3\frac{1}{16}$, $2\frac{5}{8}$, and $3\frac{3}{16}$ miles. How many more miles did he travel the second week? (a) $1\frac{37}{48}$ (b) $1\frac{1}{2}$ (c) $1\frac{3}{4}$ (d) 1.
8. Four men eat a pie. The first three men eat $\frac{1}{4}$, $\frac{2}{7}$, and $\frac{3}{11}$ of the pie respectively. How much of the pie did the fourth man eat? (a) $\frac{59}{308}$ (b) $\frac{70}{308}$ (c) $\frac{1}{3}$ (d) $\frac{1}{4}$.
9. A, B, and C are bequeathed an inheritance. A gets $\frac{1}{6}$, B gets $\frac{1}{8}$, and C gets the rest. When the estate was finally adjusted, A had to give $\frac{2}{3}$ of his share to C, and C then gave $\frac{3}{4}$ of his share to B. What part of the estate had B finally? (a) $\frac{3}{4}$ (b) $\frac{71}{96}$ (c) $\frac{75}{95}$ (d) $\frac{76}{96}$.
10. Clock A loses 1 minute a day, and clock B gains $2\frac{3}{4}$ minutes per day. If clock B is 15 minutes ahead of clock A, how many days will it take clock B to be 30 minutes ahead of clock A? (a) 7 (b) 4 (c) 6 (d) 8.

Correct Answers
(You'll learn more by writing your own answers before comparing them with these.)

1. c	3. d	5. b	7. a	9. b
2. a	4. d	6. d	8. a	10. b

PROBLEM SOLUTIONS   Fractions

1. Find the L.C.D. of $\frac{1}{8}$, $\frac{1}{7}$, $\frac{1}{6}$, $\frac{1}{10}$
   SOLUTION: Multiply Divisors to find L.C.D.
   2)8-7-6-10   (2 is a factor of 8-6-10)
   3)4-7-3-5   (3 is a factor of 3)
   4)4-7-1-5   (4 is a factor of 4)
   5)1-7-1-5   (5 is a factor of 5)
   7)1-7-1-1   (7 is a factor of 7)
    1-1-1-1   Will have 1-1-1-1
   L.C.D. = 2 x 3 x 4 x 5 x 7 = 840
   (c) Answered in text.

   ANSWER: L.C.D. = 840

2. Add: 16 $\frac{3}{8}$, 4 $\frac{4}{5}$, 12 $\frac{3}{4}$, 23 $\frac{5}{6}$
   SOLUTION: L.C.D. = 120
   $16 \frac{3}{8} = 16 \frac{45}{120}$
   $4 \frac{4}{5} = 4 \frac{96}{120}$
   $12 \frac{3}{4} = 12 \frac{90}{120}$
   $23 \frac{5}{6} = 23 \frac{100}{120}$
   $\qquad 55 \frac{331}{120} = 57 \frac{91}{120}$ (a)

   ANSWER: Sum = 57 $\frac{91}{120}$

3. Subtract 27 $\frac{5}{14}$ from 43 $\frac{1}{6}$
   SOLUTION: L.C.D. = 42
   $$43 \frac{1}{6} = 43 \frac{49}{42}$$
   $$-27 \frac{5}{14} = 27 \frac{15}{42}$$
   $$15 \frac{34}{42} = 15 \frac{17}{21} \quad (d)$$

   ANSWER: Difference = 15 $\frac{17}{21}$

4. Multiply 17$\frac{5}{8}$ by 128.
   SOLUTION:
   $17 \frac{5}{8}$ x 128
   $$\frac{141}{8} \times \frac{128}{1} = 2256 \quad (d)$$

   ```
         141
        x 16
         846
         141
        2256
   ```

   ANSWER: Product = 2256

5. What is the sum of $12\frac{1}{6} - 2\frac{3}{8}$
   $- 7\frac{2}{3} + 19\frac{3}{4}$.

   SOLUTION: L.C.D. = 24

   $$12\frac{1}{6} = 12\frac{\overset{11}{\cancel{}}}{24} \overset{28}{}$$
   $$- 2\frac{3}{8} = 2\frac{9}{24}$$
   $$\phantom{-2\frac{3}{8} =}\ 9\frac{19}{24} = \ 9\frac{19}{24}$$
   $$- 7\frac{2}{3} = -7\frac{16}{24}$$
   $$\phantom{-7\frac{2}{3} =}\ 2\ \frac{3}{24} = \ 2\frac{1}{8}$$
   $$+ 19\frac{3}{4} = +19\frac{6}{8}$$
   $$\phantom{+ 19\frac{3}{4} = +}\ 21\frac{7}{8}\quad \text{(b)}$$

   Explanation
   Reduced $2\frac{3}{24} = 2\frac{1}{8}$
   L.C.D. = 8

   ANSWER: $21\frac{7}{8}$ = Sum

6. By how much does $\dfrac{\frac{6}{7}}{\frac{7}{8}}$ exceed $\dfrac{6}{8}$?

   SOLUTION:

   $$6 \div \frac{7}{8} = \frac{6}{1} \times \frac{8}{7} = \frac{48}{7} = 6\frac{6}{7}$$
   $$\frac{6}{7} \div 8 = \frac{6}{7} \times \frac{1}{8} = \frac{3}{28}$$
   $$6\frac{6}{7} = 6\frac{24}{28}\quad \text{L.C.D.} = 28$$
   $$- \frac{3}{28} = \ \frac{3}{28}$$
   $$\phantom{- \frac{3}{28} = }\ 6\frac{21}{28} = 6\frac{3}{4}\quad \text{(d)}$$

   ANSWER: $6\frac{3}{4}$

7. SOLUTION:

   $3\frac{1}{2} = 3\frac{12}{24}$ miles first week
   $1\frac{1}{4} = 1\ \frac{6}{24}$
   $1\frac{1}{6} = 1\ \frac{4}{24}$ L.C.D. = 24
   $2\frac{3}{8} = 2\ \frac{9}{24}$
   $\phantom{2\frac{3}{8} = }\ 7\frac{31}{24} = 8\frac{7}{24}$ miles traveled first week

   $\frac{1}{4}\ = \ \frac{4}{16}$ miles 2nd week
   $\frac{3}{8}\ = \ \frac{6}{16}$
   $\frac{9}{16} = \ \frac{9}{16}$ L.C.D. = 16
   $3\frac{1}{16} = 3\frac{1}{16}$
   $2\frac{5}{8} = 2\frac{10}{16}$
   $3\frac{3}{16} = 3\frac{3}{16}$
   $\phantom{3\frac{3}{16} = }\ 8\frac{33}{16} = 10\frac{1}{16}$ miles traveled 2nd week

   (a)

   L.C.D. = 48
   $10\frac{1}{16} = 9\frac{51}{48}$ miles 2nd week
   $- 8\frac{7}{24}\quad 8\frac{14}{48}$ miles first week
   $\phantom{- 8\frac{7}{24}\quad }1\frac{37}{48}$ miles more traveled 2nd week

   ANSWER: $1\frac{37}{48}$

8. SOLUTION:
   $$\text{L.C.D.} = 4 \times 7 \times 11 = 308$$
   $\frac{1}{4} = \frac{77}{308}$ first man ate
   $\frac{2}{7} = \frac{88}{308}$ second man ate
   $\frac{3}{11} = \frac{84}{308}$ third man ate
   $\phantom{\frac{3}{11} = }\ \frac{249}{308}$ three men ate

   $$\frac{308}{308} = \text{whole pie}$$
   $$- \frac{249}{308} =$$
   $$\frac{59}{308} = \text{fourth man ate}\quad \text{(a)}$$

   ANSWER: $\frac{59}{308}$

9. SOLUTION:
   $\frac{1}{6} = \frac{4}{24}$ — A receives
   $+ \frac{1}{8} = \frac{3}{24}$ — B receives
   $\phantom{+ \frac{1}{8} = }\ \frac{7}{24}\quad$ A & B receive

   A gives $\frac{2}{3}$ to C
   $\frac{1}{6} \times \frac{2}{3} = \frac{1}{9}$ to C
   $\ \frac{24}{24} = \text{whole estate}\quad \text{L.C.D.} = 24$
   $- \frac{7}{24} = \text{A \& B receive}$
   $\ \frac{17}{24} = \text{C receives}$

   C has $\frac{17}{24}$
   $\frac{1}{9} + \frac{17}{24} = \frac{8}{72} + \frac{51}{72} = \frac{59}{72}$
   $\phantom{\frac{1}{9} + \frac{17}{24} = }\ \frac{59}{72}$ C's final share

   C gives $\frac{3}{4}$ to B

   $$\frac{59}{\cancel{72}} \times \frac{\overset{1}{\cancel{3}}}{4} = \frac{59}{96}$$
   24

   B had $\frac{1}{8}$
   $\frac{1}{8} + \frac{59}{96} = \frac{12}{96} + \frac{59}{96} = \frac{71}{96}$
   $\phantom{\frac{1}{8} + \frac{59}{96} = }\ \frac{71}{96}$ B's final share (b)

   ANSWER: $\frac{71}{96}$

10. SOLUTION:
    30 minutes — 15 minutes = 15 minutes
    more, B must be ahead of A
    $2\frac{3}{4}$ minutes + 1 minute (loss) = $3\frac{3}{4}$ minutes
    B gains over A each day
    15 minutes ÷ $3\frac{3}{4}$ minutes = $15 \div \frac{15}{4} =$
    $\dfrac{15 \times 4}{15} = 4$ days (b)

    ANSWER: It will take Clock B four days to
    be 30 min. ahead of Clock A.

DECIMALS

27. A decimal, which is a number with a decimal point (.), is actually a fraction the denominator of which is understood to be 10 or some power of 10.

    a. The number of digits, or places, after a decimal point determines which power of 10 the denominator is. If there is one digit, the denominator is understood to be 10; if there are two digits, the denominator is understood to be 100, etc.

    Example: $.3 = \frac{3}{10}$, $.57 = \frac{57}{100}$, $.643 = \frac{643}{1000}$.

    b. The addition of zeros after a decimal point does not change the value of the decimal, and if there are zeros only after a decimal point, they may be removed without changing the value of the decimal.

    Example: $.7 = .70 = .700$ and vice versa, $.700 = .70 = .7$

    c. Since a decimal point is understood to exist after any whole number the addition of any number of zeros after such decimal point written in does not change the value of the number.

    Example: $2 = 2.0 = 2.00$, etc.

    d. If a decimal point already exists with digits following it, the addition of any number of zeros after such digits will not change the value of the decimal.

    Example: $.53 = .530 = .5300$, etc.

ADDITION OF DECIMALS

28. The addition of decimals is the same as that of whole numbers with the added provision that the decimal points must be kept in a vertical line, one under the other. This determines the place of the decimal point in the answer.

    Illustration: Add: 2.31, .037, 4, and 5.0017.
    SOLUTION:
    ```
        2.3100
         .0370
        4.0000        (27c)
        5.0017
       ───────
       11.3487
    ```
    Answer: 11.3487

SUBTRACTION OF DECIMALS

29. The subtraction of decimals is the same as that of whole numbers with the added provision that, as in addition, the decimal points be kept in a vertical line, one under the other. This determines the place of the decimal point in the answer.

    Illustration: Subtract 4.0037 from 15.3
    SOLUTION:
    ```
       15.3000        (27d)
      − 4.0037
      ────────
       11.2963
    ```
    Answer: 11.2963

MULTIPLICATION OF DECIMALS

30. The multiplication of decimals is the same as that of whole numbers.

    a. The number of decimal places in the product equals the sum of the decimal places in the multiplicand and in the multiplier.

    b. If there are fewer places in the product than this sum, then a sufficient number of zeros must be added in front of the product to equal the number of places required, and a decimal point is written in front of the zeros.

    Illustration: Multiply 2.372 by .012
    SOLUTION:
    ```
        2.372   (3 decimal places)
      x  .012   (3 decimal places)
      ───────
         4744
        2372
      ────────
      .028464        (30b)
    ```
    Answer: .028464

31. A decimal can be multiplied by a power of 10 by moving the decimal point to the *right* as many places as indicated by the power. If multiplied by 10, the decimal point is moved one place to the right; if multiplied by 100, the decimal point is moved two places to the right, etc.

    Example:
    $$.235 \times 10 = 2.35$$
    $$.235 \times 100 = 23.5$$
    $$.235 \times 1000 = 235 \quad \text{etc.}$$

DIVISION OF DECIMALS

32. There are four types of division involving decimals:
    a. When the dividend only is a decimal.
    b. When the divisor only is a decimal.
    c. When both are decimals.
    d. When neither dividend nor divisor is a decimal.

33. A decimal can be cleared of its decimal point by multiplying it by a power of 10 which is indicated by the number of decimal places involved.
    Example: To clear 5.38 of its decimal point, it must be multiplied by 100.
    5.38 x 100 = 538

34. When a divisor is thus multiplied by some power of 10, the dividend must be multiplied by a similar power of 10 in order to keep the value intact.

35. TYPE A
    When the dividend only is a decimal, the division is the same as that of whole numbers, except that a decimal point must be placed in the quotient exactly above that in the dividend.
    Illustration: Divide 12.864 by 32

$$\begin{array}{r} .402 \\ 32 \overline{)\ 12.864} \\ 12\ 8 \\ \hline 64 \\ 64 \\ \hline \end{array}$$

    Answer: .402

36. TYPE B
    When the divisor only is a decimal, the divisor must be cleared of its decimal point and as many zeros must be added to the dividend as there were decimal places in the divisor. (33, 34)
    Illustration: Divide 211327 by 6.817
    SOLUTION:

$$6.817 \overline{)\ 211327} = 6817 \overline{\begin{array}{r} 31000 \\ )\ 211327000 \\ 20451 \\ \hline 6817 \\ 6817 \\ \hline \end{array}}$$

    Answer: 31000

37. TYPE C
    When both divisor and dividend are decimals, the divisor must be cleared of its decimal, and the decimal point in the dividend must be moved to the right as many places as there were in the divisor. If there are not enough places in the dividend, zeros must be added to make up the difference.

    Illustration: Divide 2.62 by .131
    SOLUTION:

$$.131 \overline{)\ 2.62} = 131 \overline{\begin{array}{r} 20 \\ )\ 2620 \\ 262 \\ \hline \end{array}} \quad (33, 31, 34)$$

    Answer: 20

38. TYPE D
    Neither the divisor nor the dividend need be a decimal and yet the problem may involve decimals. This occurs in two cases:
    a. When the dividend is a smaller number than the divisor.
    b. When it is required to work out a division to a certain number of decimal places.
    In either case, write in a decimal point after the dividend, add as many zeros as necessary, and place a decimal point in the quotient above that in the dividend.

    Illustration: Divide 7 by 50 (Case A)

$$\text{SOLUTION:} \quad 50 \overline{\begin{array}{r} .14 \\ )\ 7.00 \\ 5\ 0 \\ \hline 2\ 00 \\ 2\ 00 \\ \hline \end{array}} \quad (35)$$

    Answer: .14

    Illustration: How much is 155 divided by 40, carried out to 3 decimal places? (Case B)

$$\text{SOLUTION:} \quad 40 \overline{\begin{array}{r} 3.875 \\ )\ 155.000 \\ 120 \\ \hline 35\ 0 \\ 32\ 0 \\ \hline 3\ 00 \\ 2\ 80 \\ \hline 200 \\ \end{array}} \quad (35)$$

    Answer: 3.875

39. A decimal can be divided by a power of 10 by moving the decimal to the left as many places as indicated by the power. If divided by 10, the decimal point is moved one place; if divided by 100, the decimal point is moved two places, etc. If there are not enough places, add zeros in front of the number to make up the difference and add a decimal point.
    Example: .4 divided by 10 = .04
    .4 divided by 100 = .004

CONVERSION OF FRACTIONS TO DECIMALS

40. A fraction can be changed to a decimal by dividing the numerator by the denominator and working out the division to as many decimal places as required.
Illustration: Change 5/11 to a decimal of 2 places.

$$\text{SOLUTION:} \quad 5/11 = 11\overline{)\begin{array}{l} .45 \;\; ^5\!/_{11} \\ 5.00 \\ \underline{4.44} \\ 60 \\ \underline{55} \\ 5 \end{array}} \quad (27b)$$

Answer: .45 $^5\!/_{11}$

41. If the problem requires the fraction to be changed to the nearest decimal point, carry it out one place further. Then, if the last digit is 5 or more, add 1 to the digit before, if it less than 5, discard the last digit.

Illustration: What is 6/7 in decimal form to the nearest tenth?

$$\text{SOLUTION:} \quad 6/7 \quad 7\overline{)\begin{array}{l} .85 \\ 6.00 \\ \underline{5\,6} \\ 40 \\ \underline{35} \\ 5 \end{array}}$$

.85 to the nearest tenth=.9
Answer: .9

42. To clear fractions containing a decimal in either the numerator or the denominator, or in both, divide the numerator by the denominator.

Illustration: What is the value of 2.34/.6

$$\text{SOLUTION:} \quad 2.34/.6 = .6\overline{)2.34} = 6\overline{)\begin{array}{l} 3.9 \\ 23.4 \\ \underline{18} \\ 5\,4 \\ \underline{5\,4} \end{array}}$$
(37)

Answer: 3.9

CONVERSION OF DECIMALS TO FRACTIONS

43 Since a decimal point indicates a denominator which is a power of 10, a decimal can be expressed as a fraction the numerator of which is the number itself and the denominator of which is the power indicated by the number of decimal places there were in the decimal.
Example: .3=$^3\!/_{10}$, .47=$^{47}\!/_{100}$ (27a)

44. When the decimal is a mixed number, divide by the power of 10 indicated by its number of decimal places. The fraction does not count as a decimal place.

Illustration: Change .25⅓ to a fraction.
$$\begin{array}{ll} \text{SOLUTION:} \; .25\tfrac{1}{3} = 25\tfrac{1}{3} \div 100 & (44) \\ \qquad\qquad\quad = ^{76}\!/_3 \times ^1\!/_{100} & (24) \\ \qquad\qquad\quad = ^{76}\!/_{300} = ^{19}\!/_{75} & (8) \end{array}$$
Answer: $^{19}\!/_{75}$

45. When to change decimals to fractions.
a. When dealing with whole numbers, do not change the decimal.

Example: In the problem 12 x .14, it is better to keep the decimal. 12 x .14 = 1.68 (30)
b. When dealing with fractions, change the decimal to a fraction.

Example: In the problem ⅗ x .17, it is best to change the decimal to a fraction.
$$\tfrac{3}{5} \times .17 = \tfrac{3}{5} \times ^{17}\!/_{100} = {}^{51}\!/_{500} \quad (43, 16)$$

PROBLEMS INVOLVING DECIMALS

1. Add 37.03, 11.5627, 3.4005, 3423, and 1.141 (a) 3476.1342 (b) 3500 (c) 3524.4322 (d) 3424.1342.

2. Subtract 4.64324 from 7. (a) 3.35676 (b) 2.35676 (c) 2.45676 (d) 2.36676.

3. Multiply 27.34 by 16.943 (a) 463.22162 (b) 453.52162 (c) 462.52162 (d) 462.53162

4. How much is 19.6 divided by 3.2 **carried out to 3 decimal places.** (a) 6.125 (b) 6.124 (c) 6.123 (d) 5.123.

5. What is $\frac{5}{11}$ in decimal form? (To the nearest hundredth) (a) .44 (b) .55 (c) .40 (d) .45.

6. What is .64⅔ in fraction form? (a) $^{97}\!/_{120}$ (b) $^{97}\!/_{150}$ (c) $^{97}\!/_{130}$ (d) $^{98}\!/_{130}$.

7. What is the difference between ⅗ and ⅞ expressed decimally? (a) .525 (b) .425 (c) .520 (d) .500.

8. If 314 clerks filed 6594 papers in 10 minutes, what is the number filed per minute by the average clerk? (a) 2 (b) 2.4 (c) 2.1 (d) 2.5.

9. A man receives a monthly salary of $120 and saves .08⅓ of his earnings. How many months would it take him to save $1000? (a) 90 (b) 80 (c) 85 (d) 100.

10. A man willed his property to his three sons,—to the youngest he gave $968.49, to the second 3.4 as much as to the youngest, and to the eldest 3.7 times as much as to the second. What was the value of his estate (to the nearest penny)? (a) $16,450.50 (b) $16,444.55 (c) $16,444.90 (d) $16,444.96.

Correct Answers

(You'll learn more by writing your own answers before comparing them with these.)

1. a	3. a	5. d	7. a	9. d
2. b	4. a	6. b	8. c	10. d

PROBLEM SOLUTIONS — Decimals

1. SOLUTION:
Add:

```
   37.03
   11.5627
    3.4005
3423.0000
    1.141
─────────
3476.1342   (a)
```

ANSWER: Sum = 3476.1342

2. SOLUTION:
Subtract 4.64324 from 7

```
 7.00000
−4.64324
────────
 2.35676   (b)
```

ANSWER: Difference = 2.35676

3. SOLUTION:
Multiply 27.34 by 16.943

$$
\begin{array}{r}
27.34 \\
\times 16.943 \\
\hline
8202 \\
109360 \\
2460600 \\
16404000 \\
27340000 \\
\hline
463.22162 \quad (a)
\end{array}
$$

ANSWER: Product = 463.22162

4. SOLUTION:
Divide 19.6 by 3.2 to 3 decimal places

$$
\begin{array}{r}
6.125 \quad (a) \\
3.2)\overline{19.6,000} \\
19\,2 \\
\hline
4\,0 \\
3\,2 \\
\hline
80 \\
64 \\
\hline
160 \\
160 \\
\hline
\end{array}
$$

ANSWER Quotient = 6.125

5. SOLUTION:
$5/11$ in decimal form
.45 $5/11$ (d) $5/11$ less than $1/2$ so drop it

$$
\begin{array}{r}
.45 \\
11)\overline{5.00} \\
4\,4 \\
\hline
60 \\
55 \\
\hline
5
\end{array}
$$

ANSWER: Decimal = .45

6. SOLUTION:
$.64\tfrac{2}{3}$ in fraction form

$.64\tfrac{2}{3} = \dfrac{64\tfrac{2}{3}}{100} = \dfrac{\tfrac{194}{3}}{100} = \dfrac{194}{3} \times \dfrac{1}{100} = \dfrac{194}{300} = \dfrac{97}{150}$ (b)

ANSWER: $.64\tfrac{2}{3} = \dfrac{97}{150}$ in fraction form

7. SOLUTION:
Difference between $3/5$ and $9/8$ expressed decimally
$9/8 = 1.125$ $3/5 = .60$

$$
\begin{array}{r}
1.125 \\
- .60 \\
\hline
.525 \quad (a)
\end{array}
$$

ANSWER: Difference = .525

8. SOLUTION:
6594 papers ÷ 314 clerks = 21 papers per clerk
21 papers ÷ 10 minutes = 2.1 papers per minute filed by average clerk (c)

ANSWER: Average clerk filed 2.1 papers per minute

9. SOLUTION:

$$
\begin{array}{r}
\$120 \text{ monthly salary} \\
\times .08\tfrac{1}{3} \\
\hline
40 \\
9\,60 \\
\hline
\$10.00 \text{ saved monthly}
\end{array}
$$

$1000 ÷ $10 = 100 months (d)

ANSWER: Saved 100 months

10. SOLUTION:

$$
\begin{array}{r}
\$968.49 \text{ willed to youngest son} \\
\times 3.4 \\
\hline
387396 \\
2905470 \\
\hline
\$3292.866 \text{ to second son} = \$3292.87 \\
\times 3.7 \\
\hline
23050062 \\
98785980 \\
\hline
\$12183.6042 \text{ to eldest son} = \$12,183.60
\end{array}
$$

$$
\begin{array}{rl}
\$968.49 & \text{youngest son} \\
3,292.87 & \text{second son} \\
12,183.60 & \text{eldest son} \\
\hline
\$16,444.96 & \text{value of estate} \quad (d)
\end{array}
$$

ANSWER: Value of estate = \$16,444.96

PERCENTS

46. The per cent sign (%) is a symbol used to indicate percentage, but no operations can be performed with the number to which it is attached. For convenience, then, it is sometimes required to attach a per cent sign; but to perform operations with the number, it is necessary to remove the per cent sign.
    a. In general, to add a % sign, multiply the number by 100.
    Example: 3=300%
    b. In general, to remove a % sign, divide the number by 100.
    Example: 200%=2
    c. A per cent may be expressed as a decimal or a fraction by dividing it by 100.
    Example: 57%=.57   (39)
            9%=$^9/_{100}$ (1b)
    d. A decimal may be expressed as a per cent by multiplying it by 100.
    Example: .67=67%   (31)

47. To change a fraction or a mixed number to a per cent:
    a. Multiply the fraction or mixed number by 100.
    b. Reduce, if possible.
    c. Add a % sign.

    Illustration: Change $\frac{1}{7}$ to a per cent.
    SOLUTION: $\frac{1}{7}$x100=$^{100}/_7$
                       (16, 47a, 46a)
            =$14\frac{2}{7}$ (5, 47b)
        $\frac{1}{7}$=$14\frac{2}{7}$%   (47c)
    Answer: $14\frac{2}{7}$%
    Illustration: Change $4\frac{2}{3}$ to a per cent.
    SOLUTION: $4\frac{2}{3}$x100=$1\frac{4}{3}$x100=$^{1400}/_3$
                     (16, 47a)
            =$466\frac{2}{3}$
                 (5, 47b)
        $4\frac{2}{3}$=$466\frac{2}{3}$%   (47c)
    Answer: $466\frac{2}{3}$%

48. To remove a % sign attached to a decimal and to keep it as a decimal, divide the decimal by 100.
    Example: .5%=.5÷100=.005   (39)

49. To remove a % sign attached to a decimal and to change the number to a fraction:
    a. Divide the decimal by 100.
    b. Change this result to a fraction.
    c. Reduce, if necessary

    Illustration: Change 15.05% to a fraction.
    SOLUTION:
       15.05%=15.05÷100=.1505
                        (39, 49a)
            =1505/10000
                        (43, 49b)
            =301/2000
                        (6, 49c)
    Answer: 301/2000

50. To remove a % sign attached to a fraction or mixed number and to keep it as a fraction, divide the fraction or mixed number by 100.

    Illustration: Change $\frac{3}{4}$% to a fraction.
    SOLUTION: $\frac{3}{4}$%=$\frac{3}{4}$÷100=$\frac{3}{4}$ x 1/100
                        (22)
            =3/400
    Answer: 3/400

51. To remove a % sign attached to a fraction or mixed number and to change the number to a decimal:
    a. Divide the fraction or mixed number by 100.
    b. Change this result to a decimal.

    Illustration: Change 3/5% to a decimal.
    SOLUTION:
       3/5%=3/5÷100=3/5x1/100 (22, 51a)
               =3/500   (16)
            .006   (40, 51b)
     3/500=500$\overline{)3.000}$
    Answer: .006

52. To remove a % sign attached to a decimal including a fraction and to keep it as a decimal, divide the decimal by 100.
    Example: .5$\frac{1}{3}$%=.005$\frac{1}{3}$ (39)

53. To remove a % sign attached to a decimal including a fraction and to change the number to a fraction:
a. Divide the decimal by 100.
b. Change this result to a fraction.
c. Clear this mixed fraction.
d. Reduce, if necessary.

Illustration: change .14 1/6% to a fraction.
SOLUTION: .14 1/6% = .0014 1/6
$$(39, 53a)$$
$$= \frac{14\ 1/6}{10000}$$
$$(43, 53b)$$

$$= 14\ 1/6 \div 10000$$
$$(24, 53c)$$
$$= 85/6 \times 1/10000$$
$$(22)$$
$$= 85/60000$$
$$(16)$$
$$= 17/12000$$
$$(7, 53d)$$

Answer: 17/12000

53A. In a percentage problem, the whole is 100% (or 1).
Example: If a problem involves 10% of a quantity, the rest of the quantity is 90%.

PERCENTAGE PROBLEMS

1. What per cent is 2 5/13? (a) 239 6/13% (b) 238 6/13% (c) 237 6/14% (d) 200 6/13%.

2. What is 5.37% in fraction form? (a) 537/10,000 (b) 5 37/10,000 (c) 537/1000 (d) 5 37/100.

3. What is ¾% in decimal form? (a) .75 (b) 7.5 (c) .075 (d) .0075.

4. What is 2 3/7% in fraction form? (a) 18/700 (b) 17/800 (c) 17/1700 (d) 17/700.

5. What per cent is 14% of 23%? (a) 60% (b) 61½% (c) 60 20/23% (d) 60 2/5%.

6. The entrance price to see an exhibition was reduced by 25%, but the daily attendance increased 30%. What was the effect of this on the daily receipts? (a) 2% increase (b) 2% decrease (c) 2½% increase (d) 2½% decrease.

7. A house valued at $4,750 is insured for 4/5 of its value at 1¼%. What is the amount of premium which must be paid? (a) $47.50 (b) $47.00 (c) $46.00 (d) $48.50.

8. A certain family spends 30% of its income for food, 8% for clothing, 25% for shelter, 4% for recreation, 13% for education, and 5% for miscellaneous items. The weekly earnings are $50. What is the number of weeks it would take this family to save $1500? (a) 100 (b) 150 (c) 175 (d) 200.

9. On Monday a man deposited $360 in the bank. On Tuesday he deposited a sum 5% greater than the deposit of Monday; and on Wednesday he deposited a sum 4% greater than the sum of the first two deposits; on Thursday he withdrew 25% of the total deposit. How much did he have left in the bank? (a) $1130 (b) $1129.14 (c) $1130.45 (d) $1142.50.

10. A man owned 50 shares of stock worth $75 each. The firm declared a dividend of 4%, payable in stock. How many shares did he then own? (a) 50 (b) 52 (c) 53 (d) 54.

Correct Answers				
1. b	3. d	5. c	7. a	9. b
2. a	4. d	6. d	8. d	10. b

NOW, CHECK YOUR METHODS WITH OUR SIMPLIFIED PROBLEM SOLUTIONS, WHICH FOLLOW.

PROBLEM SOLUTIONS Percentage

1. $2\frac{5}{13} =$ what %
SOLUTION:
$2\frac{5}{13} = \frac{31}{13}$

$$\begin{array}{r} 2.38\frac{6}{13} = 238\frac{6}{13}\% \quad \text{(b)} \\ 13\overline{)31.00} \\ \underline{26} \\ 50 \\ \underline{39} \\ 110 \\ \underline{104} \\ 6 \end{array}$$

ANSWER: $2\frac{5}{13} = 238\frac{6}{13}\%$

2. 5.37% in fraction form
SOLUTION:

$5.37\% = .0537 = \dfrac{537}{10,000}$ (a)

ANSWER: $5.37\% = \dfrac{537}{10,000}$ in fraction form

3. ¾% in decimal form
SOLUTION: $\frac{3}{4}\% = \frac{3}{4} \div 100 = \frac{3}{400} = .0\frac{3}{4}$
$= .0075$
$\frac{3}{4}\% = .0075$ in decimal form   (d)

ANSWER: $\frac{3}{4}\% = .0075$ in decimal form

4. $2\frac{3}{7}\%$ in fraction form
SOLUTION:

$2\frac{3}{7}\% = \dfrac{17\%}{7} = \dfrac{17}{7} \cdot \dfrac{1}{100} = \dfrac{17}{700}$ (d)

ANSWER: $2\frac{3}{7}\% = \dfrac{17}{700}$ in fraction form

5. What % is 14% of 23%?
SOLUTION:

$$14\% \text{ of } 23\% = 23\overline{)14.00}\;.60\tfrac{20}{23} = 60\tfrac{20}{23}\% \quad \text{(c)}$$
$$\underline{13\,8}$$
$$20$$

ANSWER: 14% of 23% $= 60\frac{20}{23}\%$

6. SOLUTION:
100% $-$ 25% $=$ 75% entrance price
100% $+$ 30% $=$ 130% daily attendance

$$\begin{array}{r} 1.30 \\ \times \;.75 \\ \hline 650 \\ 9100 \\ \hline .9750 \text{ income} \end{array}$$

$$\begin{array}{r} 100.0\% \text{ daily receipts} \\ -\;97.5\% \text{ income} \\ \hline 2.5\% \text{ or } 2\frac{1}{2}\% \text{ decrease} \quad \text{(d)} \end{array}$$

ANSWER: Decrease of $2\frac{1}{2}\%$

7. SOLUTION:
Value of house $4750. Insurance $\frac{4}{5}$ of value at $1\frac{1}{4}\%$

$$\$\cancel{4750}\overset{950}{} \times \frac{4}{\cancel{5}1} = \$3800 \text{ insurance value}$$

$$\$3800 \times 1\frac{1}{4}\% = \$\cancel{3800}\overset{19}{} \times \frac{5}{\cancel{4}2} \times \frac{1}{\cancel{100}1} =$$

$$\frac{95}{2} = \$47\frac{1}{2} = \$47.50 \text{ premium} \quad \text{(a)}$$

ANSWER: Premium $= \$47.50$

8. SOLUTION:

30%	income spent
8%	" "
25%	" "
4%	" "
13%	" "
5%	" "
85%	income expenses

"or"
$30\% + 8\% + 25\% + 4\% + 13\% + 5\% =$
85% expenses

$$\begin{array}{r} 100\% \text{ income} \\ -\;85\% \text{ expenses} \\ \hline 15\% \text{ saves} \end{array} \qquad \begin{array}{r} \$50 \text{ weekly earnings} \\ \times .15 \\ \hline \$7.50 \text{ saves weekly} \end{array}$$

$$\begin{array}{r} 2\,00.\text{weeks} \quad \text{(d)} \\ \$7.50\,)\$1500.00. \text{ to save} \\ \underline{1500} \\ 00 \end{array}$$

ANSWER: 200 weeks to save $1500

9. SOLUTION:
Monday deposits $360
$360 × 5% = $360 × .05 = $18.00
$$\begin{array}{r} + 360.00 \\ \hline \$378.00 \text{ Tuesday} \end{array}$$

$$\begin{array}{r} \$378 \text{ Tuesday deposits} \\ 360 \text{ Monday deposits} \\ \hline \$738 \text{ both days deposits} \\ \times .04 \\ \hline \$29.52 \\ + 738.00 \\ \hline \$767.52 \text{ Wednesday deposits} \end{array}$$

$$\begin{array}{rl} \$360 & \text{deposited Monday} \\ 378 & \text{deposited Tuesday} \\ 767.52 & \text{deposited Wednesday} \\ \hline \$1505.52 & \text{Total deposits in bank} \end{array}$$

Withdrew 25% Thursday = ¼

$1505.52 × $\frac{1}{4}$ = $376.38 withdrew Thursday

$1505.52 (total) −$376.38 = $1129.14 left in bank (b)

ANSWER: Left in bank $1129.14

10. SOLUTION:
$75 × 50 = $3750 value of stock
$$\begin{array}{r} \$3750 \text{ value of stock} \\ \times .04 \\ \hline \$150.00 \text{ dividend} \end{array}$$

$$\begin{array}{r} 2 \text{ dividend shares} \\ \$75 \overline{)\$150} \\ 150 \\ \hline \end{array}$$

$$\begin{array}{r} 50 \text{ shares owned} \\ + 2 \text{ shares dividend} \\ \hline 52 \text{ shares then owned} \quad (b) \end{array}$$

ANSWER: Shares then owned = 52

PROFIT AND LOSS

62. The following terms may be encountered in profit and loss problems:
    a. The cost price of an article is the price paid by a person who wishes to sell it again.
    b. There may be an allowance or trade discount on the cost price.
    c. The list price or marked price is the price at which the article is listed or marked to be sold.
    d. There may be a discount or series of discounts on the list price.
    e. The selling price or sales price is the price at which the article is finally sold.
    f. If the selling price is greater than the cost price, there has been a profit.
    g. If the selling price is lower than the cost price, there has been a loss.
    h. If the article is sold at the same price as the cost, there has been no loss or profit.
    i. Profit or loss may be based either on the cost price or on the selling price.
    j. Profit or loss may be stated in terms of dollars and cents, or in terms of per cent.
    k. Overhead expenses include such items as rent, salaries, etc. and may be added to the selling price.

63. To find the profit in terms of money, subtract the cost price from the selling price, or selling price—cost price=profit.
    Example: If an article costing $3.00 is sold for $5.00, the profit is $5.00—$3.00=$2.00

64. To find the loss in terms of money, subtract the selling price from the cost price, or, cost price—selling price=loss.
    Example: If an article costing $2.00 is sold for $1.50, the loss is $2.00—$1.50=$.50

65. If the profit or loss is expressed in terms of money, then
    a. Cost price+profit=selling price.
    b. Cost price—loss=selling price.
    Example: If the cost of an article is $2.50, and the profit is $1.50, then the selling price is $2.50+$1.50=$4.00   (65a)

Example: If the cost of an article is $3.00, and the loss is $1.20, then the selling price is $3.00—$1.20=$1.80

66. To find the selling price if the profit is expressed in per cent based on cost price:
    a. Multiply the cost price by the % profit to find the profit in terms of money.
    b. Add this product to the cost price.

    Illustration: Find the selling price of an article costing $3.00 which was sold at a profit of 15% of the cost price.
    SOLUTION: $3.00×15%=3.00×.15
                                         (46c, 66a)
                          =$.45=Profit
                                              (30)
              $3.00+$.45=$3.45
                                         (65a, 66b)
    Answer: The selling price is $3.45

67. To find the selling price if the loss is expressed in per cent based on cost price:
    a. Multiply the cost price by the % loss to find the loss in terms of money.
    b. Subtract this product from the cost price.

    Illustration: If an article costing $2.00 is sold at a loss of 5% of the cost price, find the selling price.
    SOLUTION: $2.00×5%=2.00×.05
                                         (46c, 67a)
                          =$.10=loss (30)
              $2.00—$.10=$1.90
                                         (65b, 67b)
    Answer: The selling price is $1.90

68. To find the cost price when given the selling price and the % profit based on the selling price:
    a. Multiply the selling price by the % profit to find the profit in terms of money.
    b. Subtract this product from the selling price.
    Illustration: If an article sells for $12.00 and there has been a profit of 10% of the selling price, what is the cost price?

SOLUTION: $$\$12.00 \times 10\% = 12.00 \times .10$$
(46c, 68a)

$$= \$1.20 = \text{profit}$$
(30)

$$\$12.00 - \$1.20 = \$10.80$$
(68b)

Answer: Cost price $10.80

69. To find the cost price when given the selling price and the % loss based on the selling price:

   a. Multiply the selling price by the % loss to find the loss in terms of money.
   b. Add this product to the selling price.
   Illustration: What is the cost price of an article selling for $2.00 on which there has been a loss of 6% of the selling price?
   SOLUTION: $$\$2.00 \times 6\% = 2.00 \times .06$$
(46c, 69a)

$$= \$.12 = \text{loss}$$
(30)

$$\$2.00 + \$.12 = \$2.12$$
(69b)

   Answer: Cost price $= \$2.12$

70. To find the % profit based on cost price:
   a. Find the profit in terms of money.
   b. Divide the profit by the cost price.
   c. Convert to a per cent.
   Illustration: Find the % profit based on cost price of an article costing $2.50 and selling for $3.00
   SOLUTION: $$\$3.00 - \$2.50 = \$.50 = \text{profit}$$
(63, 70a)

$$2.50 \overline{\smash{)}.50} = 250 \overline{\smash{)}50.00} = .20$$
(37, 38, 70b)

$$= 20\%$$
(46d, 70c)

   Answer: Profit $= 20\%$

71. To find the % loss based on cost price:
   a. Find the loss in terms of money.
   b. Divide the loss by the cost price.
   c. Convert to a per cent.
   Illustration: Find the % loss based on cost price of an article costing $5.00 and selling for $4.80.
   SOLUTION: $$\$5.00 - \$4.80 = \$.20 = \text{loss}$$
(64, 71a)

$$5.00 \overline{\smash{)}.20} = 500 \overline{\smash{)}20.00} = .04$$
(37, 38, 71b)
(46d, 71c)

$$= 4\%$$

   Answer: Loss $= 4\%$

72. To find the % profit based on selling price:
   a. Find the profit in terms of money.

b. Divide the profit by the selling price.
c. Convert to a per cent.
Illustration: Find the % profit based on the selling price of an article costing $2.50 and selling for $3.00.
SOLUTION:

$$\$3.00 - \$2.50 = \$.50 = \text{profit} \quad (63, 72a)$$
$$3.00 \overline{\smash{)}.50} = 300 \overline{\smash{)}50.00} = .16\tfrac{2}{3}$$
(37, 38, 72b)

$$= 16\tfrac{2}{3}\%$$
(46d, 72c)

Answer: Profit $= 16\tfrac{2}{3}\%$

73. To find the % loss based on selling price:
   a. Find the loss in terms of money.
   b. Divide the loss by the selling price.
   c. Convert to a per cent.
   Illustration: Find the % loss based on the selling price of an article costing $5.00 and selling for $4.80.
   SOLUTION:

$$\$5.00 - \$4.80 = \$.20 = \text{loss} \quad (64, 73a)$$
$$4.80 \overline{\smash{)}.20} = 480 \overline{\smash{)}20.00} = .04\tfrac{1}{6}$$
(37, 38, 73b)

   Answer: Loss $4\tfrac{1}{6}\%$

74. To find the cost price when given the selling price and the % profit based on the cost price:
   a. Establish a relation between the selling price and the cost price.
   b. Solve to find the cost price.

   Illustration: An article is sold for $2.50 which is a 25% profit of the cost price. What is the cost price?
   SOLUTION: Since the selling price represents the whole cost price plus 25% of the cost price,

$$2.50 = 125\% \text{ of the cost price} \quad (74a, 53a)$$
$$2.50 = \tfrac{125}{100} \text{ of the cost price} \quad (56a)$$
$$\text{Cost price} = 2.50 \div \tfrac{125}{100}$$
$$= 2.50 \times \tfrac{100}{125} \quad (22)$$
$$= \tfrac{250}{125} = \$2.00 \quad (31, 74b)$$

   Answer: Cost price $= \$2.00$

75. To find the selling price when given the profit based on the selling price.
   a. Establish a relation between the selling price and the cost price.
   b. Solve to find the selling price.

   Illustration: A merchant buys an article for $27.00 and sells it at a profit of 10% of the selling price. What is the selling price?

SOLUTION:

$27.00 +$ profit $=$ selling price   (65a)

Since the profit is 10% of the selling price, the cost price must be 90% of the selling price.   (53a)

$27.00 = 90\%$ of the selling price   (75a)

    $= {}^{9}\!\%_{100}$ of the selling price   (56a)

selling price $= 27.00 \times {}^{10}\!\%_{90}$ (56b, 24)

    $= \$30.00$ (18, 75b)

Answer: Selling price $= \$30.00$

76. To find the selling price when given the % loss of the selling price:
   a. Establish a relation between the cost price and the selling price.
   b. Solve to find the selling price.

Illustration: Find the selling price of an article bought for $5.00 on which there is a 25% loss on the selling price.

SOLUTION:

$\$5.00 -$ loss $=$ selling price   (65b)

Since the loss is 25% of the selling price, the cost price must be 125% of the selling price.   (53a)

$5.00 = 125\%$ of the selling price. (76a)

$5.00 = {}^{125}\!\%_{100}$ of the selling price (56a)

selling price $= 5.00 \times {}^{10}\!\%_{125}$ (56b, 24)

    $= \$4.00$ (18, 76b)

Answer: Selling price $= \$4.00$

77. TRADE DISCOUNTS — A trade discount, usually expressed in per cent, indicates the part that is to be deducted from the list price.

78. To find the selling price when given the list price and the % discount:
   a. Multiply the list price by the % discount to find the discount in terms of money.
   b. Subtract the discount from the list price.
   Illustration: The list price of an article is $20.00. There is a discount of 5%. What is the selling price?
   SOLUTION:

$\$20.00 \times 5\% = 20.00 \times .05 = \$1.00 =$ discount.   (46c, 30, 78a)

$\$20.00 - \$1.00 = \$19.00$ (78b)

Answer: Selling price $= \$19.00$

79. SERIES OF DISCOUNTS—There may be more than one discount to be deducted from the list price. These are called a discount series.

80. To find the selling price when given the list price and a discount series:
   a. Multiply the list price by the first % discount.
   b. Subtract this product from the list price.
   c. Multiply the remainder by the second discount.
   d. Subtract this product from the remainder.
   e. Continue the same procedure if there are more discounts.

Illustration: Find the selling price of an article listed at $10.00 on which there are discounts of 20% and 10%.

SOLUTION:

$\$10.00 \times 20\% = 10.00 \times .20 = \$2.00$ (46c, 30, 80a)

$\$10.00 - \$2.00 = \$8.00$ (80b)

$\$8.00 \times 10\% = 8.00 \times .10 = \$.80$ (46c, 30, 80c)

$\$8.00 - \$.80 = \$7.20$ (80d)

Answer: Selling price $= \$7.20$

81. Instead of deducting each discount individually, it is often more practicable to find the single equivalent discount first and then deduct. It does not matter in which order the discounts are taken.

82. To find the single equivalent discount of a discount series:
   a. Add the first two discounts.
   b. Multiply the first two discounts.
   c. Subtract this product from the sum to find the equivalent discount of the first two discounts.
   d. If there is a third discount, add the equivalent of the first two discounts to the third.
   e. Multiply the equivalent of the first two discounts by the third.
   f. Subtract this product from the sum to find the equivalent of the three discounts.
   g. Continue the same procedure if there are more discounts.

Illustration: What is the single discount equivalent to the discount series 20%, 25%, and 10%?

SOLUTION:

$20\% + 25\% = .20 + .25 = .45$ (46c, 28, 82a)

$20\% \times 25\% = .20 \times .25 = .0500$ (46c, 30, 82b)

$.45 - .05 = .40$ (27b, 29, 82c)

$.40 + 10\% = .40 + .10 = .50$ (46c, 28, 82d)

$.40 \times 10\% = .40 \times .10 = .0400$ (46c, 30, 82e)

$.50 - .04 = .46$ (27b, 29, 82b)

$.46 = 46\%$ (46d)

Answer: The single equivalent discount of the three discounts is 46%.

PROFIT AND LOSS PROBLEMS

1. A car cost a dealer $516. He wishes to mark it so that he may deduct 20% from the marked price and still make a profit of 25% of the cost. What is the list price? (a) $806.25 (b) $805.25 (c) $800.00 (d) $805.00.

2. A dealer sells a set of furniture for $900 which is 80% more than he paid for it. At what price must he sell the same set to make 120% on the cost price? (a) $1000 (b) $1100 (c) $1200 (d) $1250.

3. A man sells two houses for $2400 each. He makes 20% of the cost price on the first, but on the second he has a loss of 20% of the cost price. How much did he gain or lose by this transaction? (a) $200 loss (b) $200 gain (c) $250 loss (d) $250 gain.

4. A merchant sells a shipment of gloves at a profit of 16%. He invests the proceeds of this sale in a lot of women's dresses which he sells at a loss of 4% of the cost. He makes a net profit of $56.80. What was the cost of the gloves? (a) $600 (b) $200 (c) $500 (d) $450.

5. After marking down a desk 20%, a dealer asked $40 for it. Being unable to sell it at this price, he gave another discount of 5% and still made $8. What was the percent above cost at which the desk was originally marked? ,a) 50% (b) 60% (c) 66⅔% (d) 33⅓%.

6. If the cost of an article is $3.80, the profit being 20% of the cost and the selling expense 5% of the sales, what is the selling price? (a) $5.00 (b) $4.40 (c) $4.50 (d) $4.80.

7. A company had been selling its pianos for $325, less 20% for cash. To increase its sales, it decided to allow an additional discount so that a piano could sell for $234. What was the second discount allowed? (a) 70% (b) 8% (c) 9% (d) 10%.

8. A manufacturer's list price is 40% above the cost of manufacture. He allows a trade discount of 10% from the list price. What is his per cent profit based on cost price? (a) 25% (b) 26% (c) 28% (d) 30%.

9. Assuming that the yearly depreciation value of a typewriter is 10%, what is closest to the original cost if the value at the end of the third year is $65.61? (a) $60 (b) $70 (c) $80 (d) $90.

10. If a man buys an article at ¾ its value and sells it for 20% more than its value, what is his per cent profit based on cost? (a) 50% (b) 60% (c) 70% (d) 80%.

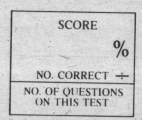

SCORE
.... %
NO. CORRECT ÷
NO. OF QUESTIONS ON THIS TEST

Correct Answers

(You'll learn more by writing your own answers before comparing them with these.)

1. a	3. a	5. c	7. d	9. d
2. b	4. c	6. d	8. b	10. b

NOW, CHECK YOUR METHODS WITH OUR

SIMPLIFIED PROBLEM SOLUTIONS, WHICH FOLLOW

PROBLEM SOLUTIONS — Profit and Loss

1. SOLUTION:
Cost of car = \$516 $\quad$ 25% = ¼

$$100\% - 20\% = \$516 + \left(\$\overset{129}{\cancel{516}} \times \frac{1}{\underset{1}{\cancel{4}}}\right)$$

$80\% = \$516 + \$129 = \$645$
$\$645 = 80\%$ of list price
List Price = $\$645 \div 80\% = \$645 \div \frac{80}{100} = \$645 \times \frac{10\cancel{0}}{8\cancel{0}} = \$806.25$

ANSWER: \$806.25 (a)

2. SOLUTION:
$100\% + 80\% = 180\%$ or $1\frac{4}{5} \times$ cost price equals selling price

$$\$900 \div 1\tfrac{4}{5} = \$900 \times \frac{5}{9} = \$500 \text{ Cost Price}$$

$120\% = 1\frac{1}{5}$

$$\$500 \times 1\tfrac{1}{5} = \$\overset{100}{\cancel{500}} \times \frac{6}{\underset{1}{\cancel{5}}} = \$600 \text{ to make}$$

120%
$\$600 + \$500 = \$1100$ Selling Price (b)

ANSWER: \$1100 = Selling Price

3. SOLUTION:
$100\% + 20\% = 120\%$ Selling Price on one house
$100\% - 20\% = 80\%$ Selling Price on another house
$120\% = 1\frac{1}{5}$
$80\% = \frac{4}{5}$
$120\% = \$2400$

$$\$2400 \div 1\tfrac{1}{5} = \$2400 \div \tfrac{6}{5} = \$\overset{400}{\cancel{2400}} \times \frac{5}{\underset{1}{\cancel{6}}} = \$2000 \text{ Cost}$$

$\$2400 - \$2000 = \$400$ profit on first house
$100\% - 20\% = 80\% = \frac{4}{5}$

$$\$2400 \div \tfrac{4}{5} = \$\overset{600}{\cancel{2400}} \times \frac{5}{\underset{1}{\cancel{4}}} = \$3000 \text{ Cost 2nd house}$$

$\$3000 - \$2400 = \$600$ loss 2nd house
\$600 loss − \$400 profit = \$200 loss (a)

ANSWER: Loss = \$200

4. SOLUTION:
$100\% + 16\% = 116\%$ Selling Price at profit of 16%
$100\% - 4\% = 96\%$ Selling Price at loss of 4%
$1.16 \times .96 = 1.1136 \quad 1.1136 - 1.00 = .1136 \quad .1136 = \$56.80$
$\$56.80 \div .1136 = \$500$ Cost (c)

ANSWER: Cost = \$500

5. SOLUTION:
$100\% - 5\% = 95\%$ second discount
$\$40 \times .95 = \$38.00$ Selling Price
$100\% - 20\% = 80\%$ first discount
$80\% = \$40$
$\$40 \div .80 = \$50$ marked price
$\$38 - \$8 = \$30$ cost
$\$50 - \$30 = \$20$ marked up

$$\$20 \div \$30 = \frac{20}{30} = \tfrac{2}{3} = 66\tfrac{2}{3}\% \qquad \text{(c)}$$

ANSWER: 66⅔% above original cost

6. SOLUTION:
$\$3.80$ = cost $\quad$ 20% profit
$100\% + 20\% = 120\% = 1\frac{1}{5} = \frac{6}{5}$

$$\$\overset{.76}{\cancel{3.80}} \times \frac{6}{\underset{1}{\cancel{5}}} = \$4.56$$

$\$100\% - 5\% = 95\%$
$\$4.56 \div .95 = \$4.80$ Selling Price (d)

ANSWER: Selling Price = \$4.80

7. SOLUTION
$\$325 \times 20\% = \$65.00$ discount
$\$325 - \$65 = \$260$ Selling Price
$\$260 - \$234 = \$26$ second discount

$$\$26 \div \$260 = \frac{26}{260} = \frac{1}{10} = 10\% \qquad \text{(d)}$$

ANSWER: Second discount allowed = 10%

8. SOLUTION:
$100\% + 40\% = 140\% = 1.40$
$1.40 \times .10 = .14 = 14\%$ trade discount
$140\% - 14\% = 126\%$
$126\% - 100\% = 26\%$ profit (b)

ANSWER: Profit = 26%

9. SOLUTION:

$100\% \times 10\% = 10\%$ $100\% - 10\% =$ 90% value at end of first year.

$90\% \times 10\% = 9\%$

$90\% - 9\% = 81\%$ value second year

$81\% \times 10\% = 8.1\%$

$81\% - 8.1\% = 72.9\%$ value third year

$72.9\% = \$65.61$

$\$65.61 \div .729 = \$90$ original cost   (d)

ANSWER: Original cost = \$90

10. SOLUTION:

$100\% =$ original value

$100\% \times \frac{3}{4} = 75\%$ cost

$100\% + 20\% = 120\%$ Selling Price

$120\% - 75\% = 45\%$ profit

$45\% \div 75\% = \dfrac{45}{75} = \dfrac{3}{5} = 60\%$ (b)

ANSWER: Per cent based on cost = 60%

INTEREST

83. Interest is the price paid for the use of money. There are three items considered in interest:
    1. The principal which is the amount of money bearing interest.
    2. The interest rate, expressed in per cent on an annual basis.
    3. The time, during which the principal is used.

84. Since the interest rate is an annual rate, the time must be expressed annually, too.
    a. If the time is given in years, or part of a year, do not change the figures given.
    b. If the time is given in months it should be expressed as a fraction, the numerator of which is the number of months given, and the denominator of which is 12.
    c. If the time is given in days, it should be expressed as a fraction, the numerator of which is the number of days given, and the denominator of which is 360. (Sometimes, it is required to find the exact interest, in which case 365 is the denominator.)
    d. If the time is given in terms of years and months, change it all to months and form a fraction, the numerator of which is the number of months, and the denominator of which is 12.
    e. If the time is given in terms of years, months, and days, or months and days, or years and days, change it all to days and form a fraction, the numerator of which is the number of days, and the denominator of which is 360 (or 365, if so required.) A month is considered as 30 days.

85. To find the interest when the three items are given:
    a. Change the rate of interest to a fraction.
    b. Express the time as a fractional part of a year.
    c. Multiply all three items.
    Illustration: Find the interest on $400 at at 2¼ % for 3 months and 16 days.
    SOLUTION: $2¼\% = \frac{9}{400}$ (50, 85a)
         3 months and 16 days $= \frac{106}{360}$
         of a year   (84e, 85b)

(30 days to a month)
$$400 \times \frac{9}{400} \times \frac{106}{360}$$
$$= \frac{53}{20} \qquad\qquad (18, 85c)$$
$$= \$2.65 \qquad\qquad (38d)$$
Answer: Interest $2.65

86. If the interest, interest rate, and time are given, to find the principal:
    a. Change the interest rate to a fraction.
    b. Express the time as a fractional part of a year.
    c. Multiply the rate by the time.
    d. Divide the interest by this product.
    Illustration: What amount of money invested at 6% would receive interest of $18 over 1½ years?
    SOLUTION: $6\% = \frac{6}{100}$ (46c, 86a)
             (84a, 86b)
         1½ years $= \frac{3}{2}$ years
         $6/100 \times 3/2 = 9/100$ (18, 86c)
         $\$18 \div 9/100 = 18 \times 100/9$
         $= \$200$ (86d, 22, 18)
    Answer: Amount = $200

87. If the principal, time and interest are given, to find the rate:
    a. Change the time to a fractional part of a year.
    b. Multiply the principal by the time.
    c. Divide the interest by this product.
    d. Convert to a per cent.
    Illustration: At what interest rate should $300 be invested for 40 days to accrue $2 in interest?
    SOLUTION: 40 days $= \frac{40}{360}$ of a year
             (84e, 87a)
         $300 \times \frac{40}{360} = \frac{100}{3}$ (18, 87b)
         $\$2 \div 100/3 = 2 \times 3/100$
         $= 3/50$ (22, 18, 87c)
         $\frac{3}{50} = 6\%$ (47)
    Answer: Interest rate = 6%

88. If the principal, interest, and interest rate are given, to find the time (in years):
    a. Change the interest rate to a fraction (or decimal).

b. Multiply the principal by the rate.

c. Divide the interest by this product.

Illustration: Find the length of time for which $240 must be invested at 5% to accrue $16 in interest.

SOLUTION: 5%=.05   (46c, 88a)

    240x.05=12   (18, 88b)

    16÷12=1⅓   (88c)

Answer: Time=1⅓ years

COMPOUND INTEREST

89. Interest may be computed on a compound basis; that is, the interest at the end of a certain period (half year, full year, or whatever time stipulated) is added to the principal for the next period. The interest is then computed on the new increased principal, and for the next period, the interest is again computed on the new increased principal. Since the principal constantly increases, compound interest yields more than simple interest.

COMPOUND INTEREST RATE

90. Since the interest rate is an annual rate, it must be proportionately reduced if the interest is compounded on less than a yearly basis. In general, if the interest is computed for some fractional part of a year, use that same fractional part of the interest rate. Specifically:

a. If the interest is compounded annually, use the rate given.

b. If compounded semi-annually, use ½ the rate given.

c. If compounded quarterly, use ¼ the rate given, etc.

91. To find the compound interest when given the principal, the rate, and time period:

a. Determine the rate to be used, and change it to a decimal.

b. Multiply the principal by this rate to ascertain the interest for the first period.

c. Add the interest to the principal.

d. Multiply the new principal by the determined rate to find the interest for the second period.

e. Add this interest to form a new principal.

f. Continue the same procedure until all periods required have been accounted for.

g. Subtract the original principal from the final principal to find the compound interest.

Illustration: Find the amount that $200 will become if compounded semi-annually at 4% for 1½ years.

SOLUTION: Since it is to be compounded semi-annually for 1½ years, the interest will have to be computed 3 times, and the rate to be used is 2%=.02

          (90b, 46c, 91a)

Interest for the first period: $200x.02=$4   (30, 91b)

First new principal: $200+$4 =$204   **(91c)**

Interest for the second period: $204x.02=$4.08   (30, 91d)

Second new principal: $204+ $4.08=$208.08   (91e)

Interest for the third period: $208.08x.02=$4.1616

          (30, 91f)

Final principal: $208.08 + $4.16=$212.24

Answer: $212.24

BANK DISCOUNTS

92. When a note is cashed by a bank in advance of its date of maturity, the bank deducts a discount from the principal and pays the rest to the depositor.

93. To find the bank discount:

a. Find the time between the date the note is deposited and its date of maturity, and express this time as a fractional part of a year.

b. Change the rate to a fraction.

c. Multiply the principal by the time and the rate to find the bank discount.

d. If required, subtract the bank discount from the original principal to find the amount the bank will pay the depositor.

Illustration: A $400 note drawn up on August 12, 1962 for 90 days is deposited at the bank on September 17, 1962. The bank charges a 6½% discount on notes. How much will the depositor receive?

SOLUTION: From August 12, 1962, to September 17, 1962 is 36 days. This means that the note has 54 days to run.

    54 days=$^{54}/_{360}$ of a year

          (84c, 93a)

    6½%=$^{13}/_{200}$ (50, 93b)

    $400x13/200x54/360=

       39/10=$3.90

          (18, 38b, 93c)

    $400—$3.90=$396.10 (93d)

Answer: The depositor will receive $396.10

INTEREST PROBLEMS

1. Find the interest on $480 at 3½% for 2 months and 15 days. (a) $2.50 (b) $3.50 (c) $3.25 (d) $4.00.

2. Find the length of time it would take $432 to yield $78.66 in interest at 4¾%. (a) 2 yrs. 10 mos. (b) 3 yrs. (c) 3 yrs. 10 mos. (d) 4 yrs.

3. A man wishes to borrow a certain sum of money for 120 days. He goes to a bank whose rate is 6%. They deduct $360 as discount. How much does the man borrow? (a) $5000 (b) $10,550 (c) $15,000 (d) $18,000.

4. One sum of money is invested at 3% and a second sum, twice as large as the first, is invested at 2½%. The total interest is $448. How much is invested at 2½%? (a) $11,000 (b) $11,100 (c) $11,200 (d) $11,300.

5. Mr. B borrowed $600 and at the end of 9 years and 6 months returned $856.50. What is the rate per cent? (a) 4½% (b) 5% (c) 6% (d) 7%.

6. A house costs $10,000. Incidental expenses and taxes amount to $360 a year. What rent per month must the owner receive to clear 6% of his investment? (a) $60 (b) $65 (c) $80 (d) $85.

7. What is the compound interest on $600, compounded quarterly, at 6% for 9 months? (a) $27.38 (b) $27.40 (c) $27.41 (d) $27.42.

8. A 90-day note was drawn up on April 16, 1934 and discounted at 6% on May 31, 1934. What was the face amount of the note if the depositor received $754.30? (a) $760 (b) $750 (c) $740 (d) $735.

9. What is the discount rate of a bank if a 60-day note for $320, discounted 45 days after being drawn, yields $319.40? (a) 4½% (b) 4% (c) 4¾% (d) 5%.

10. A 60-day note for $432 was drawn up on October 6, 1961. Some time later, it was deposited at a bank whose discount rate was 5¼% and the depositor received $430.74. When was it deposited? (a) November 15, 1961 (b) October 15, 1961 (c) December 15, 1961 (d) January 15, 1962.

Correct Answers

1. b	3. d	5. a	7. c	9. a
2. c	4. c	6. c	8. a	10. a

NOW, CHECK YOUR METHODS WITH OUR

SIMPLIFIED PROBLEM SOLUTIONS, WHICH FOLLOW.

PROBLEM SOLUTIONS   Interest

1. SOLUTION:

2 months 15 days = 75 days or $\frac{75}{360}$ of year

$3\frac{1}{2}\% = \frac{7}{2}\% = \frac{7}{200}$

$\$480 \times \frac{7}{200} \times \frac{75}{360} = \frac{21}{6} = \$3.50$ Interest

$$\frac{\$3.50}{6)\overline{21.00}} \quad (b)$$

ANSWER: Interest = $3.50

2. SOLUTION:

$\$432 \times 4\frac{3}{4}\% \quad 4\frac{3}{4}\% = \frac{19}{4}\%$

$\$432 \times \frac{19}{4}\% = \$432 \times \frac{19}{400} = \$20.52$

Interest 1 year
$78.66 Interest
$78.66 ÷ $20.52 = 3.83⅓ year = 3⅚ year

$\frac{5}{6} \times 12$ mo. = 10 mo. Therefore 3 years 10

months.   (c)

ANSWER: Time — 3 years 10 months

3. SOLUTION:

120 days = $\frac{120}{360}$ year = $\frac{1}{3}$ year

$\frac{1}{3} \times 6\% = \frac{1}{3} \times \frac{6}{100} = \frac{2}{100} = .02$

$360 ÷ .02 = $18,000 borrowed   (d)

ANSWER: Man borrowed $18,000.

4. SOLUTION

Sum #1 at 3% = Interest on #1 = 3%
Sum #2 (twice as large) Sum #1
Sum #2 at 2½% = Interest Sum #2
5% + 3% = 8% on Interest #1 + Interest
#2 (2 × 2½% = 5% Interest)
8% = $448

$\$448 ÷ \frac{8}{100} = \$448 \times \frac{100}{8} = \$5600$

Sum #1

2 × $5600 = $11,200 or Sum #2

ANSWER: Invested 2½% = $11,200 = sum

(c)

PROOF:

$\$5600 \times 3\% = \$5600 \times \frac{3}{100} = \$168.00$

Interest at 3%
$11,200 × 2½% = $11,200 × .025 = $280
$168 + $280 = $448 Total Interest

5. SOLUTION:
$856.50 — $600 = $256.50
9 years 6 months = 9½ years

$\$256.50 ÷ 9½ = \$256.50 ÷ \frac{19}{2} =$

$\$256.50 \times \frac{2}{19} = \frac{\$513.00}{19} = \$27$

$\frac{\$27}{600} = \frac{9}{200} = 4.5\% = 4\frac{1}{2}\%$ (a)

ANSWER: Rate per cent = 4½%

6. SOLUTION:
$10,000 × 6% = $600 to receive on his investment for one year
$600 + $360 = $960 profit and expenses
$960 ÷ 12 = $80 Rent per month   (c)

ANSWER: Rent per month = $80.

7. Compound interest on $600 — quarterly at 6% for 9 months
SOLUTION:
$600 at 6% for 9 months or ¾ year
$600 × .06 × ¼ = $9.00 Interest for 1st quarter
$600 + $9 = $609 due at end of 1st quarter
$609 × .06 × ¼ = $9.13½ = $9.14 Interest 2nd quarter
$609 + $9.14 = $618.14 due at end 2nd quarter
$618.14 × .06 = $37.0884 × ¼ = $9.2721 = $9.27 Interest 3rd quarter
$6.18.14 + $9.27 = $627.41 due end 3rd quarter
$9.00 + $9.14 + $9.27 = $27.41 compound Interest   (c)

ANSWER: Interest compounded quarterly = $27.41

8. SOLUTION:

Discount $754.30 @ 6% on 90-day note, April 16, 1934 to May 31, 1934
April 16 to April 30 = 14 days
May 31 days

$$\overline{45 \text{ days}} = \frac{45}{360} \text{ year}$$

$$\frac{45}{360} \times \frac{6}{100} = \frac{3}{400} \text{ Interest}$$

Explanation

$$\left(\frac{\overset{9}{\cancel{45}}}{\underset{60}{\cancel{360}}} \times \frac{\overset{1}{\cancel{6}}}{\underset{20}{\cancel{100}}} = \frac{9}{1200} = \frac{3}{400}\right)$$

$$100\% - \frac{3}{400} = \frac{400}{400} - \frac{3}{400} = \frac{397}{400}$$

$$\$754.30 \div \frac{397}{400} = \$754.30 \times \frac{400}{397} = \$760 \text{ (a)}$$

ANSWER: Face amount of note = $760

9. SOLUTION:

60 days − 45 days = 15 days
$320 − $319.40 = $.60 Interest saved in 15 days.

$$\frac{.60}{320} \div \frac{15}{360} = \frac{\overset{.04}{\cancel{.60}}}{\underset{8}{\cancel{320}}} \times \frac{\overset{9}{\cancel{360}}}{\underset{1}{\cancel{15}}} = \frac{.36}{8} = 4\frac{1}{2}\%$$

discount rate   (a)

ANSWER: Discount rate = 4½%

10. SOLUTION:

60 day note for $432 drawn up on October 6, 1961

$$60 \text{ day note} = \frac{60}{360} = \frac{1}{6} \text{ year for note}$$

Discount rate = 5¼% received $430.74

$$5\frac{1}{4}\% = \frac{21\%}{4} = \frac{21}{400} \text{ discount rate}$$

$432 − $430.74 = $1.26 = interest charged by bank

$$\$1.26 \div \frac{21}{400} \div \$432 =$$

$$\overset{.06}{\cancel{\$1.26}} \times \frac{400}{\cancel{21}} \times \frac{1}{432} = \frac{24.00}{432} = \frac{24}{432} = \frac{1}{18} \text{ yr.}$$

$$\frac{1}{\cancel{18}} \times \overset{20}{\cancel{360}} = 20 \text{ days}$$

NOTE: Since the note was deposited 20 days before the date of maturity, the bank charged a discount which could be considered interest on the face value. The number of days between the date the note was drawn up and the time of deposit, added to the number of days from the date of deposit to the date of maturity must equal the full term of the note or 60 days.

60-day note − 20 days = 40 days after it was drawn up, it was deposited.

October 6, 1961 to
October 31, 1961 =   25 da. left in Oct.
November 15, 1961 = + 15 da. left in Nov.
                    40 da.

Therefore 40 da. = Nov. 15 note deposited   (a)

ANSWER: Note deposited November 15, 1961

TAXATION

94. The following facts should be taken into consideration in taxation problems:
   a. Taxes may be expressed as a per cent or in terms of money based on a certain denomination.
   Example: The general tax rate for Unemployment Insurance in New York State is 2.7%. On the other hand, the realty tax in New York City for the fiscal year of 1963 was $4.27 per $100 of assessed property.
   b. A surtax is an additional tax besides the regular tax rate.

95. In taxation, there are usually three items involved: the amount taxable, henceforth called the base, the tax rate, and the tax itself.

96. To find the tax when given the base and the tax rate in per cent:
   a. Change the tax rate to a decimal.
   b. Multiply the base by the tax rate.

   Illustration: How much would be realized on $4000 if taxed 15%?
   SOLUTION: 15%=.15   (46c, 96a)
             $4000x.15=$600   (30, 96b)
   Answer: Tax=$600

97. To find the tax rate in % form when given the base and the tax:
   a. Divide the tax by the base.
   b. Convert to a per cent.

   Illustration: Find the tax rate at which $5600 would yield $784.
   SOLUTION: $784÷$5600=.14
                     (38a, 97a)
         .14=14%   (46d, 97b)
   Answer: Tax rate=14%

98. To find the base when given the tax rate and the tax:
   a. Establish a relation between the tax and the base.
   b. Solve to find the base.

   Illustration: What amount of money taxed 3% would yield $75?

SOLUTION: $75=3% of the base   (98a)
          $75=3/100 of the base (46c)
          Base=75÷3/100   (56b)
            =75x100/3=$2500
                 (22, 18, 98b)
Answer: Base=$2500

99. When the tax rate is fixed and expressed in terms of money, take into consideration the denomination upon which it is based; that is, whether it is based on every $100, or $1000, etc.

100. To find the tax when given the base and the tax rate in terms of money:
   a. Divide the base by the denomination upon which the tax rate is based.
   b. Multiply this quotient by the tax rate.

   Illustration: If the tax rate is $3.60 per $1000, find the tax on $470,500.
   SOLUTION: $470,500÷1000=470.5
                     (38, 100a)
         $470.5x3.60=$1,693.80
   Answer: $1,693.80   (30,100b)

101. To find the tax rate based on a certain denomination when given the base and the tax derived:
   a. Divide the base by the denomination indicated.
   b. Divide the tax by this quotient.

   Illustration: Find the tax rate per $100 which would be required to raise $350,000 on $2,000,000 of taxable property.
   SOLUTION: $2,000,000÷100=20,000
                      (101a)
         $350,000÷20,000=$17.50
                    (38b, 101b)
   Answer: Tax rate=$17.50 per $100

102. Since a surtax is an additional tax besides the regular tax, to find the total tax:
   a. Change the regular tax rate to a decimal.
   b. Multiply the base by the regular tax rate.
   c. Change the surtax rate to a decimal.
   d. Multiply the base by the surtax rate.
   e. Add both taxes.

Illustration: Assuming that the tax rate is 2⅓% on liquors costing up to $3.00, and 3% on those costing from $3.00 to $6.00, and 3½% on those from $6.00 to $10.00, what would be the tax on a bottle costing $8.00 if there is a surtax of 5% on all liquors above $5.00?

SOLUTION: An $8.00 bottle falls within the category of $6.00 to $10. The tax rate on such a bottle is
3½%=.035   (51, 102a)
$8.00x.035=.28   (30, 102b)
surtax rate=5%=.05
                  (46c, 102c)
$8.00x.05=$.40   (30, 102d)
$.28+$.40=$.68   (102e)
Answer: Total tax=$.68

TAXATION PROBLEMS

1. Lodge A with 120 men is assessed $96.75. Lodge B with 160 members is assessed $85. How much more is the average for a member of Lodge A than for a member of Lodge B? (a) $.275 (b) $.375 (c) $.475 (d) $.35

2. What tax rate on a base of $3650 would raise $164.25? (a) 4% (b) 5% (c) 4½% (d) 5½%

3. If the tax rate is 3½% and the amount to be raised is $64.40, what is the base: (a) $1800 (b) $1840 (c) $1850 (d) $1860

4. What is the tax rate per $1000 if a base of $338,500 would yield $616.07? (a) $1.80 (b) $1.90 (c) $1.95 (d) $1.82

5. On what base would a tax rate of $2.51 per $100 yield $1689.23? (a) $67,000 (b) $66,300 (c) $67,350 (d) $67,300

6. What is the premium on a $7200 policy at $.67 per 100? (a) $48.24 (b) $48.20 (c) $47.00 (d) $49.00

7. A merchant who has debts of $43,250 has gone bankrupt and can pay off only 15¢ on the dollar. How much will his creditors receive? (a) $6487.50 (b) $6387.50 (c) $6387.00 (d) $6287.00.

8. A certain community needs $185,090.62 to cover its expenses. If its tax rate is $1.43 per $100 of assessed valuation, what must be the assessed value of its property? (a) $12,900,005 (b) $12,943,400 (c) $12,940,000 (d) $12,840,535.

9. A house is insured for 80% of its value at 5/16%. The premium is $32.50. What is the total value of the house? (a) $11,500 (b) $12,000 (c) $13,000 (d) $13,500.

10. Assuming that the income tax law allows $500 personal exemption for single people and $200 for each dependent, and that the tax rates are 2½% on the first $2000 taxable income and 4½% on the next $3000 taxable income, what would be the income tax of Mr. Jones, single, who earns $5200 a year and has two dependents. There is a surtax of 3¼% on all net income, (net income after the personal exemption and dependency deductions have been made). (a) $280 (b) $293.25 (c) $290.25 (d) $284.25

Correct Answers

1. a	3. b	5. d	7. a	9. c
2. c	4. d	6. a	8. b	10. b

NOW, CHECK YOUR METHODS WITH OUR SIMPLIFIED PROBLEM SOLUTIONS, WHICH FOLLOW.

PROBLEM SOLUTIONS Taxation

1. SOLUTION:
   120 men assessed $96.75—Lodge A
   160 men assessed $85.00—Lodge B
   How much more is average for member Lodge
   A than for Lodge B?
   ($96.75 ÷ 120) − ($85.00 ÷ 160)
   $.806¼ − $.531¼ = $.275   (a)

   ANSWER: $.275 more for Lodge A member

2. SOLUTION:
   What tax rate on a base of $3650 would raise
   $164.25?

   $$?\% = \frac{\$\ 164.25}{\$3650.00} = .04\tfrac{1}{2} = 4\tfrac{1}{2}\%\quad (c)$$

   ANSWER: Tax rate = 4½%

3. SOLUTION:
   Tax = 3½%   Amount to be raised = $64.40
   Find base.

   $$\$64.40 \div 3\tfrac{1}{2}\% = \$64.40 \div \frac{7}{200}$$

   $$\frac{\overset{9.20}{\cancel{\$64.40}} \times 200}{\underset{1}{\cancel{7}}} = \$1840.00\ \text{base}\quad (b)$$

   ANSWER: Base = $1840

4. SOLUTION:
   Base of $338,500 yielded $616.07
   Find tax rate per $1000.

   $$\frac{\$338,500}{1000} = \$338.50$$

   $$\frac{\$616.070}{338.50} = \$1.82\ \text{tax rate per thousand}\quad (d)$$

   ANSWER: Tax rate per $1000 = $1.82

5. SOLUTION:
   Find base when tax rate of $2.51 per $100
   yields $1689.23.

   $$\text{Rate} = \frac{\$2.51}{100}$$

   $$\frac{\$1689.23 \times 100}{2.51} = \frac{\$168923}{2.51} = \$67,300$$
   base.   (d)

   ANSWER: Base $67,300

6. SOLUTION:
   Policy = $7200   Rate = $.67 per $100
   Find premium

   $$\frac{\$72\cancel{00}}{1\cancel{00}} \times .67 = \$48.24\ \text{premium}\quad (a)$$

   ANSWER: Premium = $48.24

7. SOLUTION:
   Debt = $43,250
   Pays .15 on $1.00

   $$\frac{\$43,250 \times .15}{1.00} = \$6487.50\quad (a)$$

   ANSWER: Creditors receive $6487.50

8. SOLUTION:
   Community needs $185,090.62
   Tax = $1.43 per $100 assessed valuation
   Find assessed value of property

   $$\frac{\$185090.62}{1.43} \times 100 = \$12,943,400\quad (b)$$

   Explanation (8th problem)
   $185090.62 × 100 = $18,509,062

   ```
                    $12943400
          1.43 )$18509062.00
                 143
                 420
                 286
                 1349
                 1287
                  620
                  572
                   486
                   429
                    572
                    572
   ```

   **ANSWER: Assessed value of property =
   $12,943,400**

9. SOLUTION:
   Insurance = 80% of value
   Rate = $\frac{5}{16}$%
   Premium = $32.50
   Find total value of house

   $$\$32.50 \div \frac{5}{16}\% = \$32.50 \times \frac{1600}{5} = \$10,400$$

   amt. for which house was insured.
   $10,400 \div \frac{80}{100} = 10,400 \times \frac{100}{80} =$
   $13,000 value of house   (c)

   ANSWER: Value of house = $13,000

10. SOLUTION:
    $500 single exemption, $200 each dependent
    Taxable income $5200
    Single exemption = $500
    2 dependents   = + 400
                        $900 deduction
                      $5200 salary
                      —900
                      $4300 net income
          $4300 — $2000 = $2300

    1st $2000 at 2½% = $ 50
        $2300 × 4½% =   103.50
        $4300 × 3¼% =   139.75
                        $293.25 (Total
                          income tax)   (b)

    ANSWER: $293.25 Total income tax

DATA SUFFICIENCY TESTS

This selection of questions is particularly important and relevant in preparing you for the exam. The questions come from many previous exams. In selecting them we discovered and eliminated a good number of duplicate and repetitive questions. So, what you have here is a concise presentation of those points in this field which examiners consider to be significant. Study and answer them carefully. Correct answers appear at the end of the set.

EXPLAINING THIS TYPE OF QUESTION

Directions: Each of the question items has two statements, labeled (1) and (2), in which pertinent data are given. In these questions, do not compute an answer but decide instead if the given data are adequate for finding the solution. Relying on your mathematical background and everyday facts (such as the hours in a day) and the data given in the problems, you are to shade space

A   if statement (1) ALONE is sufficient, but statement (2) alone is not sufficient to answer the question asked;

B   if statement (2) ALONE is sufficient, but statement (1) alone is not sufficient to answer the question asked;

C   if BOTH statements (1) and (2) TOGETHER are sufficient to answer the questions asked, but NEITHER statement ALONE is sufficient;

D   if EACH statement ALONE is sufficient to answer the question asked;

E   if statements (1) and (2) TOGETHER are NOT sufficient to answer the questions asked, and additional data specific to the problem are needed.

Example:

What is the value of x?
  (1) AB = BC
  (2) y = 40

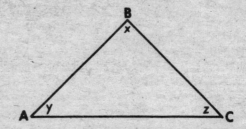

Explanation:

According to statement (1), AB = BC; therefore, △ABC is isosceles and y = z. By statement (2), y = 40; hence z = 40. It is known that x + y + z = 180; since y and z are known, this equation can be solved for x. Thus the problem can be solved, and since statements (1) and (2) are both needed, the answer is C.

The data following may be used in doing the problems.

Triangle:

The angles of a triangle added together equal 180°.
The angle BDC is a right angle; therefore,

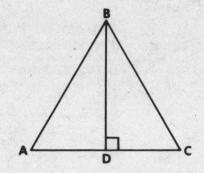

(I) the area of triangle $ABC = \dfrac{AC \times BD}{2}$

(II) $AB^2 = AD^2 + DB^2$

Circle:

There are 360 degrees of arc in a circle.
The area of a circle of radius $r = \pi r^2$
The circumference of a circle $= 2\pi r$
A straight angle has 180°.

Symbol references:

$\parallel$ is parallel to	$>$ is greater than
$\leqq$ is less than or equal to	$<$ is less than
$\geqq$ is greater than or equal to	$\perp$ is perpendicular to
$\angle$ angle	$\triangle$ triangle

Note: *In the data sufficiency questions which follow, the diagrams are generalized illustrations and are not necessarily drawn to scale.*

Now, push forward! Test yourself and practice for your test with the carefully constructed quizzes that follow. Each one presents the kind of question you may expect on your test. And each question is at just the level of difficulty that may be expected. Don't try to take all the tests at one time. Rather, schedule yourself so that you take a few at each session, and spend approximately the same time on them at each session. Score yourself honestly, and date each test. You should be able to detect improvement in your performance on successive sessions.

DATA SUFFICIENCY TEST

TIME: 20 Minutes

DIRECTIONS: Each question below is followed by two numbered facts. Decide whether the data given is sufficient for answering the question. Sometimes the two facts do not give enough information to answer the question. Sometimes the two facts give just enough data to answer the question. And sometimes one of the facts alone is sufficient to answer the question. Read each question and the two facts that follow it; then mark your answer on the answer sheet that follows.
Mark "A" if statement 1 alone is sufficient to answer the question, but statement 2 alone is not sufficient.
Mark "B" if statement 2 alone is sufficient to answer the question, but statement 1 alone is not sufficient.
Mark "C" if both statements together are needed to answer the question, but neither statement alone is sufficient.
Mark "D" if either statement by itself is sufficient to answer the question asked.
Mark "E" if not enough facts are given to answer the question.

DIRECTIONS: Explanations of the key points behind each question are given at the end of the test. They follow the key answers which we have consolidated, facilitating comparison of your answers with ours. Score boxes and answer sheets are also included there. Remember, you'll learn more rapidly if you conscientiously answer questions on your own, before deriving your score.

1. Is Denise older than Andrea?

   (1) Denise's father and Andrea's father were born the same year.
   (2) Andrea's grandfather is 5 years older than Denise's grandfather.

2. Is A less than B?

   (1) $A^2 = 25$
   (2) B = 6

3. How much did Edna spend for dress material?

   (1) The material cost 25 cents per square yard.
   (2) If she bought three times as much material, she could have made four more dresses.

4. Does Devin weigh more than 180 lbs?

   (1) If Devin loses 10 lbs., he will be less than 180 lbs.
   (2) If Devin loses 10 lbs., he will weigh less than 180 lbs. but more than 170 lbs.

5. What is the value of x?

   (1) $3x - y = 24$
   (2) $x + y = 10$

6. How many days will it take 12 men to paint 12 rooms?

   (1) Any group of 4 men can paint 3 rooms per day.
   (2) Each man can paint three-fourths of a room per day.

52037

7. Find the value of a + b + c.

   (1) abc = 0
   (2) a + b = 4

8. If ⊙ is one of the operations addition or multiplication, which is it?

   (1) 0 ⊙ 0 = 0
   (2) 0 ⊙ 1 = 1

9.

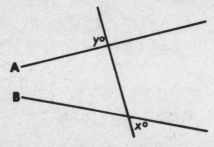

   In the figure above, are lines A and B parallel?

   (1) x = y
   (2) x + y = 180°

10. There are four plateaus on a mountain labeled A, B, C, and D.

   A is 2,200 feet above the ground.
   B is 600 feet higher than A.
   D is 1,000 feet higher than C.
   Is B higher than C?

   (1) D is 2,600 feet above the ground.
   (2) D is 400 feet higher than A.

11. If triangle ABC lies wholly within square DEFG, what is the area of the region of DEFG not overlapped by △ABC?

   (1) No point on △ABC touches any point on sq. DEFG.
   (2) The area of △ABC is 20 and the area of sq. DEFG is 50.

12. What is the distance from city A to city C?

   (1) City A is 60 miles from city B.
   (2) City B is 40 miles from city C.

13.

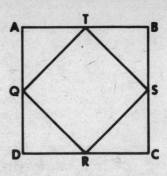

   ABCD is a square. Find the perimeter of QRST.

   (1) The area of ABCD is 16.
   (2) Q, R, S, and T are the mid-points of the four sides of ABCD.

14. If A is positive, is B more than 100 percent of A?

   (1) B = $\frac{2}{3}$A
   (2) B = A − 4

15. If Y is a member of the set of numbers {8,12,15,16,20} what number is Y?

   (1) Y is a multiple of 4.
   (2) Y is a multiple of 5.

16. Is A ÷ 5 even?

   (1) A ÷ 15 is an integer
   (2) A ÷ 10 is not odd

17. What is the value of $\frac{X - Y}{Y}$?

   (1) $\frac{x}{y}$ = 2
   (2) y = 4

18.

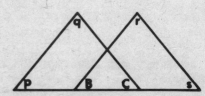

   In the two triangles above, what is the value of p + q + r + s?

   (1) p + q = r + s
   (2) B + C = 90°

CONSOLIDATE YOUR KEY ANSWERS HERE

CORRECT ANSWERS

EXPLANATORY ANSWERS

Elucidation, clarification, explication and a little help with the fundamental facts covered in the Previous Test. These are the points and principles likely to crop up in the form of questions on future tests.

1. **(E)**

Statements (1) and (2) mention only the fathers and grandfathers, no information is given about the ages of Andrea and Denise.

2. **(C)**

From statement (1) A = ±5 and statement (2) B = 6, hence B > A.

3. **(E)**

In order to do the problem, you must know how much material is required for one dress, and neither statement supplies the information.

4. **(B)**

By statement (2) if Devin loses 10 lbs., he still weighs more than 170 lbs. He must weigh more than 180 lbs. to begin with.

5. **(C)**

Add statements (1) and (2) together to get $4x = 34$ then $x = 8\frac{1}{2}$

6. (D)

    By statement (1),
    4 men paint 3 rooms in 1 day;
    1 man paints $\frac{3}{4}$ room in 1 day (divide by 4);
    1 man paints 12 rooms in 16 days (divide by $\frac{3}{4}$);
    12 men paint 12 rooms in $1\frac{1}{2}$ days (multiply and divide by 10).
    By statement (2) same as above.

7. (E)

    For three unknowns, you need three equations, and only two are given.

8. (B)

    By statement (1) the operation could be either addition or multiplication. By statement (2) it could only be addition.

9. (A)

    By statement (1) if x and y are equal, their vertical angles are also equal. Their vertical angles are alternate interior angles, thus the lines are parallel.

10. (D)

    By statement (1) A = 2,200
    B = 2,800
    D = 2,600
    C = 1,600
    B > C
    By statement (2) A = 2,200
    D = 2,600
    B = 2,800
    C = 1,600
    B > C

11. (B)

    Using statement (2), the area of square DEFG minus the area of triangle ABC equals 30, the region not overlapped by triangle ABC.

12. (E)

    This is a question on the locus of points from a fixed point. City A is within a 60 mile radius of City B and City B is within a 40 mile radius of City C. Not knowing the exact location of either city it is impossible to determine the number of miles from City A to City C.

13. (C)

    By statement (1) if the area of the square is 16, then each side is 4. By statement (2) since Q, R, S, and T are the midpoints of the four sides, it is now possible to find the 4 sides of Q, R, S, T. Using the theorem $(QT)^2 = 2^2 + 2^2$
    $$(QT)^2 = 4 + 4$$
    $$(QT)^2 = 8$$
    $$QT = 2\sqrt{2}$$
    hence, the perimeter of QRST equals $8\sqrt{2}$.

14. (D)

    By statement (1) if B = $\frac{2}{3}$A, then A > B and by statement (2) if B = A − 4, then A is also greater than B.

15. (C)

    By statements (1) and (2), 20 is the only possible answer.

16. (B)

    By statement (2) if A ÷ 10 is not odd, it must be even. Hence A ÷ 5 must also be even because 5 is a multiple of 10.

17. (A)

    $$\frac{x-y}{y} = \frac{x}{y} - \frac{y}{y} = \frac{x}{y} - 1;$$

    therefore, to solve the problem the value of x/y must be known. Statement (1) x/y = 2.

18. (B)

    The number of degrees in a $\triangle$ = 180; there are two triangles, hence angles p, q, r, s, B, and C must equal 360°. By statement (2) if angles B and C equal 90°, then angles p + q + r + s must equal 360 − 90 or 270°.

DATA SUFFICIENCY

TIME: 25 Minutes

DIRECTIONS: Each question below is followed by two numbered facts. Decide whether the data given is sufficient for answering the question. Sometimes the two facts do not give enough information to answer the question. Sometimes the two facts give just enough data to answer the question. And sometimes one of the facts alone is sufficient to answer the question. Read each question and the two facts that follow it; then mark your answer on the answer sheet that follows.

Mark "A" if statement 1 alone is sufficient to answer the question, but statement 2 alone is not sufficient.

Mark "B" if statement 2 alone is sufficient to answer the question, but statement 1 alone is not sufficient.

Mark "C" if both statements together are needed to answer the question, but neither statement alone is sufficient.

Mark "D" if either statement by itself is sufficient to answer the question asked.

Mark "E" if not enough facts are given to answer the question.

DIRECTIONS: Explanations of the key points behind each question are given at the end of the test. They follow the key answers which we have consolidated, facilitating comparison of your answers with ours. Score boxes and answer sheets are also included there. Remember, you'll learn more rapidly if you conscientiously answer questions on your own, before deriving your score.

1. What is the area of the parallelogram ABCD?
   (1) AECF is a rectangle with an area of 18 square inches
   (2) BC=CF

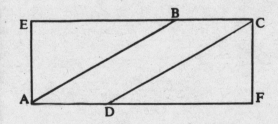

2. What month is it?
   (1) Next Friday will be the 29th.
   (2) This is leap year.

3. A man wants to cover a rectangular room with a carpet. How much will it cost him?
   (1) The service charge is $10, and each square yard costs $15.
   (2) If the room were half as large, it would cost him $165 less.

4. What is the value of x^3+1?
   (1) $x^2-x+1=0$
   (2) $x^3-1=(x-1)(x^2+x+1)$

5. Alice, Betsy, and Chris are three sisters. What is the order of their ages?

   (1) The sum of Alice's age and Betsy's age is equal to twice Chris' age.
   (2) Five years ago, Betsy was twice as old as Chris.

6. Find the number of degrees in angle *C*.
   (1) AD is parallel to BC
   (2) Angle A=45°

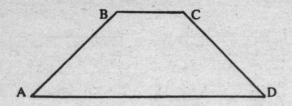

7. How many men are marching in the Odd Fellows' parade?
   (1) They can arrange themselves in three, five, or seven equal rows
   (2) There is an even number of men marching.

8. Is *F* greater than *G*?
   (1) $F=(a-1)(a^2+a+1)$ and $G=(a+1)(a^2-a+1)$
   (2) $F=2G$

9. John studies Chinese in high school. Which school does he attend?
   (1) All students at Jefferson High School take French
   (2) Maysville High School offers only Chinese

10. Find the length of one side of the square ABCD.
    (1) BE=3 inches
    (2) The area of the shaded semicircle is ¼ the area of the large circle.

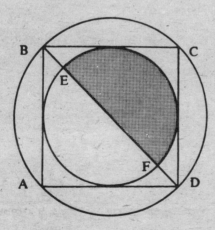

11. George and Sam go on a 300-mile trip by car. They take turns driving, each driving for 8 hours. What is the average rate of each?
    (1) George drove 48 miles more than Sam
    (2) George averaged 6 miles an hour faster than Sam.

12. There are 30 boys in a club. How many are both boy scouts and junior high school graduates?
    (1) 10 are boy scouts.
    (2) 20 are junior high school graduates.

13. What is the value of x?
    (1) $x + y = 5$.
    (2) $x - y = 1$.

14. How many pennies does a boy have?
    (1) He has 37 cents in coins.
    (2) One of the coins is a nickel.

15. In triangle RST, angle S is 90° and SR=ST. Find the area of triangle RST.
    (1) RS=7.
    (2) $RT=7\sqrt{2}$.

16. $3x-6y=5$. What is the value of y?
    (1) $x-2y=\frac{5}{3}$.
    (2) $x=3$.

17. In $\triangle ABC$, what is the length of side AC?
    (1) AB=10 inches
    (2) BC=12 inches.

18. Find three consecutive odd numbers.
    (1) The sum of the numbers is 63.
    (2) The largest number is 4 more than the smallest.

19. What is the ratio of x to y?
    (1) $x=\frac{2}{3}y$.
    (2) $7x-y=y$.

20. What is the total cost of linoleum needed for a room 9 feet by 12 feet?
    (1) Linoleum tiles are 6 inches square.
    (2) Linoleum tiles cost 52¢ per square foot.

CONSOLIDATE YOUR KEY ANSWERS HERE

CORRECT ANSWERS

ANSWER STRIPS					
	A	B	C	D	E
1					
2					
3					
4					
5					
6					
7					
8					
9					
10					

ANSWER STRIPS					
	A	B	C	D	E
11					
12					
13					
14					
15					
16					
17					
18					
19					
20					

CORRECT ANSWERS					
	A	B	C	D	E
1					■
2					■
3			■		
4	■				
5			■		
6					■
7					■
8	■				
9					■
10	■				

CORRECT ANSWERS					
	A	B	C	D	E
11			■		
12					■
13		■			
14				■	
15			■		
16	■				
17					■
18	■				
19			■		
20		■			

SCORE	.... %
NO. CORRECT ÷ NO. OF QUESTIONS	

EXPLANATORY ANSWERS

Elucidation, clarification, explication and a little help with the fundamental facts covered in the Previous Test. These are the points and principles likely to crop up in the form of questions on future tests.

1. (E) If we let CF grow larger and decrease EC correspondingly, we can change the area of ABCD without contradicting either statement.

2. (E) Just because the 29th is mentioned, there is no reason to believe it is February. It might be any month.

3. (C) The charge without service would be ($165x2)+$10, or $340.

4. (A) Since (2) is always true, it makes no difference. $x^3+1=(x+1)(x^2-x+1)=0$

5. (C) (1) tells us that Chris is in the middle, since her age is the average of the other two. (2) tells us that Betsy is older than Chris, so Betsy is the oldest, Chris is next, and Alice is the youngest.

6. (E) Not enough information is given.

7. (E) The number may be any even multiple of 210.

8. (A) $F=a^8-1$ and $G=a^8+1$, so G is greater.

9. (*E*) Statement 1 simply eliminates Jefferson H.S. Statement 2 tells us that John *may* attend Maysville H.S. However, other high schools may offer Chinese.

10. (*A*) In any case (2) is true. Since the proportions remain constant, once BE is given, the side of the square can be calculated as $6/(\sqrt{2}-1)$.

11. (*D*) From Statement 1, George drove $x + 48$ if Sam drove x. $x+48+x=300$. $x=126$ which is the distance George drove in 8 hours. We can now find his average rate. From Statement 2, we merely subtract 6 miles from George's average rate to get Sam's average rate.

12. (*E*) Statements 1 and 2 together tell us that the number of boy scouts is 10 and the number of junior high school graduates is 20. But a boy scout may also be a junior high school graduate. More information is needed to solve.

13. (*C*) Add Statements 1 and 2 to get $2x=6$ or $x=3$. We can easily determine the value of y now.

14. (*E*) Neither of the statements supplies us with the necessary information concerning pennies.

15. (*D*) The area of the triangle $= \frac{1}{2} \times 7 \times 7 = 24\frac{1}{2}$. That was from Statement 1. Now, Statement 2 will give us this information:

$(7\sqrt{2})^2 = (RS)^2 + (ST)^2$. Since RS = ST, $49 \times 2 = 2(RS)^2$. Therefore, RS = 7. From this point, we are able to find the area of the triangle.

16. (*B*) With Statement 2, we know that $3 \times 3 - 6y = 5$. Therefore, it is easy to find the value of y. The information given in Statement 1 is of no help.

17. (*E*) Neither Statement gives us sufficient information. The size of one of the angles would help us.

18. (*A*) Let the first odd number $= x$. Then, $x + (x + 2) + (x + 4) = 63$. The equation can easily be solved. The information in Statement 2 is not sufficient.

19. (*D*) From Statement 1, we find that $\dfrac{x}{y} = \dfrac{2}{7}$

The ratio is, accordingly, established. From Statement 2: $7x = 2y$. Again, we establish the ratio asked for.

20. (*B*) Since Statement 1 does not give us the cost of the tiles, it is an insufficient statement. Statement 2, on the other hand, gives us the information required—namely, the cost of the tiles. The linoleum will cost $108 \times \dfrac{52}{100} = \$56.16$.

DATA SUFFICIENCY TEST

TIME: 20 Minutes

DIRECTIONS: Each question below is followed by two numbered facts. Decide whether the data given is sufficient for answering the question. Sometimes the two facts do not give enough information to answer the question. Sometimes the two facts give just enough data to answer the question. And sometimes one of the facts alone is sufficient to answer the question. Read each question and the two facts that follow it; then mark your answer on the answer sheet that follows.

Mark "A" if statement 1 alone is sufficient to answer the question, but statement 2 alone is not sufficient.

Mark "B" if statement 2 alone is sufficient to answer the question, but statement 1 alone is not sufficient.

Mark "C" if both statements together are needed to answer the question, but neither statement alone is sufficient.

Mark "D" if either statement by itself is sufficient to answer the question asked.

Mark "E" if not enough facts are given to answer the question.

Explanations of the key points behind these questions appear with the answers at the end of this test. The explanatory answers provide the kind of background that will enable you to answer test questions with facility and confidence.

Note: *In the data sufficiency problems which follow, the diagrams are generalized illustrations and are not necessarily drawn to scale.*

1. Exactly how many inches long is the length of a certain rectangle?

   (1) If it were six inches longer it would be exactly 3 feet.
   (2) If it were six inches less it would be exactly 2 feet.

2. How much did the salesman earn from the sale of 3 cars?

   (1) Each car sold for $3,400.
   (2) He received a 20% commission on each sale.

3. Are A and B on the same committee?

   (1) B is a member of the sales committee.

   (2) A is a member of the planning committee, and members of the sales committee can be on the planning committee.

4. How many gulos are in 8 munos?

   (1) 2 bulos = 8 gulos
   (2) 16 munos = 4 bulos

5. Exactly how many pounds of frankfurters did the boys and girls eat at the party?

   (1) At the party, the boys ate three times as many frankfurters as the girls.
   (2) If the girls ate 6 more frankfurters, then the boys would have eaten only twice as much as the girls.

S2037

6.

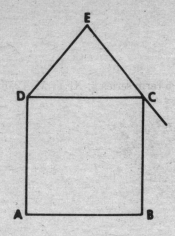

Find the area of the above figure.

(1) A side of square ABCD = 4
(2) DEC is an equilateral △

7.

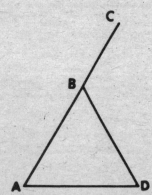

In the figure above ABC is a straight line. What is the degree measure of ∠BDA?

(1) ∠ABD = ∠BAD + ∠BDA
(2) ∠DBC = 90°

8. X and Y are two inscribed polygons whose vertexes lie on the same circle. Is the perimeter of X greater than Y?

(1) The circumference of the circle is 14π.
(2) Polygon X has 3 more sides than polygon Y.

9.

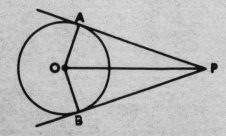

In the figure above, PA and PB are tangents to circle O at points A and B. What is the length of OP?

(1) The radius of circle O is 6 in.
(2) Tangent PA equals 8 in.

10. If A, B, and C are negative integers and t is an integer, is t negative?

(1) t = A − B
(2) tC = A

11. Does $\frac{3A - 2B}{4} = 1$?

(1) A = 2B
(2) B = 4

12.

What is the length of segment BC in the figure above?

(1) BD = 15
(2) CD = 10

13.

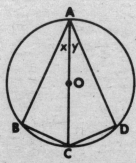

In the figure above, what is the value of the ratio $\frac{x}{y}$?

(1) The areas of triangles ABC and ACD are equal.
(2) Chords BC and CD are equidistant from O, the center of the circle.

14. If A, B, and C are the degree measurements of the three angles of an isosceles triangle, what is the value of B?

(1) A = 35°
(2) C = 95°

15. Christine has x + 5 pencils. She distributes equal amounts to her brother and four girl friends and has two pencils left for herself. Exactly how many pencils did she have originally?

(1) If Christine had only x pencils to give out in the same manner, she would still have two pencils for herself.

(2) If Christine had eleven less pencils to give out in the same manner she would have none left for herself.

16. In the 5 term series 3, $\underline{X}$, $\underline{Y}$, $\underline{M}$, $\underline{12}$, find the value of M.

(1) The third term is twice the first term.
(2) The fourth term is twice the second term.

CONSOLIDATE YOUR KEY ANSWERS HERE

CORRECT ANSWERS

EXPLANATORY ANSWERS

Elucidation, clarification, explication and a little help with the fundamental facts covered in the Previous Test. These are the points and principles likely to crop up in the form of questions on future tests.

1. (D)

By statement (1) if the rectangle were 6 inches longer, it would be exactly 3 feet, implies it must now be $2\frac{1}{2}$ feet. By statement (2) if the rectangle were 6 inches less it would be exactly 2 feet, implies also it must now be $2\frac{1}{2}$ feet.

2. (C)

Using the introduction and statement (1)

we learn the 3 cars sold for $10,200. Adding statement (2) and taking 20% of the total selling price, we find the salesman earned $2,040.

3 (E)

Neither statement (1) nor (2) indicate that A and B are definitely on the same committee.

4. (C)

By statement (1) if 2 bulos = 8 gulos,
4 bulos = 16 gulos.
By statement (2) if 16 munos = 4 bulos,
then using (1) and (2) 4 bulos = 16 gulos =
16 munos.

∴ 16 gulos = 16 munos
and 8 gulos = 8 munos.

5. (E)

Neither by statement (1) nor (2) can it be
determined how many frankfurters were
consumed by the boys and girls.

6. (C)

To find the area of the entire figure, you
must find the area of both geometric figures
shown. By statement (1) the area of the
square can be found using the formula $A = S^2$. Therefore, $A = 4^2$, $A = 16$. By statement (2) the area of the equilateral triangle
can be found by using the formula,
$A = \dfrac{S^2}{4}\sqrt{3}$.

$A = \dfrac{4^2}{4}\sqrt{3}$, $A = 4\sqrt{3}$.

Combining both statements, the area of
the entire figure is $16 + 4\sqrt{3}$.

7. (E)

Both statements do not provide enough
information to find the angle BDA.

8. (E)

Since the lengths of the sides of both polygons cannot be determined, it is impossible
to determine if the perimeter of X is
greater than the perimeter of Y.

9. (C)

The radius drawn to a tangent is perpendicular to the tangent at the point of contact, therefore $\triangle$PAO is a rt. triangle. By
statement (1) $OA = 6$ and by statement
(2) $PA = 8$. Hence using the Pythagorean
theorem $(OP)^2 = 8^2 + 6^2$; $(OP)^2 = 64 + 36$;
$(OP)^2 = 100$; $OP = 10$.

10. (B)

By statement (2) tC = A, A is negative.

To get a negative answer in multiplication,
you must multiply unlike signs. C is negative, therefore t is not negative.

11. (D)

$\dfrac{3A - 2B}{4} = 1$

$3A - 2B = 4$

By statement (1), $A = 2B$ substituting

$3A - 2B = 4$	$3A - 2B = 4$
$3(2B) - 2B = 4$	$3A - 2(1) = 4$
$6B - 2B = 4$	$3A - 2 = 4$
$4B = 4$	$3A = 6$
$B = 1$	$A = 2$

Knowing A and B, the problem can now be
determined.

By statement (2), $B = 4$ substituting

$3A - 2B = 4$
$3A - 2(4) = 4$
$3A - 8 = 4$
$3A = 12$
$A = 4$

Knowing A and B, again the problem can
be answered.

12. (C)

By statement (1) BD = 15; by statement
(2) CD = 10. Subtracting BD − CD,
15 − 10 = 5, BC = 5.

13. (B)

By statement (2) chords equidistant from
the center of a circle are equal; equal
chords have equal arcs ($\overarc{BC} = \overarc{CD}$). Angles
x and y intercept equal arcs, therefore,
x = y. Thus the ratio is 1:1.

14. (B)

By statement (2) if angle C = 95°, then
angles A and B are the equal angles and
each are $42\frac{1}{2}°$.

15. (E)

Neither statement supplies enough information to solve the problem.

16. (E)

Since the series is not defined, neither statement helps in solving the problem.

DATA SUFFICIENCY TEST

TIME: 15 Minutes

DIRECTIONS: *Each question below is followed by two numbered facts. Decide whether the data given is sufficient for answering the question. Sometimes the two facts do not give enough information to answer the question. Sometimes the two facts give just enough data to answer the question. And sometimes one of the facts alone is sufficient to answer the question. Read each question and the two facts that follow it; then mark your answer on the answer sheet that follows.*
Mark "A" if statement 1 alone is sufficient to answer the question, but statement 2 alone is not sufficient.
Mark "B" if statement 2 alone is sufficient to answer the question, but statement 1 alone is not sufficient.
Mark "C" if both statements together are needed to answer the question, but neither statement alone is sufficient.
Mark "D" if either statement by itself is sufficient to answer the question asked.
Mark "E" if not enough facts are given to answer the question.

DIRECTIONS: *Explanations of the key points behind each question are given at the end of the test. They follow the key answers which we have consolidated, facilitating comparison of your answers with ours. Score boxes and answer sheets are also included there. Remember, you'll learn more rapidly if you conscientiously answer questions on your own, before deriving your score.*

Note: *In this exam, the diagrams next to the problems should provide data helpful in working out the solutions. In certain problems the diagrams CANNOT be drawn to scale and are so indicated; but, in all others, they are drawn as precisely as possible. Again, except when specifically stated otherwise, all figures lie in the same plane.*

Lastly, all numbers are real numbers in this section.

1. In a class of 28 students, how many boys scored over 90% on the last geometry test?

   (1) Exactly 5 girls in the class scored over 90% on the geometry test.
   (2) One-fourth of the class scored over 90% on the geometry test.

2. What is the average of w, x, y, and z?

   (1) $w + x + y - 20 = z + 4$
   (2) $3(w + x + y) = 63$ and $z = 3$

3. How many members belong to club A?

   (1) All the members of club A also belong to club B.
   (2) There are exactly 40 members of club B.

4. What is the value of $a^2 - b^2$?

   (1) $a - b = 4$
   (2) $a + b = 6$

5.

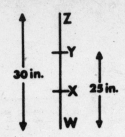

Find the length of XY.

(1) XZ = 18 in.
(2) XW = 12 in.

6. In △PQR, is the measure of ∡Q greater than 90°?

(1) The measure of ∡R is 100°
(2) The measure of ∡P is 30°

7.

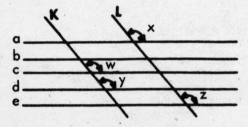

In the figure above, K ∥ L. Is x = y?

(1) a ∥ c ∥ e
(2) b ∥ d

8. What is the value of x/y?

(1) x = y − 4
(2) 3x = 2y

9.

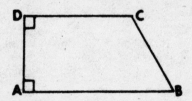

In the figure above, what is the perimeter of ABCD?

(1) AD = 3, CB = 5
(2) AB = 10

10. Pamela's weight is a whole number. What is Pamela's weight?

(1) If Pamela gains 6 pounds, she will weigh less than 130 pounds.
(2) If Pamela gains 8 pounds, she will weigh more than 130 pounds.

11.

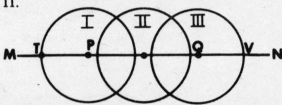

In the figure above, line segment MN contains the centers of three overlapping circles. What is the length of PQ (P is the center of circle I and Q is the center of circle III)?

(1) The radii of circles I, II, and III are 10, 6 and 8 respectively.
(2) The length of the segment from T to V is 40.

12.

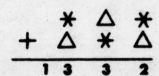

In the sum of the three-digit numbers above, * and △ are different positive integers less than 10. What is the integer *?

(1) △ = 7
(2) * + 2 = △

CONSOLIDATE YOUR KEY ANSWERS HERE

CORRECT ANSWERS

EXPLANATORY ANSWERS

Elucidation, clarification, explication and a little help with the fundamental facts covered in the Previous Test. These are the points and principles likely to crop up in the form of questions on future tests.

1. (C)

   By statement (2) $\frac{1}{4}$ of 28 = 7. It is now known that 7 in the class scored over 90%. Using statement (1) if 5 out of the 7 are girls, then 2 boys scored over 90%.

2. (B)

   To find the average of four terms you must find their total. This can be accomplished in statement (2).

   $3(w + x + y) = 63$ and $z = 3$
   $w + x + y = 21$ and $z = 3$
   $w + x + y + z = 24$

   Therefore, their average is 6.

3. (E)

   Impossible to determine from information given.

4. (C)

   The question contains two unknowns and requires 2 equations to solve. Statement (1) is an equation and statement (2) is an equation.

5. (D)

   By statement (1) add XZ and WY and subtract their total from WZ. In statement (2) subtract XW from WY.

6. (A)

   By statement (1) if one angle of a triangle is 100°, then the sum of the other two angles equals 80°. Hence ∠Q could not be greater than 90°.

7. (E)

   If a, b, c, d, and e were parallel to each other, it could be determined that x = y. But there is no indication that these lines are all parallel to each other.

8. **(B)**

    By statement (2)

    $3x = 2y$

    $\dfrac{x}{y} = \dfrac{2}{3}$

9. **(C)**

    After using both statements to find the perimeter of ABCD, the side CD must be found.

    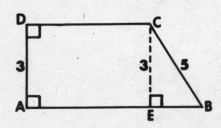

    Draw CE $\perp$ AB, CE = AD = 3. $\triangle$CEB is now a 3, 4, 5 rt. $\triangle$. EB = 4. Therefore, AE = 6 = CD.

10. **(C)**

    Let x = Pamela's weight.

    Statement (1) $x + 6 < 130$
    $x < 124$
    Statement (2) $x + 8 > 130$
    $x > 122$

    If $122 < x < 124$, x = 123.

11. **(C)**

    Using statement (1) the diameter of circles I and III are 20 and 16 respectively. By statement (2) the distance from T to V is 40, hence the distance from circle I to circle II is 40 − 36 or 4. To find the length of PQ, 10 + 4 + 8 = 22.

12. **(D)**

    By statement (1) if $\triangle$ = 7, then * could only be 5 to obtain the sum indicated. By statement (2) 7 and 5 are the only two digits whose difference is 2, that would obtain the same sum.

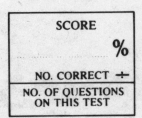

SCORE

%

NO. CORRECT ÷

NO. OF QUESTIONS
ON THIS TEST

PART FIVE

Another Model Exam and Final Advice

5

The time allotted for each Test in each Examination in this book is based on a careful analysis of all the information now available. The time we allot for each test, therefore, merely suggests in a general way approximately how much time you should expend on each subject when you take the actual Exam. We have not, in every case, provided precisely the number of questions you will actually get on the examination. It's just not possible to know what the examiners will finally decide to do for every Test in the Examination. It might be a good idea to jot down your "running" time for each Test, and make comparisons later on. If you find that you're working faster, you may assume you're making progress. Remember, we have timed each Test uniformly. If you follow all our directions, your scores will all be comparable.

FINAL VERISIMILAR EXAMINATION

In this comprehensive examination we have sought to predict the content of your test, and to provide you with the kind of practice you really require. It has approximately the same number of questions as the official test. The topics tested, the form of the questions, the level of difficulty, and the number of questions for each topic . . . all are quite similar to the official test. In every respect it simulates the actual conditions you will encounter. Test yourself to get an overview, to review your strengths and weaknesses, and to put yourself in the right frame of mind for scoring high.

The time allowed for the entire examination is 3½ hours. In order to create the climate of the test to come, that's precisely what you should allow yourself . . . no more, no less. Use a watch and keep a record of your time, especially since you may find it convenient to take the test in several sittings.

In constructing this Examination we tried to visualize the questions you are *likely* to face on your actual exam. We included those subjects on which they are *probably* going to test you.

Although copies of past exams are not released, we were able to piece together a fairly complete picture of the forthcoming exam.

A principal source of information was our analysis of official announcements going back several years.

Critical comparison of these announcements, particularly the sample questions, revealed the testing trend; foretold the important subjects, and those that are likely to recur.

In making up the Tests we predict for your exam, great care was exercised to prepare questions having just the difficulty level you'll encounter on your exam. Not easier; not harder, but just what you may expect.

The various subjects expected on your exam are represented by separate Tests. Each Test has just about the number of questions you may find on the actual exam. And each Test is timed accordingly.

The questions on each Test are represented exactly on the special Answer Sheet provided. Mark your answers on this sheet. It's just about the way you'll have to do it on the real exam.

As a result you have an Examination which simulates the real one closely enough to provide you with important training.

Proceed through the entire exam without pausing after each Test. Remember that you are taking this Exam under actual battle conditions, and therefore you do not stop until told to do so by the proctor.

Certainly you should not lose time by trying to mark each Test as you complete it. You'll be able to score yourself fairly when time is up for the entire Exam.

Correct answers for all the questions in all the Tests of this Exam appear at the end of the Exam.

Don't cheat yourself by looking at these answers while taking the Exam. They are to be compared with your own answers *after* the time limit is up.

ANALYSIS AND TIMETABLE: IV. VERISIMILAR EXAMINATION
This table is both an analysis of the exam that follows and a priceless preview of the actual test. Look it over carefully and use it well. Since it lists both subjects and times, it points up not only what to study, but also how much time to spend on each topic. Making the most of your study time adds valuable points to your examination score.

SUBJECT TESTED	Time Allowed
READING RECALL	35 minutes
DATA INTERPRETATION & PROBLEM SOLVING	75 minutes
VERBAL ABILITY	20 minutes
DATA SUFFICIENCY	15 minutes
READING COMPREHENSION	20 minutes
ENGLISH USAGE	15 minutes
PRACTICAL BUSINESS JUDGMENT	25 minutes

ANSWER SHEET FOR VERISIMILAR EXAMINATION IV.

TEST I. READING QUESTIONS

1 A B C D E   2 A B C D E   3 A B C D E   4 A B C D E   5 A B C D E   6 A B C D E   7 A B C D E   8 A B C D E
9 A B C D E   10 A B C D E   11 A B C D E   12 A B C D E   13 A B C D E   14 A B C D E   15 A B C D E   16 A B C D E
17 A B C D E   18 A B C D E   19 A B C D E   20 A B C D E   21 A B C D E   22 A B C D E   23 A B C D E   24 A B C D E
25 A B C D E   26 A B C D E   27 A B C D E   28 A B C D E   29 A B C D E   30 A B C D E   31 A B C D E   32 A B C D E

TEST II. DATA INTERPRETATION

1 A B C D E   2 A B C D E   3 A B C D E   4 A B C D E   5 A B C D E   6 A B C D E   7 A B C D E   8 A B C D E
9 A B C D E   10 A B C D E   11 A B C D E   12 A B C D E   13 A B C D E   14 A B C D E   15 A B C D E   16 A B C D E

TEST III. PROBLEM SOLVING

1 A B C D E   2 A B C D E   3 A B C D E   4 A B C D E   5 A B C D E   6 A B C D E   7 A B C D E   8 A B C D E
9 A B C D E   10 A B C D E   11 A B C D E   12 A B C D E   13 A B C D E   14 A B C D E   15 A B C D E   16 A B C D E
17 A B C D E   18 A B C D E   19 A B C D E   20 A B C D E   21 A B C D E   22 A B C D E   23 A B C D E   24 A B C D E
25 A B C D E   26 A B C D E   27 A B C D E   28 A B C D E   29 A B C D E   30 A B C D E   31 A B C D E   32 A B C D E
33 A B C D E   34 A B C D E   35 A B C D E   36 A B C D E   37 A B C D E   38 A B C D E   39 A B C D E   40 A B C D E

TEST IV. DATA INTERPRETATION

1 A B C D E   2 A B C D E   3 A B C D E   4 A B C D E   5 A B C D E   6 A B C D E   7 A B C D E   8 A B C D E

TEST V. ANTONYMS

1 A B C D E   2 A B C D E   3 A B C D E   4 A B C D E   5 A B C D E   6 A B C D E   7 A B C D E   8 A B C D E
9 A B C D E   10 A B C D E   11 A B C D E   12 A B C D E   13 A B C D E   14 A B C D E   15 A B C D E   16 A B C D E

TEST VI. VERBAL ANALOGIES

1 A B C D E   2 A B C D E   3 A B C D E   4 A B C D E   5 A B C D E   6 A B C D E   7 A B C D E   8 A B C D E
9 A B C D E   10 A B C D E   11 A B C D E   12 A B C D E   13 A B C D E   14 A B C D E   15 A B C D E   16 A B C D E

TEST VII. SENTENCE COMPLETIONS

TEST VIII. DATA SUFFICIENCY

TEST IX. READING COMPREHENSION

TEST X. ENGLISH USAGE

TEST XI. ENGLISH USAGE

TEST XII. TEST XIII. DATA APPLICATION AND EVALUATION

READING RECALL

4 passages - 26 questions

TEST I. READING PASSAGES

TIME: 15 Minutes

DIRECTIONS: This is a test to determine your ability to remember main ideas and significant details. You are to read the four passages that follow in a period of 15 minutes altogether. It is suggested that you divide your time equally among the four passages. When the time is up, you will be asked to recall certain ideas and facts about the four passages. You will not be able to refer back to the passages after 15 minutes.

PASSAGE 1

A Polish proverb claims that fish, to taste right, should swim three times—in water, in butter and in wine. The early efforts of the basic scientists in the food industry were directed at improving the preparation, preservation, and distribution of safe and nutritious food. Our memories of certain foodstuffs eaten during the Second World War suggest that, although these might have been safe and nutritious, they certainly did not taste right nor were they particularly appetizing in appearance or smell. This neglect of the sensory appeal of foods is happily becoming a thing of the past. Indeed, in 1957 the University of California considered the subject of sufficient importance to warrant the setting-up of a course in the analysis of foods by sensory methods. The book. *Principles of Sensory Evaluation of Food,* grew out of this course. The authors hope that it will be useful to food technologists in industry and also to others engaged on research into the problem of sensory evaluation of foods.

The scope of the book is well illustrated by the chapter headings: "The Sense of Taste"; "Olfaction"; "Visual, Auditory, Tactile, and Other Senses"; and "Factors Influencing Sensory Measurements." There are further chapters on panel testing, difference and directional difference tests, quantity-quality evaluation, consumer studies, statistical procedures (including design of experiments), and physical and chemical tests. An attempt has clearly been made to collect every possible piece of information which might be useful, more than one thousand five hundred references being quoted. As a result, the book seems at first sight to be an exhaustive and critically useful review of the literature. This it certainly is, but this is by no means its only achievement, for there are many suggestions for further lines of research, and the discursive passages are crisply provocative of new ideas and new ways of looking at established findings.

Of particular interest is the weight given to the psychological aspects of perception, both objectively and subjectively. The relation between stimuli and perception is well covered, and includes a valuable discussion of the uses and disadvantages of the Weber fraction in the evaluation of differences. It is interesting to find that in spite of many attempts to separate and define the modalities of taste, nothing better has been achieved than the familiar classification into sweet, sour, salty and bitter. Nor is there as yet any clear-cut evidence of the physiological nature of the taste stimulus. With regard to smell, systems of classification are of little value because of the extraordinary sensitivity of the nose and because the response to the stimulus is so subjective. The authors suggest that a classification based on the size, shape and electronic status of the molecule involved merits further investigation, as does the theoretical proposition that weak physical binding of the stimulant molecule to the receptor site is a necessary part of the mechanism of stimulation.

Apart from taste and smell, there are many other components of perception of the sensations from food in the mouth. The basic modalities of pain, cold, warmth and touch, together with vibration sense, discrimination and localization may all play a part, as, of course, does auditory reception of bone-conducted vibratory stimuli from the teeth when eating crisp or crunchy foods. In this connection the authors rightly point out that this type of stimulus requires much more investigation, suggesting that a start might be made by using subjects afflicted with various forms of deafness. It is, of course, well known that extraneous noise may alter discrimination, and the attention of the authors is directed to the work of Prof. H. J. Eysenck on the "stimulus hunger" of extroverts and the "stimulus avoidance" of introverts. (It is perhaps unfair to speculate, not that the authors do, that certain breakfast cereals rely on sound volume to drown any deficiencies in flavor, or that the noisier types are mainly eaten by extroverts.)

PASSAGE 2

The future of the American project to drill a hole through the mantle of the Earth now seems in doubt. Recently, the Committee on Science and Astronautics of the U.S. House of Representatives jibed at approving the new estimate of 28 million dollars for the cost of completing the Mohole. It remains to be seen whether the corresponding Senate committee will take the same view, but the prospects are not encouraging. For even if the Senate should consider that present costs are justifiable, the difference between the House and the Senate would somehow have to be reconciled before work could go ahead. Nobody will be surprised that those most closely associated with the Mohole project have been cast down by this latest twist in the long tortuous history of this project.

Two separate questions arise. The wisdom of the House Committee's decision is, for example, open to question, chiefly because the Mohole project is now so far advanced. A technique for drilling deep holes in the ocean floor has been developed, and orders for the drilling barges have been placed. By canceling now, Congress will save only a proportion of the total cost of the Mohole. It is capricious, to say the least of it, for the politicians to pull hard on the purse-strings at this late stage. It would have been much more to the point if they had taken a hard skeptical look at the project four years ago, for there was then good reason for believing that the drilling programme was being pushed ahead too quickly, and with too little preliminary study. A more deliberate program might have been easier to contain within the bounds of a public budget, and might have been more rewarding as well. But Congress cannot put the clock back to the beginning by a crude cancellation.

The second issue is even more alarming. Hitherto, Congress has not exercised to any important extent its constitutional right to arbitrate on the fine details of scientific programs financed by public money. It is true that plans for building—and siting—big particle accelerators have usually been examined in detail by Congressional committees, and the National Institutes of Health have occasionally been showered with more money than they could usefully spend, but the great public agencies have usually been allowed to manage their own affairs within the framework of a budget agreed by Congress. Though the details of the programmes of the National Science Foundation have been examined by Congress in the process of accounting for the spending of public money, Congress has usually trusted the judgment of its scientific public servants on the disposition of these funds. On the face of it, the Mohole decision looks like a departure from this practice. It could be a dangerous precedent.

PASSAGE 3

Hong Kong's size and association with Britain, and its position in relation to its neighbours in the Pacific, particularly China, determine the course of conduct it has to pursue. Hong Kong is no more than a molecule in the great substance of China. It was part of the large province of Kwangtung, which came under Chinese sovereignty about 200 B.C., in the period of the Han Dynasty. In size, China exceeds 3¾ million square miles, and it has a population estimated to be greater than

700 million. Its very immensity has contributed to its survival over a great period of time. Without probing into the origins of its remarkable civilization, we can mark that it has a continuous history of more than 4,000 years. And, through the centuries, it has always been able to defend itself in depth, trading space for time.

In this setting Hong Kong is minute. Its area is a mere 398 square miles, about one two-hundredth part of the province of which it was previously part, Kwantung. Fortunately, however, we cannot dispose of Hong Kong as simply as this. There are components in its complex and unique existence which affect its character and, out of all physical proportion, increase its significance.

Amongst these, the most potent are its people, their impressive achievements in partnership with British administration and enterprise, and the rule of law which protects personal freedom in the British tradition.

What is Hong Kong, and what is it trying to do? In 1841 Britain acquired outright, by treaty, the Island of Hong Kong, to use as a base for trade with China, and, in 1860, the Kowloon Peninsula, lying immediately to the north, to complete the perimeter of the superb harbour, which has determined Hong Kong's history and character. In 1898 Britain leased for 99 years a hinterland on the mainland of China to a depth of less than 25 miles, much of it very hilly. Hong Kong prospered as a centre of trade with China, expanding steadily until it fell to the Japanese in 1941. Although the rigors of a severe occupation set everything back, the Liberation in 1945 was the herald of an immediate and spectacular recovery in trade. People poured into the Colony, and this flow became a flood during 1949-50, when the Chinese National Government met defeat at the hands of the Communists. Three-quarters of a million people entered the Colony at that stage, bringing the total population to 2⅓ millions. Today the population is more than 3¾ millions.

Very soon two things affected commercial expansion. First, the Chinese Government restricted Hong Kong's exports to China, because she feared unsettled internal conditions, mounting inflation and a weakness in her exchange position. Secondly, during the Korean War, the United Nations imposed an embargo on imports into China the main source of Hong Kong's livelihood. This was a crisis for Hong Kong; its China trade went overnight, and, by this time, it had over one million refugees on its hands. But something dramatic happened. Simply stated, it was this: Hong Kong switched from trading to manufacture. It did it so quickly that few people, even in Hong Kong, were aware at the time of what exactly was happening, and the rest of the world was not quickly convinced of Hong Kong's transformation into a centre of manufactures. Its limited industry began to expand rapidly and, although more slowly, to diversify, and it owed not a little to the immigrants from Shanghai, who brought their capital, their experience and expertise with them. Today Hong Kong must be unique amongst so-called developing countries in the dependence of its economy on industrialization. No less than 40 per cent of the labor force is engaged in the manufacturing industries; and of the products from these Hong Kong exports 90 per cent, and it does this despite the fact that its industry is exposed to the full competition of the industrially mature nations. The variety of its goods now ranges widely from the products of shipbuilding and ship-breaking,' through textiles and plastics, to air-conditioners, transistor radios and cameras.

More than 70 per cent of its exports are either manufactured or partly manufactured in Hong Kong, and the value of its domestic exports in 1964 was about 750 million dollars. In recent years these figures have been increasing at about 15 per cent a year. America is the largest market, taking 25 per cent of the value of Hong Kong's exports; then follows the United Kingdom, Malaysia, West Germany, Japan, Canada and Australia; but all countries come within the scope of its marketing.

PASSAGE 4

Do students learn from programed instruction? The research leaves us in no doubt of this. They do, indeed, learn. They learn from linear programs, from branching programs built on the Skinnerian model, from scrambled books of the Crowder type, from Pressey review tests with immediate knowledge of results, from programs on machines or programs in texts. Many kinds of students learn—college, high school, secondary, primary, preschool, adult, professional, skilled labor, clerical employees, military, deaf, retarded, imprisoned—every kind of student that programs have been tried on. Using programs, these students are able to learn mathematics and science at different levels, foreign languages, English language correctness, the details of the U.S. Constitution, spelling, electronics, computer science, psychology, statistics, business skills, reading skills, instrument flying rules, and many other subjects. The limits of the topics which can be studied efficiently by means of programs are not yet known.

For each of the kinds of subject matter and the kinds of student mentioned above, experiments have demonstrated that a considerable amount of learning can be derived from programs; this learning has been measured either by comparing pre- and post-tests or the time and trials needed to reach a set criterion of performance. But the question, how well do students learn from programs as compared to how well they learn from other kinds of instruction, we cannot answer quite so confidently.

Experimental psychologists typically do not take very seriously the evaluative experiments in which learning from programs is compared with learning from conventional teaching. Such experiments are doubtless useful, they say, for school administrators or teachers to prove to themselves (or their boards of education) that programs work. But whereas one can describe fairly well the characteristics of a program, can one describe the characteristics of a classroom teaching situation so that the result of the comparison will have any generality? What kind of teacher is being compared to what kind of program? Furthermore, these early evaluative experiments with programs are likely to suffer from the Hawthorne effect: that is to say, students are in the spotlight when testing something new, and are challenged to do well. It is very hard to make allowance for this effect. Therefore, the evaluative tests may be useful administratively, say many of the experimenters, but do not contribute much to science, and should properly be kept for private use.

These objections are well taken. And yet, do they justify us in ignoring the evaluative studies? The great strength of a program is that it permits the student to learn efficiently by himself. Is it not therefore important to know how much and what kind of skills, concepts, insights, or attitudes he can learn by himself from a program as compared to what he can learn from a teacher? Admittedly, this is a very difficult and complex research problem, but that should not keep us from trying to solve it.

END OF SECTION

If you finish before the allotted time is up, work on this part only. When time is up, proceed directly to the next part and do not return to this part.

TEST I. READING QUESTIONS

TIME: 20 minutes

DIRECTIONS: Answer the following questions in accordance with the contents of the preceding passages. You are not to turn back to the passages.

QUESTIONS ON PASSAGE 1

1. The reviewer uses a Polish proverb at the beginning of the article in order to

   (A) introduce, in an interesting manner, the discussion of food
   (B) show the connection between food and nationality
   (C) indicate that there are various ways to prepare food
   (D) bring out the difference between American and Polish cooking
   (E) impress upon the reader the food value of fish

2. The reviewer's appraisal of *Principles of Sensory Evaluation of Food* is one of

   (A) mixed feelings
   (B) indifference
   (C) derogation
   (D) high praise
   (E) faint praise

3. The article points out that

   (A) many people suffered from food poisoning during World War II
   (B) at least one institution of higher learning has conducted a course in how to enjoy food
   (C) what is one man's poison is another man's meat
   (D) you must have a good sense of smell to enjoy good food
   (E) in the forties, food, in many cases, stank literally and figuratively

4. The Weber fraction was originated by

   (A) Max Weber (1881-1961), American painter
   (B) Ernest Heinrich Weber (1795-1878), German physiologist
   (C) Baron Karl Maria Friedrich Ernest von Weber (1786-1826), German composer
   (D) Max Weber (1864-1920), German political economist and sociologist
   (E) George Weber (1808-1888), German historian

5. The writer of the article does *not* express the view, either directly or by implication, that

   (A) more sharply defined classifications of taste are needed than those which are used at present
   (B) more research should be done regarding the molecular constituency of food
   (C) food values are objectively determined by an expert "smeller"
   (D) psychological considerations would play an important part in food evaluation
   (E) temperature is an important factor in the appraisal of food

6. The authors of the book suggest the use of deaf subjects because

   (A) deaf people are generally introversive
   (B) all types of subjects should be used to insure the validity of an experiment

(C) they are more objective in their attitude than normal subjects would be when it comes to food experimentation

(D) the auditory sense is an important factor in food evaluation

(E) they are more fastidious in their choice of foods

7. **The chapter headings listed for** *Principles of Sensory Evaluation of Food* **make no specific reference to the sense of**
(A) smell
(B) sight
(C) touch
(D) hearing
(E) muscular movement

QUESTIONS ON PASSAGE 2

8. The mantle of the Earth is

(A) the Earth's crust
(B) close to the Earth's center
(C) approximately halfway between the surface of the Earth and its center
(D) about fifteen miles from the Earth's surface
(E) of gaseous formation

9. The attitude of the writer toward the lawmakers is definitely *not* one of

(A) disgust
(B) obstinacy
(C) resentment
(D) skepticism
(E) fear

10. It is true that

(A) the total appropriation for the Mohole project was between twenty-five and thirty million dollars
(B) the Committee on Science and Astronautics is in favor of continuing the Mohole project
(C) both houses of Congress see eye-to-eye on the completion of the Mohole project
(D) before resumption of the Mohole project, it will be necessary to start ordering drilling equipment
(E) Congressmen demonstrated indelicacy in their Mohole decision-making

11. The article implies that

(A) the Senate favors scientific research more than the House of Representatives

(B) the National Science Foundation is a Congressional Committee
(C) the legislators are far from frugal in their allotment for the Mohole project
(D) the federal lawmakers have been manifesting an undemocratic attitude
(E) the House of Representatives has employed a watchdog attitude toward scientific expenditures whereas the Senate has been permissive.

12. The reader may infer that

(A) the project was started about two years ago
(B) the project has been discontinued because of the dangers involved
(C) the decision to continue the project is the responsibility of the lower House —not the upper House of Congress
(D) there is a question of unconstitutionality in disbanding the project
(E) the project was poorly planned at the start

13. The word "siting" used in the passage

(A) is a misspelling
(B) is a variant spelling
(C) means locating
(D) means setting
(E) means sorting

14. "Mohole" is likely derived from

(A) an Indian tribe
(B) more hole
(C) Mohorovicic, Yugoslavian geologist
(D) a follower of Mohammed
(E) Bohenjo-Daro, an ancient civilization

QUESTIONS ON PASSAGE 3

15. The article gives the impression that

    (A) English rule constituted an important factor in Hong Kong economy
    (B) refugees from China were a liability to the financial status of Hong Kong
    (C) Hong Kong has taken a developmental course comparable to that of the new African nations
    (D) British forces used their military might imperialistically to acquire Hong Kong
    (E) there is a serious dearth of skilled workers in Hong Kong

16. The economic stability of Hong Kong is mostly attributable to

    (A) its shipbuilding activity
    (B) businessmen and workers from Shanghai who settled in Hong Kong
    (C) its political separation from China
    (D) its exports to China
    (E) a change in the area of business concentration

17. Hong Kong's commerce was adversely affected by

    (A) the Han Dynasty
    (B) Japanese occupation
    (C) British administration
    (D) the defeat of the Chinese National Government
    (E) the conversion from manufacturing to trading

18. Hong Kong's population is about _____ that of China.

    (A) 1/50
    (B) 1/100
    (C) 1/200
    (D) 1/500
    (E) 1/1000

19. The author states or implies that

    (A) the United States imports more goods from Hong Kong than all the other nations combined
    (B) about three-quarters of its exports are made exclusively in Hong Kong
    (C) Malaysia, Canada, and West Germany provide excellent markets for Hong Kong goods
    (D) approximately one-half of the Hong Kong workers are involved with manufacturing
    (E) the United Nations has consistently cooperated to improve the economy of Hong Kong

20. Hong Kong first came under Chinese rule approximately

    (A) a century ago
    (B) eight centuries ago
    (C) fourteen centuries ago
    (D) twenty-one centuries ago
    (E) forty centuries ago

QUESTIONS ON PASSAGE 4

21. The word Skinnerian refers to

    (A) a plastic model
    (B) a nineteenth century textbook
    (C) a psychologist
    (D) a pedagogical principle
    (E) a culinary device.

22. The article implies that programed instruction

    (A) is inferior to other instruction
    (B) is superior to other instruction
    (C) is beneficial regardless of the type of programing used
    (D) is best for certain educational levels
    (E) is probably of temporary duration.

23. Psychologists view the results of program experiments
    (A) lightly
    (B) enthusiastically
    (C) with distaste
    (D) with complete acceptance
    (E) with risibility.

24. The article indicates that, with programed instruction, the teacher
    (A) may be dispensed with
    (B) may prove of negative value
    (C) and principal must work together
    (D) must be superior to get results
    (E) remains an important factor.

25. Programed learning
    (A) is a recent educational innovation
    (B) has been used in our schools for many years
    (C) is confined to teaching machines
    (D) refers to a student's school program
    (E) is always in linear form.

26. The expression "scrambled books" refers to a program type in which the student
    (A) eats while he learns
    (B) learns in a disorganized manner
    (C) learns by referring to various reference materials
    (D) is directed to different pages not in consecutive order
    (E) must be self-directed in his selection of research materials.

END OF PART
If you finish before the allotted time is up, work on this part only.
When time is up, proceed directly to the next part and do not
return to this part.

QUANTITATIVE PART

56 questions- 75 minutes

TEST II. DATA INTERPRETATION

TIME: 13 minutes

DIRECTIONS: Read each question in this test carefully. Answer each one on the basis of the following table. Select the best answer among the given choices and blacken the proper space on the answer sheet at the end of the test.

NUMBER OF EMPLOYEES IN CIVIL SERVICE
BETWEEN YEARS 1902 AND 1937

Year	Total Number (In Thousands)	Competitive Class (In Thousands)	Labor Class (In Thousands)	Non-Competitive Class (In Thousands)
1902	33	18	12	2
1906	43	24	16	2
1910	53	29	18	5
1914	56	31	18	6
1918	54	31	16	6
1922	60	35	17	7
1926	74	44	19	9
1930	90	52	24	12
1933	91	49	25	15
1937	107	63	27	17

1. The greatest percentage increase in the competitive class occurred between the years of
   (A) 1933 and 1937   (B) 1926 and 1930
   (C) 1922 and 1926   (D) 1906 and 1910
              (E) 1902 and 1906

2. The smallest percentage of employees in the competitive class is found in the year
   (A) 1902   (B) 1910   (C) 1914
          (D) 1933   (E) 1937

3. The greatest percentage of employees in the labor class is found in the year
   (A) 1902   (B) 1906   (C) 1910
          (D) 1930   (E) 1937

4. The approximate ratio of 54%, 27%, and 16% for competitive, labor class and non-competitive employees respectively
   (A) never occurs   (B) occurs once
   (C) occurs twice   (D) occurs three times
              (E) occurs five times

5. The most accurate of the following statements regarding the interpretation of the table is that

   (A) the percentage of employees in the non-competitive class has been constantly increasing since the World War

   (B) the percentage of employees in the competitive class has never fallen below 55%

   (C) since 1926, employees in the labor class have been increasing at a faster rate than in the non-competitive class

   (D) the average number of employees in the competitive class between the years of 1922 and 1937 inclusive was greater than the average number of total employees between 1902 and 1922 inclusive

   (E) between 1933 and 1937, the percentage increase in the competitive class was more than 3 1/2 times the percentage increase in the labor class.

S1281

307

Carefully study the table below. You are to
answer questions 6 through 10 solely on the basis
of the data given in the table.

YEAR	PRIVATELY FINANCED				Total publicly financed	TOTAL
	1-family	2-family	Multi-family	Total		
1937	267,000	16,000	49,000	332,000	4,000	336,000
1938	316,000	18,000	65,000	399,000	7,000	406,000
1939	373,000	19,000	66,000	458,000	57,000	515,000
1940	448,000	26,000	56,000	530,000	73,000	603,000
1941	533,000	28,000	58,000	619,000	96,000	715,000
1942	252,000	18,000	31,000	301,000	196,000	497,000
1943	136,000	18,000	30,000	184,000	166,000	350,000
1944	115,000	11,000	13,000	139,000	30,000	169,000
1945	184,000	9,000	15,000	208,000	18,000	226,000
1946	590,000	24,000	48,000	662,000	114,000	776,000
1947	745,000	34,000	72,000	851,000	3,000	854,000

6. "Multi-family private dwellings have been
built in greater numbers than 2-family private
dwellings." For the years covered by the table,
this statement
(A) is true (B) is false (C) is partly true
(D) cannot be determined from the table

7. Considering only the last ten years of the table,
the number of years in which the number of 1-
family private dwellings exceeded the number
of publicly-financed dwellings is
(A) 1   (B) 2   (C) 9   (D) 10

8. The number of years during which the number
of publicly-financed dwellings was more than
half the number of privately-financed dwellings
is
(A) 1   (B) 2   (C) 3   (D) 4.

9. The number of years during which privately-
financed 1-family dwellings was less than half
the total number of all dwellings is
(A) 1   (B) 2   (C) 3   (D) 4.

10. The number of years during which there was
an increase of at least 10% in the number of
private 2-family dwellings built is
(A) 1   (B) 2   (C) 3   (D) 4.

END OF TEST

*Go on to the next Test in the Examination, just as you would do
on the actual exam. Check your answers when you have completed
the entire Examination. The correct answers for this Test, and
all the other Tests, are assembled at the conclusion of this
Examination.*

TEST III. PROBLEM SOLVING

TIME: 54 minutes

DIRECTIONS: For each of the following questions, select the choice which best answers the question or completes the statement.

EXPLANATIONS ARE GIVEN WITH THE ANSWERS
WHICH FOLLOW THE QUESTIONS

1. Which of the following fractions is more than ¾?

    (A) $\frac{35}{71}$ (B) $\frac{13}{20}$
    (C) $\frac{71}{101}$ (D) $\frac{19}{24}$
             (E) $\frac{15}{20}$

DO YOUR FIGURING HERE

2. If $820 + R + S - 610 = 342$, and if $R = 2S$, Then
   $S =$

    (A) 44
    (B) 48
    (C) 132
    (D) 184
    (E) 192

3. What is the cost, in dollars, to carpet a room x yards long
   and y yards wide, if the carpet costs two dollars per square
   foot?

    (A) xy
    (B) 2xy
    (C) 3xy
    (D) 6xy
    (E) 18xy

4. If $7M = 3M - 20$, then $M + 7 =$

    (A) 0
    (B) 2
    (C) 5
    (D) 12
    (E) 17

5. In circle O below, AB is a diameter, angle BOD contains 15°
   and angle EOA contains 85°. Find the number of degrees in
   angle ECA.

    (A) 15
    (B) 35
    (C) 50
    (D) 70
    (E) 85

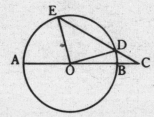

GO ON TO THE NEXT PAGE

6. The diagonal of a rectangle is 10. The area of the rectangle

   (A) must be 24
   (B) must be 48
   (C) must be 50
   (D) must be 100
   (E) cannot be determined from the data given

7. In triangle PQR in the figure below, angle P is greater than angle Q and the bisectors of angle P and angle Q meet in S. Then

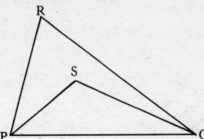

   (A) SQ > SP
   (B) SQ = SP
   (C) SQ < SP
   (D) SQ ≥ SP
   (E) no conclusion concerning the relative lengths of SQ and SP can be drawn from the data given

8. The coordinates of vertices X and Y of an equilateral triangle XYZ are (−4, 0) and (4, 0), respectively. The coordinates of Z may be

   (A) $(0, 2\sqrt{3})$
   (B) $(0, 4\sqrt{3})$
   (C) $(4, 4\sqrt{3})$
   (D) (0, 4)
   (E) $(4\sqrt{3}, 0)$

9. Given: All men are mortal. Which statement expresses a conclusion that logically follows from the given statement?

   (A) All mortals are men.
   (B) If X is a mortal, then X is a man.
   (C) If X is not a mortal, then X is not a man.
   (D) If X is not a man, then X is not a mortal.
   (E) Some mortals are not men.

10. In the accompanying figure, ACB is a straight angle and DC is perpendicular to CE. If the number of degrees in angle ACD is represented by x, the number of degrees in angle BCE is represented by

    (A) 90 − x
    (B) x − 90
    (C) 90 + x
    (D) 180 − x
    (E) 45 + x

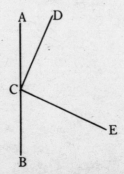

GO ON TO THE NEXT PAGE

DO YOUR FIGURING HERE

11. What is the smallest positive number which, when it is divided by 3, 4, or 5, will leave a remainder of 2?

    (A) 22
    (B) 42
    (C) 62
    (D) 122
    (E) 182

12. A taxi charges 20 cents for the first quarter of a mile and 5 cents for each additional quarter of a mile. The charge, in cents, for a trip of d miles is

    (A) $20 + 5d$
    (B) $20 + 5 (4d - 1)$
    (C) $20 + 20d$
    (D) $20 + 4 (d - 1)$
    (E) $20 + 20 (d - 1)$

13. In a certain army post, 30% of the men are from New York State, and 10% of these are from New York City. What percent of the men in the post are from New York City?

    (A) 3
    (B) .3
    (C) .03
    (D) 13
    (E) 20

14. From 9 A.M. to 2 P.M., the temperature rose at a constant rate from $-14°F$ to $+36°F$. What was the temperature at noon?

    (A) $-4°$
    (B) $+6°$
    (C) $+16°$
    (D) $+26°$
    (E) $+31°$

15. There are just two ways in which 5 may be expressed as the sum of two different positive (non-zero) integers; namely, $5 = 4 + 1 = 3 + 2$. In how many ways may 9 be expressed as the sum of two different positive (non-zero) integers?

    (A) 3
    (B) 4
    (C) 5
    (D) 6
    (E) 7

16. A board 7 feet 9 inches long is divided into three equal parts. What is the length of each part?

    (A) 2 ft. 7 in.
    (B) 2 ft. 6⅓ in.
    (C) 2 ft. 8⅓ in.
    (D) 2 ft. 8 in.
    (E) 2 ft. 9 in.

GO ON TO THE NEXT PAGE

17. In the figure below, the largest possible circle is cut out of a square piece of tin. The area of the remaining piece of tin is approximately (in square inches)

(A) .75
(B) 3.14
(C) .14
(D) .86
(E) 1.0

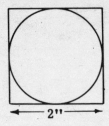

18. Which of the following is equal to 3.14×10^6?

(A) 314
(B) 3,140
(C) 31,400
(D) 314,000
(E) 3,140,000

19.

$$\frac{36}{29 - \dfrac{4}{0.2}} =$$

(A) 4/3
(B) 2
(C) 4
(D) ¾
(E) 18

20. In terms of the square units in the figure below, what is the area of the semicircle?

(A) 32π
(B) 16π
(C) 8π
(D) 4π
(E) 2π

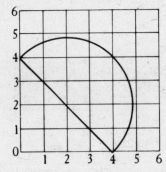

21. The sum of three consecutive odd numbers is always divisible by I. 2 II. 3 III. 5 IV. 6

(A) only I
(B) only IV
(C) only I and II
(D) only I and III
(E) only II and IV

GO ON TO THE NEXT PAG

DO YOUR FIGURING HERE

22. In the diagram, triangle ABC is inscribed in a circle and CD is tangent to the circle. If angle BCD is 40° how many degrees are there in angle A?

    (A) 20
    (B) 30
    (C) 40
    (D) 50
    (E) 60

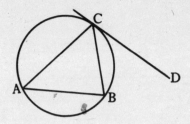

23. If a discount of 20% off the marked price of a suit saves a man $15, how much did he pay for the suit?

    (A) $35
    (B) $60
    (C) $75
    (D) $150
    (E) $300

24. The ice compartment in a refrigerator is 8 inches deep, 5 inches high, and 4 inches wide. How many ice cubes will it hold, if each cube is 2 inches on a side?

    (A) 16
    (B) 20
    (C) 40
    (D) 80
    (E) 160

25. Find the last number in the series:
    8 , 4 , 12 , 6 , 18 , 9 , ?

    (A) 19
    (B) 20
    (C) 22
    (D) 24
    (E) 27

26. A 15–gallon mixture of 20% alcohol has 5 gallons of water added to it. The strength of the mixture, as a percent, is near

    (A) 15
    (B) 13⅓
    (C) 16⅔
    (D) 12½
    (E) 20

GO ON TO THE NEXT PAGE

27. In the figure below, QXRS is a parallelogram and P is any point on side QS. What is the ratio of the area of triangle PXR to the area of QXRS?

 (A) 1 : 4
 (B) 1 : 3
 (C) 2 : 3
 (D) 3 : 4
 (E) 1 : 2

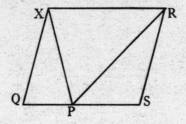

28. If x (p + 1) = M, then p =

 (A) M − 1
 (B) M
 (C) $\dfrac{M-1}{x}$
 (D) M − x − 1
 (E) $\dfrac{M}{x} - 1$

29. If T tons of snow fall in 1 second. how many tons fall in M minutes?

 (A) 60 MT
 (B) MT + 60
 (C) MT
 (D) $\dfrac{60\,M}{T}$
 (E) $\dfrac{MT}{60}$

30. If $\dfrac{P}{Q} = \dfrac{4}{5}$, what is the value of 2 P + Q ?

 (A) 14
 (B) 13
 (C) − 1
 (D) 3
 (E) cannot be determined from the information given

31. The figure shows one square inside another and a rectangle of diagonal T. The best approximation to the value of T, in inches, is given by which of the following inequalities?

 (A) 6 < T < 9
 (B) 11 < T < 12
 (C) 12 < T < 13
 (D) 9 < T < 11
 (E) 10 < T < 11

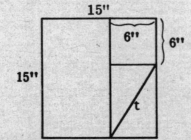

GO ON TO THE NEXT PAGE

32. What is the smallest positive integer K > 1 Such that $R^2 = S^3$ = K. for some integers R and S?

DO YOUR FIGURING HERE

   (A) 4
   (B) 8
   (C) 27
   (D) 64
   (E) 81

33. The number of square units in the area of triangle RST is

   (A) 10
   (B) 12.5
   (C) 15.5
   (D) 17.5
   (E) 20

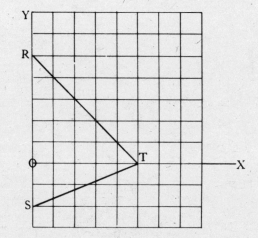

34. In the figure. PQR is an equilateral triangle of side 10 inches. At each vertex, a small equilateral △ of side X is cut off to form a regular hexagon. What is the length of X, in inches?

   (A) 3
   (B) 3⅓
   (C) 3½
   (D) 4
   (E) 4½

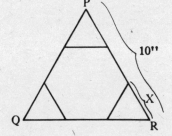

35. Which of the following has the same value as $\dfrac{P}{Q}$?

   (A) $\dfrac{P-2}{Q-2}$

   (B) $\dfrac{1+P}{1+Q}$

   (C) $\dfrac{P^2}{Q^2}$

   (D) $\dfrac{3P}{3Q}$

   (E) $\dfrac{P+3}{Q+3}$

GO ON TO THE NEXT PAGE

DO YOUR FIGURING HERE

36. A man travels a certain distance at 60 miles per hour and returns over the same road at 40 miles per hour. What is his average rate for the round trip in miles per hour?

(A) 42   (D) 48
(B) 44   (E) 50
(C) 46

37. As shown in the figure, a circular metal disc wears down to one-half of its original radius. What per cent of the original area remains?

(A) 50
(B) 25
(C) 75
(D) 40
(E) 60

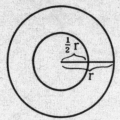

Questions 38 through 40 refer to the accompanying circle graph which shows how a certain family distributes its expenditures.

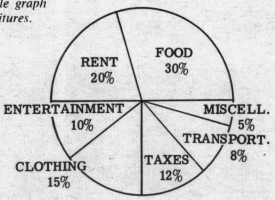

38. How many degrees should there be in the central angle of the sector for clothing?

(A) 18   (D) 28.8
(B) 36   (E) 43.2
(C) 54

39. If the family spends $320 per month, how much are its taxes? (monthly)

(A) $38.40   (D) $64.00
(B) $32.00   (E) $16.80
(C) $25.60

40. How many degrees should there be in the central angle showing clothing, taxes, and transportation combined?

(A) 100   (D) 126
(B) 110   (E) 130
(C) 120

END OF TEST

TEST IV. DATA INTERPRETATION

TIME: 8 minutes

DIRECTIONS: Read each test question carefully. Each one refers to the following graph, and is to be answered solely on that basis. Select the best answer among the given choices and blacken the proper space on the answer sheet.

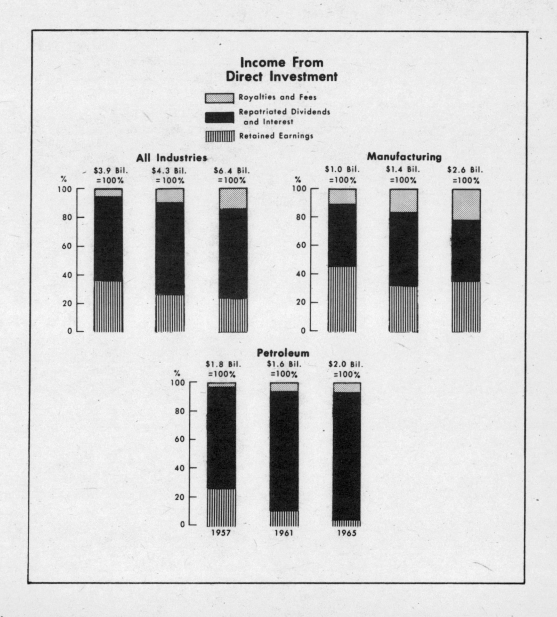

1. The manufacturing and petroleum industries accounted for what percent of income from direct investment in all industries in 1961?

   (A) 40%   (B) 50%
   (C) 60%   (D) 70%
   (E) cannot be determined from the given information

2. In 1957, how much was classified as "Retained Earnings" in the combined Petroleum and Manufacturing industries?

   (A) $400 million   (B) $450 million
   (C) $520 million   (D) $630 million
            (E) $900 million

3. The greatest percent increase of income was seen in

   (A) the manufacturing industry between 1957 and 1961
   (B) the manufacturing industry between 1961 and 1965
   (C) the petroleum industry between 1957 and 1961
   (D) the petroleum industry between 1961 and 1965
   (E) the combined statistics for all industries between 1957 and 1965

4. Which of the following does *not* represent an *increase?*

   (A) Royalties and fees in the manufacturing industry, 1961-1965
   (B) Repatriated dividends and interest in the petroleum industry, 1961-1965
   (C) Retained earnings in all industries, 1957-1961
   (D) Royalties and fees in the petroleum industry, 1957-1961
   (E) Repatriated dividends and interest in all industries, 1957-1965

5. Which represents the greatest amount?

   (A) Retained earnings in all industries in 1957
   (B) Total income from direct investment in manufacturing in 1957
   (C) Total retained earnings in the petroleum industry for all three years
   (D) Repatriated dividends and interest from manufacturing in 1965
   (E) Royalties and fees for all industries in 1965

6. How many degrees of a "pie" chart would be occupied by the manufacturing industry if the whole pie were to represent income from direct investment in 1961 for all industries?

   (A) 96°
   (B) 107°
   (C) 117°
   (D) 124°
   (E) 145°

END OF PART
If you finish before the allotted time is up, work on this part only.
When time is up, proceed directly to the next part and do not return to this part.

VERBAL ABILITY PART

39 questions - 20 minutes

TEST V. ANTONYMS

TIME: 5 Minutes

DIRECTIONS: For each question in this test, select the appropriate letter preceding the word that is opposite in meaning to the capitalized word.

1. PROFUSION:

   (A) travesty   (B) valiant
   (C) scarcity   (D) ordinance
       (E) laudanum

2. AGNOSTIC:

   (A) aged   (B) fanatic
   (C) truncheon   (D) farmer
       (E) inebriate

3. MITIGATION:

   (A) aggravation   (B) verdant
   (C) obscene   (D) restriction
       (E) interregnum

4. MISANTHROPE:

   (A) angel   (B) cauterize
   (C) supercilious   (D) biologist
       (E) humanitarian

5. INIQUITY:

   (A) equitable   (B) rectitude
   (C) noxious   (D) apostasy
       (E) taupie

6. PROTUBERANCE:

   (A) cadence   (B) habitation
   (C) indentation   (D) appanage
       (E) timbrel

7. INGENUOUS:

   (A) gimlet   (B) hypothetical
   (C) spasmodic   (D) sirocco
       (E) hypocritical

8. SANCTIMONIOUS:

   (A) contumacious   (B) flagitious
   (C) zany   (D) ingenuous
       (E) impervious

9. EXTIRPATE:

   (A) propogate   (B) helot
   (C) ingratiate   (D) emasculate
       (E) dauber

10. CAPRICIOUS:

   (A) redoubtable   (B) constant
   (C) bellicose   (D) cretaceous
       (E) ignominious

11. CASUISTRY:

   (A) wright   (B) trilogy
   (C) sedentary   (D) verity
       (E) salsify

12. CONTUMELY:

   (A) pecuniary   (B) imminence
   (C) eminence   (D) augur
       (E) tractable

13. CREDULITY:

   (A) litany   (B) drollery
   (C) ablution   (D) badinage
       (E) cynicism

14. PREDILECTION:

   (A) sobriety   (B) hostility
   (C) euphony   (D) palliative
       (E) contentious

TEST VI. VERBAL ANALOGIES

TIME: 7 Minutes

DIRECTIONS: *In these test questions each of the two CAPI-
TALIZED words have a certain relationship to each other.
Following the capitalized words are other pairs of words, each
designated by a letter. Select the lettered pair wherein the words
are related in the same way as the two CAPITALIZED words are
related to each other.*

1. ARCHAEOLOGIST : ANTIQUITY ::
   (A) flower : horticulture
   (B) ichthyologist : marine life
   (C) theology : minister
   (D) Bible : psalms
   (E) gold : silver

2. COURT : JUSTICE ::
   (A) doctor : sickness
   (B) chief : boss
   (C) machinist : product
   (D) policeman : government
   (E) auditor : accuracy

3. SCHOOL : DISCIPLINE ::
   (A) pupil : dean
   (B) report card : marks
   (C) society : conformity
   (D) underworld : gangster

4. ATOM : ELECTRON ::
   (A) sun : earth
   (B) constellation : sun
   (C) sputnik : satellite
   (D) neutron : proton

5. FINGER : HAND ::
   (A) leg : toe
   (B) dictionary : word
   (C) toe : foot
   (D) medicine : doctor

6. COOLNESS : NIGHT ::
   (A) black : yellow
   (B) humidity : sunshine
   (C) warmth : day
   (D) fear : fright

7. GIRL : WOMAN ::
   (A) student : teacher
   (B) adult : chid
   (C) black : white
   (D) infant : child

8. SHOE : LEATHER ::
   (A) passage : ship
   (B) trail : wagon
   (C) journey : boat
   (D) highway : asphalt
   (E) car : engine

9. PEDAGOGUE : LEARNING ::
   (A) teaching : books
   (B) professor : erudition
   (C) Plato : pedant
   (D) schoolmaster : ABC's
   (E) books : knowledge

10. THIRST : PARCH ::
    (A) fever : flush
    (B) water : sink
    (C) hunger : strangle
    (D) laughter : appease

11. STEP : STAIRWAY ::
    (A) staircase : banister
    (B) wood : carpet
    (C) rung : ladder
    (D) house : porch

12. FALL : PAIN ::
    (A) flying : walking
    (B) food : calories
    (C) disobedience : punishment
    (D) laugh : cry

TEST VII. SENTENCE COMPLETIONS

TIME: 8 Minutes

DIRECTIONS: Each of the completion questions in this test consists of an incomplete sentence. Each sentence is followed by a series of lettered words, one of which best completes the sentence. Select the word that best completes the meaning of each sentence, and mark the letter of that word opposite that sentence.

1. Boston's traditional swanboat rides provide a restful _____ from the city's summer heat, as they cruise the _____ waters of the Public Garden.

    (A) picnic . . . colorful
    (B) relief . . . turbid
    (C) hiatus . . . vapid
    (D) respite . . . placid
    (E) amnesty . . . gay

2. All countries in the region, who are also UN members, are _____ to join.

    (A) embraced
    (B) eligible
    (C) prohibited
    (D) tantamount
    (E) organized

3. An Australian woman _____ has discovered a way to boost the seed yield of pastureland.

    (A) agronomist
    (B) psychoanalyst
    (C) astrophysicist
    (D) phrenologist
    (E) bioscopist

4. It is usually a good thing when a discussion is taken firmly by the hand and led down from the heights of _____ to the level ground of hard _____.

    (A) ridiculousness . . . sublimity
    (B) mountaintops . . . meadowland
    (C) audacity . . . sincerity
    (D) fantasy . . . fact
    (E) speculation . . . reality

5. Electronic eavesdropping technology has become so _____ that the comparatively little law on the subject has become as _____ as the horse and buggy.

    (A) repulsive . . . fictitious
    (B) omnivorous . . . ridiculous
    (C) sophisticated . . . outmoded
    (D) clandestine . . . entangled
    (E) popular . . . homey

6. Basic research provides the _____ fund of scientific knowledge on which the applied researchers draw to give society a rich rate of interest.

    (A) depleted
    (B) endowed
    (C) capital
    (D) deterred
    (E) realistic

7. He _____ his speech heavily with jargon of the trade.

    (A) retards
    (B) brakes
    (C) disburses
    (D) inflates
    (E) lards

8. It really looked as if the outclassed Portuguese were about to make as _____ an exit from the _____ as had the Italians.

    (A) ignominious . . . competition
    (B) differential . . . forum
    (C) emphatic . . . cavern
    (D) surreptitious . . . vista
    (E) opportune . . . palladium

583

9. The growing of cereals on a large scale was the first stage in a revolution that was to replace a food-gathering _____-existence by an urban civilization based on agriculture.

 (A) paternal   (B) herbivorous
 (C) sedulous   (D) nomadic
            (E) urbane

10. But a _____ wind built up during the race, and shortly most of the summertime boats turned to and went home.

 (A) infamous   (B) helpless
 (C) snarling   (D) ravishing
            (E) vacillating

11. To be director of the most important, largest, and surely richest art museum in the country demands _____ concentration and strong personal _____.

 (A) continued . . . antipathy
 (B) invaluable . . . attachment

 (C) hectic . . . interposition
 (D) unseemly . . . charm
 (E) unflagging . . . involvement

12. The novel, describing the experiences of man who is brought back from the dead a new scientific technique, is a _____ on doctors, research foundations, and ma _____ of contemporary society.

 (A) treatise . . . remorses
 (B) satire . . . foibles
 (C) dossier . . . infallibilities
 (D) criticism . . . nostalgias
 (E) capsule . . . validities

13. The sales of Jules Verne's books continue _____ like a runaway balloon.

 (A) flit   (B) advance
 (C) revive   (D) soar
        (E) leap

END OF PART
If you finish before the allotted time is up, work on this part only.
When time is up, proceed directly to the next part and do not
return to this part.

DATA SUFFICIENCY PART

15 questions - 15 minutes

TEST VIII. DATA SUFFICIENCY

TIME: 15 minutes

DIRECTIONS: *Each question below is followed by two numbered facts. Decide whether the data given is sufficient for answering the question. Sometimes the two facts do not give enough information to answer the question. Sometimes the two facts give just enough data to answer the question. And sometimes one of the facts alone is sufficient to answer the question. Read each question and the two facts that follow it; then mark your answer on the answer sheet that follows.*

Mark "A" if statement 1 alone is sufficient to answer the question, but statement 2 alone is not sufficient.

Mark "B" if statement 2 alone is sufficient to answer the question, but statement 1 alone is not sufficient.

Mark "C" if both statements together are needed to answer the question, but neither statement alone is sufficient.

Mark "D" if either statement by itself is sufficient to answer the question asked.

Mark "E" if not enough facts are given to answer the question.

How many full jars will be needed to fill a bowl of punch with a capacity of 5 gallons?
(1) The punch bowl is hemispherical.
(2) Each jar holds one quart.

How long did Gottfried Wilhelm von Leibnitz live?
(1) He was born in 1646.
(2) He died in the year MDCCXVI.

Is a bullfrog an amphibian?
(1) The bullfrog belongs to the genus Rana.
(2) The genus Rana is part of the amphibian group.

How many degrees are there in the smaller acute angle of a right triangle?
(1) The hypotenuse is twice the length of the shorter arm.
(2) The larger acute angle is 60°.

5. How many more calories are there in a hamburger than in an apple?
   (1) A banana has twice the calories that an apple has.
   (2) A hamburger has 1½ times as many calories as a banana.

6. What is the third term in a series of numbers?
   (1) The first number in the series is 3.
   (2) The second number in the series is 9.

7. What is the amount of a deposit in the 16th week of a regular series of deposits?
   (1) A depositor starts off a bank account with $5; the next week he deposits $7.
   (2) The deposits form an arithmetic progression.

8. How much does a certain length of ribbon cost?
   (1) The length is 63 inches.
   (2) A yard and a half remains on the bolt after the ribbon is cut.

9. What is the second angle (in degrees) of a triangle?
   (1) The first angle is three times the second angle.
   (2) The third angle is 20 degrees more than the second angle.

10. How many gallons are needed to raise the water level of a rectangular swimming pool **4 inches**?
    (1) The pool is 75 feet long by 42 feet wide & 12 feet deep.
    (2) The present water level is 7 feet.

11. Is Socrates mortal?
    (1) All men are mortal.
    (2) Socrates is a man.

12. What is the meaning of the adjective *monanthous*?
    (1) *mon* means *single* (Greek).
    (2) *anthous* means *flower* (Greek).

13. What is the number of cubic feet of soil required to fill a flower box?
    (1) The box is 8 inches wide.
    (2) The box is 3 feet long.

14. What is the part of speech of *ice*?
    (1) It modifies the word *skates*.
    (2) It modifies a noun.

15. What is the difference between *testimony* and *evidence*.
    (1) Both are legal terms.
    (2) Testimony means information given orally only.

END OF PART
If you finish before the allotted time is up, work on this part only.
When time is up, proceed directly to the next part and do not
return to this part.

READING AND GRAMMAR PART

45 Questions 35 Minutes

TEST IX. READING COMPREHENSION

TIME: 20 Minutes

DIRECTIONS:
Select the word or expression that most satisfactorily completes
each statement or answers each question in accordance with the
meaning of the passage.

A vast health checkup is now being conducted in the western Swedish province of Varmland with the use of an automated apparatus for high-speed multiple-blood analyses. Developed by two brothers, the apparatus can process more than 4,000 blood samples a day, subjecting each to 10 or more tests. Automation has cut the cost of the analyses by about 90 per cent.

The results so far have been astonishing, for hundreds of Swedes have learned that they have silent symptoms of disorders that neither they nor their physicians were aware of. Among them were iron-deficiency anemia, hypercholesterolemia hypertension and even diabetes.

The automated blood analysis apparatus was developed by Dr. Gunnar Jungner, 49-year-old associate professor of clinical chemistry at Goteborg University, and his brother, Ingmar, 39, the physician in charge of the chemical central laboratory of Stockholm's Hospital for Infectious Diseases.

The idea was conceived 15 years ago when Dr. Gunnar Jungner was working as clinical chemist in northern Sweden and was asked by local physicians to devise a way of performing multiple analyses on a single blood sample. The design was ready in 1961.

Consisting of calorimeters, pumps and other components, many of them American-made, the Jungner apparatus was set up here in Stockholm. Samples from Varmland Province are drawn into the automated system at 90-second intervals. The findings clatter forth in the form of numbers printed by an automatic typewriter.

The Jungners predict that advance knowledge about a person's potential ailments made possible by the chemical screening process will result in considerable savings in hospital and other medical costs. Thus, they point out, the blood analyses will actually turn out to cost nothing.

In the beginning, the automated blood analyses ran into considerable opposition from some physicians who had no faith in machines and saw no need for so many tests. Some laboratory technicians who saw their jobs threatened also protested. But the opposition is said to be waning.

1. Automation is viewed by the writer with
   - (A) animosity
   - (B) indecision
   - (C) remorse
   - (D) indifference
   - (E) favor

2. The results of the use of the Jungner apparatus indicate that
   - (A) person may become aware of an ailment not previously detected
   - (B) blood diseases can be cured very easily
   - (C) diabetes does not respond to the apparatus
   - (D) practically all Swedish physicians have welcomed the invention
   - (E) only one analysis may be made at a time

3. All of the following statements about automated blood analysis are true EXCEPT:
   - (A) the analysis is recorded in a permanent form
   - (B) the idea for the apparatus involved an international effort
   - (C) the system has met opposition from physicians and technicians
   - (D) the machine is more efficient than other types of analysis
   - (E) the process is a means to save on hospital costs

4. The main purpose of the passage is to
   - (A) predict the future of medical care
   - (B) describe a health check-up system
   - (C) show how Sweden has superior health care
   - (D) warn about the dangers of undetected disease
   - (E) describe in detail the workings of a new machine

5. The prediction process that the Jungners use is essentially
    (A) biological
    (B) physiological   (D) anatomical
    (C) chemical   (E) biophysical

In discussing human competence in a world of change, I want to make it crystal-clear that I am not ready to accept all the changes that are being pressed on us. I am not at all prepared to suggest that we must blindly find new competences in order to adjust to all the changes or in order to make ourselves inconspicuous in the modern habitat. Let me be specific. I see no reason in the world why modern man should develop any competence whatsoever to pay high rents in order to be permitted to live in buildings with walls that act as soundtracks rather than sound-absorbers. Nor do I believe that this problem can or should be overcome by developing such novel engineering competences as "acoustical perfume"—artificial noise to drown out next-door noises. When I don't wish to be a silent partner to the bedroom conversation of the neighbors, I am not at all satisfied by having the sound effects of a waterfall, the chirping of crickets, or incidental music superimposed on the disturbance, just to cover up the incompetence or greed of modern builders.

The other day I found myself wandering through the desolate destruction of Pennsylvania Station in New York, thoroughly incompetent in my efforts to find a ticket office. Instead I found a large poster which said that "your new station" was being built and that this was the reason for my temporary inconvenience. Nonsense! my station was not being built at all. My station is being destroyed, and I do not need the new competence of an advertising copy writer or a public relations consultant to obscure the facts. The competence that was needed— and which I and great numbers of like-minded contemporaries lacked—was the competence to prevent an undesirable change. In plain language— the competence to stop the organized vandalism which, in the name of progress and change, is tearing down good buildings to put up flimsy ones; is dynamiting fine landmarks to replace them with structures that can be ripped down again twenty years later without a tear.

When the packaging industry finds it increasingly easy to design containers that make reduced contents appear to be an enlarged value at a steeper price, the change does not call for the competence of a consumer psychologist to make the defrauded customer feel happy. The change calls simply for a tough public prosecutor.

Lest I be mistaken for a political or even a sentimental reactionary who wants to halt progress and change, let me add another example of modern life the improvement of which may call for radical public action rather than for any new competence. Commuter rail transportation has fallen into decline in many parts of the country. Persons dependent on it find themselves frustrated and inconvenienced. In reply to their plight, they are given explanations such as the economic difficulties facing the railroad. Explanations, however, are no substitute for remedies. The competence required here is not technological or mechanical. After all, it would be difficult to persuade any sane citizen that a technology able to dispatch men into space and return them on schedule is mechanically incapable of transporting commuters from the suburbs to the cities in comfort, in safety, and on time.

The competence lacking here is one of general intelligence of the kind that is willing to shed doctrinaire myths when they stand in the way of the facts of modern life. To make millions of commuters suffer (and I use this example only because it is readily familiar, not because it is unique today) merely because the doctrine of free, competitive enterprise must be upheld, even after competition has disappeared as a vital ingredient, is an example of ludicrous mental incompetence. So is the tendency to worry whether a public takeover of a public necessity that is no longer being adequately maintained by private enterprise constitutes socialism or merely the protection of citizens' interests.

We ought to place the stress of competence in such a fashion that we can use it to mold, control and—in extreme instances—even to block change rather than merely to adjust or submit to it.

—by Fred M. Hechinger (reprinted with permission)

6. The attitude of the writer is
    (A) sardonic and uncompromising
    (B) critical and constructive
    (C) petulant and forbidding
    (D) maudlin and merciful
    (E) reflective and questioning

7. A "doctrinaire myth" (next to last paragraph) may be defined as a belief based on the false premises of
    (A) a deluded lexicographer
    (B) a public relations man
    (C) an insincere politician
    (D) a quack
    (E) an impractical theorist

8. In the article, the author urges us
   (A) to fight against unethical political deals
   (B) to disregard the claims of the advertiser
   (C) to be opposed to many of the changes going on in our society today
   (D) not to rent a luxury apartment
   (E) to avoid becoming a commuter

9. An appropriate title for this article would be
   (A) Antidotes for Incompetence
   (B) The Suffering Commuter
   (C) Unwarranted Destruction
   (D) Structured Vandalism
   (E) Progress and Change

10. The passage, in no way, states or implies that
    (A) much construction today is inferior to what it was in other years
    (B) the razing of the Pennsylvania Station was justifiable
    (C) consumers are often deceived
    (D) some engineering devices are not worth the trouble spent in contriving them
    (E) space scientists have made great progress

11. You would expect the author to say that
    (A) there is no reason for the United States to send nuclear-powered submarines to Japanese ports
    (B) a great deal of confusion reigns in credit card circles
    (C) a truly fundamental need in our society is honesty of thought and attitude
    (D) the damage done to our language by the structural linguists is not altogether irreparable
    (E) the world's population seems now to be increasing out of all proportion to the world's ability to provide food and education

There is a time in every man's education when he arrives at the conviction that envy is ignorance; that imitation is suicide; that he must take himself for better for worse as his portion; that though the wide universe is full of good, no kernel of nourishing corn can come to him but through his toil bestowed on that plot of ground which is given him to till. The power which resides in him is new in nature, and none but him knows what he can do, nor does he know until he has tried.

Society everywhere is in conspiracy against the manhood of every one of its members. Society is a joint-stock company, in which the members agree for the better securing of his bread to each shareholder, to surrender the liberty and culture of the eater. The virtue in most request is conformity. Self-reliance is its aversion. It loves not realities and creators, but names and customs.

Whoso would be a man, must be a nonconformist. He who would gather immortal palms must

not be hindered by the name of goodness, but must explore if it be goodness. Nothing is at last sacred but the integrity of your own mind. Absolve you to yourself, and you shall have the suffrage of the world.

A foolish consistency is the hobgoblin of little minds, adored by little statemen and philosophers and divines. With consistency a great soul has simply nothing to do. He may as well concern himself with his shadow on the wall. Speak what you think now in hard words, and tomorrow speak what tomorrow thinks in hard words again, though it contradict everything you said today. "Ah, so you shall be sure to be misunderstood." Is it so bad, then, to be misunderstood? Pythagoras was misunderstood, and Socrates, and Jesus, and Luther, and Copernicus, and Galileo, and Newton, and every pure and wise spirit that ever took flesh. To be great is to be misunderstood. . . .

12. According to the passage, the practice of adhering, at all times, to the regulations is
    (A) praiseworthy
    (B) characteristic of inadequate people
    (C) a matter of democratic choice
    (D) reserved only for the intelligent
    (E) not workable

13. The writer, in effect, is saying that one
    (A) must always change his opinions
    (B) who agrees with the findings of Newton may also agree with those of Copernicus, Pythagoras, Socrates, Jesus, Luther, and Galileo
    (C) must join a group to survive in our society
    (D) should continue to appraise the facts at the cost of changing a previous conclusion
    (E) can find solace only in a belief in the hereafter

14. You may infer that the author
    (A) was a philosopher-humorist
    (B) once remarked that Toil, Want, Truth, and Mutual Faith were the four angels of his home
    (C) was a leader of oyster pirates, a deck hand on a North Pacific sealer, a mill worker hobo, and college student for a time
    (D) achieved a reputation as a clever business entrepreneur
    (E) was a vivid personality who led a strenuous life and became president of the United States

15. Society, so the selection implies,
    (A) does not encourage an individual to be creative
    (B) wants its members to be self-starters
    (C) can thrive only under democratic rule
    (D) encourages investments in stocks & bonds
    (E) will not improve unless the quality of its leaders improve

TEST X. ENGLISH USAGE

TIME: 8 Minutes

DIRECTIONS: *This is a test of standard written English. The rules may differ from everyday spoken English. Many of the following sentences contain grammar, usage, word choice, and idiom that would be incorrect in written composition. Some sentences are correct. No sentence has more than one error. Any error in a sentence will be underlined and lettered; all other parts of the sentence are correct and cannot be changed. If the sentence has an error, choose the underlined part that is incorrect, and mark that letter on your answer sheet. If there is no error, mark E on your answer sheet.*

1. Many themes considered sacrilegious in the nineteenth
   <u>A</u>   <u>B</u>
   century are treated casually on today's stage. No error.
                     <u>C</u>   <u>D</u>   <u>E</u>

2. The color of his eyes are brown. No error.
   <u>A</u>   <u>B</u>   <u>C</u> <u>D</u>   <u>E</u>

3. All of my experience as a reporter of sports events indicate
                                                      <u>A</u>
   that the San Francisco Giants cannot possibly lose the
            <u>B</u>   <u>C</u>   <u>D</u>
   pennant. No error.
            <u>E</u>

4. We need further information before we can accede to
      <u>A</u> <u>B</u>   <u>C</u>
   your request. No error.
   <u>D</u>   <u>E</u>

5. Just between you and I, these theories won't work.
   <u>A</u>   <u>B</u>   <u>C</u>   <u>D</u>
   No error.
   <u>E</u>

6. If you would have gone into the hall, you would have met
   <u>A</u>   <u>B</u>   <u>C</u>   <u>D</u>
   your friends. No error.
                <u>E</u>

7. The Confederate Army retreated during the winter
        A   B
   in order to conserve their strength. No error.
   C   D   E

8. Let's keep this strictly between you and me. No error.
   A   B   C   D   E

9. In this type of problem, the total of all the items are
       A   B   C D
   always a positive number. No error.
                     E

10. I never have and never intend to visit foreign countries.
     A   B   C   D
   No error.
   E

11. His clothing laid on the floor until his mother picked it
        A   B   C   D
   up. No error.
      E

12. When the coach makes the decision as to which of the
         A   B
   two boys will play, you may be sure that he will choose
                                     C
   the best one. No error.
   D   E

13. He would have been more successful if he would have
           A   B
   had the training all of us received. No error.
        C   D   E

14. Mr. Martin, together with all the members of his family,
      A
   are having a good time in Europe. No error.
   B   C   D   E

15. This technique may be usable in your business if you can
       A   B
   adopt it to your particular situation. No error.
   C   D   E

END OF TEST

TEST XI. ENGLISH USAGE

TIME: 7 Minutes

DIRECTIONS: This is a test of standard written English. The rules may differ from everyday spoken English. Many of the following sentences contain grammar, usage, word choice, and idiom that would be incorrect in written composition. Some sentences are correct. No sentence has more than one error. Any error in a sentence will be underlined and lettered; all other parts of the sentence are correct and cannot be changed. If the sentence has an error, choose the underlined part that is incorrect, and mark that letter on your answer sheet. If there is no error, mark E on your answer sheet.

1. If the manager <u>would have</u> planned <u>more carefully</u>,
              A   B
   <u>bankruptcy</u> <u>might have been</u> avoided. <u>No error.</u>
       C   D   E

2. The prisoners were <u>accused of</u> robbery, <u>assault</u>, <u>embezzle-</u>
                  A   B   C
   <u>ment and forging.</u> <u>No error.</u>
       D   E

3. Since there was no evidence to indicate <u>who's</u> <u>ring it was</u>,
                                     A   B
   the <u>presiding magistrate</u> <u>dismissed</u> the case. <u>No error.</u>
           C   D   E

4. <u>Offer</u> the nomination to <u>whoever</u> commands the <u>respect</u>
    A   B   C
   <u>of the people.</u> <u>No error.</u>
      D   E

5. Two <u>astronauts</u> were disappointed because they <u>had hoped</u>
         A   B
   <u>to have made</u> the <u>first trip</u> to the moon. <u>No error.</u>
      C   D   E

6. <u>If</u> you want me to <u>express my opinion</u>, I think that
    A   B
   Report A is <u>equally as good</u> as Report B. <u>No error.</u>
       C   D   E

7. "Frank's dog is still in the yard," my father said, "perhaps
   $\underset{A}{\underline{\text{dog}}}$ $\underset{B}{\underline{\text{said}}}$
   he had better stay there until we have finished our din-
   $\underset{C}{\underline{\text{better stay}}}$ $\underset{D}{\underline{\text{finished}}}$
   ner." $\underset{E}{\underline{\text{No error.}}}$

8. He had a $\underset{A}{\underline{\text{chance}}}$ to invest wisely, $\underset{B}{\underline{\text{establish}}}$ his position,
   and $\underset{C}{\underline{\text{displaying}}}$ his ability $\underset{D}{\underline{\text{as}}}$ an executive. $\underset{E}{\underline{\text{No error.}}}$

9. The snow fell $\underset{A}{\underline{\text{during the night}}}$ so that it was $\underset{B}{\underline{\text{laying}}}$ in big
   $\underset{C}{\underline{\text{drifts on the highway}}}$ $\underset{D}{\underline{\text{the next morning.}}}$ $\underset{E}{\underline{\text{No error.}}}$

10. The $\underset{A}{\underline{\text{coach}}}$ with $\underset{B}{\underline{\text{his}}}$ entire team $\underset{C}{\underline{\text{are}}}$ traveling $\underset{D}{\underline{\text{by plane.}}}$
    $\underset{E}{\underline{\text{No error.}}}$

11. By his $\underset{A}{\underline{\text{perserverance,}}}$ he succeeded in $\underset{B}{\underline{\text{overcoming}}}$ the
    $\underset{C}{\underline{\text{apathy}}}$ of $\underset{D}{\underline{\text{his}}}$ pupils. $\underset{E}{\underline{\text{No error.}}}$

12. $\underset{A}{\underline{\text{This}}}$ is $\underset{B}{\underline{\text{one}}}$ of those $\underset{C}{\underline{\text{tricky}}}$ questions that $\underset{D}{\underline{\text{has}}}$ two
    answers. $\underset{E}{\underline{\text{No error.}}}$

13. She $\underset{A}{\underline{\text{did}}}$ the work very $\underset{B}{\underline{\text{well, however,}}}$ she showed
    $\underset{C}{\underline{\text{no interest in anything}}}$ $\underset{D}{\underline{\text{beyond}}}$ her assignment. $\underset{E}{\underline{\text{No error.}}}$

14. $\underset{A}{\underline{\text{Roberts,}}}$ a man $\underset{B}{\underline{\text{whom}}}$ we trusted with the $\underset{C}{\underline{\text{most difficult}}}$
    task of $\underset{D}{\underline{\text{all}}}$ proved loyal to his country. $\underset{E}{\underline{\text{No error.}}}$

15. It was $\underset{A}{\underline{\text{hard}}}$ to believe that $\underset{B}{\underline{\text{conscientious}}}$ pupils could
    $\underset{C}{\underline{\text{misspell}}}$ so many words in their $\underset{D}{\underline{\text{quizzes.}}}$ $\underset{E}{\underline{\text{No error.}}}$

END OF PART

PRACTICAL BUSINESS JUDGMENT

30 questions - 25 Minutes

DIRECTIONS: In testing your aptitude for business, they will ask you to evaluate a Situation and a Decision. You will be quizzed on goals, assumptions, conclusions, information, predictions, problems, options, and opinions. First, you will read a comprehensive analysis of a business situation; and then you will take two sub-tests based on your analysis: Data Application Quiz, and Data Evaluation Quiz.

Business Situation   Where to Open the Store?

The Company and the Town. The Bowton Company's supermarkets are situated in Illinois, Wisconsin, and Indiana. The company is dynamic and aggressive, having grown from 8 stores ten years ago to 26 today.

Fords Lake is a town 40 miles from the Chicago Loop. It has not shown the spectacular growth of other suburbs, but its population has increased from 16,000 to over 30,000 in the past decade. With no other Bowton supermarket within 20 miles of the area, the Bowton Company is considering opening a store in Fords Lake.

The Arguments Against. Some Bowton executives oppose the project as a poor risk. They point to the proposed site, which is in a shopping center three miles from the Fords Lake business district. Two other food chains have failed on this site because, they claim, most new residences are on the other side of the community.

Moreover, the shopping-center owners demand a five-year lease. Bowton would have to try to find another business to take over the lease should its own store fail before the end of that time.

If a Bowton market must be opened in Fords Lake, it would be far better, these executives argue, to build it in the heart of the community. But, they point out, another supermarket is already there.

The Arguments For. The majority of the executives maintain that the site has great potential. A new east-west highway is being built which will pass Fords Lake to the north and force the car-commuters to Chicago to pass by the shopping center. A housing project of 3,000 units is going to be constructed nearby. This project will have three- and four-bedroom homes. The average household is expected to consist of five people with over $15,000 of income to dispose of annually.

They also argue that the center of Fords Lake is now congested with traffic and has extremely poor parking facilities, while there is excellent parking in the shopping center. Investment in a new building in Fords Lake proper would thus be a bad risk and would prove far more costly than a five-year lease should the store fail.

They are not too concerned about the other supermarket in Fords Lake. There is enough business for both. Besides, the competitor's prices are higher than Bowton's.

They also discount past supermarket failures in the shopping center. They claim these were caused more by poor management than by the shopping center's being slightly off the beaten path.

The Decision. The board of directors listens to both sides and then votes to open a Bowton store at the Fords Lake shopping center.

Now, push forward! Test yourself and practice for your test with the carefully constructed quizzes that follow. Each one presents the kind of question you may expect on your test. And each question is at just the level of difficulty that may be expected.

TEST XII. DATA APPLICATION

DIRECTIONS: Based on your understanding of the Business Situation, answer the following questions testing your comprehension of the information supplied in the passage. For each question, select the choice which best answers the question or completes the statement. When you understand the data and interpret it correctly, you will be better prepared to evaluate Data, as required by the second part of this test.

1. In the last ten years, the Bowton Company has increased its number of supermarkets by

   (A)   18%
   (B)   26%
   (C)   200%
   (D)   325%
   (E)   480%

2. In the last decade the population of Fords Lake has increased about

   (A)   50%
   (B)   100%
   (C)   150%
   (D)   200%
   (E)   250%

3. Which of the following arguments are used by some Bowton executives to oppose a Bowton store in the shopping center?

   I. The center is far from the new residences.

   II. Another Bowton store is five miles away.

   III. The owners demand a five-year lease.

   (A)   I only
   (B)   II only
   (C)   I and II only
   (D)   I and III only
   (E)   I, II and III

4. Which of the following are arguments used to oppose Bowton's opening a store in the heart of the Fords Lake business district?

   I. A rival store is already there.
   II. Two supermarkets already failed in that area.
   III. Parking facilities are poor.

   (A)   I only
   (B)   III only
   (C)   I and III only
   (D)   II and III only
   (E)   I, II and III

5. The shopping-center site is favored by

   (A)   only a minority of Bowton executives
   (B)   the residents of Fords Lake
   (C)   the majority of Bowton executives
   (D)   less than half of the Bowton board of directors
   (E)   the stockholders of the Bowton Company

6. One argument presented in favor of the shopping-center site is that

   (A)   it is at present close to a dense residential area
   (B)   the shopping-center owners would waive rent for two years
   (C)   no supermarket has ever been in this area of the community
   (D)   a new highway will pass nearby
   (E)   Bowton has been very successful in shopping-center locations

7. The average family that will occupy the housing project soon to be constructed will

   (A) be considered as a typical lower-middle-income family

   (B) probably go into the Fords Lake business district to shop

   (C) consist of three people

   (D) be able to spend $15,000 a year after taxes

   (E) probably have little economic effect on the shopping center

8. The population increase in the Fords Lake community expected to result from the new housing project is

   (A) 3,000
   (B) 10,000
   (C) 15,000
   (D) 30,000
   (E) 46,000

9. Which of the following arguments are used to ease the fear of those who worry about competition from a rival Fords Lake supermarket?

   I.   There is enough business for both stores.
   II. The other store is badly managed.
   III. Bowton's prices are lower.

   (A) I only
   (B) II only
   (C) I and II only
   (D) I and III only
   (E) I, II and III

10. Which of the following reason(s) given explain the failure of two supermarkets in the shopping center?

   I.   Poor parking facilities
   II. Off the beaten path
   III. Poor management

   (A) I only
   (B) II only
   (C) III only
   (D) II and III only
   (E) I, II and III

END OF TEST

Go on to the next Test in the Examination, just as you would do on the actual exam. Check your answers when you have completed the entire Examination. The correct answers for this Test, and all the other Tests, are assembled at the conclusion of this Examination.

TEST XIII. DATA EVALUATION

DIRECTIONS: Based on your analysis of the Situation, classify each of the following conclusions in one of five categories. Check:

(A) *if the conclusion is a MAJOR OBJECTIVE in making the decision; that is, the outcome or result sought by the decision maker.*

(B) *if the conclusion is a MAJOR FACTOR in arriving at the decision; that is a consideration, explicitly mentioned in the passage that is basic in determining the decision.*

(C) *if the conclusion is a MINOR FACTOR in making the decision; that is, a secondary consideration that affects the criteria tangentially, relating to a Major Factor rather than to an Objective.*

(D) *if the conclusion is a MAJOR ASSUMPTION made in deliberating; that is a supposition or projection made by the decision maker before weighing the variables.*

(E) *if the conclusion is an UNIMPORTANT ISSUE in getting to the point; that is a factor that is insignificant or not immediately relevant to the situation.*

11. The residents at the projected residential development will shop in the Bowton store

12. Past growth of Fords Lake

13. No Bowton store within 20 miles

14. Poor management causing past supermarket failures

15. New east-west highway

16. Competition from another store

17. The expansion of the Bowton Company to a new location.

18. An increase of the population flow through the shopping center site

19. Failure of two supermarkets due to poor site selection

20. Bowton activities confined to three states

21. Car commuters to pass shopping center

22. Establishing a new store

23. New housing development

24. Enough business for two supermarkets

25. Five-year lease

26. Fords Lake is 40 miles from Chicago

27. Car commuters will shop at Bowton supermarket

28. New houses will have 3–4 bedrooms

29. High disposable income of expected new residents

30. Bowton's prices are lower than those of competitors

53329

END OF EXAMINATION

CORRECT ANSWERS FOR VERISIMILAR EXAMINATION IV.

(Please make every effort to answer the questions on your own before looking at these answers. You'll make faster progress by following this rule.)

TEST I. READING QUESTIONS

1.A	5.C	9.B	13.C	17.B	21.C	25.A
2.D	6.D	10.E	14.C	18.C	22.C	26.D
3.E	7.E	11.D	15.A	19.C	23.A	
4.B	8.D	12.E	16.E	20.D	24.E	

TEST II. DATA INTERPRETATION

1.E	3.B	5.E	7.C	9.A
2.D	4.B	6.A	8.B	10.D

TEST III. PROBLEM SOLVING

1.D	6.E	11.C	16.A	21.B	26.A	31.E	36.D
2.A	7.A	12.B	17.D	22.C	27.E	32.D	37.B
3.E	8.B	13.A	18.E	23.B	28.E	33.D	38.C
4.B	9.C	14.C	19.C	24.A	29.A	34.B	39.A
5.B	10.A	15.B	20.D	25.E	30.E	35.D	40.D

TEST III. EXPLANATORY ANSWERS

1. **(D)** ¾ = .75

$\dfrac{35}{71}$ is slightly less than $\dfrac{35}{70} = .5$

$\dfrac{13}{20} = \dfrac{13 \times 5}{20 \times 5} = \dfrac{65}{100} = .65$

$\dfrac{71}{101}$ is very close to $\dfrac{7}{10}$ or .7

$\dfrac{15}{20} = \dfrac{15 \times 5}{20 \times 5} = \dfrac{75}{100} = .75$

which equals ¾

$\dfrac{19}{24} = \begin{array}{r} .79 \\ \hline 24\overline{)19.00} \\ 168 \\ \hline 220 \\ 216 \end{array}$ which is more than ¾

2. **(A)** $820 + RTS - 610 = 342$
$R + S + 210 = 342$
$R + S = 132$
If $R = 2S$, then $2S + S = 132$
$3S = 132$
$2 = 44$

3. **(E)**

Area = xy sq. yd.
= 9 xy sq. ft.
9 xy·2 = 18 xy

4. **(B)** $7M = 3M - 20$
$4M = -20$
$M = -5$
$M + 7 = -5 + 7 = 2$

5. **(B)** Arc EA = 85° and arc BD = 15°, since a central angle is measured by its arc then

$$\text{angle ECA} = 1 \ (AE - BD)$$
$$= 1 \ (85 - 15)$$
$$= \tfrac{1}{2} \cdot 70$$
$$= 35°$$

6. **(E)** If we know only the hypotenuse of a right triangle, we cannot determine its legs. Hence, the area of the rectangle cannot be determined from the data given.

7. **(A)** If angle P > angle Q, then ½ angle P > ½ angle Q; then angle SPQ > angle SQP. Since the larger side lies opposite the larger angle, it follows that SQ > SP.

8. **(B)** Since Z is equidistant from X and Y, it must lie on the Y – axis. Then △ OZY is a 30° − 60° − 90° triangle with YZ = 8 Hence OZ = ½√3 = 4√3 Coordinates of Z are

(0, 4√3)

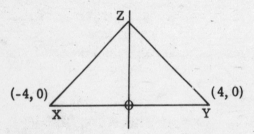

9. **(C)** (A) is a converse and not necessarily true
(B) is also based on the truth of the converse
(C) is based on the contrapositive, which is logically equivalent to the given statement
(D) is based on the converse; not necessarily true
(E) does not necessarily follow
Hence (C)

10. **(A)** Since ACB is a straight angle and angle DCE is a right angle, then angle ACD and angle BCE are complementary. Hence BCE = 90 − x.

11. **(C)** The smallest, positive number divisible by 3, 4, or 5 is 3·4·5 = 60. Hence the desired number is
60 + 2 = 62

12. **(B)** Since there are 4d quarter miles in d miles, the charge = 20 + 5 (4d − 1)

13. **(A)** Assume that there are 100 men on the post; then 30 are from New York State and ¹/₁₀ × 30 = 3 are from New York City.
³/₁₀₀ = 3%

14. **(C)** Rise in temp. = 36 − (−14) = 36 + 14 = 50° ⁵⁰/₅ = 10° (hourly rise)
Hence, at noon, temp. = −14 + 3 (10) = −14 + 30 = + 16°

15. **(B)** 9 = 8 + 1 = 7 + 2 = 6 + 3 = 5 + 4
Thus, 4 ways

16. **(A)** $\dfrac{7 \text{ ft. } 9 \text{ in.}}{3} = \dfrac{6 \text{ ft. } 21 \text{ in.}}{3} = 2 \text{ ft. } 7 \text{ in.}$

17. **(D)** Area of Square − 2² − 4
Area of Circle − π · 1² − π
Difference = 4 − π = 4 − 3.14 = .86

18. **(E)** 3.14 × 10⁶ = 3.14 × 1,000,000 = 3,140,000

19. **(C)** $\dfrac{36}{29 - \dfrac{4}{0.2}} = \dfrac{36}{29 - 20} = \dfrac{36}{9} = 4$

20. **(D)** Diameter = 4√2, since it is the hypotenuse of a right isosceles △ of leg 4
Then the radius = 2√2
Area of semicircle = 1 × π (2√2)²
= 1 × π · 8 = 4π

21. **(B)** Consecutive odd numbers may be represented as 2n + 1
2n + 3
2n + 5
Sum = ‾‾6n + 9‾‾
Always divisible by 3. Thus, only II.

22. **(C)** Angle BCD is formed by tangent and chord and is equal to one-half arc BC. Angle A is inscribed angle and also equal to one-half of arc BC.
Hence angle A = angle BCD = 40°

23. **(B)** Let x = amount of marked price.
Then $\frac{1}{5}x = 15$
$$x = 75$$
$75 - 15 = \$60$

24. **(A)** Since the ice cubes are 2 inches on an edge, there can be only 2 layers of 8 cubes each or a total of 16 cubes.

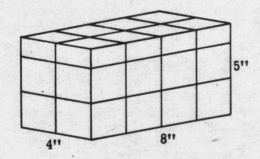

25. **(E)** There is a double recurring pattern here as indicated: Multiply by .5; then multiply by 3. Hence, the last term is 27.

26. **(A)** The new solution is $\frac{3}{20}$ pure alcohol or 15%.

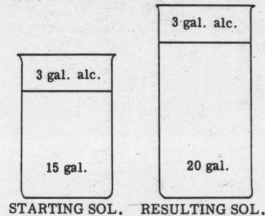

STARTING SOL.   RESULTING SOL.

27. **(E)** Area of $\boxed{P}$ = XR × altitude from P to XR.
Area of $\triangle XPR = \frac{1}{2}$ XR × altitude from P to XR.
Hence, ratio of area of $\triangle$ to $\boxed{P}$ = 1:2

28. **(E)** x(p + 1) = M Divide both sides by x.
$$p + 1 = \frac{M}{x}$$
$$\text{or } P = \frac{M}{x} - 1$$

29. **(A)** $\frac{T}{1} = \frac{x}{60M}$
$$x = 60 \text{ MT}$$

30. **(E)** If $\frac{P}{Q} = \frac{4}{5}$
Then $5P = 4Q$
However, there is no way of determining from this the value of $2P + Q$.

31. **(E)** The right triangle of which T is hypotenuse has legs which are obviously 6 inches and 9 inches.
Hence, $T^2 = 6^2 + 9^2$
$T^2 = 36 + 81 = 117$
$T = \sqrt{117}$
or $10 < T < 11$

32. **(D)** Since K is an integer and R and S are integers, K must be a perfect square and perfect cube. The smallest such number listed is $64 = 8^2 = 4^3$

33. **(D)** The $\triangle$ RST has a base of 7 and an altitude of 5. Hence the area $= \frac{1}{2} \cdot 7 \cdot 5 = 17\frac{1}{2}$

34. **(B)** Since the small triangles are also equilateral, their sides must also equal X. Hence, PR is divided into three equal parts, so that $X = \frac{1}{3} \cdot 10 = 3\frac{1}{3}$

35. **(D)** $\frac{3P}{3Q}$ is obviously reducible to $\frac{P}{Q}$
The others cannot be reduced because we may not add or subtract the same numbers to numerator and denominator, or take the square roots of them.

36. **(D)** Let the number of miles traveled each way = M

The time going $= \frac{\text{distance}}{\text{rate}} = \frac{M}{60}$

The time coming $= \frac{M}{40}$

Total time for round trip $= \frac{M}{60} + \frac{M}{40}$

$$= \frac{2M + 3M}{120} = \frac{5M}{120} = \frac{M}{24}$$

Average rate =
$$\frac{\text{total distance}}{\text{total time}} = \frac{2M}{\frac{M}{24}} = 48 \text{ miles per hour.}$$

37. **(B)** Original area — πr^2
Reduced area — $\pi(\frac{1}{2}r)^2$ — $\frac{1}{4}\pi r^2$
Hence, 25% of original area remains.

38. **(C)** Central angle = .15 × 360° = 54°

39. **(A)** Taxes = .12 × 320 = $38.40.

40. **(D)** (.15 + .12 + .08) 360° = .35 × 360°
= 126°

TEST IV. DATA INTERPRETATION

1.D	2.E	3.B	4.C	5.A	6.C

TEST IV. EXPLANATORY ANSWERS

1. **(D)** 1.6 billion + 1.4 billion = 3 billion. 3 billion is about 70% of 4.3 billion.

2. **(E)** 25% of 1.8 billion + 45% of 1 billion = 900 million.

3. **(B)** 2.6 billion minus 1.4 billion = 1.2 billion.

4. **(C)** 1957: 35% of 3.9 billion = 1 billion, 365 million. 1961: 30% of 4.3 billion = 1 billion, 290 million.

5. **(A)** 35% of 3.9 billion = 1 billion, 365 million. This exceeds the amount of each of the other choices.

6. **(C)** $\frac{1.4}{4.3}$ times 360 degrees = approx. 117 degrees.

TEST V. ANTONYMS

1.C	3.A	5.A	7.E	9.A	11.D	13.E
2.B	4.E	6.C	8.D	10.B	12.C	14.B

TEST VI. VERBAL ANALOGIES

1.B	3.C	5.C	7.D	9.B	11.C
2.E	4.B	6.C	8.D	10.A	12.C

TEST VII. SENTENCE COMPLETIONS

1.D	3.A	5.C	7.E	9.D	11.E	13.D
2.B	4.E	6.C	8.A	10.C	12.B	

TEST VIII. DATA SUFFICIENCY

1.B	3.C	5.C	7.C	9.C	11.C	13.E	15.E
2.C	4.D	6.E	8.E	10.A	12.C	14.D	

TEST VIII. EXPLANATORY ANSWERS

1. (*B*) Statement 1, in no way, contributes to the solution of the problem. Statement 2 tells us that each jar holds one quart = ¼ gallon. 20 × ¼ gallon = 5 gallons.

2. (*C*) MDCCXVI = 1716. 1716 — 1646 = 70 years.

3. (*C*) The amphibian group includes Rana (Statement 2). Rana includes the bullfrog (Statement 1). Therefore, the amphibian group must include the bullfrog.

4. (*D*)

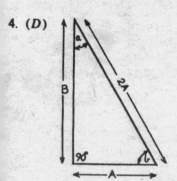

From Statement 1, we learn that side A, as shown in the diagram, is ½ side 2A.

$$\text{Sin A} = \frac{\text{length of leg opposite angle A}}{\text{length of hypotenuse}} = \tfrac{1}{2}$$

The table of sine ratios which mathematicians have constructed for all acute angles between 0° and 90° should tell us that if sin A = .5, then angle a = 30°. Statement 2 tells us that angle b = 60°. The three angles of any triangle add up to 180°. Therefore, angle a = 30°.

5. (*C*) Statement 1 tells us that the calories of 2 apples = the calories of a banana. Therefore, 2A = 1B. Statement 2 tells us that the calories in 1 hamburger = the calories in ³⁄₂ bananas. Therefore, 1H = ³⁄₂B. So 2H = 3B. Since 1B = 2A, let us substitute in the relationship of 2H = 3B.

$$2H = 3B = 3 \times 2A = 6A$$

$$H = \frac{6A}{2} \text{ and } H = 3A$$

Therefore, 1 hamburger has 3 times as many calories as 1 apple.

6. (*E*) The series pattern is not brought out by the first and second numbers of the series.

7. (*C*) Statements 1 and 2 indicate that the first three deposits are in the sequence of 5,7,9. We can, therefore, establish that we have here an arithmetic series which progresses by 2's.

8. (*E*) Statement 1 indicates the length of the ribbon. What we need to know in order to solve the problem is the cost per unit of that particular ribbon. The latter information is not provided.

9. (*C*) Statement 1 tells us that angle A = 3B. Statement 2 tells us that C = 20 + B. Since the three angles of any triangle = 180°, A + B + C = 180. Substituting, we have
3B + B + 20 + B = 180
5B = 160; B = 32°.

10. (*A*) Statement 1 indicates that the volume of the added water = 75 × 42 × ⅓ = 1050 cubic feet. 7.5 gallons of water is approximately 1 cubic foot of water. Therefore, 1050 × 7.5 = 7,875 gallons of water = Answer. Statement 2 is irrelevant.

11. (*C*) In this syllogism, Statement 1 is the major premise, Statement 2 is the minor premise, and the conclusion, by deductive reasoning, is that Socrates is mortal.

12. (*C*) By putting together the information of the two statements, we may conclude that monanthous means having but one flower.

13. (*E*) The third dimension of the box is lacking. Without this third dimension, we cannot solve the problem.

14. (*D*) A word that modifies *skates* (which is a noun) must be an adjective. Any word that modifies a noun must be an adjective.

15. (*E*) The information in Statement 1 is of too general a nature to be of any help. Statement 2 tells us what *testimony* means but tells us nothing about what *evidence* means.

TEST IX. READING COMPREHENSION

1. E	4. B	7. E	10. B	13. D
2. A	5. C	8. C	11. C	14. B
3. B	6. B	9. A	12. B	15. A

TEST X. ENGLISH USAGE

1. E	4. E	7. D	10. A	13. B
2. C	5. C	8. E	11. B	14. B
3. A	6. B	9. D	12. D	15. C

TEST XI. ENGLISH USAGE

1. A	4. E	7. B	10. C	13. B
2. D	5. C	8. C	11. A	14. D
3. A	6. D	9. B	12. D	15. E

TEST XII. TEST XIII. DATA APPLICATION AND EVALUATION

1. D	6. D	11. D	16. E	21. C	26. E
2. B	7. D	12. C	17. A	22. A	27. D
3. D	8. C	13. C	18. B	23. C	28. C
4. C	9. D	14. D	19. D	24. C	29. B
5. C	10. D	15. C	20. E	25. C	30. B

TEST XII. TEST XIII. EXPLANATORY ANSWERS

1. **(D)** The stores increased from 8 to 26.

2. **(B)** The population increased from 16,000 to slightly over 30,000.

3. **(D)** It is stated that no other Bowton supermarket is within 20 miles of Fords Lake. The opposing executives refer only to the new residences already occupied, not to the projected housing development near the shopping center.

4. **(C)** It is stated there is a rival store in the heart of Fords Lake and that parking facilities are poor. The two supermarkets that failed were in the shopping center, not in the business district.

5. **(C)** So stated in the story.

6. **(D)** So stated in the story. **(A)** is wrong since the shopping center is not as yet close to a residential area of any size. **(C)** is incorrect; we are told that two supermarkets failed in the shopping center. **(E)** is wrong; we are not told what success Bowton has had in other shopping centers.

7. **(D)** Disposable income is what is left after taxes, social security, and so forth, are taken out of a salary check; in short, it is take-home pay. **(A)** is wrong; $15,000 disposable income is far higher than lower-middle income. **(C)** is wrong; we are told the average family will consist of five people. **(B)** and **(E)** are assumptions that are not stated in the story.

8. **(C)** is correct. There will be 3,000 new housing units with an average of five people in each, or a total of 15,000.

9. **(D)** represents the correct statements; **(E)** is wrong; we don't know if the rival store is badly managed.

10. **(D)** We are told that the shopping center is off the beaten path at the moment. We are also told that poor management was the reason given by a majority of Bowton executives for failure of the two previous supermarket ventures.

LETTER CODE FOR EVALUATING DATA

(A) means that the Conclusion is a Major Objective;
(B) means that the Conclusion is a Major Factor;
(C) means that the Conclusion is a Minor Factor;
(D) means that the Conclusion is a Major Assumption;
(E) means that the Conclusion is an Unimportant Issue.

1. **(D)** is correct. It is assumed that the future development residents will go to the shopping center rather than all the way to the Fords Lake business district.

2. **(C)** is correct. The past growth of Fords Lake seems to weigh in the considerations about its possible future growth.

3. **(C)** The fact that no other Bowton store is within 20 miles is a minor factor in seeking a site in Fords Lake.

4. **(D)** Poor management of the two supermarkets that failed in the shopping center is an assumption on the part of the Bowton executives who favor opening a store in the Fords Lake area.

. **(C)** The new east-west highway is a minor factor influencing the major factor that more people will now pass the shopping center, which, in turn, influences the decision to open a store in the shopping center.

. **(E)** Competition from the other supermarket in the area does not influence the decision to open a Bowton store.

7. **(A)** The Bowton Company has shown rapid growth.

. **(B)** Increase of population through the shopping center is the major factor.

. **(D)** No one really knows why the other two supermarkets failed.

20. **(E)** The geographic area of Bowton's activities has no bearing on the decision.

21. **(C)** Many car-commuters will now pass the shopping center.

22. **(A)** The establishment of a new store is a major objective.

23. **(C)** The future residential development certainly influences the decision to open a new store nearby.

24. **(C)** A community of 45,000 or more after the new development is built certainly would be able to support two supermarkets.

25. **(C)** The five-year lease is used as an argument against opening a store in the shopping center.

26. **(E)** The distance from Fords Lake to Chicago plays no part in the deliberations.

27. **(D)** That the car-commuters will stop to shop at the shopping center is an assumption that only the future will prove or disprove.

28. **(C)** The fact that the new houses will have 3–4 bedrooms is a minor factor leading to the major factor that there will be a relatively large family in the average residence.

29. **(B)** The amount of money the average family in the development will be able to spend is a major factor influencing the decision to open a new store.

30. **(B)** The fact that Bowton has lower prices than the one rival in the area is an important factor in deciding to open a store.

TEST—TAKING MADE SIMPLE

Having gotten this far, you're almost an expert test-taker because you have now mastered the subject matter of the test. Proper preparation is the real secret. The pointers on the next few pages will take you the rest of the way by giving you the strategy employed on tests by those who are most successful in this not-so-mysterious art.

BEFORE THE TEST

T-DAY MINUS SEVEN

You're going to pass this examination because you have received the best possible preparation for it. But, unlike many others, you're going to give the best possible account of yourself by acquiring the rare skill of effectively using your knowledge to answer the examination questions.

First off, get rid of any negative attitudes toward the test. You have a negative attitude when you view the test as a device to "trip you up" rather than an opportunity to show how effectively you have learned.

APPROACH THE TEST WITH SELF-CONFIDENCE. Plugging through this book was no mean job, and now that you've done it you're probably better prepared than 90% of the others. Self-confidence is one of the biggest strategic assets you can bring to the testing room.

Nobody likes tests, but some poor souls permit themselves to get upset or angry when they see what they think is an unfair test. The expert doesn't. He keeps calm and moves right ahead, knowing that everyone is taking the same test. Anger, resentment, fear . . . they all slow you down. "Grin and bear it!"

Besides, every test you take, including this one, is a valuable experience which improves your skill. Since you will undoubtedly be taking other tests in the years to come, it may help you to regard this one as training to perfect your skill.

Keep calm; there's no point in panic. If you've done your work there's no need for it; and if you haven't, a cool head is your very first requirement.

Why be the frightened kind of student who enters the examination chamber in a mental coma? A test taken under mental stress does not provide a fair measure of your ability. At the very least, this book has removed for you some of the fear and mystery that surrounds examinations. A certain amount of concern is normal and good, but excessive worry saps your strength and keenness. In other words, be prepared EMOTIONALLY.

Pre-Test Review

If you know any others who are taking this test, you'll probably find it helpful to review the book and your notes with them. The group should be small, certainly not more than four. Team study at this stage should seek to review the material in a different way than you learned it originally; should strive for an exchange of ideas between you and the other members of the group; should be selective in sticking to important ideas; should stress the vague and the unfamiliar rather than that which you all know well; should be businesslike and devoid of any nonsense; should end as soon as you get tired.

One of the *worst* strategies in test taking is to do *all* your preparation the night before the exam. As a reader of this book, you have scheduled and spaced your study properly so as not to suffer from the fatigue and emotional disturbance that comes from cramming the night before.

Cramming is a very good way to *guarantee poor test results*.

However, you would be wise to prepare yourself factually by *reviewing your notes* in the 48 hours preceding the exam. You shouldn't have to spend more than two or three hours in this way. Stick to salient points. The others will fall into place quickly

Don't confuse cramming with a final, calm review which helps you focus on the significant areas of this book and further strengthens your confidence in your ability to handle the test questions. In other words, prepare yourself FACTUALLY.

Keep Fit

Mind and body work together. Poor physical condition will lower your mental efficiency. In preparing for an examination, observe the common-sense rules of health. Get sufficient sleep and rest, eat proper foods, plan recreation and exercise. In relation to health and examinations, two cautions are in order. Don't miss your meals prior to an examination in order to get extra time for study. Likewise, don't miss your regular sleep by sitting up late to "cram" for the examination. Cramming is an attempt to learn in a very short period of time what should have been learned through regular and consistent study. Not only are these two habits detrimental to health, but seldom do they pay off in terms of effective learning. It is likely that you will be *more confused* than better prepared on the day of the examination if you have broken into your daily routine by missing your meals or sleep.

On the night before the examination go to bed at your regular time and try to get a good night's sleep. Don't go to the movies. Don't date. In other words, prepare yourself PHYSICALLY.

T-HOUR MINUS ONE

After a very light, leisurely meal, get to the examination room ahead of time, perhaps ten minutes early . . . but not so early that you have time to get into an argument with others about what's going to be asked on the exam, etc. The reason for coming early is to help you get accustomed to the room. It will help you to a better start.

Bring all necessary equipment . . .

. . . pen, two sharpened pencils, watch, paper, eraser, ruler, and any other things you're instructed to bring.

Get settled . . .

. . . by finding your seat and staying in it. If no special seats have been assigned, take one in the front to facilitate the seating of others coming in after you.

The test will be given by a test supervisor who reads the directions and otherwise tells you what to do. The people who walk about passing out the test papers and assisting with the examination are test proctors. If you're not able to see or hear properly notify the supervisor or a proctor. If you have any other difficulties during the examination, like a defective test booklet, scoring pencil, answer sheet; or if it's too hot or cold or dark or drafty, let them know. You're entitled to favorable test conditions, and if you don't have them you won't be able to do your best. Don't be a crank, but don't be shy either. An important function of the proctor is to see to it that you have favorable test conditions.

Relax . . .

. . . and don't bring on unnecessary tenseness by worrying about the difficulty of the examination. If necessary wait a minute before beginning to write. If you're still tense, take a couple of deep breaths, look over your test equipment, or do something which will take your mind away from the examination for a moment.

If your collar or shoes are tight, loosen them.

Put away unnecessary materials so that you have a good, clear space on your desk to write freely.

You Must Have

TO GIVE YOUR Best Test PERFORMANCE

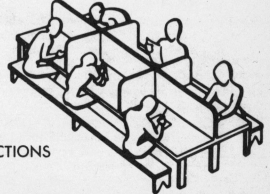

(1) A GOOD TEST ENVIRONMENT

(2) A COMPLETE UNDERSTANDING OF DIRECTIONS

(3) A DESIRE TO DO YOUR BEST

WHEN THEY SAY "GO" — TAKE YOUR TIME!

Listen very carefully to the test supervisor. If you fail to hear something important that he says, you may not be able to read it in the written directions and may suffer accordingly.

If you don't understand the directions you have heard or read, raise your hand and inform the proctor. Read carefully the directions for *each* part of the test before beginning to work on that part. If you skip over such directions too hastily, you may miss a main idea and thus lose credit for an entire section.

Get an Overview of the Examination

After reading the directions carefully, look over the entire examination to get an over-view of the nature and scope of the test. The purpose of this over-view is to give you some idea of the nature, scope, and difficulty of the examination.

It has another advantage. An item might be so phrased that it sets in motion a chain of thought that might be helpful in answering other items on the examination.

Still another benefit to be derived from reading all the items before you answer any is that the few minutes involved in reading the items gives you an opportunity to relax before beginning the examination. This will make for better concentration. As you read over these items the first time, check those whose answers immediately come to you. These will be the ones you will answer first. Read each item carefully before answering. It is a good practice to read each item at least twice to be sure that you understand it.

Plan Ahead

In other words, you should know precisely where you are going before you start. You should know:
1. whether you have to answer all the questions or whether you can choose those that are easiest for you;
2. whether all the questions are easy; (there may be a pattern of difficult, easy, etc.)
3. The length of the test; the number of questions;
4. The kind of scoring method used;
5. Which questions, if any, carry extra weight;
6. What types of questions are on the test;
7. What directions apply to each part of the test;
8. Whether you must answer the questions consecutively.

Budget Your Time Strategically!

Quickly figure out how much of the allotted time you can give to each section and still finish ahead of time. Don't forget to figure on the time you're investing in the overview. Then alter your schedule so that you can spend more time on those parts that count most. Then, if you can, plan to spend less time on the easier questions, so that you can devote the time saved to the harder questions. Figuring roughly, you should finish half the questions when half the allotted time has gone by. If there are 100 questions and you have three hours, you should have finished 50 questions after one and one half hours. So bring along a watch whether the instructions call for one or not. Jot down your "exam budget" and stick to it INTELLIGENTLY.

EXAMINATION STRATEGY

Probably the most important single strategy you can learn is to do the easy questions first. The very hard questions should be read and temporarily postponed. Identify them with a dot and return to them later.

This strategy has several advantages for you:
1. You're sure to get credit for all the questions you're sure of. If time runs out, you'll have all the sure shots, losing out only on those which you might have missed anyway.

2. By reading and laying away the tough ones you give your subconscious a chance to work on them. You may be pleasantly surprised to find the answers to the puzzlers popping up for you as you deal with related questions.

3. You won't risk getting caught by the time limit just as you reach a question you know really well.

A Tested Tactic

It's inadvisable on some examinations to answer each question in the order presented. The reason for this is that some examiners design tests so as to extract as much mental energy from you as possible. They put the most difficult questions at the beginning, the easier questions last. Or they may vary difficult with easy questions in a fairly regular pattern right through the test. Your survey of the test should reveal the pattern and your strategy for dealing with it.

If difficult questions appear at the beginning, answer them until you feel yourself slowing down or getting tired. Then switch to an easier part of the examination. You will return to the difficult portion after you have rebuilt your confidence by answering a batch of easy questions. Knowing that you have a certain number of points "under your belt" will help you when you return to the more difficult questions. You'll answer them with a much clearer mind; and you'll be refreshed by the change of pace.

Time

Use your time wisely. It's an important element in your test and you must use every minute effectively, working as rapidly as you can without sacrificing accuracy. Your exam survey and budget will guide you in dispensing your time. Wherever you can, pick up seconds on the easy ones. Devote your savings to the hard ones. If possible, pick up time on the lower value questions and devote it to those which give you the most points.

Relax Occasionally and Avoid Fatigue

If the exam is long (two or more hours) give yourself short rest periods as you feel you need them. If you're not permitted to leave the room, relax in your seat, look up from your paper, rest your eyes, stretch your legs, shift your body. Break physical and mental tension. Take several deep breaths and get back to the job, refreshed. If you

don't do this you run the risk of getting nervous and tightening up. Your thinking may be hampered and you may make a few unnecessary mistakes.

Do not become worried or discouraged if the examination seems difficult to you. The questions in the various fields are purposely made difficult and searching so that the examination will discriminate effectively even among superior students. No one is expected to get a perfect or near-perfect score.

Remember that if the examination seems difficult to you, it may be even more difficult for your neighbor.

Think!

This is not a joke because you're not an IBM machine. Nobody is able to write all the time and also to read and think through each question. You must plan each answer. Don't give hurried answers in an atmosphere of panic. Even though you see a lot of questions, remember that they are objective and not very time-consuming. Don't rush headlong through questions that must be thought through.

Edit, Check, Proofread . . .

. . . after completing all the questions. Invariably, you will find some foolish errors which you needn't have made, and which you can easily correct. Don't just sit back or leave the room ahead of time. Read over your answers and make sure you wrote exactly what you meant to write. And that you wrote the answers in the right place. You might even find that you have omitted some answers inadvertently. You have budgeted time for this job of proofreading. PROOFREAD and pick up points.

One caution, though. Don't count on making major changes. And don't go in for wholesale changing of answers. To arrive at your answers in the first place you have read carefully and thought correctly. Second-guessing at this stage is more likely to result in wrong answers. So don't make changes unless you are quite certain you were wrong in the first place.

FOLLOW DIRECTIONS CAREFULLY

In answering questions on the objective or short-form examination, it is most important to follow all instructions carefully. Unless you have marked the answers properly, you will not receive credit for them. In addition, even in the same examination, the instructions will not be consistent. In one section you may be urged to guess if you are not certain;

in another you may be cautioned against guessing. Some questions will call for the best choice among four or five alternatives; others may ask you to select the one incorrect or the least probable answer.

On some tests you will be provided with worked out fore-exercises, complete with correct answers. However, avoid the temptation to skip the directions and begin working just from reading the model questions and answers. Even though you may be familiar with that particular type of question, the directions may be different from those which you had followed previously. If the type of question should be new to you, work through the model until you understand it perfectly. This may save you time, and earn you a higher rating on the examination.

If the directions for the examination are written, read them carefully, at least twice. If the directions are given orally, listen attentively and then follow them precisely. For example, if you are directed to use plus (+) and minus (−) to mark true—false items, then don't use "T" and "F". If you are instructed to "blacken" a space on machine-scored tests, do not use a check (✔) or an "X". Make all symbols legible, and be sure that they have been placed in the proper answer space. It is easy, for example, to place the answer for item 5 in the space reserved for item 6. If this is done, then all of your following answers may be wrong. It is also very important that you understand the method they will use in scoring the examination. Sometimes they tell you in the directions. The method of scoring may affect the amount of time you spend on an item, especially if some items count more than others. Likewise, the directions may indicate whether or not you should guess in case you are not sure of the answer. Some methods of scoring penalize you for guessing.

Cue Words. Pay special attention to qualifying words or phrases in the directions. Such words as *one, best reason, surest, means most nearly the same as, preferable, least correct,* etc., all indicate that *one* response is called for, and that you must select the response which best fits the qualifications in the question.

Time. Sometimes a time limit is set for each section of the examination. If that is the case, follow the time instructions carefully. Your *exam budget* and your watch can help you here. Even if you haven't finished a section when the time limit is up, pass on to the next section. The examination has been planned according to the time schedule.

If the examination paper bears the instruction "Do not turn over page until signal is given," or "Do not start until signal is given," follow the instruction. Otherwise, you may be disqualified.

Pay Close Attention. Be sure you understand what you're doing at all times. Especially in dealing with true-false or multiple-choice questions it's vital that you understand the meaning of every question. It is normal to be working under stress when taking an examination, and it is easy to skip a word or jump to a false conclusion, which may cost you points on the examination. In many multiple-choice

and matching questions, the examiners deliberately insert plausible-appearing false answers in order to catch the candidate who is not alert.

Answer clearly. If the examiner who marks your paper cannot understand what you mean, you will not receive credit for your correct answer. On a True-False examination you will not receive any credit for a question which is marked both true and false. If you are asked to underline, be certain that your lines are under and not through the words and that they do not extend beyond them. When using the separate answer sheet it is important *when you decide to change an answer,* you erase the first answer completely. If you leave any graphite from the pencil on the wrong space it will cause the scoring machine to cancel the right answer for that question.

Watch Your "Weights." If the examination is "weighted" it means that some parts of the examination are considered more important than others and rated more highly. For instance, you may find that the instructions will indicate "Part I, Weight 50; Part II, Weight 25, Part III, Weight 25." In such a case, you would devote half of your time to the first part, and divide the second half of your time among Parts II and III.

A Funny Thing . . .

. . . happened to you on your way to the bottom of the totem pole. You *thought* the right answer but you marked the *wrong* one.

1. You *mixed answer symbols*! You decided (rightly) that Baltimore (Choice D) was correct. Then you marked *B* (for Baltimore) instead of *D*.

2. You *misread* a simple instruction! Asked to give the *latest* word in a scrambled sentence, you correctly arranged the sentence, and then marked the letter corresponding to the *earliest* word in that miserable sentence.

3. You *inverted digits*! Instead of the correct number, 96, you wrote (or read) 69.

Funny? Tragic! Stay away from accidents.

Record your answers on the answer sheet one by one as you answer the questions. Care should be taken that these answers are recorded next to the appropriate numbers on your answer sheet. It is poor practice to write your answers first on the test booklet and then to transfer them all at one time to the answer sheet. This procedure causes many errors. And then, how would you feel if you ran out of time before you had a chance to transfer all the answers.

When and How To Guess

Read the directions carefully to determine the scoring method that will be used. In some tests, the directions will indicate that guessing is advisable if you do not know the answer to a question. In such tests, only the right answers are counted in determining your score. If such is the case, don't omit any items. If you do not know the answer, or if you are not sure of your answer, then *guess*.

On the other hand, if the directions state that a scoring formula *will* be used in determining your score or that you are *not to guess,* then *omit* the question if you do not know the answer, or if you are not sure of the answer. When the scoring formu-la is used, a percentage of the *wrong* answers will be subtracted from the number of *right* answers as a correction for haphazard guessing. It is improbable, therefore, that mere guessing will improve your score significantly. *It may even lower your score.* Another disadvantage in guessing under such circumstances is that it consumes valuable time that you might profitably use in answering the questions you know.

If, however, you are uncertain of the correct answer but have *some* knowledge of the question and are able to eliminate one or more of the answer choices as wrong, your chance of getting the right answer is improved, and it will be to your advantage to *answer* such a question rather than *omit* it.

BEAT THE ANSWER SHEET

Even though you've had plenty of practice with the answer sheet used on machine-scored examinations, we must give you a few more, last-minute pointers.

The present popularity of tests requires the use of electrical test scoring machines. With these machines, scoring which would require the labor of several men for hours can be handled by one man in a fraction of the time.

The scoring machine is an amazingly intricate and helpful device, but the machine is not human. The machine cannot, for example, tell the difference between an intended answer and a stray pencil mark, and will count both indiscriminately. The machine cannot count a pencil mark, if the pencil mark is not brought in contact with the electrodes. For these reasons, specially printed answer sheets with response spaces properly located and properly filled in must be employed. Since not all pencil leads contain the necessary ingredients, a special pencil must be used and a heavy solid mark must be made to indicate answers.

(a) Each pencil mark must be heavy and black. Light marks should be retraced with the special pencil.

(b) Each mark must be in the space between the pair of dotted lines and entirely fill this space.

(c) All stray pencil marks on the paper, clearly not intended as answers, must be completely erased.

(d) Each question must have only one answer indicated. If multiple answers occur, all extraneous marks should be thoroughly erased. Otherwise, the machine will give you *no* credit for your correct answer.

Be sure to use the special electrographic pencil!

HERE'S HOW TO MARK YOUR ANSWERS ON MACHINE-SCORED ANSWER SHEETS:

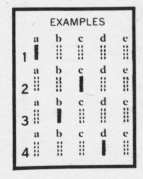
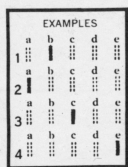

Make only ONE mark for each answer. Additional and stray marks may be counted as mistakes. In making corrections, erase errors COMPLETELY. Make glossy black marks.

Your answer sheet is the only one that reaches the office where papers are scored. For this reason it is important that the blanks at the top be filled in completely and correctly. The proctors will check this, but just in case they slip up, make certain yourself that your paper is complete.

Many exams caution competitors against making any marks on the test booklet itself. Obey that caution even though it goes against your grain to work neatly. If you work neatly and obediently with the test booklet you'll probably do the same with the answer sheet. And that pays off in high scores.

THE GIST OF TEST STRATEGY

- APPROACH THE TEST CONFIDENTLY. TAKE IT CALMLY.

- REMEMBER TO REVIEW, THE WEEK BEFORE THE TEST.

- DON'T "CRAM." BE CAREFUL OF YOUR DIET AND SLEEP.
  . . ESPECIALLY AS THE TEST DRAWS NIGH.

- ARRIVE ON TIME . . . AND READY.

- CHOOSE A GOOD SEAT. GET COMFORTABLE AND RELAX.

- BRING THE COMPLETE KIT OF "TOOLS" YOU'LL NEED.

- LISTEN CAREFULLY TO ALL DIRECTIONS.

- APPORTION YOUR TIME INTELLIGENTLY WITH AN "EXAM BUDGET."

- READ ALL DIRECTIONS CAREFULLY. TWICE IF NECESSARY.
  PAY PARTICULAR ATTENTION TO THE SCORING PLAN.

- LOOK OVER THE WHOLE TEST BEFORE ANSWERING ANY QUESTIONS.

- START RIGHT IN, IF POSSIBLE. STAY WITH IT. USE
  EVERY SECOND EFFECTIVELY.

- DO THE EASY QUESTIONS FIRST; POSTPONE HARDER QUESTIONS
  UNTIL LATER.

- DETERMINE THE PATTERN OF THE TEST QUESTIONS.
  IF IT'S HARD-EASY ETC., ANSWER ACCORDINGLY.

- READ EACH QUESTION CAREFULLY. MAKE SURE YOU UNDERSTAND
  EACH ONE BEFORE YOU ANSWER. RE-READ, IF NECESSARY.

- THINK! AVOID HURRIED ANSWERS. GUESS INTELLIGENTLY.

- WATCH YOUR WATCH AND "EXAM BUDGET," BUT DO A
  LITTLE BALANCING OF THE TIME YOU DEVOTE TO EACH QUESTION.

- GET ALL THE HELP YOU CAN FROM "CUE" WORDS.

- REPHRASE DIFFICULT QUESTIONS FOR YOURSELF.
  WATCH OUT FOR "SPOILERS."

- REFRESH YOURSELF WITH A FEW, WELL-CHOSEN REST
  PAUSES DURING THE TEST.

- USE CONTROLLED ASSOCIATION TO SEE THE RELATION OF
  ONE QUESTION TO ANOTHER AND WITH AS MANY IMPORTANT
  IDEAS AS YOU CAN DEVELOP.

- NOW THAT YOU'RE A "COOL" TEST-TAKER, STAY CALM
  AND CONFIDENT THROUGHOUT THE TEST. DON'T LET
  ANYTHING THROW YOU.

- EDIT, CHECK, PROOFREAD YOUR ANSWERS. BE A "BITTER
  ENDER." STAY WORKING UNTIL THEY
  MAKE YOU GO.

HOW TO BE A MASTER TEST TAKER

FOR FURTHER STUDY

ARCO BOOKS FOR MORE HELP

Now what? You've read and studied the whole book, and there's still time before you take the test. You're probably better prepared than most of your competitors, but you may feel insecure about one or more of the probable test subjects.

Perhaps you've discovered that you are weak in language, verbal ability or mathematics. Why flounder and fail when help is so easily available? Why not brush up in the privacy of your own home with one of these books?

And why not consider the other opportunities open to you? Look over the list and make plans for your future. Start studying for other tests *now*. You can then pick and choose your *ideal* position, instead of settling for the first *ordinary* job that comes along.

Each of the following books was created under the same expert editorial supervision that produced the excellent book you are now using. Though we only list titles and prices, you can be sure that each book performs a real service, and keeps you from fumbling and from failure. Whatever your goal. . . Civil Service, Trade License, Teaching, Professional License, Scholarships, Entrance to the School of your choice. . .you can achieve it through the proven Question and Answer Method.

START YOUR CAREER BY MAILING THIS COUPON TODAY.

ORDER NOW from your bookseller or direct from:

ARCO PUBLISHING , INC.   **219 Park Avenue South, New York, N.Y. 10003**

Please Rush The Following Arco Books
(Order by Number or Title)

....

....

....

....

....

☐ I enclose check, cash or money order for $_____(price of books, plus $1.00 for first book and 25¢ for each additional book, packing and mailing charge) No C.O.D.'s accepted.

Residents of N.Y. and Calif. add appropriate sales tax.

☐ Please tell me if you have an ARCO COURSE for the position of ....

☐ Please send me your free COMPLETE CATALOG.

NAME_____

STREET_____

CITY_____ STATE_____ ZIP # _____

Every Arco Book is guaranteed. Return it for full refund within ten days if not completely satisfied.

PROFESSIONAL CAREER EXAM SERIES

Action Guide for Executive Job Seekers and Employers, Uris	01787-2	3.95
Air Traffic Controller, Morrison	04593-0	8.00
Automobile Mechanic Certification Tests, Sharp	03809-8	6.00
Bar Exams	01124-6	5.00
The C.P.A. Exam: Accounting by the "Parallel Point" Method, Lipscomb	02020-2	15.00
Certified General Automobile Mechanic, Turner	02900-5	6.00
Computer Programmer, Luftig	01232-3	8.00
Computers and Automation, Brown	01745-7	5.95
Computers and Data Processing Examinations: CDP/CCP/CLEP	04670-8	10.00
Dental Admission Test, Arco Editorial Board	04293-1	6.00
Graduate Management Admission Test	04360-1	6.00
Graduate Record Examination Aptitude Test	00824-5	5.00
Health Insurance Agent (Hospital, Accident, Health, Life)	02153-5	5.00
How a Computer System Works, Brown & Workman	03424-6	5.95
How to Become a Successful Model—Second Edition, Krem	04508-6	2.95
How to Get Into Medical and Dental School, revised edition, Shugar, Shugar & Bauman	04095-5	4.00
How to Make Money in Music, Harris & Farrar	04089-0	5.95
How to Remember Anything, Markoff, Dubin & Carcel	03929-9	5.00
The Installation and Servicing of Domestic Oil Burners, Mitchell & Mitchell	00437-1	10.00
Instrument Pilot Examination, Morrison	04592-2	9.95
Insurance Agent and Broker	02149-7	8.00
Law School Admission Test, Candrilli & Slawsky	03946-9	6.00
Life Insurance Agent, Snouffer	04306-7	8.00
Medical College Admission Test, Turner	04289-3	6.00
Miller Analogies Test—1400 Analogy Questions	01114-9	5.00
National Career Directory	04510-8	5.95
The 1978-79 Airline Guide to Stewardess and Steward Careers, Morton	04350-4	5.95
Notary Public	00180-1	6.00
Nursing School Entrance Examinations, Turner	01202-1	6.00
Oil Burner Installer	00096-1	8.00
The Official 1978-79 Guide to Airline Careers, Morton	03955-8	5.95
Playground and Recreation Director's Handbook	01096-7	8.00
Principles of Data Processing, Morrison	04268-0	7.50
Psychology: A Graduate Review, Ozehosky & Polz	04136-6	10.00
Real Estate License Examination, Gladstone	03755-5	6.00
Real Estate Mathematics Simplified, Shulman	04713-5	5.00
Refrigeration License Manual, Harfenist	02726-6	10.00
Resumes for Job Hunters, Shykind	03961-2	5.00
Resumes That Get Jobs, revised edition, Resume Service	03909-4	3.00
Simplify Legal Writing, Biskind	03801-2	5.00
Spanish for Nurses and Allied Health Science Students, Hernandez-Miyares & Alba	04127-7	10.00
Stationary Engineer and Fireman	00070-8	8.00
Structural Design	04549-3	10.00
The Test of English as a Foreign Language (TOEFL), Moreno, Babin & Cordes	04450-0	8.00
TOEFL Listening Comprehension Cassette	04667-8	7.95
Veterinary College Admissions	04147-1	10.00
Your Resume—Key to a Better Job, Corwen	03733-4	4.00

ADVANCED GRE SERIES

Biology: Advanced Test for the G.R.E., Solomon	04310-5	4.95
Business: Advanced Test for the G.R.E., Berman, Malea & Yearwood	01599-3	4.95
Chemistry: Advanced Test for the G.R.E., Weiss	01069-X	4.95
Economics: Advanced Test for the G.R.E., Zabrenski & Heydari-Darafshian	04548-5	5.95

Education: Advanced Test for the G.R.E.,	04117-3	
Engineering: Advanced Test for the G.R.E., Ingham & Nesbitt	01604-3	
French: Advanced Test for the G.R.E., Dethierry	01070-3	
Geography: Advanced Test for the G.R.E., White	01710-4	
Geology: Advanced Test for the G.R.E., Dolgoff	01071-1	
History: Advanced Test for the G.R.E.,	04414-4	
Literature: Advanced Test for the G.R.E.	01073-8	
Mathematics: Advanced Test for the G.R.E., Bramson	04264-8	
Music: Advanced Test for the G.R.E., Murphy	01471-7	
Philosophy: Advanced Test for the G.R.E., Steiner	01472-5	
Physical Education: Advanced Test for the G.R.E., Rubinger	01609-4	
Physics: Advanced Test for the G.R.E., Bruenn	01074-6	
Political Science: Advanced Test for the G.R.E., Meador & Stewart	01459-8	
Psychology: Advanced Test for the G.R.E., Millman & Nisbett	01145-9	
Sociology: Advanced Test for the G.R.E.,	04547-7	
Spanish: Advanced Test for the G.R.E., Jassey	01075-4	
Speech: Advanced Test for the G.R.E., Graham	01526-8	

GRADUATE FOREIGN LANGUAGE TESTS

Graduate School Foreign Language Test: French, Kretschmer	01461-X
Graduate School Foreign Language Test: German, Goldberg	01460-1
Graduate School Foreign Language Test: Spanish, Hampares & Jassey	01874-7

PROFESSIONAL ENGINEER EXAMINATIONS

Chemical Engineering, Coren	01256-0	8
Civil Engineering Technician	04267-2	1
Electrical Engineering Technician	04149-8	10
Engineer in Training Examination (EIT), Morrison	04009-2	10
Engineering Fundamentals	04273-7	1
Fundamentals of Engineering, Home Study Program, (3 Vols.)	04302-4	4
Fundamentals of Engineering (Vol. I), Morrison	04234-6	1
Fundamentals of Engineering (Vol. II), Morrison	04240-0	1
Fundamentals of Engineering (2 vols.)	04243-5	3
Industrial Engineering Technician	04154-4	1
Mechanical Engineering Technician	04274-5	10
Principles and Practice of Electrical Engineering Examination, Morrison	04031-9	10
Professional Engineer (Civil) State Board Examination Review, Packer et al	03637-0	15
Professional Engineering Registration: Problems and Solutions	04269-9	10
Solid Mechanics, Morrison	04409-8	10

NATIONAL TEACHER AREA EXAMS

Early Childhood Education: Teaching Area Exam for the National Teacher Examination	01637-X
Education in the Elementary School: Teaching Area Exam for the National Teacher Examination	01318-4
English Language and Literature: Teaching Area Exam for the National Teacher Examination	01319-2
Mathematics: Teaching Area Exam for the National Teacher Examination	01639-6
National Teacher Examination	00823-7